LI
TE

GERMAN
CINEMA

ᴮᵞ

2002

Contemporary Film and Television Series

A complete listing of the books in this series can be found at the back of this volume.

GERMAN CINEMA

Texts in Context

MARC SILBERMAN

WAYNE STATE UNIVERSITY PRESS

DETROIT

99   98   97   96   5   4   3   2

Library of Congress Cataloging-in-Publication Data
Silberman, Marc, 1948–
    German cinema : texts in context / Marc Silberman.
      p.   cm.   —   (Contemporary film and television series)
    Includes bibliographical references and index.
    ISBN 0-8143-2560-2 (pbk. : alk. paper)
    1. Motion pictures—Germany—History.   I. Title.   II. Series.
PN1993.5.G3S54   1995
791.43′0943—dc20   95-20032
                                          CIP

Contents

Preface

When I first conceived this project, my intention was to write a so-cial history of the German cinema. The naive conviction that a study of such sweep could be accomplished by a single scholar in a foreseeable span of time gave way to the realization that it would require the multi-dimensional competencies of a research group. Other considerations at-tracted my attention as I gathered material, and when I began to write in 1987 the idea and my interest had taken a different shape and direction. Motivated by a lack of confidence in chronology and by increasing uncer-tainty as to what "Germany" means, I was searching for alternative ways of relating historical events to aesthetic phenomena, of mediating between the public sphere and the way individuals express themselves. Rather than some singular method or theory it was the playful relation with film texts and their systems of meanings that opened up for me new links or unex-pected connections. The result is not, I think, a study in subjective criti-cism, although my personal engagement with the films in question will often be evident. The readings of fourteen films, chosen for their para-digmatic significance, apply a range of interpretative concepts and test hy-potheses of narrative construction while establishing the discursive context in which they were produced and perceived. Thus, although I am thinking historically, I am not writing film history in the usual sense.

A long-term project like this one owes many debts to many individ-uals and institutions. Family, friends, students, colleagues, other cinema specialists, librarians, and film archivists in the United States and Germany encouraged and facilitated my work in ways that they themselves probably did not always recognize. The research and much of the writing was ac-complished with a generous grant from the Alexander von Humboldt Foundation under the auspices of Prof. Friedrich Knilli at the Technical

University in West Berlin. The manuscript was finished with financial support from the Graduate School of the University of Wisconsin. Libraries and archives at the (former) Staatliches Filmarchiv der DDR, Deutsches Institut für Filmkunde, and especially Stiftung deutsche Kinemathek were gracious hosts to a demanding guest. I thank all the individuals and institutions that contributed to the completion of this book and can only wish that they recognize in it a token of my debt.

Earlier versions of several chapters were published previously: a short section of chapter 1 in an essay on Weimar images of the French Revolution in *Framing the Past: The Historiography of German Cinema and Television*, ed. Bruce A. Murray and Christopher J. Wickham (Carbondale: Southern Illinois University Press, 1992); the central section of chapter 4 in *Medien/Kultur: Schnittstellen zwischen Medienwissenschaft, Medienpraxis und gesellschaftlicher Kommunikation*, ed. Knut Hickethier and Siegfried Zielinski (Berlin: Volker Spiess, 1991); chapter 5 in *Intertextuality: German Literature and Visual Art from the Renaissance to the Twentieth Century*, ed. Ingeborg Hoesterey and Ulrich Weisstein (Columbia, S.C.: Camden House, 1993); chapter 7 in *Widergänger: Faschismus und Antifaschismus im Film*, ed. Joachim Schmitt-Sasse (Münster: MAkS, 1993); chapter 9 in *The Films of G. W. Pabst*, ed. Eric Rentschler (New Brunswick, N.J.: Rutgers University Press, 1990); and chapter 11 in *Germanic Review* 66, no. 1 (Winter 1991).

Finally, this book was researched and written during ten years that witnessed memorable and unsettling events in Germany. At no other time have I ever been so aware of history as a construction, of the past as a burden. But also my work on the German cinema constantly forced me to acknowledge the way culture serves us by containing the unbearable truths of memory.

Introduction:
Setting the Limits

Historical overviews of world cinema emphasize three German contributions to the international canon: the innovative use of the camera in expressionist films of the early twenties; the unprecedented politicization of the entire cinema apparatus during the Third Reich; and the emergence of a "new wave" cinema in the seventies that combined innovative aesthetics with socially conscious narratives. The focal points in the history of German cinema have been the object of intense and sophisticated investigation, but at the same time the efforts to highlight these historical contributions have produced gaps. What were the contexts of the achievements? The present study begins to close the gaps by examining the links between the focal points. The readings of fourteen paradigmatic films cover the span of German cinema from the twenties through the eighties, describing the cultural, institutional, and textual systems that grounded and transformed the acknowledged historical achievements.

Readers of this history will find neither an elaborated narrative about the periodic rises and declines of a national cinema nor an overview of the technological discoveries and stylistic traits identified with German films. As discrete elements all of these aspects enter into the proposed readings, but the goal is not to (re)constitute the canon of German films or to describe a tour through an imaginary museum of the German cinema where the past becomes history. Instead, the process of reading closely a series of exemplary films aims at situating them in the present. Reading is understood as an open process of interpretation, of returning to the past in order to conceptualize retrospectively the context in which particular meanings circulated. An interest in determining the issues, struggles, and blockages that have shaped the terrain of cinema culture in Germany guided the selection of films. Over time they have changed, arising variously in response to different constraints and influences. As a result, each reading seeks its own specific intersection of textual analysis and cultural context.

This approach needs explanation. The cinema is a site of collective production and reception, and many kinds of social activity traverse it: industrial, technological, financial, ideological, aesthetic, consumerist. My point of departure assumes that both films and their contexts are constructs. Every film is constructed as a form or vehicle of communication within the public sphere, in respect to the cinematic institution which produces it and to the historical spectator who watches it. Likewise every film is (re)constructed in the present, in respect to me (the spectator) who tries to make sense out of it in my own time. Cinema and history, then, are discourses that bring the film spectator into an imaginary relation to the present by constructing a way of seeing. My readings of films probe how the cinematic institution in Germany and specific film texts construct this way of seeing for the viewing subject.

Cultural studies have ushered in a paradigm change in recent years, a fundamental shift from an understanding of history as ontology (the truth about social events) to history as discourse (a signifying practice).[1] From this latter position history does not consist of the physical past that was experienced, available later in an unproblematic way for analysis and interpretation. Rather it is the past reworked and resignified from the perspective of contemporaneous events. Cultural studies stress the intersections of various practices: theory and analysis, interpretation and empiricism, text and context. This stress in turn foregrounds the ideological nature of categories that define discourses. Politics, class, economics, and authorship, for example, are not events or identities external to the film text but rather they organize the film narration and are organized by it. Hence, the cinematic discourse of history is not constructed only or even most pertinently in representations of the past (the genre of the "historical film") but rather in the relations of the spectator to history and to the past represented in the film. A film's meaning is produced in a context, and every film is historical in the way it positions the spectator in relation to this context through characters, narrated events, atmosphere, facts, and fictions.

To consider the cinema as discourse in relation to the real focuses attention on modes of representation as a way of examining reality. This is not a matter of accuracy or verisimilitude in the traditional sense of realism but rather of textual coherence, the representational coherence embedded in story, event, character, setting, etc. Frequently this coherence is figured within family constellations (parents/children) or couples (men/women), creating tensions whose historical and national specificity will become the object of investigation. The focus on signifying practices shifts critical attention from the prevailing hierarchical relationship between form and content to narrational strategies. Narration is a process and a product of the reciprocal determinations between the spectator's eye and the camera "eye." It is the work that makes a particular film understandable, irreducible to any one set of signifiers (i.e., camera placement, mise-en-scène, editing, etc.).[2] It follows, then, that what a film means is less important in the interpretative readings than how the film produces meanings at a specific, historical juncture. This raises questions too about the way utopian aspirations and counter hegemonies are imagined, for as a signifying practice the cinema partakes of power struggles by contributing to the discourses of how change operates and possibly by contesting such change.

Because the spectator is a point or space where individual perception, social determinants, and textual strategies come together, spectatorship has become one of the central critical categories in film theory and criticism. It emerged within the more general discussion of structural linguistics as film scholars in the sixties rethought how the cinema produces meaning in contradistinction to literature or the other arts. Over the next twenty years psychoanalysis and feminism richly inflected the debate by foregrounding the unconscious work of the spectator and the gendered nature of the look.[3] All films engage specular relations by soliciting the audience as viewer. They address their audiences textually and contextually by constructing a relation between the protagonist, the camera, and the spectator. This leads to considerations about the structures that enable a film to be understood, as well as questions of style, form, and conventions in the cinema. Equally important are considerations that address how a spectator is subject to ideological effects and determinations such as class, gender, or nationality. Point of view, visual perception, spectator pleasure are all means of negotiating subjectivity through spectator positioning. The textual spectator, then, fills the subject position constructed by the text and inscribed as a fictional space in the film's narration. It is not "unreal," that is, existing only in the imagination, but rather defines where and how imaginary operations take place in the course of the film.

The spectator also exists contextually as the audience in a historically constituted public sphere. Spectator reaction can never be reconstructed completely, but it is possible to elucidate the limits and the terms of possibility by attending to a film's reception. The notion of the spectator written into the text, to be elicited only by interpretation, suggests an ideal spectator already constituted prior to the film text or determined by the ideology of the text that stands in opposition to the historical viewer. Yet spectators are neither victims of a film's aesthetic structure nor a mere reflection of society's political structures. Articulating the relation between textual and viewing subject is both an empirical and a metaphysical problem that can be "described" only through accurate textual readings. The readings I propose oscillate between the textually inscribed spectator, which tends to undermine historicity in its perpetual present of formal and narrative patterns, and the socioculturally differentiated spectator with a political and institutional identity.

To establish what goes on in people's imagination is a speculative undertaking, but to analyze the imaginary activity involved in looking and watching is important for relating spectatorship to aesthetic experience. Not illusion, fantasy, or the image *of* something in the sense of "reflection," imaginary activity is transitive, functioning through rhetorical figures, narrative forms, visual images, and the projections that lead to meaning through representation.[4] As an aesthetic construct a film invents imaginary and formal resolutions to real contradictions. These imaginary relations and operations pertain to retroactive interpretation. The spectator perceives the cinema world as subjective, exaggerated, full of gaps, and incomplete in a way that triggers the imagination, and the imaginary (retro)activity of producing meaning operates through the positioning of a film's spectator. If the cinema proposes an imaginary relationship to the real conditions of existence, then it is also produced by these conditions and constantly reworks the relation between spectator and sociohistorical context. Nonetheless, imaginary activity cannot be circumscribed by a notion of dominant ideology or use value. The relationship between the film text and spectator, between representation and reality, is much more complex than such a rigid or simple law of mediations could possibly explicate. Imaginary activity intersects all of them in ways that must allow each its own momentum, and the work of interpretation consists of teasing out these operations and their transformations.

The German cinema offers a rich field of study for an investigation of culturally specific imaginary activity. Radical ruptures in continuity, identity, and memory mark twentieth-century Germany in a way that requires vigorous creative operations for constructing the imaginary resolutions in film narratives. Striking narrative and visual negotiations of the anxieties and excesses that haunt the German past emerge in the following readings as a major component in the specificity of this national cinema. The establishment of the cinema as the quintessential modern medium corresponded in the twenties to the search for new forms of visual pleasure that could contain the threat of the Other associated with the modernist crisis, an experience that was brutally lived out under Weimar Germany's social and political transformations. The Third Reich presumably ended the modernist crisis and banned modernism as degenerate, but in the circulation of its visual imagery the fascist regime combined modern technology and administration to produce powerful narratives about excluding and eliminating difference for the sake of the fatherland. The postwar German cinema quickly bifurcated along the cold-war fault lines: the state film production company in the East attempted to revitalize the socially critical tradition of Weimar filmmaking, while the many small film producers in the West pursued superficiality and escapism in order to compete with the commercial Hollywood cinema. Common to the films produced through the fifties in both countries were the qualities of absolute visual transparency and absolute narrative closure, even if the ideological orientation was diametrically opposed. In the sixties and seventies the rise of new media, especially television broadcasting, shifted the function and the audience for the cinema in both East and West Germany. In the German Democratic Republic film culture attempted to address within the confines of a controlled public sphere issues of self-realization and social alienation that appealed to a younger audience. In the Federal Republic an unusual combination of state subsidies, public television, and a young generation of independent filmmakers blossomed into a hybrid, noncommercial cinema that saw itself as the social conscience of the nation, asking hard questions about the past, political emancipation, social equality, and national identity.

The fourteen films that constitute the corpus for this historical discourse on the German cinema do not necessarily interrogate historical events or problems but rather transform historical traumas into narrative and visual representations. *Passion* (chapter 1) stands at the inauguration of a viable commercial German film industry. Ernst Lubitsch's extravagant historical spectacle about the French Revolution belongs to the genre that under the pretext of retelling the past seeks to reorganize social relations in the present, in this case those of revolutionary Germany in 1919. Central to this undertaking was his innovative visual style based on artifice and the articulation of cinematic address through the look that could translate class relations into terms of gender and erotic desire. While *Passion* ushers in a new visual dominance that would soon become identified with the stylistic distortions and narrational idiosyncrasies of the art or expressionist cinema in early Weimar Germany, *The Last Laugh* (chapter 2) already marks a culminating point and transition to the new realism that characterized the second half of the twenties. One of the major contributors to the refinements of cinematic illusion through new camera techniques, Friedrich Wilhelm Murnau thematized seeing and being seen in this paranoid parable about the power and vulnerability of the (self-) image. As a tale of threatened subjectivity set in the contemporary metropolis, it also registers the social tensions that marked Germany's transition into modernity during the twenties. Murnau's success confirmed the international competitiveness of Germany's commercial film industry, whereas *Kuhle Wampe or Who Owns the World?* (chapter 3) with its overtly ideological aesthetics indicates not only the larger institutional and discursive context of Weimar filmmaking but also the hopes and failures in addressing an oppositional public sphere. The collective experiment under the direction of Slatan Dudov and Bertolt Brecht engages the topical problem of unemployment and impoverishment through an anti-illusionistic use of montage, yet the allegorical images of solidarity aim at a working-class audience that was already showing serious signs of disintegration under the pressure of political change in the early thirties.

The political instrumentalization of the cinema by institutions of power can be found in any country, but during the Third Reich it reached a new level of sophistication in the effort to monopolize the public's visual imagination in Germany. The well-known, seductive images and camera work of a Leni Riefenstahl or the celebrated high production values of propaganda films were typical neither for the quality or quantity turned out by the studios. Three films illustrate less familiar but more characteristic aspects. *To New Shores* (chapter 4) demonstrates on the one hand the continuity beyond 1933 in technical craftsmanship and stylistic perfection schooled during the twenties and on the other the narrow margins and lost opportunities for social criticism in a studio system committed to escapist fantasies. Using genre conventions of the pathos-laden melodrama set in another place and time, Detlef Sierck (later in Hollywood exile known as Douglas Sirk) plays off erotic excess against aggressive evil in a way that reveals the moral confines of cinematic illusions in an authoritarian society. In contrast *Request Concert* (chapter 5) is a topical film by Eduard von Borsody that combines the entertainment qualities of a musical love story with overt war propaganda. Its wooden, theatricalized dramaturgy typifies the way fascist film narration eliminated specular playfulness in favor of kitsch images that reinforce the links between private emotions and the national interest of an imperialistic war. Finally, *Romance in a Minor Key* (chapter 6), an adaptation of a nineteenth-century literary text, gauges the challenge of projecting escapist fantasies even as the discipline of everyday life under fascism became increasingly brutal. Helmut Käutner's sentimental tale of a woman's attempt to break out of a suffocating marriage folds back her desire and resistance into tropes of self-sacrifice and resignation to the patriarchal order that reproduce the reality of fascist society.

The postwar cinema reestablished itself in Germany to a large extent with the same personnel but under policies implemented by the victorious Allies and subject to the tensions of the cold war. In East Germany the centralized, state-controlled and financed Deutsche Film Aktiengesellschaft (DEFA) studio began releasing films already in 1946 with a distinct ideological commitment to humanist and realist aesthetics. Meanwhile in West Germany a decentralized, undercapitalized private studio system committed to Hollywood-type entertainment values provided the basis for a chronically crisis-prone film industry. *Rotation* (chapter 7) typifies the DEFA studio's effort to create "the new film" in the tradition of Weimar cinema's realism. Reconstructing the social relations that led to and sustained fascist authority by means of a family narrative, Wolfgang

Staudte explicitly addresses a historically complicit spectator through visual metaphors of blindness and vision in order to convey his moralistic message of individual responsibility. If *Rotation* exemplifies the classical, antifascist humanism in the East, the comic *Heimatfilm Black Forest Girl* (chapter 8) represents the West German defense in the fifties against both the flood of American movies and memories of the recent past. Hans Deppe uses sanitized images of local nature and folklife as a projection screen. Read against the grain, it reveals the unresolved traumas that dominated the public sphere: the desire for security and a stable national identity in a world where dissemblance and existential uncertainty determined social relations. *The Last Ten Days* (chapter 9), one of the first war films exhibited in the midfifties in West Germany, attempts to confront directly the catastrophe of the recent past. Georg Wilhelm Pabst unfolds with documentary sensitivity the last days of the Nazi leaders in an underground bunker in Berlin. The melodramatic narrative finds striking, apocalyptic images for the demise of political power and institutional legitimacy but, like all the films of the fifties, it is unable to express directly and realistically the pain, melancholy, and sorrow vis-à-vis the past.

When East Germany closed its borders in 1961, many intellectuals felt that a breathing space opened in which cultural expression would be unhampered by direct ideological competition with the West. Yet by the midsixties the effects of general economic mismanagement had become noticeable, and the government reverted to punishing measures of ideological conformity to shore up its power. A massive critique of art and culture was staged, resulting in the shelving of almost the entire year's production of DEFA films in 1965 and a crackdown in the wake of the Prague Spring events in 1968. This was the difficult production context of *I Was Nineteen* (chapter 10), which retreated to the proven safety of the antifascist film genre of the earlier *Rotation* but with the crucial structural difference that it was an autobiographical feature. Konrad Wolf, whose Jewish Communist family fled Germany in the thirties to Moscow, relates his own unheroic story of returning home to Germany in 1945 in the form of a quest narrative for self- and national identity. The story's intimacy and unusual perspective marked a breakthrough to the younger viewers who no longer recognized themselves in the heroic epics of the previous generation. With the serious effort at economic modernization ushered in by a new government in the early seventies, DEFA directors found it possible to address this younger audience about its own sense of alienation, often through narratives about strong, rebellious women. In the early eighties *On Probation* (chapter 11) was one of the last examples in this shift to "problematic" female protagonists before the final phase of stagnation began in East Germany. Hermann Zschoche presents the case study of a young, asocial, single mother caught between the state's power to discipline aberrant behavior and a sympathetically portrayed vitality that transgresses bound-aries. That his protagonist still moves within the confines of traditional pa-triarchal representations of women as the Other does not detract from the carefully drawn critique of institutionalized power but also is symptomatic of the narrow margins of critique ventured in the East German cinema.

West Germany too experienced in the sixties a crisis in the com-mercial film industry. Brought to a head through competition with televi-sion and changing leisure-time patterns, it produced a situation that a younger generation of filmmakers could use to its own advantage for re-forming the state subsidy system. Like *Kuhle Wampe* in the early thirties, *Artists under the Big Top: Perplexed* (chapter 12) probes the limits of an al-ternative cinematic discourse in the public sphere. At the threshold of what was to become the internationally celebrated New German Cinema, Alexander Kluge's parable of the artist's struggle in consumer society in many ways set the agenda for the next decade: the search for new, subver-sive narrative and visual strategies that link the subjective experience of cin-ematic pleasure to the desire for social change; the conviction that enter-tainment and art are not mutually exclusive; and the awareness that the gaps in German memory about the recent past are constitutive of German identity. If Kluge's circus film anticipated the new wave cinema of the sev-enties, then the internationally honored *Marianne and Juliane* (chapter 13) is a kind of culminating point. Margarethe von Trotta's insistence on coupling domestic terrorism with the Nazi past in order to expose the in-tersection of personal and national identity through family dynamics as well as her status as one of the most successful woman filmmakers to emerge in Germany suggest both the dominant themes and the crucial role of outsiders in the New German Cinema. Finally, *Paris, Texas* (chapter 14) demonstrates the challenges the German cinema faced as the new wave energies became established and dissipated. Ironically Wim Wenders's move to the United States, his internationally financed project produced with American scriptwriters and a multinational team, throws into relief the specificity of the German dilemma in relating (film) narration to the search for roots, for family continuity in the face of a ruptured past, and ul-timately for a place in history. At the same time he is one of most thought-ful and radical directors in the best tradition of the German cinema to seek new ways of seeing one's own relation to the present.

The close readings that follow seek to deepen and complicate the connections summarized here. Each chapter presents a single film, bring-ing together authorial aspects such as personal style and intentions with textual aspects such as genre, modes of narration, and address. In addition, the films are situated within a wider production and reception context in order to show how political issues and social transformations intersect with narrative and visual strategies. The chronological sequence and grouping into familiar periods is less a matter of adhering to traditional historiography than of providing a convenient framework to argue against. The selection of paradigmatic films is guided, of course, by considerations of exemplarity rather than exhaustivity. To avoid overlap and repetition, films were excluded that other scholars have treated at length within the context of historical and historicizing discourses. Nonetheless, some familiar, even canonical films were included in order to resituate them and examine their imaginary operations. With the intent of widening the pool for critical discussion, other films were chosen because they were popular upon their release but are now rarely mentioned. This very neglect can be an element that exposes the historical nature of imaginary strategies. Needless to say, many aspects of the German cinema go unmentioned: for example, early cinema before 1918, documentaries, avant-garde and experimental films, short and animated films, television feature films, films by Germans in exile, and the Swiss-German cinema. I will be pleased if readers of these interpretations discover their own gaps in German cinema history and develop new imaginary strategies for closing them.

Part 1

The Weimar
Cinema

1

Specular Presence
and Historical Revolution:
Ernst Lubitsch's *Passion*

OR AT LEAST two reasons, September 18, 1919 marks a historic date in the German cinema. On that day the new flagship cinema of the Universum-Film Aktiengesellschaft (UFA) film company in Berlin, the UFA-Palast am Zoo, opened to a capacity crowd of 2,000 and with a full symphony orchestra to accompany the screening of a silent film. It was Ernst Lubitsch's *Passion* (*Madame Dubarry*), the box office success that established the recently organized film production company as a major competitor on the international scene.

Founded before the end of the war in December, 1917 with the tacit support of the war ministry under the direction of Army General Erich Ludendorff, the UFA was a corporate entity that drew its initial capital from secret government bonds, major banks, and heavy industries as well as three production companies with their distribution and exhibition arms. Aimed at guaranteeing a financially viable film industry to serve both the public's entertainment needs and the government's propaganda purposes, UFA was Germany's first fully integrated cinema corporation. Under the control of the Deutsche Bank after the war it emerged in an advantageous position to compete in the international market with its production capabilities having expanded under the mantle of the war economy.[1] The UFA-Palast—the first of those many richly decorated cinema palaces that contributed to Berlin's reputation as a film metropolis in the ensuing years—represented only one of the more bombastic statements about the increasing cultural impact of this new popular entertainment. Through government intervention and sponsorship—institutional factors that repeatedly play a significant role in the German cinema—the motion pictures were seeking to become culturally respectable, a status they had yet to achieve. Constructing Germany's largest and most luxurious cinema less than one year after the country's military defeat and despite the ongoing economic hardships in postwar Germany not only shows UFA's optimism about its commercial role in the future of the cinema, it demonstrates as well that UFA intended to move the cinema in Germany from its subproletarian and suburban grounding to the urban centers of bourgeois culture.[2] The building's theatrical design, the integration of other arts through the elaborately painted interior, the symphony orchestra, and the aura of spectacle at a premiere with invited journalists and celebrities were all factors calculated to appeal to the tastes of the middle classes familiar with traditional cultural norms.[3]

Passion, a historical costume film set during the French Revolution, was also part of UFA's strategy to differentiate its "product" and to attract audiences by developing its expertise with grandiose spectacles, strong narratives, and an expanded star system. Indeed, Lubitsch's film was praised for its narrative sophistication and for its high production values which, despite the industry's relative impoverishment after the war, compared favorably to Hollywood productions of the time (e.g., D. W. Griffith's treatment of similar historical subject matter in *Orphans of the Storm*, 1922). More importantly, after an unprecedented run of over three months to capacity crowds in Berlin and other German cities, *Passion* went on to break the postwar blockade of German films in England, France, and the United States, opening the way for what was perceived by some as an "invasion" of German art films during the following years.[4] September 18, 1919, then, marks a notable transition in the development of the German cinema from a local, marginal product to the forceful contestant in the cultural domain that it would become during the Weimar years. More than that, the film's success in the domestic and international markets suggests that this story about a historical revolution introduced new ways of seeing and imaginary strategies that effectively addressed the fascination and anxieties of an audience faced with the threat of social collapse and change.

The Weimar period of German cinema, stretching from the collapse of the Wilhelmine Empire in 1918 to Hitler's rise to power in 1933, is usually considered a nationally and stylistically coherent entity comprised of more or less fantastic and realist films. Its reception, at least among cinephiles and the community of film scholars, has been fatefully overdetermined by two strikingly incompatible but nonetheless complementary studies authored by contemporaries who watched these films as they were released. Siegfried Kracauer's *From Caligari to Hitler* proposes a psychosociological reading of over 200 film narratives based on the assumption that the cinema, as collectively produced and popularly consumed entertainment, reflects a nation's mentality and its psychological dispositions.[5] Reasoning by analogy, he shows with remarkable consistency how the films narrativize displacement or projection onto an Other—

vampire, monster, automaton, woman—of anxieties and desires tied to the middle class's fear of its own social instability. The second classic study, Lotte Eisner's *The Haunted Screen*, pursues the project of defining expressionist style in the German cinema by showing how it drew on literary, theatrical, and art historical sources. Eisner argues that metaphysical categories of German interiority and emotional ecstasy, of vision and abstraction, explain the evolution of innovative cinema technology in such areas as lighting, editing, and camera movement.

In each case Kracauer and Eisner are compelled to smooth over ambiguities that fall outside the totalizing systems they develop in order to account for relations between Weimar films and German fascism in the thirties. As a result, neither one is able to recognize that this period of German cinema is characterized precisely by its contradictions, by its destabilization of notions like an autonomous self or preconstructed subject expressed in the film text. At a time when Germany's antiquated economic, political, social, and cultural structures were undergoing a rapid transformation into modernity, the cinema apparatus, that very child of modern technology and perception, was asserting itself as the dominant vehicle for representing a new way of seeing social relations. Only recently have critics suggested it might be useful or even necessary to consider issues of historicizing spectatorship.[6] For the innovations in the new visual medium present ways of negotiating spectator positioning and visual pleasure through imaginary strategies that define the historical and national specificity of Weimar cinema.

Following Kracauer's crypto-Freudian readings, in the case of *Passion* the film's subtext is a classical Oedipal drama in which the father-son generational conflict is organized along sexually determined class lines defined by the French Revolution, to wit the libertine aristocracy and the family-oriented bourgeoisie. Jeanne and Armand, the simple seamstress and the student, are wrenched out of their love when Jeanne responds to the flirtations of the aristocrat Don Diego. He represents a third term, the Father, who disrupts the exclusive couple in a role that other males, including King Louis XV, will also occupy in the course of the plot. In a standard projection of sublimated desire, Armand represses sexuality into rage against the Father by joining the revolution. Having established his identity by overthrowing the Father and usurping the site of his power, Armand experiences the return of the repressed, of his desire for Jeanne. As president of the Revolutionary Tribunal he must sentence Jeanne, who has become Countess Dubarry. He condemns her to death, winning the applause of the Tribunal delegates, but in a last, desperate attempt to allay his castration anxiety, the Oedipal trauma against which identity is constituted, he tries to help her escape from her prison cell and is shot by his comrades.

Kracauer reads and identifies with the film in this way when he criticizes Lubitsch for considering history "an arena reserved for blind and ferocious instincts, a product of devilish machinations forever frustrating our hopes for freedom and happiness," and he goes on to claim (as does an entire tradition of film criticism after him) that the story shows contempt for historic fact as well as disregard for the meaning of the revolution, thus exposing the film's antidemocratic tendencies.[7] Yet this conclusion misconstrues the structure of the film's imaginary logic. As a representation of the French Revolution *Passion* is of course wrong in its details, privileging the anecdotal over the central event and collapsing the political into the play of eroticism and vanity. As a whole, however, its system of address, that is, its positioning of the spectator within an imaginary relation to the narrative, reveals the ambivalence that accompanies social upheaval and the search for a new self-, gender, and national identity. As such, the film can be situated within the rupture and dislocation in postwar Germany of 1919. Lubitsch does not examine these tensions through plot but rather in the interplay of narration and mise-en-scène. Kracauer, in other words, validates only one aspect of the film's narrative logic, denying the epistemological force of the imaginary in a medium based on spectacle.

Lubitsch was a major contributor to the articulation of cinematic address, a central factor in the elaboration of Hollywood's classical narrative structures.[8] He devised numerous "tricks" for positioning the spectator by foregrounding the look through point-of-view shots; he also developed a highly economical system of punctuation between shots dominated by principles of symmetry, variation, inversion, and doubling. Indeed, Lubitsch was one of the first German directors to be called to Hollywood because of his achievements in these areas. There he perfected the interplay between the complete and the incomplete, the seen and the unseen—and later the heard and the unheard—in order to codify the process, or activity, of spectatorship. In this regard *Passion* deserves particular attention. Inaugurating the period of Weimar cinema, the way it plays off narrative logic against mise-en-scène already suggests a number of characteristics that will come to distinguish the German cinema of the Weimar period as a national alternative to the emerging Hollywood model.

The fact that the film plot draws on a historical event—the French Revolution—for its narrative framework seems to be more a coincidence than a calculation of political or overt ideological significance. Although the historical drama dominated the stage at this time, the genre of the historical film really gained popularity only toward the end of the Weimar Republic, and then it turned its attention to Prussian history.[9] In the cinema historical themes were channeled into the costume film, a genre that had been developed in Italy beginning already in 1912 and was to be perfected in the United States under the innovative direction of D. W. Griffith and Cecil B. DeMille. Based on a notion of universal history that could encompass events from biblical anecdotes and Egyptian mythology to military battles in ancient Rome or in recent European history, it elicits parallels to contemporary developments from an organic view of the past that knows no causes, only effects. Furthermore, the costume film had incorporated popular elements of the Italian opera tradition such as complicated intrigues, exaggerated emotions, large casts, and extravagant sets.[10] In contrast Lubitsch combines elements from the drawing-room comedy's irony, the social drama's eroticism, and the psychological drama's strength of motivation to produce the specifically German genre of the historical spectacle or period film.[11]

UFA's production manager, Paul Davidson, regarded a feature about the French Revolution as a way to gain entry into the French market, a major concern for UFA's postwar stabilization because the French film industry had dominated the German market with its exports until the war started. He chose Lubitsch as director not for the latter's experience with historical spectacle (it was his first historically oriented film) but because of his success with *The Oyster Princess* (*Die Austernprinzessin*, 1919) earlier that year, a satirical comedy about an American millionaire, packed with visual tricks in a fairy-tale-like setting. For Lubitsch, who had a virtually unlimited budget for the first time in his directing career, it was an opportunity to indulge fully his well-developed sense of detail: in costume, set design, and group blocking for hundreds of extras. Moreover, he could draw on his experience as an apprentice actor in Max Reinhardt's theater ensemble at the Deutsches Theater in Berlin where mass spectacle and festival theater had become a trademark.[12]

Typically in *Passion* historical event is displaced to the margins and historical ornament (dress, gesture, and decor) dominate the mise-en-scène. Not simplicity or documentary directness but aesthetics and artifice dominate the film's visual style. Although political events and tensions shimmer through, Lubitsch structures the film around plot (narration), character (acting), and spectacle (appearance), adapting more from the conventions of popular literature than historical narratives or historiography. For example, the film draws details from the traditional social drama's plot structure that was familiar to the audience both through popular novels and the cinema: a conflict between rich and poor in which the former are portrayed reductively as lazy, erotic, and decadent and the latter as honest, unerotic, but exploited. Thus, although Lubitsch was not pursuing political aims, like all his films from the German period (until 1922), *Passion* engages the relations of the powerful to their subjects. The common denominator among his comedies, vaudeville extravaganzas, and historical spectacles is the interplay of the look, of desire, and of power.

The film's fictional plot revolves around sexuality and desire. Counterposed to each other are the male obsessions of possession and voyeurism on the one hand and female objectification through spectacle and display on the other. Lubitsch quickly establishes the framework for their interplay. It is no coincidence, for example, that the narrative opens in a dress shop.[13] Jeanne, whose meteoric rise into the world of wealth and noble titles depends on her beauty as exchange value and her eroticism as promise of untold pleasures, makes explicit the connection between the store and patriarchy. Both are ideological edifices that engage relations of power and rely on a system of repressive authority. The first shots in Madame Labille's store clearly portray Jeanne as an energy that must be tamed so that the store's commodity circulation can function. This same energy, however, will enable Jeanne to cross all social thresholds as she liberates herself from patriarchal notions of sexual identity in order to become a narrative agent able to control the look of the (male) Other. Moreover, the representation of this energy coincided with UFA's concern about the film's circulation as commodity by means of Pola Negri's star personality: a mix of innocence and sensuality that has more to do with the changing gender relations in the Weimar Republic than with historical verisimilitude. This personality, revealed most effectively in Jeanne's adeptness at role-playing and in games, becomes increasingly obvious in contrast both to the male characters, who are calculating and motivated by considerations of self-interest (Armand's anger, Diego's and Dubarry's instinctual drive, Choisseul's hunger for power, Louis's masochism), and to the other female characters, who are associated with authority (Mme. Labille), death (Mme. Paillet), and failure (Countess Gramont). The dress shop, itself a world of costume and masquerade, is the ideal point of departure, then, for a film narrative that will focus on woman as the site where appearance and spectacle intersect.

Meanwhile Armand is the site where sexually motivated fears and desire meet generational and class conflict, structuring the plot through a series of confrontations between him and his Other. The first in this metonymic sequence is Don Diego. Along with all the aristocrats he is associated with qualities such as wastefulness and libertine sexuality. Indeed, these are precisely the social class attributes against which the ascendent bourgeoisie historically forged its notions of productivity and repression. Jeanne triggers the conflict between Armand and Diego when she must decide whose invitation to accept for a Sunday afternoon. In the first of several role-playing situations that allow Jeanne a measure of self-control, she introduces a game of chance by counting the ribbons on her bodice to determine the winner. Chance and desire do not coincide, however, when Armand wins this game the first time around, so she begins to count once again, reversing the order in Don Diego's favor and giving in to desire and curiosity. This "decision," this assertion of female sexuality, activates a chain of encounters in which Jeanne, the medium of circulation, mediates male desire.

Jeanne enters a hierarchical social organization as object, exchanged and used by men as a kind of currency in the circulation of male desire. Her positioning as the absolute object of the commodity form is based on her appearance, on characteristics of excessive beauty, ornament, costume, and masquerade. She is a proto–femme fatale, a male fantasy of aggressive sexual allure combined with inaccessibility, a signifier of both desire and fear of that desire. A crucial scene, again one presented as a game situation, illustrates the dialectical tension of passivity and activity inherent in the figure. Furious with Jeanne because she failed to extract money from the king's finance minister, Choiseul, the debt-ridden Dubarry instrumentalizes her beauty during his evening card games in order to attract the attention of the king's chamberlain, Lebel. The intricate play of point-of-view shots and looks across the card table visually foregrounds Jeanne both for the spectator and for Lebel as the site of visual fascination. She is appearance on display, framed or sometimes masked in shots that heighten the voyeuristic quality but also emphasize the relation between male and female as one between their looks. At the same time, this drama of the look, which links the narrative aesthetics inherent in the visual medium to the historical event of revolution, prompts the spectator's imaginary response to the promise of erotic desire, to that which is never seen, shown, or possessed.[14]

The play of appearance engaged by the mise-en-scène allows Jeanne to negotiate the social organization as narrative agent because it confuses the very absoluteness of the distinction between subject and object. Thus, in her excessiveness she is the object of the male gaze but she appropriates in turn and controls the look for herself. The first sequence in Mme. Labille's dress shop charts out the terms of excess and control through a series of shot/reverse shots that will be elaborated in the course of the film. Jeanne, laughing and playful while working on her hats, is repeatedly reminded to behave properly by Mme. Labille's reprimanding stare, a vested authority subsequently born by Choiseul and later by Citizen Paillet and the executioner as representatives of revolutionary justice. Jeanne too is invested with a look, at this point purely intransitive: she peeks at herself in the mirror before leaving the store to see if she *looks* attractive, interrupted once again by a reverse shot of Mme. Labille's contemptuous stare, which puts an end to her narcissistic self-apprehension. The next sequence introduces the logical extension of Jeanne's narcissism by reproducing the spectator's position as an onlooker from within the film. As she walks in the street, men turn to look *at* her, positioning Jeanne as the object of their desire and binding specularity (being-looked-at) to sexuality (desire for the female). The terms of patriarchal discourse have been explicitly and efficiently established within a few moments of the film's first shot. Yet, as the rest of the film will show, Jeanne's sexual identity cannot be contained within these terms. She learns, very quickly, that her look too has a transitive power, disrupting social barriers and leveling thresholds of

Madame Labille reprimands Jeanne with her look while Jeanne looks at herself in the mirror, the beginning of a process in which she learns to control the look (used by permission of Stiftung deutsche Kinemathek, Berlin).

desire. The look, then, begins to emerge as the most forceful language of communication, an ideal vehicle for seduction in a silent film about changing gender relations in the modern world.

This process of appropriating the look for her own purposes begins when Don Diego arrives at the dress shop to reimburse Mme. Labille for the hat his horse accidentally crushed. In a series of eye-line cuts between close-ups of Jeanne's and Diego's faces we see how she becomes aware of the impact her appearance makes on this cavalier. Later, when she enters his house for the Sunday afternoon tryst, she has a moment to survey the richly appointed surroundings. Her look takes possession of the space as the camera pans slightly to the left and then back (one of the few panning shots in the entire film). The implication of her look as a mark of agency becomes clearer in the mirror scene that follows Count Dubarry's interruption of their flirtation. Peeking over the top of the screen behind which Diego has concealed her, the camera frames her in a large mirror hanging

Dubarry watches Jeanne in the mirror looking at Don Diego (used by permission of Stiftung deutsche Kinemathek, Berlin).

above the two men seated at the table across from her. She and Diego mischievously flirt with each other via the mirror while Dubarry concentrates on his meal until the latter, looking up from the table, sees her and, fascinated by her image, also throws her a kiss. The camera cuts to a medium shot (without the mirror) as Jeanne tumbles down from her perch, collapsing the screen and upsetting the ruse of concealment.

Jeanne flaunts her desire, and this positions her as an agent, not only as an object of the look: she entices men to seduce her through her look. At the same time, her power rests in her ability to complicate if not reverse the spectator/spectacle opposition of patriarchal discourse. Women's desire unsettles (men), and the disorientation caused by the collapse in this mirror scene enables Jeanne in an emblematic sense to cross a social and sexual boundary. Increasingly the spectator watches not only the object Jeanne (framed by the camera, looking in mirrors, pinned down by a male gaze) but also the subject Jeanne looking at men or at men being seduced by her beauty, so that the men too become objects of spectacle.

Jeanne's excess splits the spectator's identification, and the mise-en-scène foregrounds her as desired object: through her elaborate costumes and headdresses, through the repeated close-ups of her animated face, in the frequent shots where she looks at herself in a mirror (preparing herself for presentation to a man), and not least of all in the king's demonstrative gesture of using his lorgnon to frame and pin down her image. For those who look these narcissistic images promise a stable identity as unity through possession. Yet when Jeanne looks, she sets herself in relation to other looks and to the looks of an Other, robbing the image of its unity and providing spectators with a position from which we can be looked at. The play of control and loss of control constructs, then, an imaginary relation that oscillates between visual pleasure and anxiety. Inscribed in a network of power and loss of power, this imaginary relation describes a paradigm that will be worked and reworked by many of the most famous features produced during the Weimar period of German cinema. Here Jeanne is the vehicle who in her innocence confirms patriarchal logic and at the same time she is the outsider or Other who violates it by becoming the most powerful woman in France (albeit through the absolute commodification of her body).

Woman as innocent and tempting source of pleasure: Lubitsch's female protagonists are always strong, aggressive women whose strength derives not from manipulative calculation but from an instinctual talent for artifice and the play of appearances. Appearance becomes a real factor in this constellation, and conflicts in Lubitsch's films are carried out between this scandalous power of female artifice and the representatives of social order who fall prey to its seduction. Jeanne, the simple girl of the folk, rises to the position of the king's mistress. She literally makes Louis into her slave, as the sequence following the king's seduction does not hesitate to show. Louis kneels before her, kissing her feet as she languishes on the bed, while the affairs of state wait upon her whim, as Choiseul complains. The camera then frames Louis watching Jeanne with great delight as she dresses behind a screen, until she forbids him to watch. Next the king manicures her fingernails (while two maids look on and laugh), obeying her orders to sit down or exit her chamber as she wishes. Jeanne's assumption of the master's role makes manifest the vulnerability of male control when exposed to the fascination of the erotic and, because this is not a comedy, it explains why she must be eliminated at the end of the film.

Jeanne tries to extend this control not only over the king but also over Armand. At the apogee of her power Jeanne sends for her original lover, whom she has saved from execution for the murder of Don Diego, and at her bidding he is led blindfolded to her chamber. Just as Louis is politically blinded by Jeanne, so Armand is unseeing and unknowing in the romantic tryst she plans. The past, however, cannot be reactivated; rather it has a tendency to return, and then with a vengeance, as a symptom of that which was repressed. When Armand discovers that his beloved Jeanne was his protector but also has become Countess Dubarry, the king's mistress, he

King Louis kisses
Jeanne's foot in a
playful inversion of the
master/slave
relationship (used by
permission of Stiftung
deutsche Kinemathek,
Berlin).

demands that she choose between him and Louis, which she refuses to do, just as she had refused in that original game of counting ribbons on her bodice:

> [title—Jeanne:] You know that I love only you. Ask of me what you will, but not that!

He leaves her, gives himself up to helpless weeping, and eventually leads the mass revolutionary rebellion. Armand's repression of desire and rejection of sexuality allows him to identify fully with the bourgeois revolution. When Jeanne later confronts him (notably in a male disguise, another example of her control of appearance) and elicits a promise from him not to let his comrades destroy her, she asks what wish of his she may fulfill in return:

> [title—Armand:] My only wish is that you disappear from my memory.

History has caught up with the love story, transforming excessive desire into the immediacy of aggravation, rupture, and erasure contained in the sign "French Revolution." Thus, Jeanne comes to symbolize in her very power the most vulnerable point in a moribund system of authority and identity based on exchange: Choiseul hates her because she has undermined his own power; Armand turns against her out of jealousy because he cannot possess her; the "masses" call for her downfall because she represents what all men desire and what all women want to be. Hence, aggression is played out *on* Jeanne, the site where the stability of the entire system is threatened. Arrested by the police, Armand gains his freedom from Choiseul on the condition that he join him—in an ironic parody of class collaboration—to drive out the excess female sexuality threatening the country (Jeanne). Meanwhile the king is stricken by smallpox when playing blindman's bluff in the garden (Jeanne, of course, fastens the blindfold on him), and the entire system of power relations turns against the social outsider and female threat. The revolution erupts in Paris, the masses storm the Bastille as well as the king's residence, and Jeanne, her hiding place divulged by her former servant, is brought before the Revolutionary Tribunal where Citizen Armand now reigns as judge.[15] Although her look can still awaken his desire, he condemns her to death, but—closing the circle of attraction and (self-)destructive repression—he makes one last, desperate attempt to help her escape from prison. Discovered by his comrades, he is shot, and Jeanne is executed on the guillotine while the crowd cheers.[16]

The tremors of revolution, scenes of unrest and conspiracy against the throne, slowly begin to dominate the narrative. Lubitsch was praised for the powerful choreography of the mass scenes in *Passion*. Already in the early opera ball sequence, which culminates in the duel between Armand and Don Diego, the carefully timed rhythm of shot length (long, medium, close) and the variation in camera angle from low to bird's-eye shots reveal a complexity and richness in the creation of on- and offscreen space that was entirely new in the German cinema. Even more striking is the movement of crowds within the frame. Circular, snaking, or lateral lines moving in opposite directions create the maelstrom effect in the scene of dancers at the ball, for example, and in some shots the layering effect of crowds on the dance floor and groups in the theater loges above, or of crowds in public squares and flags waving on poles above, intensifies the dynamization of space. In the court scenes and street scenes Lubitsch effectively employs motion along a diagonal axis from the top to the bottom of the frame (or vice versa) to energize the space between the foreground and the background of the image. In the scenes of revolutionary violence and at the guillotine the combination of groups moving simultaneously back and forth conveys a further sense of the mass dynamic.

Characteristic for all of these scenes, the balls, games, processions, or street clashes, is the way the editing juxtaposes the image of pulsing movement with shots of those individuals whose fate is at stake. Nei-

The opera ball scene molds the space with the depth of field extended along a diagonal axis, the layered balconies, and the choreographed movements of the many dancers (used by permission of Stiftung deutsche Kinemathek, Berlin).

ther the backdrop for an individualized story nor Kracauer's "mass orna-ment," these masses represent a monumental enlargement of the power strategies and erotic play of desire that motivates the protagonists. The careful spatial composition of these scenes produces an effect similar to that of Jeanne's excess. In both cases the material's stylization tends to break down or inhibit narrative progress.[17] That is to say, the shots' tableau quality or theatricality invites the spectator to enter into the play of mise-en-scène, to indulge in the pure contemplation of the image qua image. These effects of narrative hesitation and instability are structurally imbricated with opposing effects of narrative progression. For example, point-of-view shots establish antagonisms and sympathies that invite the spectator's identification, and visual ellipses (understatement, empty shots, deserted frames) cut away just enough to solicit spectator curiosity. Lubitsch's ability to offset nondiegetic moments of excess and stylization against the narrative's economy is one of the film's major achievements. Their modulation—the discrepancy between high drama and its elabo-rate staging—corresponds to the split in spectator identification analyzed above.

It is useful to compare the historical with the textual spectator elicited by the film's narrational structure. In his 1930 study *Die Angestellten* Kracauer established a prototype of the Weimar film spectator as the white-collar, middle-class, urban worker.[18] In *From Caligari to Hitler,* his later analysis of the Weimar cinema written in the forties, he projects this prototype back for the whole period. This allows him to expose the strikingly stable relation between social anxieties expressed in the Weimar films and later experiences under the fascist dictatorship as a symbolic prefiguration. Yet, as critics have argued, this spectator describes a sociological reality that emerged in Germany at the earliest after 1924 in the period of economic stabilization and thus at most only refers to a potential target audience for films produced during the immediate postwar years.[19] A more likely sociological description of the audience in 1919 might be generalized from Emilie Altenloh's 1914 field study of film audiences in the city of Mannheim. Altenloh provides empirical evidence that the cinema audience was much more complex both in class and gender than Kracauer allowed.[20] In light of the continuity in types of films produced before and immediately after the war, one may assume that the cinema was just beginning the transition to that prototype Kracauer suggested. Indeed, UFA's very strategy was to expand its market and therefore its commercial viability by attracting new audiences. Lubitsch's film proved to be the first to address the real and potential needs of this broader mass audience successfully, and in this respect it might be considered prototypical for the Weimar cinema's formal strategies to multiply the possibilities of audience identification inscribed in the narration. Familiar plot devices from popular genres, a fascination with the wealth and decadence of the aristocracy, opportunities to exploit visual spectacle: all were formulaic elements designed to appeal to the viewing dispositions and imagination of the traditional working-class cinema public on whom the social dimension of this voyeurism was certainly not lost. Concurrently, the possibilities of identifying with Jeanne's social mobility as well as Armand's indefinite class position (as student, lieutenant in the king's guard, citizen leader of the revolution, chair of the Revolutionary Tribunal) and the projected triumph of bourgeois rationality and repression offered a middle-class public fantasies of economic and political power that were, in the real context of Germany in 1919 under the influence of the Bolshevist Revolution, just beginning to assert themselves. Lubitsch's balance of extravagance and suggestiveness (in acting, visual images, plot reversals), always just at the edge of the probable and the proper, promised something to both audiences.

For today's spectator Lubitsch's film also raises germane questions about the historical nature of patriarchal discourse on woman as amoral, unknown, and unknowable, a disintegrative force. Jeanne is specifically the hyperbolized figure of excess female sexuality, ignoring or negating all

(socially) acceptable boundaries. Her desire is uncontainable and ultimately fatal (to her and the society around her), yet at the same time its
promise makes her into the most desirable object to possess. The constant
play of the gaze, mirror images, and looks mediated through someone else's
eyes suggests that the activity of watching, the position of the spectator, is
the object of desire rather than the object itself. It is not Jeanne who is desirable but the imaginary activity her figuration allows, precisely because it
acts as a projection screen for spectator fantasies. This radical formalization
of visual elements suggests that the Weimar cinema must be recognized not
only, as critics have argued, for the way it negotiates social anxieties in a
popular entertainment format but also for a specific contribution by the
German cinema to the historical and technological possibilities of spectatorship. The Weimar cinema specialized in the effects of seeing and being
seen, formulating power relations as an instrument of perception and representation. *Passion*, then, marks for the director Lubitsch and for the star
Pola Negri, who later came to embody the femme fatale, an important advance in the cinematic discourse of sexuality and desire. The collapse of
appearance and reality as two separate spheres explains further why *Passion*
can serve neither as a commentary upon history nor as a critical object in
the realist cinema. It contradicts the illusion of immediacy through the
foregrounding of the image. In this respect the film has a paradigmatic
value for the German cinema's development during the twenties. It reveals
some of the basic strategies that will be perfected for structuring a split or
ambiguous position of spectator identification through representation and
narration; it situates the cinema as an apparatus for the production of the
look; and finally its editing and mise-en-scène organize subjectivity and difference around the specular relations.

   For this reason it would be a misreading of *Passion* to claim (based
on this film, at least) that Lubitsch is either reactionary or misogynist. He
clearly distinguishes between the hierarchy among the nobility based on
class and wealth and the revolutionary claim to power based on the look. In
neither case does the director suppose a moralistic attitude nor place the
spectator in a position of contempt. The revolution can either undo the established reign of power or serve it, and when it betrays the power of the
look as a revolutionary weapon, Lubitsch turns against it. Thus, the film invites the spectator to assume a position that recognizes both political revolution and the patriarchy as ideological discourses, while on the level of
narration Lubitsch advances the reign of the look as the mediator of power
relations.

   Offering to the spectator the pleasure of performance and play as
the means to manage repression and disavow anxieties, the imaginary in
Passion belongs to that reversal of the look typical in the Weimar cinema. Unlike Murnau, however, whose concern, as we will see in the next chapter, is

the anxiety of being seen by the Other, Lubitsch's imaginary produces through its specular play a distancing effect close to the tradition of comedy from which he emerged. The resulting ambivalence in spectator positioning disrupts any direct identification on the spectator's part with the protagonist and the tragic end. This distancing effect places Lubitsch as well in a developmental line with the epic qualities that Bertolt Brecht refined for the cinema at the end of the Weimar period, as we will see in chapter 3, a connection that the contemporary filmmaker Jean-Marie Straub has noted.[21] Unlike Brecht, Lubitsch was not interested in the image or in representation as a means of transforming reality but at most in the possibilities of subverting it. This is an attitude the enthusiastic audiences of 1919 seemed to perceive more readily than the (bourgeois) critics, who in the charged postwar atmosphere saw the film as German propaganda against democratic change. Rather it is an imaginary construct for interrogating power strategies that realign sexual roles and sexual repression among the bourgeoisie, a process that was well under way in Germany after the collapse of the Wilhelmine Empire and the defeat of the war in 1918. Less a denunciation of social revolution in the form of the historic French Revolution, the Bolshevist Revolution of 1917, or the revolutionary activities in Germany itself in 1919, *Passion* is an anticipatory critique of emergent bourgeois social life. It not only marks UFA's and Germany's historic entry into the international cinema market, it also offers historical evidence for discourses that were to become more and more threatening in the Weimar Republic: the instability of social authority and gender identity, the unprecedented commercialization of economic life, and the challenge of popular entertainment to traditional cultural values.

2

The Modernist Camera and Cinema Illusion: Friedrich Wilhelm Murnau's *The Last Laugh*

F LUBITSCH'S *PASSION* captures the liberatory sense of impending social change at the outset of the Weimar Republic, then Murnau's *The Last Laugh* (*Der letzte Mann*, 1924) exposes the oppressive anxieties about social destabilization. Both films develop new forms of visual representation to deal with the possibility of reversing power relations through the look, but the former plays with the possibilities of control through exhibitionism (display and seeing), whereas the latter engages paranoid fantasies of loss of control (invisibility and being seen). The imaginary strategies the two films develop represent paradigmatic patterns of the Weimar cinema that can be situated historically within the cultural discourses of modernism. In particular the production dates of these two features (1919 and 1924) frame what has been generally identified by film historians as the period of classical German cinema, that is, a nationally and aesthetically coherent movement referred to as cinematic expressionism and amalgamated to a canon of the world's great films. Indeed, the years between 1919 and 1925 witnessed the development of a strong art cinema in Germany that, from a purely commercial point of view, did not appeal to a mass audience. What became identified as the expressionist cinema by contemporary critics and spectators in Germany and abroad in retrospect comprised probably no more than forty films among the hundreds of productions exhibited during these few years.[1] Yet its importance for the German film industry cannot be underestimated. The idea of an avant-garde art cinema produced in Germany provided the industry with a distinct image of cultural legitimacy which became a competitive factor both for domestic and international audiences. That both Lubitsch and Murnau were invited to produce films in Hollywood is only the most visible (and certainly an unintended) effect of Germany's identification with this art cinema.

The importance of expressionism for the Weimar cinema lies in the evolution of spectator interaction with film narration and in the combination of technology and imagination that intensified the illusion of reality. Expressionism in the cinema emerged as the last manifestation of a broader art movement that in the fine arts, music, literature, and theater had already established itself prior to and during the war. It shares, in other words, the initial impulse of expressionist protest: visionary, ecstatic, and apocalyptic images, an emphasis on the irrational, self-conscious distortion as a formal property, and a consistently antibourgeois social critique.[2] Beyond that, however, cinematic expressionism introduced innovative modes of representation and functional changes in the status of art and entertainment for the middle classes. With its almost originary reinvention of the image's pictorial quality through perspectivally distorted sets, exaggerated gesture, unusual editing rhythms, and the mobile camera, the expressionist film not only developed new habits of seeing that oscillated between distraction and concentration, it also assumed a degree of privatization and fragmentation of social life that on the one hand expanded the horizon of self-identification and on the other enhanced the effects of psychological manipulation. The expressionist aesthetic in the cinema as well as in other arts, with its formal strategies of interiorization, aims at reappropriating an alienated universe by transforming it into a private, personal vision. Expressionism is, then, an aesthetic reaction to a society undergoing radical changes in its social relations and power hierarchies, but it exposes in a privileged way broader and more fundamental shifts as Weimar society sought to adjust to the effects of modernity. Expressionist films contributed to the emergence of the cinema as the most important imaginary domain of modern life, figuring the exemplary modernist response to the structural crisis of the subject.[3]

These changes and the repercussions for their institutionalization are nowhere more evident than during the Weimar period of German cinema, particularly during those postwar years before and after economic stabilization was introduced through American financial guarantees in 1924. Expressionist films opened up new aesthetic ways of creating and organizing social fantasies: by valorizing the autonomous subject against the oppressive rationalism imposed in industrial society, by prioritizing myth and the fantastic over the reality principle, and by instrumentalizing the growing independence of visual perception from the other senses. In numerous ways the implementation of the "expressionist image" broke decisively with the idea that it can reflect or transmit a pregiven reality through the self-sufficiency of the medium, the philosophical foundation of aesthetic realism. This "crisis" in representation was a point of departure that Friedrich Wilhelm Murnau exploited in his systematic understanding of the camera as an instrument of seeing and that Bertolt Brecht would push to its extreme by the end of the Weimar period. The typical modernist reaction to the crisis—already prefigured in Lubitsch's *Passion* — was to seek new ways of confronting and transforming the "real" by splitting the self into a fundamental opposition of subject and object. Many of the formal and thematic innovations of the expressionist cinema derive from this opposition. Yet, if such compositional strategies "reflect" the expressionist response to fragmentation and reification in modernity, they also articulate its protest against the loss of the subject's authenticity and integrity. This accounts for the consistent anticapitalism and the aesthetic critique of bourgeois society in the expressionist films of the early Weimar period, a position shared with modernist aesthetics in general.

The Last Laugh marks a hiatus in the Weimar cinema, drawing on the lessons both of the stylized expressionism in the gothic horror films and of the psychological realism in the *Kammerspielfilm* or intimate melodrama, while already transforming them into the contours of postexpressionism's new objectivity. To understand this shift, it is necessary to retrace the representational strategies that characterize the expressionist cinema. Some film historians stress its elements of style or atmosphere: the dynamization of space through oblique light and shadow, the geometrical or angular composition of filmic space along diagonals or in triangular patterns, or the subordination of set design to oppressive inner states.[4] Others concentrate on philosophical and thematic issues: fables of innocent victims threatened by unknown or irrational forces and haunting images of a dislocated world in which human beings are reduced to automatons, somnambulists, vampires, Golems, and the like.[5] Both approaches recognize that the Weimar cinema found its own "signature" in the expressionist film by redefining specular relations through the camera, different from Griffith's organic editing principles in America, the Soviet dialectics of montage, and the French techniques of impressionistic composition. As a modernist, avant-garde movement cinematic expressionism was committed to constructing the image before the camera and thus guaranteeing the conscious appearance, if not the reality, of the filmmaker's autonomy to shape the world and reality. *The Last Laugh* extends this challenge to renegotiate the terms of spectatorial activity through formal innovation. In doing so, it articulates the historical vicissitudes of the early Weimar period by inventing or imagining a place in a collective and historical process of seeing.

A typically expressionist feature of the cinema crucial to Murnau's filmmaking is the role of abstraction. In expressionist literary texts one finds its poetic correlative in verbal reductionism, the radical condensation of grammar and meaning into single words strung together in a "telegraphic" style. In the theater the growing popularity of pantomime and dance witnessed a similar reduction in the use of language in favor of gesture as the vehicle for expression. In this connection, the influence of Max Reinhardt's theatrical experiments on the Weimar cinema points to the tension between literary ambition and popular culture which accompanied the growing acceptance of the cinema as a legitimate cultural activity.[6] Reinhardt's theater style was antinaturalistic, stressing the stage as a poetic space in which imagination would be kindled not by the realism of the staging but rather by stylized architecture, lighting, gesture, and ultimately language and story. His intimate chamber dramas and monumental spectacles as well as his few film productions anticipated many of the visual effects identified with expressionist cinema. Translated into the silent film, where the word as a vehicle of meaning is available only in intertitular form, this stylization of the "poetic space" took on a life of its own. Moreover, the function of the camera as the "eye" that structures the filmic space quickly revealed its own logic for producing meaning, a logic that in Murnau's hands surpassed even Reinhardt's theatrical innovations.

In their tendency toward wordlessness Murnau's films invented and perfected a technology and a set of cinematic codes corresponding to the complex interplay of word and image. The power of the new medium seemed to reside in the image's photographic authenticity which could communicate without verbal explanation. This apparently unmediated reality of the moving image tended to level literary or theatrical nuance but it also invited filmmakers to elaborate imaginary negotiations for real situations. Structures, forms, and themes no longer acceptable in traditional media were revived successfully in their most trivialized modes for the cinema (pathos, melodrama, slapstick, happy endings, etc.), and that became in itself a reason for the general public to accept the cinema.[7] Murnau and other early Weimar filmmakers adapted this familiar material while seeking to expand the perceptual possibilities of spectatorial activity. Robert Wiene's 1919 film *The Cabinet of Dr. Caligari* (*Das Cabinet des Dr. Caligari*) is, of course, generally considered the preeminent example in German film history for the expressionist style. From the rather thin tradition of the prewar art film it adapted the uncanny ambiguities of doubles, doppelgänger, and the sense of the unknown as part of the visible image. More significantly it established the parameters of imaginary strategies in the Weimar cinema that included interweaving the real and the fantastic, narrativizing the anxiety of the destabilized spectator position with the consequent loss of visual control as a source of pleasure for the viewer, and negating the photographic surface of realism by distorting line, perspective, and objects.[8] *Caligari*, then, indicates a new level of awareness on the part of the producers, the audience, and the critics that specularity—the play of illusion in seeing and being seen—could become the cinema's most creative contribution to the arts and at the same time legitimate it as an acceptable art form.

The Last Laugh, produced in 1924 at the UFA film studios in Berlin, signals a turning point in the financial, cultural, and aesthetic development of the Weimar cinema after the success of the expressionist art film.[9] In contrast to other sectors of the economy, the increasingly uncontrollable inflation between 1918 and 1924 served the expansion of the film industry well and helps explain the tolerance for an artistic avant-garde within the commercial film industry. Inflation favored, on the one hand, the export of German films because they were relatively cheap on the international market and, on the other hand, protected the domestic market from imports because foreign production companies could not earn enough from distribution in Germany. The stabilization of the Reichsmark under the terms of the American-financed Dawes Plan of 1924 ended this expedient situation and quickly reversed the export-import relation, transforming an advantage into a trap for German production companies. Murnau's film was the last UFA prestige production that could benefit from the unstable and inflationary market by capitalizing on its successful international distribution (particularly in the United States), a situation which, for example, Fritz Lang's *Metropolis* no longer enjoyed one year later.

The expansion of the cinema audience in Germany from a primarily working class to a mass public had become by 1924 not only a film industry marketing strategy but also one of the integrative illusions that fed cinematic dreams. The burgeoning ranks of state employees in the new Republic and of service sector employees in the new consumer market constituted that historical spectator with middlebrow tastes whom Murnau addressed in his film allegory of economic degradation and redemption.[10] The urban, white-collar worker, who is economically dependent like the traditional wage laborer but who identifies subjectively with middle-class status and values of stability, had become a determining factor in culture consumption in the rapidly expanding metropolitan areas. Together with his production team Murnau devised new visual means of narrativization that intensified for this modern mass audience the fantasy of cinematic omnipotence. Moreover, by 1924 the role of experimental art films gradually diminished as competition from another sector of the media, radio broadcasting, appeared on the horizon. This changing cultural context corresponded to a shift in audience demands for more realism instead of the typical stylization of expressionist films. UFA was clearly concerned about competition from the technologically superior American film industry but also aware that the German industry could maintain the loyalty of its domestic audience and compete internationally by supporting the innovations identified with the expressionist cinema. The introduction of the *entfesselte* or unchained camera in *The Last Laugh* was a sensational achievement that marked both the endpoint and turning point in the gradual narrativization of the dynamic relationship between spectator and action. Not only was it able to represent psychic disruption through camera movement, it also could bind the

The *entfesselte Kamera* or unchained camera was a contraption attached to the chest of the camera operator (used by permission of
Stiftung deutsche Kinemathek, Berlin).

spectator more effectively than anything yet attempted in the cinema by
positioning the camera as the ultimate, all-knowing voyeur.

The film narrative—drawing on a banal story about the vanity of an
elderly man who is caught and ultimately crushed between the equally
stultifying social rituals of the wealthy and the poor—moves between two
social sites: the posh hotel with its lights, glistening surfaces, up-scale clien-
tele, and bustling activity, and the tenement building with its cramped,
poorly lit spaces. The protagonist is a doorman at the hotel who, too old to
shoulder the guests' heavy baggage, is demoted to the position of lavatory
attendant in the hotel's cellar and must exchange his flashy uniform for a
simple white smock. An epilogue transforms the pathos of his demise and
gives the proper twist to the title.[11] Although the lowest in the social pecking
order, the lavatory attendant was the last man to serve the American millionaire A. G. Monney before his death and according to the testament in-
herits his entire fortune. The film spins out a fantasy on the power and
function of wealth, while it subordinates these story elements to a parable
about the difference between identity and false image. On another level,
however, *The Last Laugh* can be understood as a modernist text that

protests reified social life by constructing the anxiety of being seen as the imaginary power of the Other.

Producer Erich Pommer entrusted the project for this representative prestige film to a practiced team identified with successes of the avant-garde expressionist cinema. Reputedly inspired by a newspaper account of the suicide of a lavatory attendant, the sensationalistic story was transformed by Murnau and his scriptwriter Carl Mayer into an imaginative drama between the unseen as potential threat and the seen as potential illusion. Film histories generally overlook the care Mayer took to write for the camera, describing in detail perspectives, positions, and movements. He also continued to involve himself in productions after completing the scripts, not only for revisions but also to consult with and advise the technical crew and the director.[12] *The Last Laugh* was the third in a trilogy of *Kammerspiel* or chamber films written by Mayer.[13] The chamber film genre—to a large extent elaborated by Mayer—revived naturalist themes and coupled them with formal qualities Reinhardt had employed in his intimate (*Kammerspiel*) theater productions. Like other expressionist films, those belonging to this genre radicalize a fatalistic and oppressive atmosphere, but instead of a destructive interruption from an unknown, outside source which decenters the protagonist, here obsession and instinct, the protagonist's own projections of inadequacy, lead to the downfall. Parallel to this inward focus of the protagonist are the classical dramatic unities of time, place, and action and the abstraction of characters to nameless ciphers (i.e., the doorman, the hotel manager). Within this sparse, reduced narrative framework other visual elements signify even more powerfully: gesture, facial expression, objects, costumes, light/dark contrasts, reflective surfaces, movement within the frame, etc. To stress the characters' pathological nature, Mayer limited more and more the role of language in his film scripts by suppressing the use of intertitles. *The Last Laugh* achieved a reputation as the most perfect German silent film because it almost totally eliminates the written word, heightening the narrative's pace, its fluidity, and tension.[14] Without the crutch of written titles, however, the task of narrativizing the silent film falls either to montage editing (as developed at this time by Soviet directors) or to the camera. Murnau, Mayer, and cameraman Karl Freund pursued the latter option, unchaining the camera and transforming it into an instrument of voyeurism par excellence with a life of its own.

For Murnau the unchained camera was a logical extension of his antitheatrical approach to the cinema and the culmination of his attempts to place the spectator in the mise-en-scène instead of in front of a set. Some examples illustrate the technical virtuosity he focused on this goal. After the doorman becomes drunk on the evening of his daughter's wedding, he hears one of the musicians in the tenement courtyard play a melody on his trumpet. The trumpeter turns his horn to the camera, its opening fills the frame, and as the shot cuts to a bird's-eye angle from the doorman's perspective at his apartment window above, the camera tracks quickly backwards, as if the sound of the trumpet were visibly flying up to his ear. A similar (mute) visual image for the movement of sound through space is used in the scene where the doorman's neighbors are calling the news of his humiliating demotion from one balcony of the tenement to another, the camera tracking rapidly forward from a mouth to a waiting ear. Even more striking is the scene that reputedly led to the "discovery" by Freund of a technological solution for unchaining the camera.[15] The disclosure of the doorman's demotion to the lavatory ensues when the aunt of his new son-in-law comes to the hotel with a pot of hot soup for his lunch. A messenger fetches the doorman from below while she waits at the top of the stairs. As actor Emil Jannings's face, seen from a high angle, slowly emerges from the lavatory door, the camera in a reverse shot frames her angry face; her mouth opens to a horrified cry, and the camera tracks quickly to a close-up of her nose and gaping mouth followed by another reverse shot in close-up of Jannings's nose and mouth as his head retreats behind the door. Although these drastic camera movements threaten to overpower the narrative, they are an effective means for positioning the spectator as voyeur of this man's inner psychic world, literally visualizing the unseeable with "images" of sound and psychic states.

There are many instances of other complicated camera maneuvers: first, the spectacular movement of the introductory sequence lasting over a half minute as the camera descends in an open elevator and then tracks forward through the lobby and up to the hotel's revolving door; second, the pans around and through doors (the revolving door in the hotel lobby, the glass door of the hotel manager's office, the lavatory's opaque glass swinging doors, the tenement's apartment doors and portals); third, the sequences in the darkened hotel corridor as the doorman steals and later returns his elegant uniform, accompanied by pans and tracking shots as well as by the eerie flashlight beam of the night watchman; and finally, the doorman's drunken scene after the wedding party where the unchained camera literally dances around his living room as an introduction to his dream, in its symbolic distortions the most "expressionistically" stylized sequence of the entire film. The numerous tracking and panning shots often have less of a dramatic function in the theatrical sense than one of focusing the spectator's attention on the offscreen space, on that which is not seen but yet constantly hovers as a threat.

Other visual effects reinforce the power of the look over this man without a self-image. Subjective shots convey the doorman's sense of fear after stealing the uniform: on the street in front of the hotel a low angle shot makes the buildings seem to be collapsing on him. His morning-after hangover is shown with trick shots of a double coffee pot, the contorted face of

Visual effects like double exposures exteriorize the subjective confusion of a hangover (frame enlargement by Kristin Thompson, Madison).

a neighbor woman, and the blurred facade of the tenement. And his neighbors' contemptuous laughter at his fall climaxes in superimposed close-ups of several grimacing mouths. In each case the anxiety of being seen is projected into the punishing, disintegrating look of the other through the distorted camera perspective. Contrasting shot angles have a similar function. The rapid oscillation between high and low angles when the doorman unloads an enormous trunk from a taxi emphasizes the threatening situation. Generally the doorman's size (and importance) is exaggerated by low angle shots before his fall, whereas later high angle shots intensify his humiliation and reduced, bowed demeanor. With diagonal constructions and movements that alternate with more balanced ones, the frame composition frequently reinforces the effect of such shot manipulation. For example, after stealing the uniform, the doorman's bent frame leans against a blank wall and then strains against a strong wind, cutting the image in half along a diagonal axis. In addition, repeated and distinct gestures—the doorman's vain twirling of his moustache, his whistle-blowing to hail the taxis, and his arrogant hand signals for them, but also later the slow, measured moves of his old body—constitute a pictorial dramatization that is independent of camera movement or montage.

Lighting also contributes to the figuration and dynamics of space in which the interplay of seeing and being seen takes place. Murnau's careful mise-en-scène of light and shadow to create a unique plasticity and depth for the image has been the object of much comment.[16] Striking instances in *The Last Laugh* include the night scenes where sparkling light emanates from splashing raindrops or pools of water on the streets, the doorman's rain coat glistening in the rain or his uniform glowing with an inner light when hanging in the hotel manager's cupboard, the lighted windows of the tenement or the neon signs on the city buildings, and the many mirror or glass surfaces. Light here is not the reflection of an outside source or even an ornamental element (as is often the case in Fritz Lang's films) but rather suggests in its intensity and dispersal another world, the unseen world of darkness and lurking shadows opposed to such clarity. Objects too are infused with a life of their own, with the latent and as yet unknown. Even the most harmless object seems to conceal fatality, thus destabilizing its own immobility or the equilibrium of the image. The doorman's umbrella, a button that detaches from his uniform, his whistle, the trunk he carries, the various coats (his rain coat, his uniform, the night watchman's overcoat) play an active role in narrating the story. Unlike Lubitsch, for whom objects and clothes are externalities that a person uses to "stage" the self, for Murnau they convey an essence. When the doorman loses his uniform, it is removed from him like a second skin and brings about a metamorphosis in his personality. Likewise the architecture—the blank walls, the many doors, the windows that block or transmit light, the mirrors into which the doorman gazes—is not just the background for the characters but an expressive framework for their actions. The doorman defines his spaces as much as he is defined by them.

Beyond these properties of movement and dramatization within shots, Murnau also employs various editing and montage effects to connect shots, although in *The Last Laugh* he is more reserved in this practice than in the earlier *Nosferatu* or the later *Faust*, both of which have more shots and suggest greater visual fragmentation. While dissolves, fades, masks, irises, and shot/reverse shots are used conventionally to concentrate spectator perception and to punctuate the narrative, other kinds of editing are less routine.[17] The visual rhyme achieved through the repetition of the revolving hotel door with its modulations in the elongated door in the doorman's dream of revenge and the swinging doors of the lavatory builds on associational editing. These doors are barriers but pervious ones that enable people to pass one another without seeing each other. The way the camera stops when the manager enters the lavatory to check on a guest's complaint about the demoted doorman and waits until he emerges several seconds later (in contrast to other instances of the camera "moving through" doors) is an example of elliptical editing that encourages the spectator to construct

Elements of the architecture like swinging doors contribute to the expressive framework of the protagonist's actions (used by permission of Stiftung deutsche Kinemathek, Berlin).

meaning from what is *not* seen.[18] This narrational technique reinforces the paranoid and voyeuristic play of sight by calling attention to the camera as narrator, even when it is not used subjectively.

The precision and variety of imaginative camera techniques suggest a visual surplus whose significance conceals a second text or context for meaning production. The first two shots, for example—the vertical descent in the elevator and the horizontal tracking shot through the hotel lobby, stopping at the revolving glass entry door which looks out from the brilliantly lit space to the darker street—establish a set of oppositions before they are implicated in the narrative. Thematically these oppositions of vertical/horizontal, movement/blockage or movement/boundary, and light/dark will become the context for the affectivity of the doorman's fall, worked and reworked in innumerable combinations. Likewise the emphatic, lingering camera that frames objects and clothing tends to humanize them, while the person whose story they tell is increasingly reified and dehumanized. The doorman "becomes" part of the revolving lobby door and later of the swinging lavatory doors. His uniform "is" his self-identity and at the same time the externalized form of his self-alienation, blinding him to the reality of the system that exploits him.

Another kind of opposition is introduced in the figure of doubling. The shock of recognition the old doorman experiences when faced with the newly hired, younger counterpart is a scene symbolically situated by the camera *in* the revolving door with the frame split vertically by the door's axis. This self-assured, strong doorman has usurped the protagonist's place in front of the hotel and donned an exact copy of his uniform. The double, like the doppelgänger so familiar from earlier German films, is the visual projection of the Other who deprives the self of identity and thereby controls the past of a character. The fundamental crisis leads to a loss of authority, here communicated by the camera through shots of Jannings's catatonic reaction: frozen poses of the broken, humbled doorman. The reversibility he experiences is another version of that modern reification mentioned earlier, the experience of the self as object in the crisis of subjectivity. For the doorman the image of the double confronts him with the power he has invested in being seen in the uniform. The semimilitary disguise endows him in his own eyes with authority but blinds him to its anachronistic symbolic value of servility. Obsequious toward the hotel hierarchy and its social clients who can so arbitrarily exert their authority over an old man no longer able to perform his function adequately, yet foolishly vain and arrogant toward his neighbors because he sees himself, dressed in the uniform, as better than they, the doorman is caught at his moment of insight literally in the revolving door and symbolically in a contracted social space. Having lost his uniform, he also loses his sense of self, which he gained at the price of dependency. Moreover, without this sign of respect his family and neighbors also exchange their regard for scorn and contempt, a specular image in reverse of his own arrogance toward them because they share his belief in the power of the image. In other words, the film portrays the spiteful, vicious, and petty behavior of the lower class just as critically as the inhumanity of the upper class, and the doorman falls prey to both because he has no identity of his own.

The only indication of an alternative behavior in the film are several scenes where the doorman displays compassion. The appreciation he shows toward a young bellboy who brings him a glass of water, his playful flirtation with two young women he escorts to a waiting taxi, the attentions toward a small girl who hurt herself in the tenement courtyard, and most obviously, the solidarity he feels with the old night watchman who understands the depth of his obsessive desire: these point to a humane, grandfatherly nature that exists outside the system of status and respectability symbolized by the uniform and beyond the oppositions that motivate his fall. Yet, at the end of the main part the doorman's shame derives from his blindness to the reality of a system manifested by this uniform, for it eliminates socially useful qualities such as naive playfulness, generosity toward children, and circumspection toward fellow workers. In the face of this in-

Only outside the social hierarchy of status and respectability symbolized by the uniform is the porter able to show compassion, for example, toward a girl who hurt herself (used by permission of Stiftung deutsche Kinemathek, Berlin).

difference he is ready to die. The epilogue, however, shows the doorman redeemed through money, itself no more than a substitute uniform that demonstrates an even more delicate stability in the circulation of identity and image. Money too can provide him with an external image, that is, with status that can be seen and the power it implies.

The context of modernity figured in *The Last Laugh* is constituted by the perception of the leveling effects of economic instability and inflation coupled with the effects of commodification in a technologically oriented industrial society. Murnau's film articulates these alarming perceptions in a paranoid parable about the terror of the look. The emergence of formal and technical innovations that perfect the narrativization of this threatened subjectivity suggests how a modification in aesthetic properties can reveal social and ideological value. Simply put, the unchained camera with its implications for the emancipation of the spectator's look also corresponds to the social mobility experienced in the Weimar years, both positively and negatively. The Weimar cinema developed a textual system distinct from other national cinemas precisely through an elaboration of visual and editing techniques that relate sight/seeing and the power it concedes. This film joins together the internal rendering of the doorman through the use of the subjective camera with a socially critical view of his reified destiny as the marginal victim. The double focus produces an imaginary relation for the spectator in which the anxiety of proletarianization or class decline is projected as the paranoia of not being seen or of not seeing those who look. The doorman's tragic struggle for the unseen reveals, then, a psychological dimension of subject decentering that could be generalized for the Weimar period. The epilogue seeks to reassure the spectator that the imaginary relation produced by the film is a secure position, although the exaggerated happy ending also hints at its illusory nature.

Less controversial in its subsequent reception than the frame story attached to Wiene's *The Cabinet of Dr. Caligari*, the explosive, provocative epilogue to *The Last Laugh* offers an equally well-tuned instrument for rereading the film. Supposedly suggested by producer Erich Pommer because he found the unrelieved pathos of the main part to be uncommercial, it has been interpreted variously as a parody of the Hollywood happy ending or as its emulation.[19] In either case, the inversion is not merely sentimental or a capitulation to what Pommer might have considered popular taste. The narrative device of the unknown millionaire's bequest and the doorman's subsequent eating orgy together with the night watchman in the hotel's dining room is so contrived that it suggests the kind of ferocious, aggressive caricature of George Grosz's contemporaneous drawings.[20] Despite, or maybe owing to this contrivance the resolution's poetic justice is convincing because it offers the spectator a satisfying sense of closure. The doorman rewards the compassionate (the night watchman) and the needy (the new lavatory attendant and the entire staff of hotel lackeys), ignores the haughty (the bourgeois guests in the dining room and the hotel manager) and apparently forgets his family and neighbors, who do not figure in the epilogue at all. Yet, the invitation to the spectator to enjoy the justice is offset by its self-serving nature. The epilogue's dramatic triumph perpetuates the aggrandizement of a system that cannot fulfill the needs it awakens, nor can it reestablish the framework that provided the originally stable identity for the doorman at the beginning. The line of hotel employees waiting for tips in the last sequence stresses one last time the role of money in a corrupt and unstable system, and the final sequence only reiterates how capricious and fragile respectability is and how little it has to do with external appearances. A panhandler who approaches the doorman's carriage is pushed away by the new doorman, but Jannings invites him to take a seat and, as the carriage lurches forward, the beggar is jolted onto the floor. The eternal return of success/failure undermines the optimism that one might ever control the system of winning and losing.

The grotesque contrast of utter degradation and gratuitous wealth traced along clear class lines indeed leaves no middle ground. Produced in 1924, at a crucial juncture in the Weimar Republic's evolution after a period of inflationary chaos, economic crisis, and political instability, Murnau's film projects not so much the trauma of proletarianization for a threatened middle class but rather the modernist crisis of the subject. There is no structural or institutional place between the alternatives presented in the film except compassion, and thus, the film's social dilemma is less one of leveling than of loss, the loss of stable identities in a society regulated by consumerism and appearances. The imaginary position allowed by the reconciliation corresponds to nostalgic or utopian notions of subjecthood. While the film's aesthetics, in particular its narrational devices and its carefully structured play of the look, rely on socially critical oppositions, its effect is to defuse these subversive figurations and their critical content through the constant shifts in specular relations, a process that the epilogue only underscores. Weimar cinema presents a privileged space to analyze the way aesthetic pleasure derives from the ambivalent oscillation or reversals between decentering identifications and the delimiting or mastery of that activity through the narrative closure of a film story. In other words, the epilogue displaces the spectator's desire for the secure subject, for meaningful life or for justice, into an imaginary relation that merely compensates for the doorman's earlier humiliation. The anarchic energy behind this exaggerated inversion suggests less an awareness of the rottenness of the system, which generates in the first place such degradation, than a capitulation to the system's all encompassing power. The alienated existence of the doorman is not undone by the epilogue, only reversed by a turn of fate. An unalienated otherness in the form of an identity somehow not dependent on a signifier like the uniform or money is projected only halfheartedly in the doorman's compassionate behavior, a compromise that corresponds to the handshake between the workers and the employers at the end of Lang's *Metropolis*. As a result, the happy ending seems to suggest that redemption from social degradation, humiliation, and nonauthenticity (individualistic values so important to traditional culture) lies in consumerism and the status it bestows, a recognition that resonates with the wide-ranging economic and social transitions that were under way in Germany in 1924.

3

The Rhetoric of the Image:
Slatan Dudov and Bertolt Brecht's
Kuhle Wampe or Who Owns the World?

WHILE *PASSION* AND *The Last Laugh* illustrate how the early Weimar cinema evolved specific visual, narrational, and technological effects to depict the volatile social relations of the period, *Kuhle Wampe or Who Owns the World?* (*Kuhle Wampe oder Wem gehört die Welt?* 1932) marks a more radical, overtly politicized appeal to spectatorial activity in the context of the noncommercial cinema in the Weimar Republic. Indebted to the example of Soviet montage, the film demonstrates how a politicized cinema that goes beyond issues of radical content tries to mobilize the audience. In this model, seeing context and recognizing connections as an empowering cognitive process rather than voyeurism and spectacle describe the spectator's imaginary activity. Produced collectively under the protection of the Communist Party and with the participation of many prominent leftist artists, *Kuhle Wampe* was released less than a year before the fascist takeover in 1933. In this respect the project reveals symptomatic deficits and illusions on the part of the Left at this time of social crisis but it also marks a watershed in discussions concerning the nature of cinematic representation as well as the abrupt endpoint in a decade-long development of leftist filmmaking in Germany that would not be revived for over twenty-five years.[1]

For the film industry the latter half of the twenties was characterized by increasing centralization and monopolization in all sectors including technological development, production, distribution, exhibition, and even marketing and reception through the press. The economics of stabilization introduced in 1924 and 1925 with the guarantee of American financial support created a situation in which the German market suddenly became highly vulnerable to the export intentions of other countries, especially in the cinema branch. American films flooded the German cinemas, and the German film industry became more and more dependent on Hollywood.[2] Added to this was the constant drain of film talent hired away by Hollywood studios throughout the twenties. By 1926 all the major production companies that had not yet fused or gone bankrupt entered into capitalization arrangements with American film companies, thus formalizing their financial dependency and effectively neutralizing Germany as America's most important competitor in the international market.

One year later in 1927 Alfred Hugenberg reorganized the premiere German film company UFA with the participation of domestic investors and with the support of politically conservative and nationalistic interests. As a result, it became part of one of the world's largest media conglomerates including newspapers, a major publishing house, and a news agency. The competition for investment capital to underwrite film production began to influence film content and form.[3] Not only did the commercial cinema increasingly standardize its offerings for what it considered a homogeneous urban public, abandoning the commitment to differentiated audiences as had been the case, for instance, with the expressionist "art cinema" or with the melodramatic *Kammerspielfilms* appealing to female spectators, but it also sought to gentrify production values and material by imitating Hollywood standards. Although there was still a place for isolated examples of experimental filmmaking (e.g., Walther Ruttmann's *Berlin, Symphony of a Great City* [*Berlin, Die Symphonie einer Grossstadt*], 1927, or the collaborative film *People on Sunday* [*Menschen am Sonntag*], 1929) and even for sophisticated, socially critical films (e.g., G. W. Pabst's *The Joyless Street* [*Die freudlose Gasse*] or Gerhard Lamprecht's *Slums of Berlin* [*Die Verrufenen*], both 1925), the studios directed their energies primarily toward the few expensive, international prestige films like Joe May's *Asphalt* (1929) or toward the many low-cost, lowbrow films that avoided controversy in favor of the obvious and the formulaic.

Kuhle Wampe fell outside the boundaries of commercial film production and stands as an example of ambitious efforts during the twenties to develop in Germany an independent, noncommercial cinema for the political and entertainment needs of the organized working class. Even before the war working-class organizations and industrial unions had supported a network of social and cultural agencies. With the split of the working-class movement into a social-democratic and a communist wing after the war, these efforts expanded further and led at times to a competitive, sometimes politically counterproductive rivalry. As far as the cinema was concerned, both working-class parties were tardy in recognizing its revolutionary technological and aesthetic implications, thus misjudging the political potential inherent in the medium. Basically the Left positioned itself defensively in a critical posture defined by conservative and traditional cultural values.[4]

The Social Democratic Party (SPD) slowly became concerned with influencing the production side of the film industry by creating new distribution outlets under its own control and by raising the taste of the working-class public through information and film journalism. By the midtwenties the party had established a central distributor for cultural, informational, and high quality studio films. In addition, it organized and trained mobile projection teams for film screenings among union groups and at educational meetings in order to circumvent the ever increasing impact of state censorship or the boycotts organized by commercial distributors. Direct investment in film production was minimal and had ceased entirely by 1929.[5] The German Communist Party adopted a somewhat different, more defensive policy. Despite Lenin's stress on the cinema as the most important of the arts, Clara Zetkin, a highly respected German Communist leader, in 1919 defined the party's position when she rejected the cinema as a tool in the hands of the capitalist class to divert the attention of the workers from the class struggle. Of course, she was judging the cinema as it existed in the form of commercial entertainment films. Nonetheless, this suspicious attitude toward the mass media as a manipulatory instrument continued to define the party's policy throughout the twenties. The cinema with its suggestive images was seen as a means of influencing public opinion, and the party's goal was to harness this power in conventional forms of critical realism in order to manage the purported emotional and identificatory effect for its own ideological ends.[6]

By focusing attention on the medium's content rather than its signifying and representational systems, the leftist critics remained blind to the emancipatory, cognitive possibilities of the medium. Although the Communist Party had begun as early as 1922 to produce short newsreels and documentaries in an attempt to counteract the misinformation of the dominant media about the revolutionary developments in the Soviet Union, it was not until 1925 that a more comprehensive film policy began to emerge in its cultural programs. There were a number of practical reasons for this shift. First, with the stabilization of the economy in 1925 it became clear that a political revolution was not imminent in Germany, and therefore more effort came to be focused on cultural work and propaganda rather than direct political intervention. Second, the introduction of a contingency ruling in 1925 regulating the import of foreign films made it necessary for the Left to produce its own films in order to be able to screen features from the Soviet Union that commercial exhibitors boycotted. Third, the new Soviet films by Eisenstein, Pudovkin, and Vertov, which were distributed in Germany beginning in 1926, offered not only a different model for the cinematic medium with their visual and agitational properties but also seemed to prove that there was a viable Left alternative to the commercial industry. Willi Münzenberg, a party functionary and Communist member of parliament, played the key role in implementing an organizational model for Communist media agitation in the Weimar Republic. He established the Prometheus-Film Corporation in 1926 as a distribution outlet for Soviet films and, more importantly, as a firm with sufficient capital to underwrite worker-oriented films produced in Germany.[7] *Kuhle Wampe*, the last production planned by Prometheus before its collapse in 1932, reveals the contradictions in the notion of a proletarian counter public sphere under the conditions of economic collapse prior to the Nazis' appropriation of power in 1933.

The Prometheus initiative appeared to challenge the commercial film industry, but the actual results were not impressive. The examples of Russian innovations in film narration had less impact on the German cinema than on literary and dramatic arts, where discussions concerning realism and montage techniques dominated leftist circles.[8] Both documentary and feature-length entertainment films produced by Prometheus stressed the proletarian content as a contrast to the commercial industry at the expense of formal innovation. Thus, many productions celebrated their status as "class-conscious" alternatives to the dominant cinema although they merely imitated already popular successes of the major studios.

Piel Jutzi's *Mother Krause's Journey into Happiness* (*Mutter Krausens Fahrt ins Glück*, 1929) is a case in point. Banking on the established taste for "Zille films," a subgenre of the naturalistic social drama drawing on anecdotes and characters from Berlin's slums, which the graphic artist Heinrich Zille had memorialized, Jutzi tells the melodramatic tale of a family in which the mother commits suicide out of financial desperation while her daughter finds new meaning in her life by sharing her lover's political commitment to the working-class movement. The film highlights images of working-class misery aimed, on the one hand, against the idealizing illusions of the "dream factory" and, on the other, at awakening empathy in the spectator through the pathos and victimization of the young heroine. These images of urban misery are set off against beautiful images of nature, where the workers spend their free time. The everyday working world, then, is not portrayed as a site of contradiction and struggle, as the Left's political program proclaimed, but rather as an oppressive world to be tolerated. Although the final sequence, with its optimistic images of the heroine being swept away in a street demonstration, is an unmotivated, mechanistic resolution to the entangled love affair and its tragic consequences for the mother, at the time it signaled a milestone since this was the first fictional feature film from Germany that pointed directly to class struggle as an alternative to political resignation among the proletariat.[9] Yet, the declamatory conclusion reveals in the portrayal of the heroine's spontaneous "coming to class consciousness" under the authority of her male companion a voluntarism characteristic of Communist Party cultural policy in general.

Mother Krause's Journey into Happiness marked the high point of Prometheus's commercial success, for 1929 witnessed two crucial developments that exacerbated the weaknesses of an independent Left cinema: the introduction of the sound film and the onset of the international market crash. For the commercial film industry the coming of sound was a blessing in disguise, a new technology that despite its high investment costs promised to increase flagging audience attendance owing to its novelty. An undercapitalized firm like Prometheus, however, found it impossible to compete. The worldwide depression only complicated these tendencies. The major studios produced more and more escapist fare for an audience that had less and less discretionary income to buy admission tickets, and Prometheus, which had released as many as fifteen productions a year between 1927 and 1930, had cut back to only four shorts in 1931 and two shorts and *Kuhle Wampe* in 1932. Other leftist support foundered as well. The growing polarization of German society affected working-class cultural agencies, which were devoting reduced resources to battle ever harsher state censorship. By 1929 the SPD had ceased investment in film production, and the Communist Party abandoned its support of feature-length entertainment films in favor of agitational and informational shorts.[10] This latter move simply underscored the party's political commitment to an authoritarian discourse in which it assumed the role of the vanguard, a position figured in the *Mother Krause* film in the final images of the political demonstration. *Kuhle Wampe* is an anomaly, then, in more than one sense. Whereas the Left's strategy in both politics and culture had evolved on a hierarchical model in which an elite represents, informs, and acts for the interests of the masses, the Dudov/Brecht film argues for a dialectic of political form and social content that constitutes the imaginary relation of the spectator as a participatory, cognitive process.

As Prometheus's financial situation became more precarious, it hit upon the idea of making a feature-length film on the youth movement and its sports organizations as a means of cashing in on and supporting the idealism among leftist youth.[11] Early in 1931 Slatan Dudov approached the company with a film sketch about unemployment and resignation in a working-class family.[12] Despite its financial difficulties, Prometheus accepted the project with an eye to integrating the sports theme into what would become its first sound film. Before it was finished, the firm went bankrupt, and only with financial support from the Swiss Praesens-Film company was *Kuhle Wampe* finally finished.[13] The Bulgarian Dudov, who after studying theater in Berlin had become involved with Erwin Piscator's political stage, met Brecht in 1929.[14] He was also interested in the cinema, having worked as Fritz Lang's assistant on the *Metropolis* set as well as on several documentaries for Prometheus. For Brecht, these were the years during which he was formulating his "materialist aesthetics" through the study of Marxist texts. Seeking new answers to the question "what is political art?" he was experimenting with models for linking cultural production to social change in his *Lehrstücke* (didactic plays), in film scenarios, and in theoretical essays such as those that accompanied his court case against the producers of the *Threepenny Opera* film. Brecht's *Threepenny Opera*, the most successful play of the Weimar years, had placed the author in the international limelight, and G. W. Pabst's film version of the play had opened in February 1931 to rave reviews. Brecht, who was concerned with the implications of his play's success in a capitalist theater institution, had written a new film scenario in order to radicalize both the formal means of distanciation and the anticapitalist message. The producer and Pabst had refused, however, to recognize Brecht's rights as author to revise the play, so he went to court and, in a widely publicized trial immediately preceding the shooting of *Kuhle Wampe*, Brecht undertook what he called a "sociological experiment" to unmask the contradiction between bourgeois ideologies of autonomous art and the demands of capitalist production in the culture sphere.[15]

The collective that came together around Brecht and Dudov was in part dictated by difficult and impoverished production conditions but also reflected the attempt to counteract the hierarchical studio arrangements in the commercial industry. Dudov brought in novelist Ernst Ottwald, to whom the film scenario is attributed along with Brecht, because of his intimate knowledge of the working-class environment. Hanns Eisler, who was working with Brecht and Dudov on the stage production of *The Mother*, also joined the team. He had experience writing modernist film music (e.g., for a revised version of Walther Ruttmann's *Opus* 3, 1927, and for Viktor Trivas's *Hell on Earth* [*Niemandsland*], 1931) and enjoyed a reputation for his popular workers' songs.[16] Helene Weigel, who sings one of Eisler's ballads, and Ernst Busch, who plays the lead role Fritz, were also well-known actors in the workers' theater movement. Finally, the appearance of the leading agitprop theater group, The Red Megaphone (*Das rote Sprachrohr*), as well as the participation of thousands of enthusiasts organized in workers' sports clubs for the final section of the film brought an unusual degree of visibility and public interest to the collective project.[17]

Kuhle Wampe's theme is a departure from the "traditional" proletarian film productions supported by Prometheus and the Communist Party. In what seems to have been a conscious effort to respond to the discourse of authority in *Mother Krause's Journey into Happiness*, it takes up similar plot elements from the social drama, including a suicide, a love affair, leisure activities, and the emancipation of the daughter through her political work. *Kuhle Wampe*, however, thematizes petit bourgeois behavior as a reality of the working class, contrary to the denunciatory position more typical of official leftist party views. Hence, the film problematizes precisely the issue that in the early thirties was proving to be a fertile basis for the other, fascist discourse of authority as well. In the period of crisis characterizing the last years of the Weimar Republic the structural instability of the proletariat caused by unemployment and impoverishment made it particularly susceptible to middlebrow ideologies of social harmony and classless statism proposed by the National Socialists. *Kuhle Wampe* addresses various aspects of this issue not so much to clarify its causes but to show the powerlessness effected by the desire to escape from politics altogether. In this respect, the film differs radically from Jutzi's melodrama and other socially critical portrayals of petit bourgeois family life (e.g., Leo Mittler's *Harbor Drift* [*Jenseits der Strasse*], 1929, or Hans Tintner's *Cyanide* [*Cyankali*], 1930) as well as from the industry's attempts to capitalize on the effects of the depression with escapist comedies and musicals (e.g., Wilhelm Thiele's operetta *The Three from the Filling Station* [*Die Drei von der Tankstelle*], 1930).

Beyond its thematic and political distinction *Kuhle Wampe* introduces a different structural approach. It draws formally on the rhetorical model of Soviet montage in order to elicit cognitive activity such as persuading, deciding, and seeing.[18] Premised on interruption, montage editing connects the spectator with the image by insisting on being "read." Seeing the context that has been interrupted becomes the basis of a pedagogical model of spectatorial activity. *Kuhle Wampe* was, in fact, an important opportunity for Brecht to test his Epic Theater principles in the film medium, which, he considered, utilized the most advanced artistic means of representation and thus promised the greatest political impact. The cinema confirmed his notion that technological changes have a massive stake in constituting and interpreting reality, yet just as Brecht's dramaturgical practice was directed against the "culinary" theater, so he rejected the idea of transforming film into a "high" art form as an alternative to the trivial products of the entertainment industry. Rather he saw the cinema as a mass art with revolutionary potential.[19] In addition, his interest in realism, in how images produce knowledge about "reality" under specific and changing historical conditions, dominated his theoretical and practical work during the years 1928 to 1933. Finally, Brecht's interest in Marxism made him increasingly critical of bourgeois cultural institutions so that he welcomed the opportunity to address what he perceived as the mass audience in a direct way through a film that would couple issues of class struggle and pedagogical discourse.

Brecht considered the cinema closer to visual arts like painting or photography than to the dramatic or narrative arts. For that reason his attention focused on the organization of the images within the cinematic frame as well as between frames, privileging the disjointed quality of montage. Dudov, Brecht, and Ottwald also shared an interest in the documen-

THE RHETORIC OF THE IMAGE

tary nature of the cinema and its promise of referentiality and authenticity. Hence, they avoided the mimetic notion of realism that relies on the reproduction of an illusion of reality and instead invested their energy in the conscious selection and composition of reality. This explains why the camera work in *Kuhle Wampe* is relatively restrained, even uninteresting, when compared to the virtuosity and expressiveness of the earlier Weimar cinema. On the other hand, Dudov and Brecht integrated from the Soviet cinema an awareness of cinematic punctuation, which they exploited to the full. *Kuhle Wampe* resembles, then, *Passion* and *The Last Laugh* insofar as the image dominates the word and composition draws attention to its construction, but it constructs images not as spectacle but rather as rhetoric, that is, the film relates images to the context in order to reveal social processes.

To shift spectator interest from the story to dramatized acts of cognition, the plot contains a minimum of story elements presented as a loose sequence of episodes divided into three sections. Section 1 introduces the Bönike family and its disintegration under the pressure of unemployment. Section 2 pursues the family problems through the complications in the daughter's relationship to her lover. Section 3 suggests a resolution in the young couple's tension and an alternative to the parents' resignation in the face of impoverishment when the lovers reunite at the Workers' Sports Festival. Counterbalancing this narrative continuity and its temporal unfolding, however, are the rhetorical effects that establish the relationship between seeing and persuasion. The first section, for example, opens not with an establishing shot but with a collage of quick takes from dynamically contrasting camera angles, localizing the action geographically in Berlin (image of the Brandenburg Gate), in a working class quarter of the city (shots of a factory and tenements), and temporally during the depression (sequence of newspaper headlines indicating the steep rise in unemployment figures). The printed title and the overture-like opening music — highly theatrical markings of this and each subsequent section reminiscent of Brecht's stage productions — cue the spectator to the film's structural pattern: a self-conscious narration unfolds to solicit the spectator's active role in a cognitive process.

The next sequence continues to develop strategies that stress the way of looking. Introduced by the printed title "The Job Hunt," the rhythm retards with a long take of a group of job seekers gathering at a corner and waiting for the daily classified ads to be distributed. When the delivery boy arrives, they grab the leaflets, scan them with trained eyes, and jump on their bicycles. The pace quickens with rapid shots, often from extreme angles, of bicycle wheels, feet pumping the pedals, and quick turnarounds at factory gates when the job seekers are turned away. Accompanying these introductory segments is Eisler's pulsating music — fast, staccato, and unharmonic—underlining the abrupt montage editing that condenses the bicycle race into a few images in order to convey desperation through speed and repetition. After the rush of disjointed images and its musical commentary, the third sequence introduces the Bönike family: unemployed father, housewife, working daughter Anni, and son Franz, who was one of the disappointed bicyclists. The family's impoverishment, exacerbated by the parents' platitudes, leads the son to commit suicide, showing how isolation, indifference, and anonymity bring self-destruction to this family. The section closes with a woman looking directly at the camera and commenting: "He still had the best life before him." The front-face address brings into play the rhetoric of subject-object relations by suggesting the spectator too as a watched person. The dialectic of looking and seeing is expanded to include the spectator who is implicated directly in a self-conscious process by being caught up in the network of social looks.

These first sequences introduce several crucial aspects that are central for Brecht's understanding of the cinema's political potential. His theory of Epic Theater, which in many respects was tested in this film, stresses the social *gestus* as a central performance and representational principle for structuring meaning.[20] This *gestus*, understood as a mental attitude and a physical bearing, informs all aspects of performance, including acting,

The montage sequence of bicycles condenses into a few images the desperation of the job search by the unemployed workers (frame enlargement by Kristin Thompson, Madison).

THE RHETORIC OF THE IMAGE

The impoverished Bönike family reproduces petit bourgeois behavior (used by permission of Stiftung deutsche Kinemathek, Berlin).

music, dialogue, and set. It concentrates and amplifies details in order to emphasize the context and conditions of what is shown or done. In contrast to the Epic Theater, *gestus* in *Kuhle Wampe* shifts from the actor of the performance to the camera and editing, in particular to their functions of interrupting and citing reality. Breaking the illusion of total visibility, montage becomes a means of deconstructing everyday actions and expressions into their social determinants and inscribing in them the conditions of their construction. The persistent montage in *Kuhle Wampe* is rhetorical: interruptions (expository titles, inserts, songs, choruses), contrasts of sound and image (commentary, voice-off, autonomous music), documentary-like quotes (Berlin streets and architecture, newspaper headlines), and disruptive editing (unusual camera angles spliced together, sudden extreme close-ups, direct address to the camera). It grasps images and action in the context of their political and institutional conditions, signaling the spectator that this film is being constructed as an act of interpretation. For Brecht reality is not what the spectator sees but what the spectator re-cognizes, that which is behind the visible. The "epic cinema," then, results precisely from the control of vision and seeing produced by montage.

After the son's suicide the narrative's second part focuses on the daughter as a counterpoint to the pointless death. Once again a collage sequence opens the section, but this time with a more lyrical overture consisting of nature images and accompanied by symphonic music. The following episodes alternately portray Anni's dilemmas and the useless hypocrisy and resignation of her parents. In a sequence parallel in structure and message to Franz's job hunt, for example, Anni appears in a series of elliptical shots at various offices trying to prevent her family's eviction from their apartment owing to unpaid rent. Characteristic for the rhetorical construction is the eviction "scene" itself, reduced to a synecdoche or part standing for the entirety. One shot only frames the mother who stands on a ladder and unfastens a lamp from the ceiling while an offscreen voice (a judge) reads the eviction notice in a bored monotone. Anni's lover Fritz invites the family to join him at Kuhle Wampe, a tent city in a Berlin suburb where, as a voice-over commentary and the quick sequence of images suggest, middlebrow patterns of behavior are reproduced in the settlement's

While father Bönike reads about the sexual exploits of Mata Hari, mother Bönike struggles with her accounts for the week (frame enlargement by Kristin Thompson, Madison).

pedantic cleanliness and in the inhabitants' efforts to escape the reality of impoverishment through the illusion of normalcy.

The Mata-Hari sequence is a paradigmatic example of this behavior modelled after Sergei Eisenstein's notion of the polyphonic montage that produces an abstract idea from the collision of the parts. While Anni's father reads with fascination a passage from the newspaper about the adventures of the vamp Mata Hari, tripping over foreign words and deliciously enjoying the suggestive sensuality in the description of the dancer's body, the mother calculates the weekly food expenses, oblivious to the father's voice which continues throughout the sequence. The montage juxtaposes their two very different facial expressions with close-ups of price tags for food items, setting in relation through speech, written signs, and contrasting images the boredom and emptiness fed by the pulp press, on the one hand, and their everyday distress, on the other. The following sequence contextualizes the relation of fantasized sexuality and poverty by contrasting the consequences of Anni and Fritz's love affair, for Anni has become pregnant and seeks an abortion. A lyrically composed montage renders in a kind of stream of consciousness her apprehensions about bearing a child. Images of children, toys, store windows with infants' clothes and baby products dissolve into shots of her work termination notice, a midwife's office sign, burial caskets, and her brother's covered body, accompanied throughout by musical themes from the film and from children's songs. This sequence is striking because it is the film's sole concession to realist conventions of psychological motivation.[21] The last sequence in the second section, the family's celebration of Anni's engagement to the reluctant Fritz, brings full circle the exposition of alienation and regression in the petit bourgeois family that began in the first section. Through slapstick and hyperbole the scene shows in a few grotesque strokes the family's collapse into a drunken brawl. Anni, confronted with this model of family life and Fritz's own regret at losing his freedom through marriage, breaks off the engagement.

The third section opens with the printed title "Who Owns the World?" and opposes to the destructive individualism displayed in the film's first two sections the collective spirit invested in the Workers' Sports Festival. Consistent with the stress on collective action, the family's story is subordinated now to the larger framework of class solidarity as an alternative to family disintegration. By far the most didactically structured section, it too opens with a collage, composed of industrial motifs coupled with musical themes from the Solidarity song which, through repetition, becomes a veritable refrain. Four parts present different aspects of the workers' organizational and educational work that contrast and respond to the family dilemmas in the narrative's first two parts: cooperative planning, group activities, noncompetitive races, and an agitprop skit about neighbors' solidarity to prevent a family's eviction. The final scene transfers the lesson of solidarity from the sports festival to a political discussion, from image to word. Pressed into the subway car is a sociopolitical cross section of the city's inhabitants, each of whom comments on the outrageous newspaper report that twenty-four million pounds of coffee were burned by the Brazilian government to protect the falling commodity price. The quick, polemical argument, mirrored by a camera cutting fast within the cramped space from one face to another, climaxes in the question: "who will change the world?" Anni's friend Gerda, speaking face-front to the camera in a direct challenge to the spectator, responds: "those who don't like it."

Kuhle Wampe is an early and exceptional example of how to link questions of representation, social change, and the subject who will effect that change. It presents a visually rhetorical argument that intends to persuade the spectator. Corresponding to the foregrounding of rhetorical means is the subordination of character and causality. Characters lack psychological depth, and causality is extraindividual, suggested by the collage sequences and brief references to macropolitical conditions. A realistic motivation for events arises only from the "verisimilitude" of the images' documentary quality, whose referentiality "quotes" the real like a case study rather than projecting the illusion of a seamless reality as totality. The narrative relies, then, on a complex web of fragments in which the autonomy of the scenes draws attention to the spectator's cognitive process of connecting them.

Dudov, Brecht, Ottwald, and Eisler produced the film with a historical spectator in mind, the class-conscious worker who in the early thirties was familiar with and sympathic toward the political demand for solidarity projected in the last section. Although its rhetorical structure reveals a consistent logic drawn from that assumption, the filmmakers play on a tension between the expected and expectable message of political practice and the complication of that synthetic message through the narrational rhetoric. The film's reception indicates the consequences of such an open structure. As Brecht himself recognized, the politically sympathetic critics of the Left and even those in the Communist Party understood *Kuhle Wampe* less well than the censors who initially forbade its distribution. The latter, like Brecht, were most concerned with the film's overall impact and identified the power of the critique in the rhetorical structure that the filmmakers implemented, whereas the former reproached them for a lack of partisanship and clarity.[22] In contrast to other leftist films of the twenties, which bind the spectator to the spectacle through conventional narrative patterns of identification and catharsis, *Kuhle Wampe* constructs a dynamic relation of contradiction between continuity and discontinuity. It does not aim at providing an answer for the spectator but at the spectator's recognition of the possibility of change. This emphasis on the spectator as pro-

The cramped space of a subway car encompasses a cross section of the city's inhabitants who engage in a polemical debate about changing the world (frame enlargement by Kristin Thompson, Madison).

ducer of meaning is inscribed in the disjointed representation and in the different set of relations to "reality" which it implies. Hence, an imaginary relation is constituted through a subject whose position is only provisional, projected in the space between the film's final question (who will change the world?) and answer (those who don't like it!).

Although the film's successful but short-lived run in 1932–33 seems to indicate that there did exist historically a class-conscious spectator who could respond to the imaginary activity elicited by such a construction, the total elimination of the left-wing public sphere with the onset of National Socialism in March 1933 raises questions about the provisional subject projected in the film narration. Thus, the stress on solidarity can be read symptomatically as a utopian and compensatory reaction to the real threat posed to the Left by the Nazis in competing for the loyalties of unemployed working-class youth. The remarkable absence of workplace politics, or rather their displacement into recreational activities in the sports festival, suggests a much less monolithic image of the proletarian spectator than the production team (or the German Left) wanted to admit in that crucial transitional period between the 1929 market crash and the onset of fascism in 1933. In addition, the scenes of mass enthusiasm (marches, competitive sports, streaming crowds), which for the filmmakers represented a political aesthetics, became in just a few years the dominant aesthetics of fascist politics.[23]

Kuhle Wampe's impact as a model for a politically motivated revolutionary cinema and as an alternative to studio conventions has in fact been negligible. The conditions under which the film was conceived and produced—always with an eye to the eventuality of censorship problems and to its precarious financial backing—necessitated compromises at every level of its realization. This meant that the already complicated filmic structure, drawing on avant-garde Soviet practices, had to camouflage further its agitational thrust behind the relatively harmless allegory of sports races and the appeal of the youthful participants.[24] Moreover, the National Socialists' accession to power shortly after its release meant both an interruption in the film's distribution and, more significantly, in the working-class struggle which was the film's subject. For today's spectator, with a fundamentally different historical experience behind us, this space where the struggle for change was to take place seems abstract and naive: we can no longer rely in an unreflected way on categories such as "the proletariat" or a Communist Party to change the world. In a more indirect way, however, this film has indeed established itself within a tradition of political cinema through Brecht's ideas on the nature of cinematic representation and more generally his reflections on political art.[25] Here Kuhle Wampe has become an example for the dialectical relation between aesthetic innovation and political commitment in the cinema, demonstrating that any discourse about the real and the cognitive relations that govern it cannot escape an examination of how we represent "reality" and how those representations constitute that very reality.

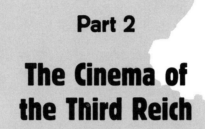

Part 2

The Cinema of
the Third Reich

4

Probing the Limits:
Detlef Sierck's *To New Shores*

WHEN ZARAH LEANDER at the end of Sierck's *To New Shores* (*Zu neuen Ufern*, 1937) acknowledges the failure of her passion for Willy Birgel by giving her "yes" to Viktor Staal before the altar, a boys chorus breaks into a triumphant "Gloria in excelcis deo." The musical overstatement is typical for melodramatic pathos, an expressive amplification of the sublime emotions. At the same time, the exaggerated "happy end" is typical for Detlef Sierck's treatment of his characters' suffering. The disparity between the heroine's renunciation and conjugal exile into the Australian desert and the religiously intoned celebration of her union with a man she hardly knows underscores the contradictions this resolution must accommodate. Sierck, who later in Hollywood under the name of Douglas Sirk came to be identified as the master of the melodramatic "weepie," produced in this German feature a remarkable example of the limits and possibilities of visual imagination in the early years of the Third Reich.[1]

All the elements of cinematic melodrama are present and organized into a characteristic antithetical structure: excessive emotion in pathos-laden situations, social contrast, coincidence played off against the vicissitudes of fate, self-sacrifice, suffering, music, and spectacle. Extreme oppositions permeate the entire film, and their emplotment traces the boundaries to imaginary activity in the specific historical circumstances of prewar fascism. To foreground this system of contrasts, Sierck employs a highly refined style based on the visual implications of the illusory and the unseen, of blindness and the unrecognized. In melodrama this visual play circulates around erotic sexuality, a site of human desire generally disavowed entirely or associated with death in the fascist discourse. Sierck's film asserts this eroticism without attempting a fundamental critique of the reactionary story and its patriarchal logic, but it does allow for an exploration of social attitudes otherwise repressed in this discourse. Thus, Sierck's film raises pertinent questions about the utopian nature of the imaginary elicited by the film's narration and the role of escapist illusions in the Nazi cinema.

Produced four years after the National-Socialist takeover of power in Germany, *To New Shores* is situated in a context where Nazi leaders attributed to the cinema a key role in stabilizing fascist domination. Their efforts to establish a completely controlled production and reception process arose from the conviction that the cinema could be effectively integrated into the fascist ideological strategy of monopolizing and disciplining imaginary relations. To this extent, the cinema of the Third Reich presents an extreme moment of state authority in the film industry, a moment where art and social need were to coalesce in an affirmative ideology. This ideology aimed at empowering a particular social reality to establish the authority of the system and to justify a group identity that would differentiate or exclude the Other.

Many commentators on the cinema of the Third Reich have pointed to the rapid and seemingly unproblematic reorganization of the film industry's administrative and economic sectors in 1933.[2] Within a year after the new regime took command it had established itself as the major agency of regulation in film production, distribution, and consumption. Explaining his Enabling Act for usurping power in a speech on March 23, 1933, Hitler mentioned the need for a "vigorous moral sanitization" of German culture. His minister of propaganda, Josef Goebbels, was responsible for implementing the act through new organizational forms and principles in the film sector. "Sanitization" meant first the withdrawal from the German exhibition market of films that contradicted National-Socialist ideology, films like *Kuhle Wampe*.[3] Second, it led to the exclusion of virtually all individuals from the film industry who were Jewish or identified with the Left. Finally, it presumed a rigidly hierarchical institutional structure based on the principle of synchronizing all public activities through absolute control from above (*Gleichschaltung*). The "legal" policy for codifying the amalgamation of state authority and the cinematic institution was achieved through a revision passed in February, 1934 of the Motion Picture Law (*Lichtspielgesetz*), a product of the Weimar Republic's 1920 Constitution which set out criteria for film censorship. Besides its provisions for excluding "undesirables" from the industry in order to protect the country's "national film culture," its most important innovation was the extension or transformation of censorship into a "positive" procedure. All scripts and projects were to be reviewed (by Goebbels personally) *before* pursuing financial backing, thereby guaranteeing a kind of precensorship. One of the more striking aspects of the law's revision is the fact that only minor changes were necessary in the wording of the Weimar document in order to implement the functioning of a new state authority.[4]

This continuity in legal restrictions also prevailed on other levels, most noticeably in the industry's capitalist structure and production forms, especially during the first four years of the Third Reich. Not only did the majority of the (non-Jewish) financial and industry leaders remain in their positions of power, but Goebbels's offer of a form of cooperation through guaranteed state credits for film production in return for political control of film content also assured the continuance of a relatively autonomous competitive market. The international crisis in the film sector during the early thirties had sorely strained the German industry's profits and led to further concentration in ownership. Despite the political control and disciplinary limitations, the industry accepted the government's compromise with its investment and tax incentives.[5]

Economic efficiency was never completely subordinated to ideological considerations, and this was nowhere more apparent than in the ongoing competition with the products from Hollywood.[6] During the thirties, the National Socialists controlled the best studio park and technical capacities in all of Europe, enabling them to compete with American developments in color technology and three-dimensionality. Indeed, the cinema in the Third Reich remained one of the strongest European producers through the onset of the war in 1939 with an average of eighty feature-length films per year as well as documentaries, shorts, and newsreels.[7] Production standards were also measured against American studio models.[8] This explains the almost slavish imitation of the American cinema and, even more importantly, the pressure on the part of the German film industry to develop a star system that could compete with that of the American studios. Goebbels's equation did not succeed, however, and the economic problems were a direct result of decisions motivated by political and ideological dictates. Not only were the production companies unable to raise the quality of their films in accordance with Goebbels's expectations but their already shaky financial stability further eroded. To be sure, the number of tickets sold—and thus profits—increased substantially between 1933 and 1937. At the same time, however, production costs grew much more quickly, and the loss of foreign export markets for German films after 1933 only exacerbated the sinking profit margins.

Detlef Sierck entered the film industry just prior to this crisis and under conditions that were not atypical at the time. The exclusion of many talented professionals for racial or political reasons created a virtual vacuum for new talent in the film industry. Trained and active onstage, he had directed and administered theaters since 1921. After the passage of the "Race Laws" at the Nuremberg Party Congress in 1935, Sierck, whose wife was Jewish, must have found it expedient to move from the ideologically more restricted stage to UFA, where the demands of international prestige still allowed a slightly more indulgent atmosphere.[9] During his short UFA career before he left Germany in 1938, he perfected in films like *Pillars of Society* (*Stützen der Gesellschaft*, 1935), *Final Chord* (*Schlussakkord*, 1936), and *La Habanera* (1937) the melodrama's inherent antithetical structure as one of the few outlets for social criticism in the mass media of a repressive society.[10] Contrary to Goebbels's assumption that the intentions of filmmakers and censors can determine a film's impact, *To New Shores'* genre and formal qualities raise questions about the consensus at which such a program aims. Furthermore, it provides evidence that Nazi ideology was unable to occupy entirely its public's cinematic imagination, manifested by the fact that the psychosocial situation of the Third Reich posed narrative problems—especially in gender relations—which narration could only resolve through blatant escapism.

    To New Shores takes up the characteristically threadbare plot of a melodrama but turns the social and psychological reversals of an unhappy love relationship into the vehicle for representing gender and power relations in a repressive culture.[11] Consistent with the demands of the genre, such problems of domination and exploitation are displaced into their consequences: pathos, sacrifice, victimization, suffering, and despondency. Gloria Vane, a popular singer in 1846 London, has the ill-fortune of being in love with the aristocratic but unworthy Sir Albert Finsbury. Pursued by debts, he seeks an appointment in the colonial army in Australia, swearing his love to Gloria before leaving. When it is discovered that Finsbury wrote a bad check, Gloria selflessly protects his name by saying she committed the deed. Convicted of forgery, she is sentenced to prison in Sydney. The only way Gloria can be released from prison before her term expires is to accept a marriage with one of the colonial settlers. When kind Henry Hoyer chooses her from among the prisoners, she sees an opportunity to escape and find Albert, who in the meantime is engaged to the daughter of Sydney's governor. Gloria is forced to seek a job singing at the local sleazy bar where the unsuspecting Finsbury arrives on the eve of his wedding. He learns the consequences of his deceit and kills himself. Meanwhile abandoned, fired from her job, and with no place to go, Gloria seeks refuge in the local church, where Henry discovers her, and she now agrees to marry him.

    The narrative's antithetical structure clearly separates the film into two parts reflecting two contrasting social systems: the first quarter set in traditional Victorian London with its social stratification and hypocrisy and the rest in a kind of Wild West colonial Australia with its pale reflection of English gentility but also with its opportunities for vindication and social mobility.[12] The first sequences establish the network of social and sexual oppositions that will weave their way throughout the story. The film opens with Finsbury and his friend "Pudding" playing billiards, a competitive game of strategy that allegorizes their social positions. Low camera angles position Finsbury as the dominant figure, and his deep voice, suave figure, and graceful gestures contrast with Pudding's nervous mannerisms. Their brief dialogue reveals that Pudding, the son of a wealthy cheese merchant, is a social climber who strives to become a gentleman under Finsbury's tutelage. He, in turn, is an impoverished aristocrat, dependent on Pudding's wealth and good will but full of disdain for his bourgeois virtues. A voice from outside their club window introduces the transition to the next scene as the camera cuts to a crowd of properly dressed citizens listening to a philistine's harangue about the upper-class immorality that is beginning to threaten the middle class. If Albert and Pudding are positioned as class rivals who use each other, then their shared commitment to the decadence of the gentleman's way of life opposes them in turn to these Victorian puritans with their stifling constraints and hypocritical attitudes toward sexuality. Anticipating the vengeful wrath of Pudding's traditionalist father, who will demand that the state punish Gloria for immoral behavior, this scene establishes the nature of the authority that guards social order. The prime example of someone who flaunts that order is, the haranguer tells his audience, a courtesan in revealing dress who sings lascivious songs to the jubilant applause of the sons of the bourgeoisie.

A dissolve to an audience applauding at the elegant Adelphi Theater seamlessly introduces this singer, Gloria Vane, with the effects of excess and exhibitionism familiar already from Lubitsch's *Passion*. She is the glamorous woman of the world who knows how to use her physical beauty and sexual allure, male signifiers of desire and fear which the previous scene pointedly formulated. The camera sensuously dollies in as she moves forward on the stage and later returns to her repeatedly in close-ups from various angles. Dressed in black lace with a plunging décolleté, playing with a huge black fan to exaggerate her flirtatious gestures and eyes, framed against a huge round bed in the background, Gloria sings her showstopper, "Yes, Sir!":

> They're afraid I might meet their protected nephews
> in the marriage bed or at the club,
> I might seduce them with a thousand tricks
> to do something they might not yet know.

This is exactly the threat against Victorian morality that triggered the earlier fulminations and will bring down the wrath of the state.

Gloria Vane's sexual threat reveals an ideological contradiction in the patriarchal system, one of the fissures in the social façade that this melodrama so carefully reveals and yet conceals at the same time. For Gloria's stage personality, her shameless and aggressive sexuality, turns out to

Gloria Vane's shameless and aggressive sexuality is only a stage role that conceals her true personality (used by permission of the Bundesarchiv-Filmarchiv Berlin, from the former Staatliches Filmarchiv der DDR).

be just that, a role she plays which hides her true, backstage personality. What she sings is a lie:

> That's how I am from head to toe,
> That's how I am and that's how I'll stay, yes, Sir!
> That's how you see me here, that's just how I am, yes, Sir![13]

Gloria is not the frivolous courtesan she appears to be, a fact emphasized in her later appearance at the Sydney Casino where in an inversion she is preceded by a favorite performer who sings: "I am a virgin," as all the men knowingly laugh. Already at the Adelphi Theater, however, her song augurs the real Gloria that will soon emerge from behind this mask. At the end it shifts abruptly to a full major chord and a long, drawn out "Hallelujah" as chanted in church chorales. This spirituality in the form of an ironic conclusion to the song distinguishes her from every other character: from the irresponsible decadence of the demimonde as well as from the hypocritical moralism of the bourgeoisie. It gains prominence through repetition on various cinematic levels, for example, her Madonna-like reflection in a mirror in the next scene with a humbly tilted face and a shawl swathed around her head, her identification as one of the "chorus of angels" later in the Sydney church, and the marriage ceremony with its choral accompaniment closing the narrative.

Among the admirers at the performance are two of the citizens from the previous scene, visually marked by their somber black suits, top hats, and unnaturally angular bodies and movements. Prodded by voyeuristic curiosity (later in the scene they will be looking through the keyhole into the theater) and fascinated by Gloria's sensuality, they nonetheless interrupt her song in feigned outrage at its immorality. At this moment Albert Finsbury enters his box near the stage and intervenes, putting the hecklers in their place, outside the theater. In a gallant gesture he steps down from his box onto the stage, crossing the boundary between audience and performer, between society and stage, and lays the bouquet of flowers he just appropriated from Pudding at Gloria's feet as an expression of admiration. Structurally this is Gloria's moment of perfect happiness: the public but theatrical declaration of love, whose loss will motivate the rest of the plot. Happiness always precedes loss in the melodramatic formula, and the heroine will become an agent of her own destruction as she tries to prolong or recover this happiness, even at the price of self-denial. Later Gloria hides her tears from Albert before his departure for Australia—only the splashing raindrops, she assures him falsely—and tells him that "lovers belong together." Meanwhile the camera frames them sitting in their carriage in a two-shot separating them clearly along a vertical axis. Dialogue and behavior, plot and mise-en-scène are often at variance, but as in this sequence sentimentality and visual fascination implicate the spectator's identification with Gloria on an emotional level while awakening a sense of fatality through the knowledge of Albert's blindness to her profound love.

The tension of social, sexual, moral, and emotional oppositions introduced in the first three sequences comes to a provisional resolution in the court scene at the end of the first part. This scene is significant for a number of reasons. First, a trial, like the stage at the Adelphi Theater and later at the Sydney Casino, provides a highly dramatic focus for suspense, sudden reversals, accusations, defenses, and judgments, all formulaic elements of the melodrama genre. In this trial the court accuses Gloria Vane of forging a check based on her (false) confession, which she will retract but then reacknowledge under pressure. Second, Sierck employs the camera and mise-en-scène to create that mixture of pathos and fatalism that characterizes the entire film. In an over-the-shoulder perspective shot the camera voyeuristically looks down on the courtroom through a high window with its protective bars in the foreground. Panning from the accuser to Gloria, who is behind another set of bars, and then around the court room,

The antinaturalistic lighting creates an aura of sentimental dreaminess (used by permission of the Bundesarchiv-Filmarchiv Berlin, from the former Staatliches Filmarchiv der DDR).

it emphasizes the spectator's privileged position vis-à-vis the protagonist. The spectator is placed at this point in a position of seeing more than any one of the characters, and only from that position is the total configuration of oppositions accessible. Moreover, this position solicits the spectator's emotional identification to compensate for the protagonist's blindness: the spectator shares in Gloria's private truth but also realizes the hopelessness of her noble act. Meanwhile the pathos arises from Gloria's eloquent silence that protects her lover from public accusation.

Finally, this scene is the most remarkable in the film for its dialectical montage of the courtroom action with a commentary by a street singer outside the courtroom window. In an obvious imitation of the ballad singer in Brecht's *Threepenny Opera*, also used by G. W. Pabst in his 1931 filmed version, the scene opens on a board with a series of four cartoons entitled "The Deed," "To Australia," "Sydney," and "Paramatta," while the droning, nasal singer's voice relates the moralistic tale of how unvirtuous girls will end up in the notorious women's prison (Paramatta) near Sydney. Couched in religious imagery, the singer tells how Paramatta is purgatory, a place that offers many a "sweet torture," a sorrowful journey to be avoided at all

The courtroom scene provides a highly dramatic focus where the defendant is already semi-incarcerated by the bars surrounding her (used by permission of the Bundesarchiv-Filmarchiv Berlin, from the former Staatliches Filmarchiv der DDR).

costs, and concludes—not unlike Gloria's earlier stage song—with a long, plaintive "amen." The ironic parallel between the trial as an exemplary demonstration of state authority and the ballad with its more popular but no less didactic warning underscores the melodramatic reversal at the film's nodal point while anticipating what further trials lie in store for Gloria in this purgatory to which she has been condemned for seven years. In addition, it assures a smooth transition as the camera dollies back from the cartoon with Paramatta's barred and chained gate and dissolves slowly to a real gate hung with chains and a padlock.

The simple but elegant coupling of the first part in London and the second in Australia opens a further set of structural oppositions. The rough Australian landscape and the architecture in the pioneer settlement of Sydney contrast with the London theater, club, and salon environment. The oppressive heat and bright light of the Australian summer replaces the chilly, foggy English climate. The London demimonde becomes a collection of uncouth rowdies, while bourgeois authority is displaced to the prison directress and the colonial military. The geographical shift also brings a crucial change in the character constellation. No longer counterposed to Pudding's social mobility and money, Albert is now confronted symbolically with a new kind of patriarchal authority. Henry Hoyer, independent farmer, honest and contemptuous of bourgeois pretension, is the first character who is not blind to Gloria's inner self. As the chained women prisoners emerge from the church at the beginning of the second part, for example, he comments spontaneously that "she doesn't look like a criminal." Later he will choose her from among all the potential "brides" in the prison and ultimately win the heroine, since he alone is unfettered by traditional social and moral hypocrisy and can therefore recognize her true virtue. Gloria, too, has undergone a radical change in this new environment, at least outwardly. At her nadir she has become a prisoner: her sumptuous clothes traded for a formless sackcloth chemise, her singing talent degraded to monotonous hand labor, her reputation as a famous actress reduced to the anonymity of a number, prisoner 218. Yet within Gloria there is a strength and a will that sustains her and produces the pathos to motivate spectator identification.

Identification with patriarchal and authoritarian values is solicited by means of this pathos. Pathos functions by showing and containing disruptive emotions that usually remain hidden in public discourse: desire, distress, confusion. It is produced through inconsistency or blockages in the narrative economy and builds on the spectator's emotional suspense in reaching a resolution. That emotional energy, however, is deflected into the consequences of the conflict, concealing the narrative inconsistency or blockage. Gloria's eloquent silence and noble suffering are the main vehicles for pathos in this film. They have a touch of masochism to them, but this is typical for the hysteria that characterizes the female protagonist in melodrama.[14] It is a hysteria just below the surface, the affect of repressing feminine desire, and equally typical is the transformation of that hysteria into song as in the climactic confrontation between Gloria and Albert.

After untold humiliations Gloria recognizes that she was deceived in her love for Albert. She returns to the stage as a singer, but now at the tacky Casino in Sydney, and she is dressed once again in a shimmering black gown, but one so shabby that it seems more a parody of her earlier glamor. The narrative "coincidence" that brings Albert to her first performance here finally offers Gloria the opportunity for a cathartic outburst when she sings "to" Albert. Once again she intones the song of yearning she had sung at Albert's going-away party in London, but now it is rephrased as an accusation against the man who abandoned her:

The only people who always wait are those who really love!
Aren't you coming yet?
How the falling drops splash from my sleeve!

I'm standing in the rain and waiting for you, for you!
On all the paths I'm expecting only you, always only you![15]

Gloria's cathartic violence is directed inwards, and her accusation is at the same time the swan song of her yearning. Since this is not the kind of entertainment the Casino audience is accustomed to, the performance is once again rudely interrupted like at the Adelphi Theater, but this time the audience ridicules her. Listening from the back of the bar, Albert is framed by the camera among a series of beams, a visual metaphor for the paralysis that prevents him from intervening as he had done in London to restore the performance. This, however, is not performance but the externalization of Gloria's suffering and disillusionment. Albert's helplessness is, then, only one of a number of dramaturgical devices used to prolong that expected moment of reconciliation which will finally end in the climactic reversal when Gloria refuses to marry him. The more abrupt the narrative disruption, the stronger the pathos; the stronger the pathos, the more difficult it becomes to achieve narrative closure by containing Gloria's yearning; and the more difficult this containment, the more satisfying will be the resolution for the spectator. As an astute critic of melodrama asserts, its strength lies in the amount of dust raised along the road which will not settle in the last five minutes.[16]

The complex network of reminiscences, repetitions, and mirrorlike oppositions gradually trace a figure of circularity in the second part. The rhyming effect of the church at the beginning and end of the second part, Gloria's two theatrical performances, her unsuccessful attempt to return to prison, the cigars and the broom seller's haunting call (both products made by the women at Paramatta prison) which pursue Albert, the characters' long stares at themselves in mirrors: these are just a few examples of recurring events, motifs, and behavior patterns in the film. Similarly, the frequent religious allusions are situated within a broader context that relates systematic coincidence to fate, that is, to the belief that nothing happens by accident. The catastrophes that accompany Gloria on her "sorrowful journey" through purgatory, those "sweet tortures" of which the street singer warned, turn out to be providence in disguise. Gloria's suffering as well as Albert's suicide are the necessary expiation without which narrative closure cannot be negotiated. The torrential rainstorm that accompanies Albert's suicide as a kind of cleansing act before the new beginning (a biblical quotation of the Deluge), the preacher's parable at the marriage ceremony about St. Peter's liberation from his chains, the redundancy of Gloria's name in the choral "Gloria" as the marriage bond is blessed: all point to an unswerving belief in the possibility of a new beginning, which is the eternal return of the identical and as such a constitutive element of the melodramatic genre. Providence, however, is secularized into the social compliance which the happy end extorts from the heroine. That explains the impression conveyed by the film of a constrained and limited world. The elaborate mise-en-scène and its dramatic artifice are signs for the closed and ordered universe in which this melodrama unfolds, a world where human will has little effect.

To New Shores conforms closely to the hundreds of escapist films produced during the Third Reich in which a happy end, prompted by social authority, can redeem even the most complicated and morally questionable situations. Moreover, the negative portrayal of English society and its brutal colonial politics coincides with the official National-Socialist view of British perfidy.[17] Yet this interpretation only partially recuperates the specificity of the melodrama's antithetical structure. The critical discussion of the melodramatic genre suggests that as an ideological construction it produces meaning differently under differing historical conditions and that it can articulate the very irrationality of the authoritarian system it serves. From this perspective the first part of the film presents a retrospective allegory of the social forces vying for power at the end of the Weimar Republic: the decadent and impoverished upper middle class, the vulgar but ambitious middle class and the traditionalist petit bourgeoisie. The plot's displacement to the New World in Australia, a clearly marked visual shift that corresponds to the National-Socialist goal of creating a new Reich, projects in the second part an image of its reality that aligns the imaginary resolution with the patriarchal and authoritarian ideology of the fascist discourse. Contrary to the collectivist class struggle envisioned by Dudov and Brecht in Kuhle Wampe (chapter 3) or to the harmonious community projected in Request Concert (chapter 5), Sierck's allegory still insists on the private, individualistic utopia of the middle-class family. In the context of National-Socialist family policy and the instrumentalization of women's bodies for the fatherland, this regressive, bourgeois fantasy maintains a critical edge, even in the ambivalence of its melancholy affirmation of female subordination.

Melodrama, then, provides a supple texture in which traditional norms and their disruption coexist. The conventionality of the narrative closure in To New Shores fits this model. Gloria, helpless and abandoned in a society that has no place for the independent woman, is saved by Henry Hoyer's second marriage proposal. Gloria reconciles herself to the most traditional of female roles, and metaphorically the religious framework of her "salvation" suggests that a higher order has been reestablished through her reconciliation. Similarly, she conforms to the National-Socialist image of the woman who sacrifices herself and renounces her career voluntarily in order to establish the heterosexual couple and begin a family.[18] The narrative makes clear that this is the best of all possible resolutions for a woman, since all other possibilities are structurally marked as less desirable. The second couple in the double marriage ceremony consists of Gloria's friend Nelly and an older, unattractive man who regards women with skepticism and hostility. This second marriage is purely expedient. Other males who choose brides at the prison are even more contemptuous, one sex-starved fellow claiming that all women are interchangeable. Fanny, the young wife of Henry's elderly uncle, represents another type. Bored with her marriage, she chases Albert while her husband treats her with a mixture of humor and paternal indulgence, explicitly referring to her as an immature child. Among these possibilities Gloria has, of course, won the best of the lot with Henry Hoyer. Although he possesses none of the eroticism or sexual attractiveness that actor Willy Birgel radiates in the role of Finsbury, Henry is a manly, self-employed farmer who stands for the loyalty, stability, and authority propagated by Nazi "blood and soil" ideals. The one structural position that remains unoccupied and nonexistent in the film's (heterosexual) discourse is a partner relationship based on mutual respect and love, eroticism and commitment. This explains why throughout the film Gloria's look is almost constantly directed outside the frame. She looks neither at other characters nor at the world around her but at some imaginary space. Her gaze is an expression of yearning for an unfulfilled promise that underscores the irony of the title's new shores.

To New Shores implements narrational strategies that counsel resignation to an established and all-powerful order but at the same time it formulates contradictions in the order's authority. The portrayal of female eroticism and desire gives it a special place within a public discourse of prewar fascism that officially denied female subjectivity. Melodrama can always accommodate this kind of contradiction, but sometimes at the price of subversive parody. For example, when Gloria has reached the lowest point of degradation in Sydney, she perceives as her only possible recourse the return to Paramatta prison, the ultimate symbol of victimization. Arriving at the gate, she learns that a woman can be readmitted to prison only with the permission of her husband, and she has none (yet)! Formal means too can underscore the irrationality underlying the authoritarian social structures. Tight framing distinguishes the mise-en-scène. The court room is seen through the bars of a window, for instance, and the procession of "brides" at Paramatta prison — itself hinting at a parody of the popular Nazi genre of the revue film — is framed in images crisscrossed with the beams and yarn of hand looms worked by the women prisoners. This kind of composition suggests a claustrophobic world in which characters are caught in a web of circumstances, acted upon and doomed to resignation despite their emotional pathos and despite that last moment of unmediated and unmotivated optimism in the happy end. This impressive camera work together with the remarkable lighting indicates that at least into the midthirties the Weimar cinema's visuality could still assert itself. Filtered through fog, mist, smoke, gauze curtains, a lace head scarf or an elaborate fan, the antinaturalistic lighting creates an aura of sentimental dreaminess for the imaginary utopian space of desire associated

The claustrophobic world of the heroine is suggested by the image composition which catches her in the yarn of her loom (used by permission of the Bundesarchiv-Filmarchiv Berlin, from the former Staatliches Filmarchiv der DDR).

with a new beginning and a new order that seemed to resonate deeply in the German public with its memory of economic and psychological degradation in the postwar period. It also reinforces the artificial quality of the world in which the characters grope around blindly.[19]

By 1937 it was apparent to Goebbels that the German film industry was not successfully producing the kind of entertainment he demanded despite the enormous subsidies provided by the state. Therefore he quietly set out to restructure the industry as a state-held trust, a project he completed in 1942 with the formal establishment of the wholly state-owned and controlled UFA-Film Corporation (UFI) holding company.[20] *To New Shores* was to play a special role in this strategy as the vehicle for launching a new female star on the German cinematic horizon. Zarah Leander, Swedish by birth and with an established career as stage actress and singer, came to UFA's attention in an operetta role in Vienna. Sierck's melodrama provided the film role that would become the star's trademark: the glamorous woman of the world with an independent nature, the femme fatale in low cut dresses who, despite everything—and here is the typical National-Socialist twist—always reveals a warm heart or returns home in the end.[21] From UFA's perspective Leander combined two unbeatable qualities: her strikingly beautiful, calm, and meditative face together with her Swedish background immediately called to mind a second Greta Garbo, and her deep, baritone voice promised a replacement for Marlene Dietrich, who had refused to remain in Germany despite UFA's handsome offers. Moreover, Leander's foreign accent in German—perfect for playing roles such as the English singer Gloria Vane—projected an image of internationality and the illusion of a connection to the outside world for Nazi culture.[22]

Zarah Leander's star image did not project the National-Socialist ideal of the feminine but yet was tolerated and even promoted as a symbol for the counterworld of erotic decadence, private desire, and female sexuality so opposed to the usual images of middlebrow self-contentedness that tended to monopolize the imaginary potential of the cinema in the Third Reich. In a repressive culture the representation of sexual difference, especially in disruptive, dramatic forms, can serve as a safety valve for ideological contradictions centered on power relations, especially when the power is attributed to a female Other. To New Shores' unabashed escapist resolution, its repression of difference through its narrative displacement onto an outcast, and its context of British colonialism set a hundred years earlier would seem to corroborate such an affirmative view. Yet melodramatic representation can also work to the surface contradictions of domination and exploitation, even while it insists on denying them. Moreover, its escapism and the guarantee of stability despite change is not specifically fascist. Rather it is the extension of something real in the imaginary, an expression of the desire to transform one's relation to reality.

The contradictions Sierck constructed so carefully in this film eschew a surface reading. Indeed, its very reliance on formulae, conventions, excess, exaggeration, and clichés invites a discursive reading of its representational system. Whether this functioned for the historical spectator of 1937 is impossible to determine.[23] One would have to assume either a politically sophisticated or sufficiently skeptical spectator to respond to these resistances. Their textual inscription—in the formal play and the thematization of the visible and the invisible—provides the spectator with a possible position from which to judge and evaluate the action in a way that none of the film characters can. This intricacy of narrational patterns alone distinguishes Sierck's film from the dominant fare of the Third Reich. He succeeded in devising a system of representation to convey not so much a political critique (which the circumstances in any case hardly allowed) but rather the limits to imaginary activity. In retrospect, his fatalistic, melancholic vision with its motifs of regression and futility and with its focus on obstacles to change seems woefully inadequate for the political reality of 1937, but the dilemma Gloria Vane confronts at the end of the film, the lack of any choice, makes intelligible to the historical spectator the real contraction of imaginary space under the fascist regime.

5

The Fascist Discourse:
Eduard von Borsody's *Request Concert*

WHEN GERMANY ATTACKED Poland in September, 1939, triggering World War II, the German film industry entered a new phase in its economic, political, and cultural development. Behind-the-scenes efforts to restructure the industry as a state-held trust were being undertaken already in 1936–37 to resolve its chronic financial woes. Goebbels appointed as trustee economist Max Winkler, whose Cautio Trust Company (Treuhandgesellschaft) had already bought out newspaper chains for the government and was poised to achieve a similar success in the film industry. By 1939 Cautio had acquired or was in the process of acquiring in the government's commission all the major film companies; and although the impression of decentralization was maintained with separate production firms in Berlin, Vienna, Prague, and Munich, in fact ownership, organization, and planning were in the hands of Cautio, acting—sometimes covertly—in close cooperation with the propaganda ministry. Goebbels's goal was to coordinate on a sound financial basis film production and distribution with the artistic and political interests of National Socialism. The initial efforts at rationalization sought to diminish what he perceived as the destructive competitiveness between the major studios and then to divide up the tasks of production, distribution, and exhibition. As a result, by 1940 the government possessed not only political control (consolidated in the first years of the regime) but also economic control of the German film industry and could proceed to regulate the market for its own ends and profits.[1]

Several factors contributed to the industry's improved stability at the end of the thirties as well as to the cinema's cultural impact in German society, not least of which was the role of German military expansionism. The annexation of Austria in March and Silesia in October, 1938; the installation of a protectorate in Czechoslovakia in March, 1939; as well as the occupations in Eastern and Western Europe after the war began (Poland, France, Belgium, Holland) led to increased audiences and production capacities. This resolved the serious problem of diminished exports that had plagued the industry after 1933 by guaranteeing not only adequate distribution markets but also enormous profits, which could cover the increasing production costs of prestige films. In addition, audience attendance was rising, owing as much to effective government campaigns during the thirties to entice the public into the cinemas as to the real audience interest in newsreels and information shorts, which were especially popular during the war's first year.[2] By 1940, then, the German film industry was well on the way to controlling the entire film production and distribution capacities in Europe, representing an instrument of enormous ideological hegemony in the hands of the National-Socialist state and one of its most important forms of public discourse.

Scholars have in retrospect variously divided up the approximately 1100 feature-length films produced during the twelve years of the Third Reich, but most agree that about 90 percent of these films can be classified as entertainment features while about 10 percent are overt propaganda films.[3] The production of the propaganda films clusters around specific caesuras in the Third Reich: the Nazi Party films of the early years (1933–35), the anti-Semitic hate films of 1938–40, and the war films of 1940–42. Eduard von Borsody's 1940 *Request Concert* (*Wunschkonzert*) was the first successful propaganda film in this last group and among the most popular films of the early war years.[4] A politico-musical with a love story set against the backdrop of war mobilization, its popularity can be attributed to the contemporary subject matter with which the whole population was familiar. Furthermore, as one of the relatively few films commissioned directly by the propaganda ministry (there were only ninety-six such films produced in the Third Reich), it marked an important step for the German cinema in the consolidation of propaganda motifs with mass entertainment values, here in the form of war as amusement. The film's narrational strategies illustrate central features of affirmative fascist narratives, including the instrumentalization of gender relations within a static framework in which women wait (for their men) and their waiting is consecrated by the government, the utopian projection of a nonconflictual, unified German community, and the rewriting of history as a linear construct with a self-evident meaning. Such a fascist narrative rewrites German social life through an ideology of unity that can achieve closure only by excluding all aberrant discourses. In contrast to Sierck's *To New Shores*, then, here visual and narrational conventions eliminate any possible contradiction in order to monopolize the mass public's imagination and to channel escapism into an explicit ideological project.

Goebbels's conception of the cinema as a privileged sphere of mass ideological influence was a theme he never tired of reiterating. With the onset of war and the mass mobilization of the German population for the war effort at home and on the front, this ideological appeal became even more urgent, as Goebbels emphasized in a speech in 1941: "We cannot overlook the fact that the film as an important and intense mass art must serve entertainment. Yet at a time in which the entire nation assumes such heavy burdens and cares, entertainment too becomes a matter of special value for state politics. Thus, it does not stand at the margins of public life nor can it escape the demands placed on it by the political leadership."[5] *Request Concert* provides a good index for the immediate impact on film production which Goebbels's strategy implied for serving the mass market with the best possible escapist entertainment. Not only did the state commission the film but it also specified the technical team and the cast as well as details concerning the plot, such as the inclusion of footage from the 1936 Olympic Games, a narrative resolution set in the war, and the integration of the popular radio program "Wunschkonzert" (Request Concert).[6] Moreover, contrary to the prior practice of excluding all topical references to Hitler and Nazi symbols in contemporary entertainment films, a practice instituted early in the regime's control of film production, *Request Concert* includes both images of Hitler (documentary footage from the Olympic Games, portrait photos hanging in offices) and numerous swastikas, Nazi insignias, and *Heil* salutes. Most striking, however, is the way the film combines entertainment and repression, distraction and mobilization.

Formally *Request Concert* is anything but innovative, sharing rather in what has variously been referred to as the theatricalization of specularity in the cinema of the Third Reich and its reduction to plot dominated by the word.[7] In contrast to the visual play and the autonomy of the image discussed in earlier films, here clarity and visibility dominate. Conventional, fourth-wall dramaturgy defines both movement and framing, and the camera is anchored at a frontal disposition. This retreat to a type of filmed theatrical presentation has implications for all cinematic aspects: the time-space continuum is remotivated with a premodern notion of causality; narrational elements such as costume, lighting, and gesture are informational rather than appealing to spectator subjectivity through visual qualities; the camera moves relatively little, and long and medium shots prevail, stressing the abstract over the concrete; and, finally, the primacy of plot over spectacle valorizes dialogue and scenic structure over the visual. This restrictive lack of referentiality indicates the fundamental structural law governing fascist film narrative in Germany: a sense of completeness, stability, and immobility that tends to dissolve the distinction between the imaginary and the real.

Director Eduard von Borsody, Austrian by birth, joined UFA as a cameraman after World War I and beginning in 1933 worked mainly as a film editor.[8] He became involved in directing in 1932 but not until 1937 did he assume responsibility on his own for the unremarkable detective film *Diamonds* (*Brillanten*). His subsequent features *Rubber* (*Kautschuk*, distributed in the United States under the title *Green Hell*, 1938) and *Congo Express* (*Kongo-Express*, 1939) are both adventure films characterized by their spectacular wildlife photography in exotic settings (Brazil and the African Congo).[9] Together with scriptwriter Felix Lützkendorf, who as an experienced war-film scenarist wrote several scripts for propaganda–film director Karl Ritter, Borsody produced in *Request Concert* a panorama of German society showing a variety of activities and destinies tied together in a community spirit symbolized by the radio show Request Concert.[10] Because of this structural commitment to showing a representative cross section of the German community, the film plot is complicated with too many characters and subplots. Essentially, however, it is a story of "boy meets girl" and the various obstacles they encounter before they can finally unite in harmony and marriage. Here the usual intrigues—including a second suitor, retarding moments, and inopportune reversals—are augmented by the necessities of war, a theme constantly foregrounded by visual images and through the radio show Request Concert.

The fictional couple consists of shy Inge Wagner and the professional air force officer Herbert Koch who accidentally meet at the 1936 Berlin Olympics and spontaneously fall in love. Herbert, who is on a short leave, proposes marriage within a few days after meeting Inge but that very evening he is ordered to Legion Condor, a flight battalion formed for deployment against the Republican forces in the Spanish Civil War. Because of the secret nature of the undertaking, he is forbidden to communicate with anyone about his mission. Three years later the war has begun, and Herbert nostalgically requests the Olympic fanfare on the "Request Concert" radio program. Inge, who happens to hear this request, has not forgotten Herbert, despite the attentions of her childhood friend Helmut Winkler, and she sets out to find him. They arrange to meet, but once again at the last minute duty calls Herbert on an urgent bombing mission, leaving Inge waiting at a restaurant. During the mission Helmut, who is now Herbert's copilot, is wounded, and when Herbert saves him from their downed plane, he discovers among his personal papers a photo of Inge. Assuming that she has become Helmut's betrothed, Herbert abandons the idea of winning her back. Finally, at Helmut's hospital bedside, the confusion is straightened out, and Herbert and Inge are reunited.

The narrative aims at linking the personal relationship between Inge Wagner and Herbert Koch to the more general framework of a society mobilizing for war in order to show the limitations imposed on such a love relationship under these conditions. A number of dialogues and scenes establish a rigid set of dichotomies that define the parameters of the ideal relationship along the coordinates of private happiness and public interest, emotions and duty, having and waiting. The couple's initial meeting and falling in love is typical for the kind of courtship they will play out and the vicissitudes to which they will be subject. After their chance encounter at the Olympic Stadium, Herbert convinces Inge to go dancing with him, and they both conspire to exclude Inge's aunt as chaperon, anticipating the generational issue that will become important in a later context. More importantly, Herbert treats the encounter as a tactical problem: he pulls out his calendar and dictates to Inge the course of their relationship: "This evening we will share a friendship drink. Tomorrow we will make our first excursion to the country. The day after tomorrow the first kiss. And in eight days we will be engaged." The cool, cheerful manner in which Herbert treats his and Inge's emotions indicates a fundamental economy of desire along gender lines that will surface again and again. Inge, and women in general, wait, yearn, and desire while Herbert and the other males find time for feelings of love as long as nothing "more important" intervenes, specifically the demands of war. For example, when Herbert considers appointing Helmut as his private pilot, he has only one question: whether he is engaged to be married. Helmut equivocates ("not yet") because his hopes for Inge have gone completely unanswered, and Herbert goes on to explain his question: "I am only concerned whether you will be somewhere else with your thoughts while flying." The antierotic, desexualized, even cold behavior that generally characterizes the heterosexual couples in this visually restrained film is here (as in other scenes of male camaraderie) clearly offset by an undercurrent of homoeroticism.

The message conveyed here to the (male) spectator implies that individual happiness is no longer a personal choice. Emotional moments, the love of a woman, are finite (limited to the time on leave) and random, whereas war is the real test for devotion and trust. For the female spectator the situation is more complicated. *Request Concert* portrays a "modern" romantic couple that exists only insofar as it is removed from war. Thus, there is an obvious tension between the private experience of love and its renunciation for the greater public cause. If war is the greatest test of love, then the war romance must demonstrate convincingly why the couple's private space has lost its protective character and what has been gained by its becoming part of the war machinery.[11] In *Request Concert* this entails a process of learning to discipline the emotions and the libido as well as an alignment of femininity with patriotism. The opening sequences suggest the way this will be achieved in the repetition by three characters of what appears to be a harmless, casual verbal aside: "I'd like to, but . . ." [Wollen schon, aber . . .]. The confirmation of desire and its simultaneous denial describes the internalized role model of the hero/heroine, who finds true strength not through isolation in a couple relationship but through acceptance of one's place in a restricted community.

The various women in the film offer a number of discursive possibilities for representing the essentially double movement in the narration between desire and repression.[12] From the outset Inge is marked as a child-woman. She arrives at the Olympic Stadium chaperoned by her aunt, remains almost speechless while the latter tries to gain them entry without tickets and, as if to remove any further doubt, when the aunt returns to find that Inge is not waiting for her, she engages in a lengthy dialogue with the gatekeeper about her lost "child," which he understands literally to be a little girl. Otherwise only her love for Herbert defines Inge. Although she apparently has parents, she lives with her matronly grandmother, and there is no indication that she is employed at a time when the entire female population in Germany was under increasing state pressure to enter the labor force. In fact, Inge seems to spend most of her time waiting for Herbert, even three years after she last saw him or heard from him, which explains why she "happens" to hear his request on the radio program. Nonetheless, when toward the end of the film the two lovers finally meet for the first time in years outside of Helmut's hospital room, he accuses her of not being honest (*aufrichtig*) with him because he believes she is now Helmut's fiancée. Women in the fascist discourse are always undependable, irresponsible, and the source of all troubles, thereby justifying their treatment as children at the hands of men.

Mrs. Eichhorn, Inge's aunt, is a sort of female foil to her niece. She is portrayed as the fussy, somewhat helpless but lovable old lady whose views are hopelessly out of date under the new circumstances (i.e., wartime). The story Inge elicits from the aunt about her past is symptomatic for the way the plot promises an imaginary space and then quickly forecloses on it. In a direct parallel to the romance Inge is about to experience, Mrs. Eichhorn relates how she fell in love with an officer who one day disappeared without a trace because duty called, and how she ended up marrying another man. Inge disputes that her situation could turn out similarly because "if you really love someone, then there is nothing in the world which can separate you." The aunt goes on to explain that there was another factor, the social disparity between the lieutenant and her own working-class family. In the next scene, the lovers' outing to the lake, Inge shyly mentions to Herbert that her father is only a low-level employee, but—and this will become significant in the community image sustained throughout the film—class is quickly rejected as a possible consideration for this modern young officer. He is marrying Inge, not her father. Another antiquated view of love is represented by Inge's grandmother, who encourages her to forget the lost officer and respond to Helmut's advances. Her comment that you find "true love" only in marriage stands in opposition to Inge's deep conviction and ultimate vindication that waiting for Herbert is the only thing that really matters. Inge's aunt and grandmother voice the prejudices of an older generation that are no longer germane. They correspond to a feminine model that Inge will transform into something more appropriate for wartime and at the same time realize as a more perfect version of that model: believing in true love and discovering it in self-denial. This collapse of boundaries between the past and the present while projecting the transformation of the past in the present is one of the fundamental imaginary operations in the fascist discourse.

While Inge occupies the space denoted as the romantic young woman who must learn to understand the necessity of denial as the foundation for true love, three other women, all wives of common soldiers, represent additional possibilities for the sublimation of desire. Mrs. Kramer is the butcher's wife who is suddenly helpless in running the shop when her husband is recruited for active duty. Her appeal to him—"Max, can you help me? . . . What will I do without you?"—illustrates one aspect of the Nazi program to integrate women into responsible positions in the labor sphere vacated by the men recruited for war. Mrs. Hammer, the baker's wife, is, in contrast to Mrs. Kramer, a physically large woman who dominates not only her husband but also the bakery, commandeering the young (male) bakers and ordering her husband out of the baking room. As several characters emphasize, including her husband, Mrs. Hammer's domineering personality is only a shell. In other words, the competent, "manly" woman also has a place in this community, and even more so if her male qualities are only a mask. Finally, Hanna Friedrich, the school teacher's wife, is distinguished only by her pregnancy. Usually shown in close-up and soft-focus, she represents sentimentalized motherhood and encourages her husband to accept his marching orders because, as she puts it, giving birth is a woman's affair. A common lesson for all of the women introduced in this film is they must retain their love for the absent male, but that love must not become so excessive that it could jeopardize the partner's commitment to the war. The private love relationship has a higher purpose in binding the soldier via his family to Germany and ultimately to victory over the enemy.

If the war romance stylizes emotional relations in the loving pair or married couple as the fulfillment of happiness, it projects all social relations into the image of a harmonious network in which true strength comes from accepting one's place in a hierarchy of intersecting and complementary groups. Thus, the fascist discourse in Germany encompasses concurrently the clear separation of gender roles into waiting women and fighting men and the unification of the entire *Volk* as a collective of equals transcending class, age, profession, region (signified by dialect differences in the film), and gender. *Request Concert* articulates this discourse on three levels: in the projection of a fascist past by means of the narrative configuration of a popular myth, in the radio concert (and music generally) as an acoustic bridge that harmonizes conflicts and private needs with the public interest, and in a series of images of everyday life that chronicle fascism as a social equalizer. Fascist discourse, then, is an affirmative discourse constructed on the premise that reality can be represented from a monocular, absolute vantage point. It offers a narrative means for telling a story by a coherent subject from the perspective of a single, closed set of values. Disregarding all aberrant discourses, it does not have to make explicit a propaganda message because it relies on the "reality effect" of the visual image as natural. The ostensibly casual observations produce a specific representation of the German everyday that eliminates contradiction and conflict as the source of narrational activity in favor of a shared ideological vision of social harmony.

The construction of a historical antecedent for the fascist perspective implies that memory is an important part of the struggle for power, and that those who control memory control social change. In this film historical memory is drawn from the recent past, the Olympic Games of 1936, which are invoked as a great national triumph, and the Legion Condor operation during the Spanish Civil War, which anticipates the onset of World War II three years later. The opening images from the Olympic Games, intercut with the initial encounter between Inge and Herbert, draw on documentary footage, including images from Leni Riefenstahl's two-part *Olympia* film (*Olympia*, 1938). The editing pace, rapid camera movements, and mise-en-scène distinguish these sequences from the wooden dramaturgy of the rest of the film. Low-angle, superimposed shots of the tolling Olympic carillons with the German eagle insignia and Olympic flags waving in the wind alternate with aerial shots of the stadium filled to capacity, and a lengthy, smooth tilt catches the architecture's vertical symmetry and geometrical ornamentation as a symbolic framework for the rigid coherence sought on a personal and national level. Newsreel footage shows Hitler and his entourage entering the stadium, accepting a bouquet of flowers from a young girl, and responding to the crowd's cheers and raised-arm salutes, all accompanied by strains of the "Badenweiler March." The first sequences stress the populist impulse that motivates the film's historical mythology. The section's final segment with the Olympic fanfare trumpets on the soundtrack, the lighting of the Olympic torch against the setting sun, the release of thousands of doves, and, once again, the tolling bells, suggests a sacral rite that the German nation hosts as a peace-loving participant.

The Legion Condor sequence is much shorter and its connection to the present more direct. The scene in which Herbert learns that his mission is absolutely top secret fades into a map of Spain followed by a series of newsreel images of tanks, (German) bombers flying in formation, and aerial shots of bombs exploding on the ground. As that last image fades out, another image of falling bombs fades in with the newspaper-like headline title "September 6, 1939" (the day the Polish Operation and World War II effectively began). The temporal jump is offset by the continuity of the march music and the images, creating an equivalence, a nontemporality, which symbolically rewrites history from a perspective equating the present and past triumphs.

The fascist narrative constructs an imaginary relation through a specific kind of story linking an ambiguous present (mobilization for war) and a nostalgic past (the successes of the Olympic Games and the Legion Condor) by focusing on events with an allegorical relevance to the war. Furthermore, integrating documentary images familiar to the cinematic public of 1940 is a narrational strategy for quoting the verisimilitude of a "historical" film. These images not only function as a guarantor for the historical discourse but also partake fully of the realist illusion, offering the credibility of events and places already full of meaning because of their historical referentiality. The documentary authenticity, the use of props like the map and the embedding of flags, Nazi insignias, and the "Heil Hitler" salute are examples of visual elements the film employs to enunciate this imaginary relation to the past.

The symbolic rewriting of the past as mythology invokes the present wartime experience as a national contest and a popular victory combining sports, technology, consumerism, adventure, and maleness. It is a mythology grounded on the projection of class unity sustained by a concept of leveling. The discourse of the common person rewrites class difference as a spontaneous collectivity while maintaining class stratifications without apparent value judgments.[13] In *Request Concert* people from all walks of life cooperate to mobilize for war on the battle front and the home front. Young officers, a butcher, a baker, a teacher, and a music student come together in battle to form a comradeship that transcends their individual backgrounds. During the last request concert, a montage of images of the rapt listeners creates a parallel collective among the entire nation—soldiers in the trenches, bomber pilots, a mother at her sewing machine, a dog (!), a young woman writing a letter, a shoemaker, a carpenter, and a machinist. The projection of an organic community condenses all the contradictions of modernity into the solidarity of the *Volk*. Notably absent in this projection, of course, is the industrial laborer, belying the romantic anticapitalism that characterized Third Reich cinema from its very beginning to its demise. Moreover love and heroism are limited to the upper class, the officers, and elegant, intelligent young women, whereas the ordinary people are simple souls in civilian life and simple soldiers in the military who know their place and obey orders. Typically the comic moments in the film develop at the expense of crude stereotypes derived from such simple souls (for example, a silly subplot concerning "captured" French pigs).

Contrary to many other Third Reich films about the ideology of unity, *Request Concert* does not introduce an explicit Other as the scapegoat, be it the enemy other (British or French) or the racial other (the Jew).[14] The nostalgia for a collective identity, which was so skillfully exploited by National-Socialist ideology, usually resorted to some form of mythological construct in which a hypothetical golden age is troubled by the intrusion of a foreigner who must be eliminated to restore order. In this case the Other is absent or only peripherally evoked as an unnamed but presumably well-known war enemy. More important in this film than developing images of the Other to be excluded is the channeling of desire and identification for the immediate goal of war mobilization.

Just as images of a cross section of the German people reinforce the idea of a spontaneous collective, so does music manifest a "natural" talent that unites the spirit and emotions of the *Volk*. This understanding of music as the voice of the collective may account for the large number of music films produced during the Third Reich. In addition, the economics of film production sought increasingly to amortize production costs through records and radio exploitation of film music, so that almost every entertainment film produced during the Third Reich included at least two hit songs.[15] *Request Concert* specifically picks up on the strong tradition of the German music film, going back to the Viennese operettas produced by UFA in the early thirties and drawing on the popularity of the UFA revue films, modelled on American musicals, which UFA continued to produce after 1933.[16] The "Wunschkonzert" of the film title refers to one of the most successful attempts in the propaganda ministry's efforts to use the broadcast medium as a means of mass influence (in Nazi German the radio was called the *Volksempfänger* or people's receiver). It was a popular Sunday afternoon program that played musical favorites requested by soldiers at the front or at home on leave or convalescing.[17] By collecting donations for the war effort, announcing personal messages (e.g., births of children to soldiers in the field), and expressing sympathy and grief with those who lost family members in combat—all aspects included in the film—the radio program was both an effective tool for bridging the spatial gap between home and the front lines and a kind of national, secular substitute for the church congregation.

The request concert in the film not only connects the soldier at the front with the civilians who remain home but also succeeds in "uniting" Inge and Herbert through his request for the Olympic fanfare music. Excerpts from three actual concerts are included, and these sequences are especially static in their visual dramaturgy and mise-en-scène, alternating

The military pilots listen intently to the broadcast of the radio program "Request Concert," hoping for news from home (used by permission of Deutsches Institut für Filmkunde, Frankfurt).

between long shots of the audience from stage front and reverse shots of the stage framed by two banners with large swastikas. As an institution the request concert consists of a potpourri supposedly reflecting the musical tastes of the whole nation—humorous, light, serious, and martial music.[18] In contrast to *To New Shores*, where the songs function diegetically to express emotions, comment on the narrative, or poetically resolve a conflict, music in *Request Concert* is performed in the radio concert program for a consumerist public or it fills the sound track as background accompaniment. It is a major component in the film's continuity, often providing the key to transitions from one sequence to another, and the few sequences without musical scoring stand out.

The most important figuration of music as a unifying spiritual force beyond the entertainment value of the radio program develops around the figure of the music student Schwarzkopf. One of the group of neighbors to be mobilized in a company (including Hammer, Kramer, and Friedrich), Schwarzkopf, who lives in an apartment with his mother upstairs from the school teacher, is introduced aurally. Friedrich hears strains of Beethoven's "Moonlight Sonata" and goes up to invite Schwarzkopf and his mother for

The wooden dramaturgy of the concert sequences with symmetrical compositions and unimaginative camera work is typical for the rigid coherence sought in the entire film narrative (used by permission of Deutsches Institut für Filmkunde, Frankfurt).

coffee and cake which Hammer has just brought by. One by one Friedrich, Hammer, and Mrs. Friedrich enter the Schwarzkopf living room, drawn intuitively by the music, and sit down to listen with transfigured faces as their heads all sway in rhythm. In contrast to the other music in the film, classical music represents a moment of introversion, an opportunity to indulge serious emotions as a substitute or alternative for the distinct cheerfulness associated with the war. Interestingly the Beethoven piano sonata is gradually overwhelmed by an offscreen marching song coming from outside the window, at which point the camera cuts to an aerial pan of a large formation of marching soldiers in the street. This in turn introduces the actual scene of mobilization in the street and then at the train station, an event portrayed as a festive occasion in which the whole city turns out to send "the boys" off to war as if it were to a game. The hierarchy of group identity, beginning with the family and moving to neighbors and finally to the whole city, prefigures in different stages the projected community of the German people.

Marching off to war is a festive occasion that brings the whole community together (used by permission of Deutsches Institut für Filmkunde, Frankfurt).

Schwarzkopf's musical talent reemerges later in the film as a crucial weapon in the struggle against the enemy. Schwarzkopf and Friedrich are left behind as lookouts in a church while the rest of their battalion engages in a surprise nighttime raid. Owing to a sudden thickening of the fog, the soldiers lose their way, so Schwarzkopf plays at full strength a Bach toccata on the church organ to signal the direction. The powerful music has the desired effect but also draws enemy fire to the church. As a result Schwarzkopf is shot just as his comrades reach him, his head falling with great pathos on the organ keyboard to sound the last mighty chord. The combination of sacral music and flames surrounding the dead Schwarzkopf mark the organ player's sacrificial death as that of a hero. It is also the only casualty actually documented in this war film other than Helmut's minor injury and another soldier's wound during the nighttime raid. This suggests that war claims only a few victims and that even an unsoldierly musician can make a tactical contribution through his musical talent to the higher cause.[19] Logically it is also Schwarzkopf who focalizes the perfunctory but necessary expression of grief for the war's victims, an emotion the radio concert moderator identifies exclusively as the responsibility of women: "A mother, one of the many mothers whose sons have fallen, called us. His comrades sent his mother his identification tag and everything he owned. The mother called us. She said, 'I have the notebook of my beloved son; on the last page there is a song which he always liked to sing: "Gute Nacht, Mutter." May I request the song once more?'" Meanwhile the camera tracks around the Schwarzkopf living room—past the piano, music notes, a portrait of the dead soldier, a Beethoven bust—and comes to rest on Schwarzkopf's mother weeping at the window where previously she had listened to him playing Beethoven.

Schwarzkopf's death and the acknowledgement of grief related to that death expose moments of perturbation in the narrative economy that can barely be concealed. A war film that completely ignores the casualties of battle would sacrifice its claim to verisimilitude and thwart the genre's conventions. On the other hand, the ideology of war romance that rewards patient waiting with true love excludes the possibility of the lover's death. The narrative's effort to generate specific figures of mediation who take sides in this conflict can succeed only by limiting death to one of the few characters not in a couple relation (Schwarzkopf's "only" connection to a woman is to his mother, who is signified as family and as belonging to another generation) and prototypically an outsider (the serious, sensitive music student). A second example of narrative stress that evolves from the attempt to repress all contradiction in the closure relates to the figure of Helmut. Although Inge insists from the beginning that he is only a childhood friend and that therefore his erotic overtures are unwelcome, his insistence on courting her leads to the mix-up that retards the romantic couple's reunion. The narrative resolution then leaves Helmut alone, without a (female) partner. His relation to Herbert, more that of a younger brother to an older, protective sibling than that of comrades, compensates to a certain degree, and the long, mouth-to-mouth kiss with which Inge rewards him at the end is even more than Herbert gets but suggests no eroticism. Helmut's desire has led nowhere and now he too must learn renunciation; but rather than waiting for true love, he reverts to the role of the injured and petulant "child" of the newly constituted couple.

The affirmative fascist narrative describes an extreme moment in which different discourses are focused for the spectator in order to empower a particular social reality, in this case the need for individual renunciation for the sake of the collective goal of winning the war. *Request Concert*, with over twenty-three million viewers by the end of the war, was the tenth biggest box office hit of the Third Reich.[20] To a certain extent this can be explained by the propaganda ministry's efforts to promote the film, awarding it four predicates or distinctions and carefully directing its exhibition and reception.[21] Beyond that, however, its success can be ascribed to an eclectic synthesis of important cinematic factors: the popular "Wunsch-konzert" radio broadcast with its stars and musical entertainment, here augmented by a visual documentary dimension; the effective integration of newsreel footage to authenticate the fictional plot; the focus on normal citizens in wartime rather than great men who "make" history; and the portrayal of German society through positive images of the conventionally familiar and agreeable in an easily comprehensible narrative form. It is difficult if not impossible to judge or reconstruct the subjective experience of a film for the historical spectator, especially in the context of the Third Reich where the propaganda ministry even manipulated a film's "critical" reception. Yet a film like *Request Concert* is part of a historical period and part of the fascist way of coming to terms with reality. The reassuring portrayal of a cheerful, orderly community and the fantasy of a just war makes politics with repetitive kitsch images while subverting any suggestion of responsibility for having begun the war. This is not the product of ideology or propaganda alone, of the director's or Propaganda Minister Goebbels's intentions, but must be regarded as the imaginary signification of a particular society's need to situate itself in the past and to open in the present a space of its own. In this respect *Request Concert* is an important historical example of the place occupied by cinematic seduction and illusion in conditioning the public for everyday life in a repressive society through mass entertainment.

6

The Illusion of Escapism:
Helmut Käutner's *Romance*
in a Minor Key

ERMANS DID NOT live *only* a regimented existence under National
Socialism, propelled by the state ideology of making over the
world in an image of racial purity and community cohesion. This
was the social practice supported by the state's authority, and a film
like *Request Concert* combines images and narrative to convey the affirmative fascist consensus underlying that social practice. Yet everyday experience as well as fascist ideology also were capable of triggering other imaginary ways of living the contingencies of the moment, even exactly opposite
ones: resignation, fear of social disintegration, and extreme interiority. This
is the subject of Helmut Käutner's *Romance in a Minor Key* (*Romanze in
Moll*, 1943), a film that cannot be reduced to an ideological or propagan-
distic prescription but rather suggests a way of mediating between the internalized desires fueled by fascist ideology and the ever harsher realities of
social existence under National Socialism. Such a film undermines the impression of the Third Reich as a public consensus, but its problematization
of the fascist order is displaced onto an emotional conflict still within the
terms of patriarchal hierarchy and domination defined by the fascist system. As a result its aberrant discourse is finally folded back into an abstract
moralism.

Despite general agreement about the totalitarian nature of German
fascism, cinema historians have insisted on a distinction between unpolitical entertainment and propaganda when considering the films produced
during the Third Reich. By disengaging form from content, much research
has reduced the issue of fascist aesthetics to overt political convictions expressed in these films.[1] That the majority of feature films produced during
the Third Reich were "apolitical," consisting of literary adaptations, dramatic melodramas, operettas, musical revue films, and farces, points to the

continuity in genres already established before 1933 (and points forward as well to the fifties). Yet to write them off as harmless, escapist, or humanistic in intention *because* they do not manifest the blatant slogans or images associated with National Socialism, ignores the complexity of cultural discourses that empower fascism as a totalitarian system.

Käutner is counted among the directors who produced high quality, unpolitical entertainment films in the second half of the Third Reich. He is claimed to be one of the few representatives of "film art" in German fascism.[2] Others detect in his filmmaking a sign of political opposition in the resistance to the aesthetics of the fascist narrative.[3] From this perspective the absence of violence, heroic themes, and visual monumentality opens a space for playfulness and formal concerns which were otherwise considered suspect if not decadent by the film censors. Common to both of these positions is, first, an appreciation of the filmmaker's technical competence and, second, the wish to vindicate that quality as something beyond fascism. Yet the film industry was a priority interest for Goebbels's propaganda ministry, one of the most highly scrutinized and carefully controlled branches of an administered culture and subject to intervention at every step. Hence, to recognize artistic or creative achievements as exceptions to the rule does not obviate the need to understand how these films too produce illusions of escapism within the fascist system.

Helmut Käutner is particularly interesting in this respect because the nine films he completed during the Third Reich have been recognized as his most successful, despite a long career as director extending into the seventies.[4] He is often singled out as the most brilliant film talent to have emerged during the National-Socialist regime, a director whose early films evoke an atmosphere identified with the tradition of Ernst Lubitsch and Max Ophüls and whose style reflects the influence of the French cinema identified with names like René Clair, Jean Renoir, and Marcel Carné.[5] His most striking achievement within the norms of Goebbels's film industry, however, was the ability to combine the talents of scriptwriter and director, for Käutner was unique among Third Reich filmmakers for having written or coauthored the scripts for all his films. This enabled him to exercise a rigor few other directors enjoyed, especially those involved in the production of entertainment features. Käutner's witty dialogues, the careful dramaturgy with its superb sense of timing and rhythm, the mobile camera, the varied editing techniques, and the meticulous handling of light and shadow reveal a high degree of subtlety and a sensitivity for visual detail while highlighting the utter impoverishment of aesthetic understanding among the majority of film directors.

Romance in a Minor Key adapts the short story "Les Bijoux" by the nineteenth-century French writer Guy de Maupassant.[6] The literary text treats the tragicomedy of a low-level bureaucrat who marries a beautiful young woman with a weakness for the theater and for ostentatious, fake jewelry. Thrown into despair after her sudden death, he drifts into poverty and finally decides to pawn one of his wife's baubles. He is shocked and shamed to learn that the jewels are not fake at all but a wealthy admirer's gifts to his wife, who was leading a double life. Confronted with his ruined honor, he realizes that the wife he lost (but in truth had never possessed) is a source of wealth. From Maupassant Käutner appropriated the core idea of a triangle story, its corollary of betrayed honor, the details of the husband's blindness as well as the cinematically rich motifs of role-playing (theater) and narcissism (jewelry). Unlike Maupassant, whose third-person narrator adopts the perspective of the husband, Käutner focuses only secondarily on this character's disgrace and instead transfers the spectator's emotional identification to the many blockages of the wife's desire. Thus, by shifting attention from the husband to the wife, Käutner transforms Maupassant's ironic anecdote about the dialectic of fate and freedom to a chamber drama about escapism and renunciation.

Käutner situates the modest love affair between a housewife and a successful composer in an unidentified setting, clearly not Germany in 1943 but perhaps provincial France in the late nineteenth century. Madeleine is married to a bank clerk who demands from himself and from others strict accountability and an unwavering sense of propriety and virtue. His one weakness, a love of cards and gambling, allows him to buy small gifts for his wife. Their humble and ordered life is disturbed when Michael, a distracted composer, accidentally jostles Madeleine on the street while she is admiring an expensive chain of pearls in a jewelry store window. Her enigmatic smile provides the inspiration he has been seeking to complete his *Romantic Symphony*. On a whim he buys the pearl necklace and commissions the jeweler to present it to the mysterious lady. What began as a playful adventure soon turns into a more serious relationship. Michael asks Madeleine to marry him, but she refuses out of loyalty to her husband. Caught in a double bind of duty and desire, she avoids Michael but is forced nonetheless to pay a price for her moment of happiness. By chance a hunting party had interrupted the lovers' tryst at the country estate of Michael's brother, who introduced them as husband and wife in order to avoid embarrassing explanations. When Victor, the newly named president at the husband's bank, turns out to have been one of those hunters and realizes the compromised situation of his subordinate's wife, he uses his position to blackmail her. To protect her husband's honor, she gives in but then commits suicide.[7]

Like Jeanne in *Passion* and Gloria in *To New Shores*, Madeleine evokes male desire and male fantasies of domination. Unlike Jeanne, however, Madeleine engages none of the play Lubitsch invested in the female look that can throw into question the autonomy and control of male desire. Käutner confines his protagonist's look by situating it always within the dynamic of the shot/reverse shot, a technique of the classical narrative cinema that produces narrational coherence and binds point of view to a privileged narrator position.[8] Moreover, actress Marianne Hoppe's subdued costumes and austere, almost masculine physique in the role of Madeleine share little of the physical or visual sensuality that mark Gloria's otherness in the repressive, antierotic society imagined by Sierck. Rather, Käutner's narrative uses the female as an object of male desire to thematize the clash between individual happiness and social norms and by this means it displaces the conflict onto the plane of possibilities and limits of expression in an authoritarian regime. Käutner's film further resembles the classic melodrama *To New Shores* in that it provides a space — removed in time and place — in which the contradictions of personal happiness and social constraint can be worked through. Contrary to Sierck's film, however, where the New World still offers a context or foil to project critically the possibility of an ideal community in a happy ending, Käutner's romantic sentimentalization of helplessness and escapism denies even that hypothetical renewal. Contrary also to *Request Concert*, which projects a mystically harmonious community as the explicit point of intersection between public need and personal desire, *Romance in a Minor Key* withdraws entirely into the private sphere and ends with the collapse even of that reduced marginal space. In this respect the crucial years of National-Socialist megalomania and defeat between 1937 and 1943 leave their traces in the narration.

The remarkable opening sequence, comparable to Murnau's splendid camera work at the beginning of *The Last Laugh*, signals that the film narrative will be removed from the public space. In one languid movement the camera pans over a city skyline at dusk and tilts down to follow the husband as he approaches the door to an apartment building. Tilting back up to a close-up of a window, open and lit from the interior, it dollies forward through the window and enters a bedroom, coming to rest finally on a close-up of a motionless woman's face on a pillow. This first extended shot leads the spectator visually and structurally from the exterior through the window, a traditional symbol for the entrance to the soul, into that most intimate of chambers, the bedroom. In addition, it introduces the motif of intrusion that will dominate the reversals in the film's narration: Michael's fateful entry into Madeleine's life, the intrusion of the hunting party at the country estate, Victor's invasion into Madeleine's home, Michael's insistence on interpreting Madeleine's smile, and even the film's flashback structure which retrospectively makes Madeleine into the voyeuristic spectacle of male memory. The camera's intrusion into the private sphere projects a system of contingency in which individuals are the passive victims of an outside, unpredictable power.

Consistent with this power of the camera is the way human interactions are constructed around a dynamic of blindness and seeing or silence and saying. Each relationship is premised on a state of nonknowledge that always leads to an action with destructive consequences. Madeleine's husband exemplifies the first alternative. Unnamed throughout the film, he typifies the self-contented, self-righteous individual. In the first scene he returns to the apartment after an evening of cards, the gambling suggesting early in the narrative the husband's metaphorical position within a system subject to chance and risk. The camera registers every movement: he lights the hall lamp, hangs his coat on a hook, tiptoes with squeaking shoes into the living room, removes them, yawns, stretches. This is a correct man who executes each movement with the same pedantic attention that has earned him respect as a bank clerk. Entering the bedroom, he sees Madeleine lying on the bed and begins to tell her about his winnings. When she does not answer, he remarks: "I know you aren't sleeping," ironically confirming the blindness that will characterize him throughout the film. Only several seconds later does he notice that she has swallowed poison. For this husband Madeleine is the "little wife" whom he spoils with gifts, whom he allows to indulge a small extravagance now and then, whom he treats, in sum, as a child. Fittingly Käutner has this claustrophobic relationship unfold in a small apartment with simple furnishings. Tightly framed interior shots visually exaggerate the suffocating spatial impression, and Madeleine's tendency to throw open the window whenever she enters the apartment makes the oppressiveness even more tangible. The husband's pet bird in a cage near the window is an obvious symbol for the physical, social, and emotional prison he has constructed for Madeleine.

In his antierotic conjugal life and his subaltern position, the husband represents the authoritarian personality that so readily accepted the dictates of German fascism.[9] A strong identification with authority coupled with an equally strong rejection of the Other, especially of those considered socially inferior, feeds his rigorous sense of conformity and moralism. The bank clerk, for example, self-righteously condemns the employee whose fraud he uncovers: "All guilt comes home to roost, my friend. No one escapes his proper punishment in the long run, and that is right. . . . I only did my duty." When another investigator explains that the culprit had troubles at home (a wife whom he no longer loved but for whom he felt responsible), the clerk rejects such laxity out of hand as a character flaw and thus in his blindness condemns too his own wife. Crosscut with the scene at the country estate where Madeleine for a moment experiences the happiness of her illicit love, this exchange establishes the momentum of the fate that will inevitably destroy both of them. Similarly, when Madeleine later relates that a neighbor woman who left her husband for another man

Madeleine's husband looks but does not see that she is dead (used by permission of Stiftung deutsche Kinemathek, Berlin).

The physical, social, and emotional prison of conjugal life is symbolized by the husband's pet bird cage and Madeleine's habit of throwing open the windows (used by permission of Stiftung deutsche Kinemathek, Berlin).

　　　　　　　　　　　　　　THE ILLUSION OF ESCAPISM

had returned home and been forgiven, her own husband's comment—"Such a thing can't be forgiven!"—reiterates his judgmental stringency and confirms Madeleine's worst fears about the consequences of her behavior. Here the husband's moral ideology is a form of protective nonseeing, a kind of self-preservation at the expense of knowledge.

The arrogant dissociation from anyone who cannot fulfill his strict moral principles is the obverse of the husband's slavish identification with those who wield power over him. Duty, honor, orderliness, and status are the obsessions of the authoritarian personality. He lives out a double bind in which freedom is equated with the will to obey authority and equality means accepting the oppression of everyone under that authority. The reception at which Victor officially assumes the directorship of his bank reveals the nature of that authority. The crucial scene begins with Madeleine's entry to the formal reception on the arm of her husband. A quick shot/reverse shot shows Madeleine's distress and Victor's surprise at their reencounter after he had met her in the "role" of Michael's wife at the country estate. The central segment then begins with a high angle shot of the guests seated around a dining table. Only as the camera tilts down to pan around the table, resting momentarily on Victor, Madeleine, and her husband, does the import of the initial image become clear. It escapes neither Madeleine nor Victor that he wields power over her because he knows of her double life and because of his social and economic position. Reflected in a huge mirror hanging behind the table, the tightly framed and severely symmetrical composition suggests the play of appearance and reality. It serves too as a warning that the power and wealth visually framed and richly highlighted in this image have their shadows. Meanwhile the bank president is introducing Victor as his successor in a long speech which celebrates and appeals to the continuance of "healthy, bourgeois moral principles." Madeleine's husband nods with profound approval while she plays nervously with her plate and Victor watches her with bemused detachment. The full irony of the toast that Victor offers her following the speech—"to bourgeois morality"—will quickly reveal its force when he exploits her vulnerability for his sexual pleasure.

If Madeleine's husband represents the authoritarian personality whose self-identity rests on subordination, then Victor embodies the arbitrary power of authority to bring catastrophe or salvation. Heir to the status associated with his uncle's bank, he shares none of its traditional moral integrity and mutual respect. Thus, Victor is at one and the same time the instrument of authority, who in her husband's name punishes Madeleine for her transgression, and the husband's foil, the projection of arbitrary power that can turn against the subordinate. Invested with the power that guarantees the system's solidity upon which the husband depends, Victor also has access to the violence inherent in that power. Furthermore, he is not constrained by the husband's willful blindness; indeed, among the three antagonists he sees most lucidly and uses that knowledge opportunistically. Yet Victor too becomes a victim, for he surrenders himself to desire, telling Madeleine in a helpless tone of voice that he cannot do otherwise. With that the entire system and its precarious hierarchy is disrupted.

Michael is the third term between these two opposites or, more accurately, he stands at an idealized position outside the antithetical poles of reproducing or corrupting the authority they describe. He is mentioned for the first time in the introductory flashback—when the jeweler describes the encounter between Madeleine and Michael to her husband—as a mad man because he acts impulsively and extravagantly. Later Michael will use the same epithet to explain his behavior to Madeleine: "Every artist is mad. I am a composer." Specialized in the role of the elegant lover, the actor Ferdinand Marian was one of the most talented and popular male leads in the Third Reich cinema, remembered perhaps unfairly for his notorious role as the suave, Jewish seducer in Veit Harlan's anti-Semitic film *Jew Suss* (*Jud Süss*, 1940). As artist in *Romance in a Minor Key* he adapts the convention of the feminized male lead from the romantic melodrama, a traditionally female-oriented film genre and one that could have expected a popular reception on the "home front" where the cinema audience consisted mostly of women by 1943. Art is a sphere of feminine activity also culturally sanctioned for males, so Michael can simultaneously play the worldly, well-bred seducer and the free, self-directed, independent male. For Madeleine he represents the outsider who treats her neither as subordinate nor with violence, neither as child nor whore. Not surprisingly Madeleine enters his life as a muse, a common male fantasy of woman as nonsexual threat. Thus, she enables him to express his feelings through art, and conversely Michael awakens emotions and desires in her she had never before experienced.

As an artist Michael is preoccupied with expression, and this accounts structurally for his bond to Madeleine, who lives in a world that denies her self-expression and imposes silence. Moreover, he is also related to the realm of illusion, that socially sanctified activity of the imagination that plays with truth and falsehood. Madeleine accuses him jokingly of deception—he lures her into a restaurant by walking off with her packages, he pretends he is a thief who wants to reform himself to gain her sympathy, he transforms day into night by closing the drapes after she refuses to drink champagne in broad daylight—and she means that he has the ability to create the world as he pleases. She, on the other hand, is denied the will that could create or transform her world:

MADELEINE: I must go.

MICHAEL: Don't lie. You don't have to go, you want to. That is, you don't even want to. You don't have to want. You women have it easy when you don't have an answer.

MADELEINE: How so?

MICHAEL: Then a smile is your excuse.

For him Madeleine is an unending source of erotic attraction, a projection and confirmation of his own expressive capacity because she is passive and without will.

Madeleine's smile fascinates and inspires Michael, and he searches her face to decipher its hidden meanings.[10] For example, in the garden of the country estate the two lovers, outsiders and transgressors both, experience a moment of idyllic happiness beyond the domain of domestic oppression and violent authority:

MICHAEL: Your smile has so many faces, Madeleine. What does it mean now?

MADELEINE: Can't you see it?

MICHAEL: Of course. But I want you to say it.

MADELEINE: If I say it, then it will already have disappeared.

MICHAEL: I'll take the risk. I want to hear it.

MADELEINE: I would like to stay here. This silence, peace, space.

Madeleine's fear that the act of expression, of speaking will frustrate her desire to escape causes her to don silence and repression for her self-protection. Moreover, when she does express the wish to extend in time the perfect moment she shares with Michael, it is immediately exposed as a fantasy only possible outside of time and leads Michael to propose marriage in hopes of possessing her forever. Madeleine's sense of a lyrical or passive nontemporality stands in sharp contrast to this and other forms of regimented time stressed in the film. The ubiquitous clocks, the stultifying repetitiveness of home life, the timetable of hours she can spend with Michael are all aspects of necessity, of those uncontrollable outside forces that intrude upon her and block her imagined avenues of escape.

For Madeleine there will be no escape from the everyday, and the following scenes at the country estate, each of which produces a new blockage, reiterate that inevitable conclusion. First, Michael's brother interrupts their idyllic walk in the park and reminds her that she is returning to the city already the next day. Then, the hunting party intrudes on them, triggering a conversation in which a poet teasingly explains why he finds Madeleine, despite her beauty, uninspiring as a literary subject. Not as Michael's wife—and so she was introduced—but only as his lover could she fire his imagination, he explains. Yet, even when the lovers playfully hint at the real nature of their relationship, the poet—insisting on his

Michael searches Madeleine's face to decipher the hidden meanings of her enigmatic smile (used by permission of Stiftung deutsche Kinemathek, Berlin).

version of the truth—rejects this possibility as "imaginative fiction" and "typically feminine," for "real life looks completely different." This scene is crosscut with the two short scenes concerning the fraud of a bank employee mentioned above in which the husband expresses another but equally undiscerning view of reality based on the notion of just punishment. Käutner himself plays the cameo role of the poet, constantly toying with his small, round spectacles (in his hand) as he talks about "reality," and he underscores his final comment by demonstratively fixing them on his nose. The irony of his and the husband's blindness to Madeleine's real experience of love—neither one will allow the possibility of female desire— underscores the theme of male blindness and more generally the broken relation to reality that characterizes all the males.[11]

In the next scene Victor throws further doubt on the durative strength of any relationship with Michael when he surmises that an artist needs new inspiration for each creation and therefore would not bind him-

The poet (played by director Helmut Käutner, sharing the sofa with the heroine) is blind to her real dilemma (used by permission of Stiftung deutsche Kinemathek, Berlin).

self to one woman. When the lovers are alone again, Madeleine recognizes that out of pity and gratitude she cannot leave her husband.

MICHAEL: But you love me and not him!

MADELEINE: Then I cannot be happy.

MICHAEL: But you have a right to be happy.

MADELEINE: Do we really have a right to be happy?

MICHAEL: Wouldn't it be better if we parted?

Madeleine's rhetorical question formulates bluntly the consequence of passivity and points to the self-pity it engenders for those who experience the world as a place that offers no other alternative but subordination. Under these conditions her earlier inhibition about speaking and naming desire emerges now as a defense, albeit illusory, against losing the self by removing the "right to happiness" to the sphere of the imaginary and the unspoken. The escape to the country estate proves, then, to be no more than a brief interlude. Subject to interruption, intervention, overturning, and reversal, the idyllic moment leads to their final separation. The last scene of the fateful interlude ends appropriately under the sign of death: a farmer with a scythe on his shoulder crosses the foreground of the image as the lovers part at the rural train stop.

Michael is not just an artist but a composer, a fact that helps justify diegetically the almost excessive, even narcotizing use of music in the film. The "romance" of the title denotes a musical form that resonates with associations of love, the musical romance being an instrumental melody often coupled with a strophic song describing a tragic love. This theme song dominates the sound track as background music and becomes in the course of the film a major narrational element as well. It can reinforce point of view, heighten a dramatic moment, or recall or anticipate the bond between the lovers. In addition, different kinds of music can signal fundamental contrasts among the characters, as in the case of the music from the record player in the husband's café or his preference to attend the circus rather than Michael's orchestral concert.

The scene where Michael falls deeply in love with Madeleine revolves precisely around the composition of this concert "Romance" inspired by her smile, a Romance in a major key. Music is a medium that expresses forceful emotions and desire, and in this scene it provides Madeleine for a moment with a substitute voice. Her entire subjectivity is invested in music, and when she insists that the Romance must be in a minor key, she is communicating her central dilemma as a woman:

[sitting next to Michael at the piano, playing in a minor key]

MICHAEL: Major, not minor. It must radiate. The melody of a happy love. Romance in a major key.

MADELEINE: No, in a minor key.

MICHAEL: Renunciation?

MADELEINE: Yes! A parting melody.

[Michael joins her in playing]

MICHAEL: Romance in a minor key? You are right. You are indeed right!

The next scene dissolves to Madeleine dreamily playing the Romance at her piano with the chain of pearls around her neck. The well-placed ellipsis following her refusal in the previous scene to see Michael ever again or to accept his gift of expensive jewels is typical for Käutner's ability to employ the visual and aural dimension of the cinema rather than relying on dialogue. Her love affair with the composer—fatefully consummated under the sign of

Romanze in Moll

aus dem gleichnamigen Film

Worte: Helmut Käutner

Musik: Lothar Brühne

Reproduction of Lothar Brühne's title song for *Romance in a Minor Key*; text by Helmut Käutner (copyright © 1943 by Wiener Bohème Verlag, used by permission of BMG UFA-Musikverlage Munich).

renunciation and accompanied by the chain of pearls, themselves a symbol for the ominous causality of events that began as an adventure and end in a death wish—will continue to be bound to this piece of music.

The public performance of the *Romantic Symphony* draws together the narrative's major visual, musical, and thematic motifs into a densely interwoven network. Madeleine arrives at the concert after having surrendered to Victor, who arranged to have her husband delayed at the bank. He, in turn, joins her after the concert has begun, whispering to her with unintended irony as he sits down, "Did I miss anything?" Madeleine, however, who has shared so little of herself with this man, does not respond. She is mute, while the music literally speaks her desire and anxiety in the lyrical text embedded in the Romance motif of renunciation:

> Just one hour between day and dreaming
> My soul might turn to you,
> I want to send my heart on a journey
> off to you.
> I never want to miss this hour,
> already in the morning I want to think of it,
> every day anew let it be conferred
> on you and me . . .
> All my yearning should surround the path
> to lend its far journey strength.
> Please don't send it with empty hands
> home to me.[12]

Once again the music acts as a vehicle of subjectivity for Madeleine, this time leading to a rush of memories. The camera freezes the suffering expression on her face in a close-up frontal shot, eyes wide open and staring at some indefinite point beyond the camera, while a series of visual "quotes" superimposed over this mask recapitulate the important narrative events. Madeleine mobilizes the past in order to make the monumental choice of death over life, and that choice is constructed as a visionary spectacle, accompanied by the musical score of the "Romance in a Minor Key" and ratified by the audience's thunderous applause as the music and the memories reach their crescendo at the same moment. Roused from his sleep, her husband asks whether "it" is over, and Madeleine answers with grave finality: "Yes, it is over."

Romance in a Minor Key constructs its plot as a classical narrative, that is, its structure is determined from the beginning by the chronology of events that leads to closure. This movement toward closure constitutes the classical narrative's order and inflects shot punctuation, sound transitions, and visual continuity to create the impression of a constant flow of action.[13] Madeleine's decision for death brings the narrative back to its point of departure—the penetration into the sphere of intimacy coming to rest on the image of a lifeless Madeleine—and marks a moment of provisional closure. This suicide transforms the imaginary escape from reality into a desperate wish to transfix the past as memory and to deny the present. It is the most radical break possible with the past and at the same time it is an admission of helplessness in confronting reality. The other characters are similarly victims of their desperate wishes and self-destructive actions. Victor, the formal defender but actual abuser of authority, is killed in a duel with Michael because his desire for Madeleine blinds him. His death revalidates the order he had upset but only at the price of a catastrophe which resembles a fantasy of vengeance. It seems to compensate justly for the defeat and disappointment suffered by Madeleine at the hands of the power he represents. Madeleine's husband is ruined after Michael reveals to him why his wife sought death. Drunk and dishevelled, he is lost in a world that no longer allows him to be blind. Michael, finally, who wanted to possess Madeleine as an instrument of his artistic expression, is left physically maimed. His hand was wounded in the duel so that he can no longer play the piano and conduct.[14]

The film's textual structure orients spectator identification precisely to this position of powerlessness and victimization. After the military defeats and reversals associated with Stalingrad in the winter of 1942, it was a position not unrelated to that of Hitler's admirers, especially those recruited from the working and middle classes who had been most susceptible to the ideology of renewal and community projected in a film like *Request Concert*. By early 1943 morale at home was beginning to sink seriously owing to expanded air attacks against German cities and the growing difficulties in supplying the civilian population with necessary goods. Already in 1942 Goebbels had directed the propaganda ministry to increase the production of light entertainment films at the expense of heroic dramas and overt propaganda, and within a short time any catastrophe in a film narrative was grounds for withholding it from distribution. This may be the reason for the delay in the release of Käutner's film within the Reich. After passing the censor in January, 1943, it was distributed only in occupied areas, in foreign countries, and for troops at the front.[15] By June, however, the film had become so successful that the propaganda ministry decided to release it also for distribution in the Reich with a predicate of artistic merit, and film critics chose it as best foreign film at the Stockholm Film Festival in 1944, the only feature of the Third Reich to receive this distinction.[16] In this respect *Romance in a Minor Key* indicates once more to what extent Goebbels saw the film industry not only as an ideological tool but also as a financial enterprise. In 1942 the highly efficient UFI monopoly controlled the second largest film market in the world, and if the war had not destroyed so much studio capacity after 1943, it would have become a profitable source of state income and the only serious competition to Hollywood.[17] Therefore, he promoted this well-made film although it played on feelings of existential loss at a time when the official cultural policy encouraged light, uncomplicated comedies. Similarly Goebbels was willing to accept filmmakers like Käutner, although they were clearly not Nazis.

Discussions of films in the Third Reich have been especially dependent on an institutional and agency approach which sees meaning and patterns imposed through political directives from above. Although a totalitarian regime like the Third Reich derived its power exactly from the extent to which it could control administrative structures, it was never able to eliminate all aberrant practices. This is not to suggest, however, that such practices are necessarily subversive. Individual films are neither inevitable apologies for such a regime nor a concerted resistance against its power. *Romance in a Minor Key* is an example of a film whose ambivalences and formal tensions expose fundamental divisions in a society that can no longer sustain a previously guaranteed equilibrium, and hence the ambivalences and tensions could not be resolved in the conventional UFA style. Käutner's point of view is, of course, untheorized, and in none of his films produced during the Third Reich does he assume an explicit political position.

Romance in a Minor Key constitutes a narrative discourse on the loss of illusion, elaborating an imaginary, protected space of privacy identified with a spectator position of helplessness and escapist desire at a historical juncture when many Germans were beginning to expect the impending collapse of the fascist regime. As a classical cinematic narrative it eliminates through identification with the protagonist's knowledge the possibility of critique or distance and reinforces the pleasure of self-pity in metaphysical suffering. Thus, the imaginary operation in this film effectively displaces the perception of victimization onto the spectator by privatizing conflict and camouflaging its topical relevance through symbolism, coded references, and complicated, even manneristic formal means. The film's desperate escape into interiority explains why it lacks a sense of external reality.[18] Betrayed and abandoned, the spectator can transfer any sense of responsibility to those who misuse their authority while maintaining the very system of hierarchy and subordination which supports it. The destabilizing potential of utopian hopes for change—always a factor in a medium that plays emotional anxiety and desire against each other—are channelled into a direction that could not threaten the regime. In this respect Käutner anticipates a narrative strategy that would under different circumstances of production and reception govern virtually the entire German postwar cinema through the sixties.

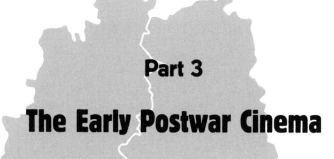

Part 3

The Early Postwar Cinema

7

The Discourse of Powerlessness: Wolfgang Staudte's *Rotation*

THE UNCONDITIONAL SURRENDER accepted by the German Military Command on May 7, 1945, summons at first glance the image of rupture and a clean break with the twelve years of fascist dictatorship. Indeed both the victors and the defeated harbored the wish, if not the conviction, that the slate could be wiped clean and that the people who had perpetrated two world wars within the span of thirty years could be recast in the role of a peaceful, democratic country under the tutelage and control of the "civilized" nations. The initial Allied policy—agreed upon by Britain, France, the Soviet Union, and the United States—of dismantling the National-Socialist administrative apparatus and economic infrastructure was not meant so much as a punitive measure but rather as the first step in achieving that tabula rasa. Coupled with the social disorder and psychological uncertainty following the military capitulation, the situation seemed to place the German people at a historical crossroads. Yet other realities—the Allies' economic interests in the rapid reestablishment of the German market and the ideological pressures of cold-war conflict—modified the original agenda for the country's reconstruction. Rebuilding Germany under these conditions was to become a question of using to a large extent the resources, structures, and individuals identified with the fascist past while guaranteeing the impossibility of a repetition of that past. Denazification, reeducation, and democratization were the catchwords for policy guidelines implemented variously in all four occupied zones of Germany.[1]

The recovery and reorganization of the German cinema and its film industry in the immediate postwar years is in retrospect prototypical for the complicated, problematic relation of rupture and continuity which determined all social structures prior to the economic miracle in West Germany and the introduction of a socialist command economy in East

Germany. Not only did the film industry inherit the Third Reich's dubious legacy of using the cinema as the most important form of mass influence but it also faced a public whose taste had been conditioned by the entertainment priorities of a fascist regime. No longer the Third Reich but not yet the two conditionally sovereign states with opposed systemic identities, Germany had to confront in this interim period the difficulties of satisfying the most elementary physical needs of feeding and housing the war-decimated population. At the same time, the desire to explain or account for the experience of fascism politically, intellectually, and emotionally was acute and at the center of Allied efforts to reeducate the German people. Among the first orders, issued in summer 1945, were guidelines that regulated the control of all information production and transfer. Each occupation zone assumed the responsibility for licensing the individuals permitted to work in the information sector and for censoring the content of materials in its respective area. The aim was to disassemble the centralized organizational structure of Goebbels's propaganda ministry as well as to counteract the effect of twelve years of information manipulation.

Film production, distribution, and exhibition fell under these general regulations, but because the Allied Control Commission—charged with addressing all suprazonal questions concerning Germany as a whole—deliberately discouraged a centralized film industry that could once again become a state-controlled monopoly, each zone developed its own policies and agencies to carry them out.[2] In all zones, but especially in the Soviet zone, the military authorities had recourse first of all to their own films for public distribution. Within one month after the German capitulation, the Soviet Military Administration in Germany (SMAD) had commissioned German technicians to refit a synchronization studio in Berlin for dubbing Soviet films for the German audience. Undamaged cinemas were quickly licensed for exhibition purposes, and Sovexport, a film distributor under Soviet management, was chartered to supply them with the necessary features.[3] These included comedies but also political and informational films from over twenty years of Soviet production. The Western zones followed suit, although not until after the 1948 currency reform enabled the transfer of profits into hard currency was the market flooded with British, French, and especially American productions.[4] German rereleases were another source of cinema entertainment in all four zones, in so far as the respective zonal censorship commissions deemed them acceptable. Screened as early as 1946, these included some pre-1933 sound features but primarily comedies and so-called apolitical dramas produced during the Third Reich. In addition, unfinished and unreleased films already in the pipeline before the surrender were readied for premiere showings.[5] Almost from the beginning, then, the diverse interests of the occupation powers themselves defined the possibilities and limitations for the development of the postwar

German cinema. In the Western zones, where print media were considered the primary instruments for information dissemination and reeducation, the film industry was reorganized largely under American direction for entertainment purposes and according to the economic priorities of the Hollywood studios and their marketing needs. In the Soviet zone the cinema was regarded along with schools as the preferential means for reeducation, so SMAD rapidly implemented measures to reorganize German film production.

In August 1945, five German exiles from Moscow met in Berlin to discuss plans for a new German film industry. With the support of SMAD's Central Administration for Education (Zentralverwaltung für Volksbildung) they convened the first public meeting in November—including numerous directors, scenarists, actors, and technicians—to lay the groundwork for an antifascist, humanistic, and democratic cinema in the Eastern zone.[6] Besides technical difficulties such as procuring capital, repairing the technical park, and obtaining sufficient raw stock for film production, there had been—in contrast to other media—virtually no antifascist film production in exile that could have provided the experience and personnel for a rebirth of the German cinema.[7] The enthusiasm and good will of those committed to a program of humanism and to the process of ideological clarification could not disguise the fact that the majority had worked for UFA during the Third Reich; yet despite this fact, or perhaps because of it, there was general agreement that the new German film could *not* simply continue the old UFA-style.[8]

Already early in 1946 a German film team was working in the Soviet Sector of Berlin. The first documentary shorts, cultural films, and newsreels appeared in the cinemas there in the spring under the name of DEFA, Deutsche Film-AG, and on May 17, 1946, when SMAD granted the official commercial license to DEFA, three feature films were in production under makeshift conditions, with financing by the Soviet distributor in the Eastern zone. During the next years DEFA consolidated its facilities—the former UFA studios located in Babelsberg near Potsdam, confiscated by the Soviet Army immediately after the war, were given over to DEFA and rebuilt in 1948–49—and expanded its production quota to twelve films in 1949. In that year Wolfgang Staudte's *Rotation* was released, one of the most highly regarded in a series of films that would come to be identified later as DEFA's antifascist classicism.[9] Staudte's film career is not atypical for the continuity obscured by the rupture of 1945. The son of actors, he himself became an actor during the Weimar Republic on major Berlin stages and as a film extra. Although he was not politically active, the Nazi regime excluded him from the stage in 1933 because of his association with progressive political theater circles. Staudte continued to appear occasionally in minor film roles (including several notorious propaganda films such as Karl Ritter's *Pour le mérite*, 1938; *Legion Condor*, 1939; Veit Harlan's *Jew Suss* [*Jud Süss*], 1940; and Arthur Maria Rabenalt's *Riding for Germany* [. . . *reitet für Deutschland*], 1941) but found regular employment first in a synchronization studio, then in radio broadcasting, and finally in a firm that produced film ads. In 1941 the Tobis film company invited him to make a series of test films, and by the end of the war he had directed five comedies, only two of which though were completed and actually released.[10]

Staudte's DEFA film productions were among the most interesting and consistently successful attempts to find an alternative to the UFA tradition and represented for many what they hoped would become the new German film. One of the first directors to join the original group of Moscow exiles who were organizing DEFA, he began shooting semidocumentary sequences in December 1945, some of which found their way later into *Rotation* (the flooding of the subway tunnels by the SS). In March 1946 he was already filming studio interiors for *The Murderers Are Among Us* (*Die Mörder sind unter uns*, 1946), a topical story that directly addresses the national catastrophe and personal guilt for fascist war crimes. Not only did this film establish Staudte's international reputation but formally it also indicated a will to overcome the constraints of UFA dramaturgy.[11] Staudte's second DEFA film, *The Strange Adventures of Mr. Fridolin B.* (*Die seltsamen Abenteuer des Herrn Fridolin B.*, 1948), was a stylistically uneven comedy. As a remake of his 1944 *The Man Whose Name Was Stolen* (*Der Mann, dem man den Namen stahl*), which had never been released during the Third Reich and was lost in the final chaos, it demonstrated the pitfalls of recirculating former UFA material.[12] Although the film employs visual detail for satirical and symbolic purposes in a way that anticipates Staudte's later films, especially his 1952 masterpiece *The Subject* (*Der Untertan*), it represents a reversion to UFA's hallmark of nonpolitical, light entertainment that the DEFA founders had intended to repudiate.

Rotation returned to the antifascist realism of Staudte's first postwar film and, more than any other DEFA film of this early period, attempted to revitalize the tradition of the Weimar proletarian cinema. Once again Staudte took up the question of personal culpability and complicity. The plot follows the fate of a "typical" worker, Hans Behnke, over a twenty-year period and paints in the process an ambitious portrait of the years from 1925 to 1945. His young family leads a marginal existence, victims of the unemployment caused by the depression in the early thirties. Hans is unpolitical, sharing with both the Communists and the Nazis a vague wish for social change but convinced that alone he can better guarantee his family's well-being. The Nazis' rise to power brings him employment and a better apartment for the family, while he lives the regimentation of everyday fas-

THE DISCOURSE OF POWERLESSNESS

cism only as an external constraint. At most Hans cooperates to protect his job, his security, and his family. His brother-in-law Kurt, a Communist active in the underground resistance, convinces him to repair their printing press, but Hans's son Helmut, who has become an enthusiastic member of the Hitler Youth, betrays him when he discovers some of Kurt's anti-Nazi leaflets. Hans experiences the war's end in a Gestapo prison, while Helmut is drafted and taken prisoner of war. Ridden by guilt, he is finally reunited with his father, who shares the conviction of their responsibility toward future generations that the past will not be repeated.

In 1955, seven years after he wrote the scenario for *Rotation*, Staudte explained his reasons for making the film as a protest against the first signs of political restoration he perceived already in 1948: "In this film I tried to position myself against current calamitous tendencies—the development in everyday politics resembles in a frightful way the period after the First World War. I tried to show how it came to that unimaginable catastrophe in a way that would contribute to the prevention of an even greater catastrophe in the future."[13] In other words the film narrative represents history in order to deploy it within a contemporary political argument in the immediate post–World War II years. Consistent with the genre of the historical film, *Rotation* reconstructs the past by bringing together images that quote reality through the force of documentary verisimilitude with a discourse on that reality. The story of a well-meaning, sympathetic, and industrious worker who finds himself implicated in the crimes of the fascist regime treats a subject with which the large majority of Germans, who were neither fanatic Nazis nor members of the resistance, could identify. The film narrative addresses this historical spectator, suggesting a resolution that perpetuates the idea of individual victimization but yet allows for an imaginary transformation of guilt into the positive virtue of the individual as an agent of civic responsibility. For many Germans the international condemnation of the Nazi crimes against humanity expressed at the Nuremberg trials after the war and the insistence on the part of the Allies that the Germans collectively carried the guilt for the past only reinforced an attitude of powerlessness. Using conventions of the realist narrative, *Rotation* negotiates the real and historically substantiated anxiety of complicity with fascism by locating passivity and resignation as the source of powerlessness.

Staudte was concerned with reconstructing the past, with ordering social relations in a fictional framework so that he could rewrite them in the present and create a coherent position of knowledge and insight for the spectator. His vehicle for rewriting history is the petit bourgeois family constellation, a unit of social relations understood to be situated at the margins of major events but representing in a microcosm historically typical behavior patterns that transcend individual destinies. He aimed to expose the moral ambiguity and antisocial attitudes that result from social values centered on individualism and exploited by the fascist regime. *Rotation* presents the family history episodically, choosing a series of pertinent excerpts from everyday life that chronicle the crucial years of social upheaval beginning in the Weimar Republic and extending through the Third Reich's collapse in 1945. Embedded as a retrospective in a historicizing frame, it is loosely divided into three segments revolving around the protagonist's struggle to protect the family from the vicissitudes of "politics": his desperate attempt to find employment in the early thirties, his personal compromises after the Nazis come to power in 1933, and his helplessness when the family disintegrates under the pressure of war.

Alternating between private and public scenes, the film begins with a series of contrasts that show the impact of political or social changes on family behavior. The first segment executes this structure around the theme of unemployment. Several short sequences show Hans and Lotte's first encounters, but the romantic involvement is immediately juxtaposed to the lovers' economic vulnerability: Hans waits in an endlessly long line at an employment office for a job that will not materialize, while in a parallel montage Lotte listens to an offscreen voice that explains she will not be rehired at her former job. The next set of contrasting sequences repeats the opposition of the private and the public. Lotte's announcement that she is pregnant and Hans's enthusiastic optimism that he can support the future family is followed by a visual commentary on his meagre opportunities: Hans pushing like a mule the rotating wheel of a carousel in an amusement park; Hans parading with a sandwich board advertising a night club; Hans at a loading dock straining under a heavy sack slung over his shoulders. A more complex montage sequence follows which develops the motif of entrapment. Hans's son framed behind the bars of a playpen dissolves to Hans watching a pampered girl in the yard of a villa through the bars of a fence. This in turn dissolves to Hans watching a waiter from behind a fence serve champagne to a couple in a garden restaurant, followed by a further dissolve to the protagonist in front of a barred factory gate with a sign that no positions are available. As music swells up on the sound track ("The International"), the camera once again dissolves to a sea of placards held aloft by demonstrating workers, Hans among them, and then pans down to frame the sticks holding the placards which now resemble a fence. This fence then becomes the jail bars enclosing Hans in a cell, and the final dissolve frames Hans from a high angle through the bars on his basement apartment window as he bitterly complains about the injustice that results in his son being undernourished.

Like Dudov's and Brecht's montage of the bike race in *Kuhle Wampe*—also conceived around the topical problem of unemployment—the rapid cutting and repetition of more or less static images in this open-

Sticks with strike placards seamlessly dissolve into the prison bars which Hans grasps in a similar way (used by permission of Stiftung deutsche Kinemathek, Berlin).

ing segment convey a sense of desperation that transcends the protagonist's individual dilemma and points to its social context. Unlike Dudov and Brecht, however, Staudte structures the narration of the family history not to elicit from the spectator an analytical process but to create the identificatory potential for a moral judgment. Characteristic for *Rotation*'s narration in this respect is the pronounced use of associative dissolves, fades, and thematic montage for smooth transitions between shots. This technique creates a seamless narrative flow and achieves the discursive goal of tracing causality and convincingly motivating characters with whom the spectator can identify through the protagonist's point of view. In contrast, the abrupt editing in *Kuhle Wampe* emphasized a fragmentary, nonfictional quality that subordinated causality and character to the rhetoric of persuasion and the process of cognition.

The formal allusion to the Dudov/Brecht film of 1932 that shimmers through *Rotation*—most convincingly in the first segment about the years prior to 1933—is not simply the product of coincidence. To be sure, in an interview published in 1966 Staudte admitted that he was ignorant of film history and insisted that he neither emulated particular cinematic models nor felt himself subject to historical influences.[14] Yet, ample evidence points to conscious retrieval of the tradition of proletarian cinema. Certainly one factor in this development was Brecht's return to East Berlin in October 1948, and the spectacularly successful staging of his play *Mother Courage* by Erich Engel in January of the next year, at the very time when Staudte was shooting his film.[15] Brecht had no direct contact with DEFA at this time, but his decision to settle in the Soviet Zone, in part arranged with the help of Slatan Dudov, resolved at least momentarily any skepticism on the part of cultural functionaries toward his modernist aesthetic views, also for the cinema. Thus, it is no surprise that besides *Rotation*, two other historical films were released in 1949 with a clear debt to the tradition of proletarian cinema in the Weimar Republic: Dudov's own *Our Daily Bread* (*Unser täglich Brot*, about a working-class family's adjustment problems in the postwar Soviet Zone), and Kurt Maetzig's *Life in the Ticking* (*Die Buntkarierten*, a working-class family history reaching back four generations).

The most obvious reference to Brecht in *Rotation* occurs in the first segment's wedding scene where one of the guests sings excerpts from two songs in the *Threepenny Opera*. The homage to Brecht is intentional and obvious, yet it comprises less an adaptation of that play's satire and cynical heroics than a quote or reminder of its social critique.[16] The identity of petit bourgeois ethical ideals with blatant crimes was Brecht's way of exposing deception as the major weapon of capitalist exploitation in the *Threepenny Opera*. For Staudte this offered a potent and authoritative context for his own critique of conformity to fascist power structures, since his audience, at least those who were old enough to remember the most popular play of the Weimar Republic, could reestablish the relevance of a leftist social critique. Beyond that the filmmaker seemed to have been less interested in specific aesthetic qualities with which Brecht (and Dudov) had earlier experimented than in the pedagogical discourse of persuasion. *Rotation's* theme concerns the consequences of petit bourgeois individualism under the specific conditions of German fascism. To this extent it addresses a contradiction in the German working class that was constitutive of National Socialism. Like Brecht, Staudte thematizes this contradiction—the desire for individual social stability at the price of ignoring political activism and the need for class solidarity—not by denouncing the petit bourgeoisie but by representing the system of social oppression to which it fell victim. Unlike Brecht, however, Staudte constructs a narration based on identification and emotional catharsis rather than on the cognitive terms of epic distanciation.

Staudte pursues this goal in the second segment by elaborating the protagonist's illusory sense of family integrity and the disciplinary power of political coercion on which it depends. After the Nazi takeover Hans is em-

A historical reference to Bertolt Brecht's *Threepenny Opera* in the wedding scene (used by permission of Stiftung deutsche Kinemathek).

ployed by a Nazi Party newspaper. The new prosperity is visible in the move from the basement quarters to a bright and well-furnished upper-floor apartment. Hans's ability to sustain this newfound security, however, demands compromise and blindness, for the party slowly begins to affect every aspect of life, down to the human relationships in the family itself. One day a party inspector comes to his home to check why Hans did not attend a local meeting and points out that he has no Hitler portrait hanging in the living room. This political intrusion into the home parallels the politicization of his job when the personnel manager later makes clear to him that party membership counts for advancement as much as professional qualification. Hans gradually relinquishes his resistance to these small, seemingly impersonal signs of acceptance. He responds to the Hitler salute, a Hitler portrait hangs in his home, and he even becomes a Nazi Party member, all steps in the process of accommodation to power that the narration indicates in an almost casual way. By this point the protagonist's isolation and political passivity prevent him from recognizing the boundary between opportunism and willful blindness. Hence, he naively wonders why the Communist Kurt, who has fled Germany, does not return; and when the Gestapo picks up the friendly Jewish couple downstairs, he can only shut the window and draw the curtains in a helpless gesture of powerlessness. Staudte's figuration of Hans's gradual accommodation to fascism is without contempt. He portrays the protagonist as the victim of a social structure he does not understand, and he shows how that lack of understanding is the necessary social mechanism engaged by those in power to maintain the status quo.

The disturbances of the family idyll become a cataclysm in the third segment when the Nazi war regime uses its power overtly to subordinate the family to its political goal of domination. Whereas in the first two segments Kurt represented the antagonist—the nagging conscience of political responsibility to whom Hans turned a deaf ear—and his son Helmut justified the personal compromises necessary for a stable family life, the last segment reverses the equation's terms. The reversal is underscored by the juxtaposition of a series of scenes alternating between Helmut's Hitler Youth training and his growing susceptibility to Nazi ideology with Kurt's resistance activities. Hans's decision to help him repair a printing press for anti-Nazi pamphlets is motivated less by political conviction than by emotional commitment. Helmut, however, turns in the illegal leaflets he finds at home out of political conviction (i.e., ideological indoctrination), which results in Kurt's execution. That betrayal becomes the first step toward the complete disintegration of the family unit and Hans's insight into his social responsibility. Staudte's careful combination of editing, rhythm, and sound conveys in one of the film's strongest scenes the full emotional impact of the reversal. A close-up of Kurt's death warrant cuts to the forgotten tea kettle whistling on the stove, an unpleasantly shrill sound that accompanies the next shots. The camera cuts back and forth between Lotte, who walks slowly to the bedroom and falls onto the bed in tears, and Hans, framed from the back, standing immobile in front of the Hitler portrait in the living room. Helmut enters the kitchen in his Hitler Youth uniform and turns off the kettle, followed by a cut first to an extreme close-up of Hans's eyes staring straight ahead, then to his hand lifting an ashtray, and finally to the ashtray flying at the portrait as the uncanny silence on the soundtrack is broken by the noise of shattering glass.

The emphatic close-up of Hans's eyes preceding the emotional outburst suggests a moment of insight into the loss of personal freedom which has resulted from his accommodation to fascist discipline. The perverse consequences of this behavior are demonstrated in the last scene of the family history when father and son confront each other under the observing eyes of the police chief. Helmut had seen his father's gesture of rebellion against the symbol of everything he held dear and subsequently testified against him. Now he enters the police office with a "Heil Hitler" salute while the heavy orchestral chords of the overture to Beethoven's Fifth Symphony sound from the radio, underscoring ironically the total misuse of everything meaningful in classical German culture. The following short takes of Hans's, Helmut's, and the officer's eyes capture an emotionally charged but almost wordless dialogue. At this point the family constellation becomes evident as Staudte's metaphor for the experience of the fascist regime. Helmut's betrayal of his father is the result of the systematic misleading of an idealistic youth. Likewise, Hans's prioritization of family duty over responsibility toward the victims of fascism is the result of his experience of class oppression. Victims of their own blindness and passivity, complicit Germans, Staudte is suggesting, must recognize the collapse of their illusions. The consequences for the family are devastating: Hans faces execution, Lotte is killed in the final bombing of Berlin, Helmut is taken a prisoner, and Kurt, the family's social conscience, is dead.

The process of the Behnke family's disintegration is a retrospective explanation filtered through Hans's memory and embedded in an elaborate frame structure that opens the film and once again closes the historical reconstruction of the family catastrophe. In the first images, Hans stares at the wall in his prison cell with the muffled sounds of battle in the background and flashes of light from exploding bombs casting the symbolic shadow pattern of bars across his face. A close shot of graffiti on the wall reveals messages of hope and despair in different languages scrawled by prisoners who were likewise awaiting their death. As Hans concentrates on these messages, a superimposed title fades in—"It began twenty years ago"—and the image and sound dissolve in a smooth transition to the first narrative sequences. The same wall with graffiti, the same shot of a staring Hans, merges the completed chronicle with the frame. Like Madeleine in Käutner's *Romance in a Minor Key*, when facing death, he contemplates the past to give a meaning to his life, but Hans's retrospective narrative leads to a conversion rather than to death. The film proposes that this "new man," who has (re)lived the death of the "old man," now recognizes the truth of his past and invites the textual spectator to learn his lesson.

The narrative's flashback structure offers a pedagogical and polemical model for motivating the process of self-reflection. Hans Behnke is blind to the import of the events taking place around him. The flat image of the prison wall he faces and the numerous images of bars, cages, and grids associated with entrapment are examples of blockages that hamper a line of clear vision throughout the film. The visual geometry extends likewise to the symbolism suggested by the title. The film begins with the credits, superimposed over spinning wheels accompanied by the sound of machines, followed by the camera pulling back to a medium shot of newspapers coming off a rotary press. This rotary press, at once a reference to Hans's job and to the figure of circularity, returns at regular intervals to punctuate the narrative. It stops spinning as the camera cuts to a newspaper headline that provides a narrational cue to the date or to a significant historical event.[17] Images of a rotating gramophone record or carousel and the very circularity of the frame story with its closure all contribute to the

Hans stares at the graffiti on the prison wall, the introduction to the flashback that constitutes the film's plot (frame enlargement by Kristin Thompson, Madison).

density of this symbol for the threat of history's repetitiveness. Furthermore, the motif of sight suggested by the many close-ups of Hans's eyes reinforces the contemplative attitude of looking, of insight. It invites the spectator to share in a process of reflecting on the past in order to comprehend the historical circumstances that led to the rupture and collapse in the present.

The frame story's provisional closure generalizes the consequences of Hans's antisocial individualism before proceeding to the epilogue and the resolution. Two scenes demonstrate the strategies involved here. In the first Staudte reenacts one of the most cruel episodes perpetrated by Hitler during the last days of the war when he ordered that a Berlin subway used as a shelter for women, children, and invalids be flooded to halt the advance of the Red Army. With characteristic rhythmic editing and attention to visual detail, the filmmaker captures the crowd's desperate fear as the water rushes in on them. Just as Behnke sits in prison, so are the masses imprisoned in the tunnel, at the mercy of the system that they tolerated and unable to escape through their own strength. The high-angle shot of a crowd behind a metal grill groping to open the air shaft and the following image of a bird cage floating on the rising water until the bird drowns visually summarizes Staudte's view of entrapment by the fascist regime. The

THE DISCOURSE OF POWERLESSNESS

The subway tunnels in Berlin are flooded in the final days of the war, entrapping the women, children, and invalids hiding there (used by permission of the Bundesarchiv-Filmarchiv Berlin, from the former Staatliches Filmarchiv der DDR).

second scene concerns Helmut, who watches his respected officer cynically exchange his uniform for a baggy suit and defect in the face of defeat. The transformation of this hero into a deserter opens Helmut's eyes to the deception to which he has fallen prey. The frame story closes then on a parallel to the father in which Helmut recognizes his victimization by a cynical system of domination.

This insight provides the basis for the resolution in the epilogue. Apprehensive about his father's feelings because of the betrayal, Helmut avoids him after returning from a POW camp. Hans, however, is overcome with emotion upon seeing his son, and when Helmut asks for his forgiveness, he insists rather that the sons must forgive the fathers. This generational message is extended into the concluding scene which—taking up the motif of circularity—reproduces the first scene of the family history when Hans and Lotte originally met at a railroad crossing. Now Helmut and his girlfriend meet at the same crossing and articulate explicitly the filmmaker's message:

HELMUT: My father and mother always met here twenty years ago.

INGE: I guess everything in life repeats itself.

HELMUT: Everything? No! Everything cannot repeat itself if we prevent it.

INGE: We? Oh, Helmut.

HELMUT: Yes, you and I, and all the other people who want peace.[18]

Staudte's recourse in the film's epilogue to a generational solution to the problem of complicity—the children can atone for the parents' mistakes—shifts the responsibility for the past into the present and onto the younger generation, a strategy that surfaced in many of the youth-oriented films produced by DEFA in the late forties and, in fact, a dominant motif in films from both East and West Germany concerned with accounting for the Nazi past.[19] It is an imaginary solution, here presented in a particularly wooden dialogue, for the difficult undertaking of sustaining the notion of victimization while effacing the guilt of complicity in order to gain a measure of dignity in the present. By overlaying the imaginary solution onto the generational bond of fathers and sons, Staudte suppresses an overt representation of guilt (only the scar on Hans's forehead, a Cain-like sign, indicates this guilt). Moreover, he offers a positive identification with an acceptable Other in the guise of the prodigal son. In this case the fact that the father actually cooperated with the underground resistance—rather atypical behavior for the large majority of Germans who tended to be active, if reluctant participants in the war—and the fact that the son denounced the father to the Gestapo, augments the pathos of reconciliation. It responds to the wish that anyone could have resisted the regime whereas it obscures the reality that almost no one did. In addition, Hans's acceptance of the responsibility for his son's betrayal at one and the same time confirms his love and places the burden of active intervention for the future into his son's hands. Staudte relies, then, on family relations as the primary arena for constructing the narrative but he also exposes the inherent limitations of the family under the stress of the Third Reich. That it remains the context for the father/son reconciliation and the son's marriage in the epilogue is possibly a concession to the fundamentally conservative attitudes of the postwar audience he was addressing. For the historical spectator was not especially sensitive to appeals of solidarity with larger political or social groupings, most of which had been tainted in one way or another.

Rotation was the most expensive DEFA production up to that point and among the most popular of its antifascist films.[20] It was originally scheduled for release in May 1949, but the Soviet licensing office delayed its premiere until September 16, 1949, almost exactly a year after the production start.[21] Critics in the East responded most strongly to what they perceived as the film's honesty and straightforward condemnation of the Nazi past, a confirmation of the specific contribution DEFA could make to the process of not forgetting. The fact that the central character was a worker, and not an intellectual as in *The Murderers Are Among Us*, also conveniently overlapped with the more general program of winning the working class over to the idea of constructing a socialist German state. Finally, the film's realist style was seen to confirm DEFA's break with the UFA tradition, especially in the understated acting, the use of documentary footage, and the conscious avoidance of flashy or seductive images. *Rotation* was first screened in the West in 1950 on the art-house and film-club circuit. It represented an important alternative to Western film production, which—when it ever did address the issue of mass support of the Nazi regime—generally treated it apologetically or as a moral failure.[22] In 1958 West German television broadcast the film, triggering a typical cold-war political controversy about its alleged Communist propaganda line.[23]

Staudte's view of history is based on the premise that events like fascism are catastrophes that befall mankind. *Rotation* was produced during the Berlin Blockade crisis of 1948–49, another catastrophe that "befell" the Germans and confirmed for them once again how little they in fact controlled their own destiny.[24] That might explain the weak conclusion Hans draws in his final, long speech to Helmut, which resembles more an editorial than a film dialogue.[25] The promise of joining the "family of nations" and the conviction in the justice of Kurt's legacy of love for all the oppressed in the world were consistent with Staudte's hope of gaining his audience's sympathy against totalitarianism and for democratic reconstruction in Germany. Yet, if the imaginary operations in *Rotation* insist on the possibility of a position of potential change where the self is the agent in history, then the appeal to patient love both by Kurt and Hans as an antidote to history's repetition seems entirely inadequate for realizing it. This discrepancy may account in the narrative for Hans's unexpected and almost voluntaristic metamorphosis into a sympathizer with the resistance and for Helmut's equally sudden transfiguration from a fanatic Nazi into a repentant son. More importantly, it describes the real limits to the ideological perception of powerlessness at a crucial juncture in postwar German history.

8

The Return of the Familiar:
Hans Deppe's *Black Forest Girl*

N THE SOVIET zone, and after 1949 in the German Democratic Republic, the government-directed film industry was a main factor in reconstituting the public sphere with a commitment to cinematic realism and to antifascist thematics that represented a conscious break
with UFA traditions. The conditions and intentions in the Western zones
were oriented from the outset more toward commercial and entertainment
values that had characterized the film industry of the Third Reich and the
conventional spectator habits it had nurtured. Symptomatically, the first
film produced and exhibited in the West was Helmut Weiss's insipid situation comedy *Tell the Truth* (*Sag die Wahrheit,* 1946), based on a script that
had been completed already in 1944 but that could be used without revision under the changed circumstances two years later. Other filmmakers
did turn their attention to more pressing topical problems such as the disruption caused by the war, the uncertainty and anxiety about the future,
and the plight of refugees and demobilized soldiers. In these "rubble films"
motifs of black-market trade, hording, cigarette currency, rationing, frater-
nization, and sex among the ruins captured the atmosphere of Germany's
devastated cities.[1] In contrast to the realism of the on-location shoots in
bombed-out urban landscapes, though, the characters in these films rarely
convey a feeling of reality because they slip too quickly into symbolic or
ideological conflicts marked by cold-war antagonisms.

The currency reform in the Western zones in June 1948 not only
signaled the beginning of a fragile stabilization and a return to normalcy
but also transformed the conditions for film production and distribution.[2]
The resulting economic and political restoration of the fifties encouraged
conformist attitudes and profit-motivated interests of film producers and
distributors. Hence, the rubble films produced between 1946 and 1948

with their sense of misery and interiority represent in retrospect an interim, a hiatus between the "no longer" and the "not yet" in an otherwise linear continuity of cinema forms, themes, and personnel from the Third Reich into the fifties. Indeed, some critics even identify a "late UFA-style" in West Germany's films of the fifties, a style aimed at reproducing dramaturgical structures, image composition, and editing techniques developed during the thirties.[3] Inconsistent and artificial plots organized for easy comprehension, exaggerated and awkward emotions, stereotypical characters in novelistic conflicts moving among theatrical sets, and visual conservatism dominated the cinematic fare emerging from West German studios. The cinema audience too registered its preference for obviously escapist films. Although some of the rubble films earned box office profits, their real competition consisted of rereleases and holdovers of light entertainment features from the Third Reich, which accounted for as much as 90 percent of the distribution market in the Western zones until 1948. After the currency reform, when the market once again became attractive to foreign companies for amortizing their films, a wave of foreign imports, especially from Hollywood, flooded the German cinemas.[4]

Under these conditions the many small, undercapitalized film production firms in West Germany had to find some way to differentiate their product in order to attract an audience. Committed to the precept of profit through entertainment and unable to compete in the international export market, they withdrew to one of the few free spaces left, the *Heimatfilm*. An exclusively German cinema genre, it was little known outside Germany but remained massively popular among domestic audiences throughout the fifties because it was distinct from foreign imports and at the same time directly addressed sensitivities of the German public faced with fundamental social changes. Its popularity reached a high point in 1955 when one-third of the film production consisted of *Heimat* features, and the genre accounted for nearly 25 percent of all releases during the fifties.[5]

Because the word *Heimat*—usually rendered by "home" in English—is untranslatable, so too the genre *Heimatfilm* has no counterpart in other national cinemas. The closest non-German adaptation is perhaps John Wise's 1965 *The Sound of Music*, a remake of Wolfgang Liebeneiner's 1956 Heimat film *The Trapp Family* (*Die Trapp-Familie*). *Heimat* describes an unfulfilled yearning with echoes of an unattainable utopia and of a lost past. It is associated with the nostalgia and drama of childhood security and family identity, of benevolent nature and mythical fate. The word gathered momentum as a concept in post-Romantic Germany and at the end of the nineteenth century as a militant rallying cry in the context of rising modernism, when the Heimat art movement began to articulate an ideology aimed against naturalism, social democracy, intellectualism, modern technology, and urban decadence. The main channel for expressing these sentiments was Heimat literature, especially by popular authors like Ludwig Anzengruber, Ludwig Ganghofer, and Hermann Löns.[6] Distinguished by descriptions of landscape and atmosphere, their stories were in fact ideal for silent films and they were adapted for the cinema already in the teens (i.e., Anzengruber's *The Fraudulent Farmer* [*Der Meineidbauer*] for the first time in 1916 and Ganghofer's *The Hunter von Fall* [*Der Jäger von Fall*] in 1918). Nature motifs were also widespread in early shorts and cultural films shown before main features, and in Bavaria an entire industry specialized in nature and peasant spectacles for the south German audience under the guidance of producer Paul Ostermayer.

In the early cinema "nature" scenes were still being filmed in the studios, but in the course of the twenties directors like Arnold Fanck and later Luis Trenker and Leni Riefenstahl moved out of the studios to make their films in the mountains. The mountain film (*Bergfilm*) celebrated nature as the protagonist in an almost documentary manner. Heroes tested themselves against the all-powerful mountains, which symbolized the eternal laws of human dependency, while love stories were usually resolved against the backdrop of catastrophic natural forces.[7] The projection of human psychology in nature, the motif of escape from the urban industrial ills and labor, and the mythicization of unconquerable fate mark the Heimat film as an important site for registering the affects of modernity in the sphere of popular culture. It reached a first apogee in the blood-and-soil ideology (*Blut und Boden*) of the fascist regime in the thirties. The word *Heimatfilm* was even coined early in the Third Reich to describe film adaptations of Ganghofer novels, and the genre went on to become a staple in its film industry with such well-known examples as Hans Steinhoff's *Vulture Wally* (*Die Geierwally*, 1940) and Veit Harlan's *The Golden City* (*Die goldene Stadt*, 1942).

Hans Deppe's 1950 comedy *Black Forest Girl* (*Schwarzwaldmädel*) took up the Heimat genre once again. Together with his next film, the family drama *Green Is the Heather* (*Grün ist die Heide*, 1951), it revitalized and defined for the entire decade the terms of an equation that made the Heimat film into the most enduring and commercially successful, if not aesthetically or visually interesting cinematic fare emerging from West German studios. Trained at the Max Reinhardt Theater Seminar in Vienna, in the twenties Deppe was considered one of the young hopefuls in Berlin theaters and cabarets. In 1931 he accepted his first film role and in 1934 codirected his first feature, a Heimat film based on a classic Theodor Storm novella. He went on to direct thirty more films during the Third Reich, including adaptations of three Ganghofer Heimat novels, and most are considered apolitical entertainment features that conform to the rigid aesthetics of the UFA tradition.[8] After 1945 Deppe reestablished himself as a director with two DEFA productions in the Soviet zone and after 1948 with thirty-five features in West Germany. Of these, fourteen were Heimat films, ranking him among the most prodigious producers in the genre. Deppe's breakthrough in 1950—*Black Forest Girl* was the biggest box office success in 1950–51 and won the Bambi, the German Oscar, in 1951—came as a complete surprise to the film industry, but it was not owing to any particularly innovative strategies on the part of the director.[9]

Black Forest Girl was by no means the first postwar Heimat film. According to one source, twenty-six such films were produced between 1947 and 1949, and in 1950 alone twenty-one more were released.[10] In contrast to the prewar Heimat film, which despite its contrived plots was frequently able to transform powerful emotions into convincing nature images, now the Heimat "feeling" became schizophrenic: nostalgia for the security of home and fear of the phantoms in that home. Nature became a consumable product, domesticated and fake as in a poorly rendered still life rather than a hypostatized site of freedom. Moreover, many of the fifties Heimat films were remakes, as if presenting the familiar past could banish the uncomfortable and uncontrollable questions about the present. Familiar stars from the thirties and forties reappear again and again; in the case of *Black Forest Girl* Paul Hörbiger, Gretl Schörg, Hans Richter, and Lucie Englisch were all well-known faces. Finally, the genre itself developed rigid formulaic attributes, repeated from film to film if they proved to be commercially successful. This led in turn to Heimat series such as the three *Sissi* films with Romy Schneider. These strategies aimed at appealing to a heterogeneous audience in order to market a cinema product, but they were also strategies that bound the audience to a historically specific imaginary relation to reality characterized by transparency and superficiality.

Black Forest Girl was the remake of a 1933 version, and both were adaptations of a popular operetta of the same name.[11] Deppe integrates elements from the tradition of the operetta film, a typical characteristic for the eclecticism of the Heimat film genre, drawing on conventions from such diverse sources as the costume film, the social drama, or the comedy of errors. Like *Request Concert*, a "boy meets girl" story unfolds, but unlike the earlier film, where war creates the blockages that retard a happy end, here—and this is symptomatic for the film's imaginary relations—the lovers and the intrigues surrounding them derive from a basic uncertainty about what is real. The narrative engages a group of marionette-like characters in a stylized space and abstract temporal situation. It constructs a series of ironic contrasts between appearance and reality, elaborated in various registers of performance, imitation, disguise, and play. The first sequence is paradigmatic: using the conventional opening of a musical revue, the narration begins in medias res with a stage show on ice that reaches a climax when the two stars, Malwina and Richard, emerge to sing a duet about the power of music to make everyone happy. The unusually wooden ice spectacle dissolves in applause as the closing curtain wipes the frame in order to cut backstage as everyone hurries to the dressing rooms. Not the show itself but the opposition of backstage reality to theatrical illusion introduces the film's central motif that motivates the hide-and-seek games of desire and denial among the characters. In this environment, perhaps because work seems like play and there is no boundary between life and art, the only problem that concerns any character is love. At a time when West Germany was just launching its economic miracle of reconstruction and the Korean War was just getting under way, all the characters' productive energy is directed at finding the right marriage partner.

In the world of illusion Malwine is the central figure, an actress referred to as the "Ice Queen" and furnished with all the attributes of a femme fatale: excessive dress (tight-fitting clothes which exaggerate her hips and breasts; elegant, low-cut gowns; elaborate hats), aggressive eroticism (she plays with men and fights to keep Hans as her lover), and narcissism (framed in mirrors as she dresses or puts on makeup). Because she does not differentiate between role-playing on stage and in real life, she is as likely to break into song over breakfast on the balcony as to give an impromptu performance at a costume ball. In the latter case her duet with Richard, ending in the verse "Who would be able to resist coquettishness?" expresses her proper role emblematically. Harmless playfulness deflects the aggressive female manipulator who potentially threatens the stable order of sexual relations. That her stage partner Richard finally becomes her "real life" partner after a series of mix-ups is only reasonable. As an actor he can distinguish between illusion and reality and accept coquettishness with self-irony. Hence, their reconciliation at the end is highly self-conscious:

MALWINE: Should we continue dancing? Otherwise this will become a novel. Is this the famous "happy end" for us?

RICHARD: Had you imagined it differently?

MALWINE: No, just like this. . . . (they kiss)

RICHARD: That this happens to the two of us?! Do we really love each other?

MALWINE: Yes. We really love each other!

RICHARD: Wonderful!

MALWINE: How wonderful!

Malwine and Richard are professional actors, but all the other characters engage in disguise and role-playing as well. In the costume ball sequence Malwine's lover Hans meets and falls in love with Bärbele, a secretary at a jewelry store. He offers her his explanation of the principle underlying

The film opens with a theatrically staged show on ice (used by permission of Deutsches Institut für Filmkunde, Frankfurt).

Backstage reality extends the theatrical illusion of spectacle (used by permission of Deutsches Institut für Filmkunde, Frankfurt).

this particular form of self-representation: "Nowhere can you see through people so clearly as at a costume ball. Everyone is disguised as he wishes to be." Indeed, this insight could be generalized as a metacritical approach for the fifties cinema: reading against the grain reveals the desires and anxieties fuelling repression. Yet, as Hans goes on to demonstrate, the practice cannot be mechanically applied. He confides to Bärbele that his turban suggests his wish to be a Maharaja with a large harem, although "in reality" the narrative will reveal that he is seeking a wife to marry. Bärbele, on the other hand, is not disguised at all, even though she looks like a toy doll, for her authentic Black Forest dirndl and the genuine Black Forest apples in her basket present her exactly as she "is," the titular "Black Forest girl." Hans's admission that he cannot figure out who she is, that she is either very naive or very sly, says more about his blindness than about her role as an innocent seductress (the Edenic allusion to knowledge and seduction is obvious when Hans bites into the red apple she offers him).

The visual motifs of disguise and blindness draw this Heimat film into the proximity of a comedy of errors. Caught in a torrential downpour while driving through the countryside, Hans and Richard find shelter in a shed and fall asleep while their clothes are drying. They awaken to find that their motor scooter, clothes, and money were stolen so that they are forced to don the clothes of the vagabond who robbed them and of a scarecrow in the field. Now "disguised" as itinerant singers, they merrily wander through the forest and meadows singing for money, a diegetic opportunity for footage of the beautiful Black Forest landscape and for another song. Another episodic disguise involves the jeweler Bussmann, who is also chasing Malwine. Richard arranges a rendezvous for him in the small village where they all meet, but instead of Malwine he sends simpleminded Lorle, the daughter of the innkeeper who is seeking a husband. Later at a folk festival Bussmann again has to disguise himself to avoid the jealous attention of Lorle's village suitor, this time by cross-dressing in the costume of a Black Forest widow. These farcical interludes expose a source of the comic Heimat film in rural caricatures. Typically they draw neither on the comic screwball or slapstick traditions but rather on humiliating situational humor. Like the comedy of errors, this kind of farce is based on a theatrical convention in which characters are not who they seem to be. By means of this dramatic otherness it is possible to transform a real conflict into one that seems to be only apparent, and eliminating the mistaken identity resolves the conflict. In a narrative that draws its energy from the opposition of appearance and reality and that was produced at a point in German history when the very notions of individual and national identity were still suffering from the political and psychological rupture of 1945, this conflict avoidance by denial of the self indicates one imaginary strategy for dealing with the difficult relation to the Other.

The values of performance, imitation, disguise, and display merge in the motif of jewelry. For her stage act Bussmann lends to Malwine a jewelled necklace in exchange for a free advertisement in the program. The commodity nature of the trade-off is only hinted at in passing, but it points to the more general status of human relations. When she asks to wear the jewels to the costume ball, Bussmann reveals to his employee Theo, who has guarded the necklace during each performance, that it is in fact just an imitation:

> THEO: I had to guard the fake jewels every evening?
>
> BUSSMANN: Do you think I would send real jewels to the theater? The sensational effect was the same in any case. . . . Anyway people want to be deceived. You can't do anything about it.

On his own Theo lends Malwine the real necklace, but when Bussmann arrives at the ball as well, Theo must quickly retrieve it from Malwine. Bärbele, who discovers that he is showing around the jewelry, takes them, thinking they are the fake ones, in order to prevent the embarrassing truth from coming out that her employer was sending an imitation to the theater. The confusion between real and fake, which surfaces in every relation, signals a more fundamental uncertainty that underlies existence in this narrative world.

The uneasiness these characters experience is that of a society in rapid transition and demanding adaptability in order to survive. This is urban postwar German society, associated with the high-life resort of Baden-Baden where the film narrative begins and manifested most bluntly in Theo, the nervous and ambitious young salesman in Bussmann's jewelry store. Although he has much in common with the *Hanswurst* or clown figure who is the victim of pranks in traditional farces, he is also set apart as the upwardly mobile beneficiary of capitalism in this film. He carries away a huge basket of exotic fruits and liqueurs at the costume ball raffle, and when he is arrested for "borrowing" Hans's motor scooter, his jail is a village restaurant pantry where he proceeds to finish off all the dry sausages and canned goods. Like the grand prize Bärbele wins at the raffle, a brand new Ford convertible, this good fortune represents the antithesis of economic degradation and hunger imposed by postwar hardship, the proof that consumerism is a magical blessing. Theo also wins a large sum of money at the gambling casino with a new "system." Accordingly he has no place in the final dance spectacle, for he is in the process of cementing a new loyalty, not to *Heimat* but to the values of conspicuous consumption. As the incarnation of the German economic miracle, Theo stands for the promise of the future when to look back at the past was perceived as paralyzing.

Bärbel's luck in the lottery wins her the symbol of economic prosperity in the impoverished postwar years, a Ford convertible (used by permission of Stiftung deutsche Kinemathek, Berlin).

Counterposed to this urban realm of unbridled wealth acquired innocently by good fortune is the fictional space called *Heimat* and identified in the narrative as the village St. Christoph.[12] The characters from the city (Malwine, Richard, Theo, Bussmann) are alienated from this intact natural world. Their context is unstable, defined by commerce, gambling, and theatricality, and contrary to the folk songs and church chorale in the village, the music in Baden-Baden is nervous, exotic, and jazzy, in a word, modern. Less a geographical place than an amalgam of values revolving around static concepts like tradition, norms, and custom, the fictional St. Christoph and its surrounding Black Forest region is an elaborately conventionalized, synthetic product including blue sky, summer sun, mountain panoramas, green meadows, cows and horses, dancing rural people, picturesque half-timber farmhouses with pots of geraniums on the window sills, church steeples, and splashing fountains and wells. It is an illusory site, a trope expressing the nostalgic image of rural peace and simplicity that might offer a refuge for the German "soul" corrupted in the city and by modern life. The many shots and breathtaking pans in vibrant colors of the forested mountains and valleys or the blossoming fruit orchards must have provided the historical spectator of 1950 with a welcome escape from the ubiquitous gray ruins in Germany's war-bombed cities.[13]

Unlike many later Heimat films of the fifties, which rigidly play off the dichotomy of the imputed eternal village values against urban decadence, the irony in Deppe's *Black Forest Girl* suggests how pervious this opposition can be. City life has a positive value even among some of the rural folk. The innkeeper Jürgen, for example, will only consider a monied suitor from the city for his daughter Lorle. In turn the rural characters are portrayed as simplistic, if not stupid and mean. Jürgen is a self-important village tyrant, Lorle's behavior is infantile, and Gottlieb is a physically threatening brute who jealously watches over Lorle.[14] Most importantly Bärbele, and to a lesser extent Hans, are able to move between these two worlds and feel comfortable in both. Bärbele is a modern city girl, Bussmann's competent secretary, and the proud owner of a sporty American car. Yet she also wears a dirndl because she is "really" from the Black Forest. She can slip back to her village without a second thought and ultimately she is chosen as the "Black Forest Bride," the most beautiful village girl who rides in the St. Cecilia festival parade. Untouched by theater and disguise, she has a deeper bond to reality. In one of the few visually striking sequences, Bärbele dances with the tea tray as the church organist Blasius practices a waltz on the piano. As an orchestra takes up the melody, the subjective camera pans to her shadow thrown on the wall as another shadow, her male partner in a turban, joins in the waltz and kisses her. The dream sequence culminates in her song that verbalizes directly, without pretense, her wish: "Beautiful dancer, where will I find you? Come back and fetch me!" Hans too has an intuitive bond to this idyllic rural world. Although he is unable to determine who Bärbele "really" is at the costume ball, he later sketches her as the paradigmatic Black Forest poster girl and fulfills the prophecy of the "Black Forest Girl" song sung by Bärbele: "Girls from the Black Forest are not easy to get. . . . Only men from the Black Forest can have them."

Nonetheless, Bärbele and Hans, like the other city people, are only temporary visitors to the village, which resembles more a vacation resort than a rural locale. Thus, the place of the farmer or peasant in the traditional Heimat film has been assumed by the innkeeper, and many of the most important scenes are set in the inn itself, the quintessence of holiday transience. For these visitors the village and its surrounding nature represent a vacation from city life, a respite that makes it palatable. This consumerist attitude, an aspect that became stronger and stronger in the course of the fifties until the Heimat film resembled tourist publicity, is consistent with the commodification of nature that distinguishes the fifties Heimat film. Nature becomes an architectural effect that can be constructed for the film narration to generate certain kinds of feelings but yet describes no real space.[15] Another element in this vacation atmosphere and an equally important setting for some key dramatic scenes is the local history museum (*Heimatmuseum*) with everyday objects collected from the region. The self-consciousness about and distance from these objects has removed them from a lived relation to custom and transformed them into folkloric pieces for urban visitors (and cinema spectators) to enjoy. The experience of community and rootedness exists only on display, in quotation marks, in the museum. No wonder that Hans assumes Bärbele had rented her dirndl from a costume shop and that Bussmann is concerned only with a jewel's effect! And when Malwine asks Jürgen where all the traditional folk dresses will come from for the festival parade, he responds that people simply have them, but then insists that she visit the museum to see them. Accompanying this sanitized preservation of folk culture in the museum is the normalization of dialect to a colorful but comprehensible accent and the simplification of regional dance to a generally recognizable waltz.[16]

Among the secondary characters, the narrative's choirmaster Blasius is especially interesting because he represents the only explicit link to the past. An older, silvery-haired gentleman, typecast with the popular Austrian actor Paul Hörbiger, he is introduced as a somewhat helpless bachelor to whom the motherly housekeeper Traudel is still trying to teach manners and whose main concern is finishing the church chorale for the St. Cecilia festival ("Santa Cecilia, ora pro nobis," sung by a boys' choir in the mandatory Heimat film church sequence). That he also jokes with her about marriage, claiming to be only outwardly old while inside a "lecherous Casanova," situates him too within the parameters of appearance and reality that define everyone's behavior. Twice Blasius articulates a kind of melancholic attitude toward the past, which barely hints at the recent and all-too-familiar history of the film's German spectators. When Bärbele suggests that the waltzes she loves would not be compatible with his religious music, he protests: "Earlier I also had high-flown dreams, opera and song compositions. But then I was forced by necessity to take this post and I renounced them." Much later he consoles Bärbele who thinks she has lost Hans to Malwine by telling her the wisdom of his experience: "Life is like that; it doesn't always work out the way you want. When I think of the hopes I've had to bury!"

Blasius's resignation can be understood as the German bad faith about the past. It rarely surfaced overtly in the fifties cinema, as if there were public agreement not to ask any embarrassing questions, but it was always present in the background. Blasius's adolescent behavior is a regression that allows him to escape the burdens of anxiety and responsibility toward the past. Traudel's motherly attitude, which he gladly tolerates, his childlike conspiracy with Bärbele to smoke cigars and play waltzes while the reproving Traudel is away, the way he falls in love with Bärbele—a woman one-third his age—by misreading a kiss she plants on his cheek, and his devotion to the boys' choir are the ingredients of a wishful escape from adulthood. His attempts fail, however, and he is literally marginalized to make room for the younger generation. At the film's end, when everyone has been paired off, the church dean invites him to join the other elders and watch the young people dance. The camera travels in to a close-up of the choirmaster as he stares reflectively into space and sings with melancholy the last verse of the waltz inspired by his love for Bärbele: "In Spring you can meditate [about love] but when Autumn comes, seize it."

Blasius's awareness of the opposition between youth and age, between hope and renunciation, does not lead to more fundamental questioning about past experience. Indeed the fifties Heimat film cultivates its timelessness precisely through stories that take place in an ambiguous present, what one critic has called a "vacation from history."[17] The characters have no past and hence no personality, so that their interaction lacks decision or conscious control. Conflicts are not personal but only apparent, motivated by external circumstances and resolved by a dramaturgical detail in the plot. Similarly the ubiquitous traditional folk dress, houses, and farms are not historical or anthropological elements but pure ornament. St. Christoph is a place outside of time and history, beyond political power struggles, existing only in rich potentiality. It is the imaginary substitute for a divided nation and a lost *Vaterland* in a country whose people had bargained away political autonomy in the war and now commanded national sovereignty only with the consent of the former enemies.

The St. Cecilia festival summarizes this abstract resolution of the conflicted relation between the Germans and their past. It culminates in an allegorical dance of a newly established community of couples where the "Black Forest Bride," who wears the traditional "bridal crown" from the local museum, is presented. Similar to the ice revue that opened the film, this final dance sequence marks an alternative to the boredom or prosaic pragmatism of everyday life and is thus a fitting conclusion to the narrative. Contrary to the other dance sequence of the costume ball with its modern music and a snake dance, this spectacle offers an image of resolution and provides the setting in which the urban characters can experience their integration into the putative *Heimat*. That a fist fight interrupts the dance—jealous Gottlieb still thinks Bussmann is flirting with his Lorle—indicates how fragile the social structure really is. Yet Blasius can save the day by sitting down at the piano and pounding out a waltz until all the couples are overpowered by its rhythm and return to the dance. As Malwine's and Richard's opening duet already anticipated, music has the power to make everyone happy and here it transforms the aggression just below the surface into an image of swirling couples. The community has been reestablished:

The St. Cecilia festival brings together the city dwellers with the folklorishly costumed peasants in an allegorical community called *Heimat* (used by permission of Stiftung deutsche Kinemathek, Berlin).

Hans is united with Bärbele, who wears the bridal crown; Malwine and Richard discover that they belong together; Lorle finally realizes that Gottlieb is an acceptable partner; and Blasius and Bussmann, who have no partners and thus do not participate in the dance, are situated on the margins as comic outsiders. The sentimental yearning for an intact world may be completely abstracted from the sociohistorical circumstances in which it is imagined, but the traces of the effort to eliminate those circumstances suggest that the resistance to reality was strong. The unquestioned continuities of tradition and belonging projected in a film like *Black Forest Girl* with its fund of clichés that can be called upon at will barely conceals the fissures in this imaginary operation.

It is hard to reconstruct the reasons why Deppe's Heimat film was such a success among cinema spectators in the early fifties. Certainly the distributor's Hollywood-like publicity campaign preceding and surrounding the film's premiere contributed to the public interest it garnered. Posters featuring the lead actors Sonja Ziemann and Rudolf Prack and banners announcing local runs decorated the streets in major West German cities before each opening. At the premiere in Stuttgart the entire cast was presented along with the cultural minister of the state of Baden-Württemberg, and gala receptions and press conferences were orchestrated around it. Even gags like dressing the cinema personnel in traditional Black Forest costumes and having the Federal Post Office issue a special cancellation stamp helped draw attention to the film. Undoubtedly an additional element in its commercial success can be attributed to the fact that it was the first postwar color feature in West Germany, picking up on a technology that the UFA studios had pioneered and used to great effect during the Third Reich.[18] Film critics, however, were almost unanimous in rejecting *Black Forest Girl*. Ziemann's weak voice, the unrealistic image of the Black Forest, the obvious inconsistencies in the script, and the disparity in age between Prack and Ziemann were some of the common complaints.[19] Later critics have also rejected the Heimat film in general for its escapism and apolitical stance.[20] Yet the film's box office success and its influence for the rest of the decade on the Heimat film genre indicate that a perspective which criticizes entertainment values for satisfying "false" needs among the audience shifts the terrain of the imaginary from the social to the moral.

By 1957 the Heimat film as genre had reached its apex both in production and distribution numbers, at least in large cities. To a certain extent the genre had simply exhausted its conventions, but an additional factor was the spread of television broadcasting in the late fifties. A poll conducted in 1961 showed that by this time the audience for Heimat films consisted mainly of elderly people and women who generally had a relatively low education and belonged to lower social strata.[21] Television programming was especially attractive to this audience, satisfying their needs for family entertainment outside of the cinema. In the sixties the Heimat film all but disappeared, metamorphosing into commercially successful rural sex comedies which became popular in the soft pornography wave late in the decade. It continued a shadow existence with an attempt at reutilizing the genre conventions for a socially critical Heimat film among New German Cinema directors, and most recently in Bavarian comedies by experimental filmmakers like Herbert Achternbusch and Walter Bockmeyer.[22] It appears that the Heimat film continues to avoid history in order to seek timely anachronisms for unresolved frustrations.

9

Privatizing the Past:
Georg Wilhelm Pabst's
The Last Ten Days

EORG WILHELM PABST'S 1955 fictionalized documentary *The Last Ten Days (Der letzte Akt)* is among the early war films distributed in postwar West Germany. Set in the Führer bunker in Berlin during the last ten days of the war, it figures images of evil in order to convey the catastrophe that war meant for Germany. While produced in Austria and filmed by one of the few celebrated directors of the Weimar cinema who remained in the Reich during the war years, the film's strength and weaknesses are symptomatic for a fifties feature that resisted the dominant cinematic image of a healthy Germany with beautiful landscapes and honorable Germans.

If the Heimat film is a specifically German genre whose calculated apoliticalness promised escape from history through timelessness and the familiar, then the war film with its international conventions for the portrayal of friend and enemy, good and evil, and patriotic defense of the homeland posed special problems for the postwar German film industry. Like the Heimat film, the war film reaches back at least to the early thirties in German cinema history with a stock of standard motifs, characters, formalized filming techniques, and visual symbols.[1] After 1945, however, the situation had changed, for the representation of Germany's role in the most recent war immediately raised the question of responsibility. The post-1945 German war film in one way or another implied the problem of guilt and the widespread political passivity during the Third Reich. This may explain why it took almost a decade for the film industry to produce its first war films. In addition, during the immediate postwar years the Allied policies of denazification and demilitarization, coupled with the Nuremberg Trial controversy concerning the collective guilt shared by Germans for the atrocities committed in the name of National Socialism, inhibited public discussion about the war. Established under the shock of Nazi crimes, the West German state was grateful to align itself with the Western powers under the sign of cold-war anticommunism and to focus its energies on economic reconstruction rather than to begin a time-consuming and potentially factious discussion about the past. Similarly, the shock of the Third Reich's capitulation hindered cinema directors in the West—most of whom had advanced their careers during its heyday—from probing into the causes and effects of the defeat.[2] Thus, the political quietism that characterized the fifties restoration in West Germany found its counterpart in the cinema in a highly developed rhetoric of avoidance. After 1948, when the brief wave of rubble films with their contemporary thematics had subsided, topical issues and the context of National Socialism disappeared almost completely from the cinema until the war film genre was revived.

The timing of the war film's reappearance in West German cinemas was not entirely accidental. Critics have recognized and commented on the political function the release of war films had at a time when the Federal Republic's remilitarization was on the agenda of the Western alliance.[3] The escalation of the cold war after NATO was established in 1949 and the Korean War erupted in 1950 called for a military alliance with German participation. The majority of West Germans welcomed this signal of political trust, yet many were not prepared for the rearmament process itself. It took six years for the government to convince its constituency, and even then there were numerous organized efforts to prevent the country's integration into a military alliance. Parliament changed the constitution in 1954 to establish a regular military force, and the first military officers for the new *Bundeswehr* (Federal Army) were appointed on January 1, 1956. Six months later the first law for a mandatory draft went into effect, the same year that the highest number of war films was released in the Federal Republic.

War films were not simply a parallel phenomenon, they were also indirectly used as state propaganda for remilitarization. A system of state financial guarantees (*Bürgschaften*) for film production had been introduced in the Federal Republic as early as 1951, and these subsidies enabled government agencies to exercise oblique control over the industry.[4] War films became a vehicle for official public opinion formation and they were commercially among the most successful films at the box office as well, capturing both political and cinematic interest until their ebb in the early sixties.

The first war films released in West Germany were not, however, German productions. Among the rush of foreign releases introduced after the 1948 currency reform were many British and American war features.[5] Indeed between 1948 and 1959 American war films accounted for over 50 percent of the those screened in West German cinemas while Austrian and German productions together made up about 40 percent of that total.[6] In particular, a film like Henry Hathaway's *The Desert Fox* (1951) about Field Marshall Erwin Rommel, depicting the German commander of the Africa Corps as a courageous and fair officer who clashes with ignorant Nazi political leaders, was a powerful model for the rehabilitation of the German military and for making acceptable once again to the public the idea of war as cinema entertainment. As early as 1952 the first domestic war films appeared, but these were historical barracks farces.[7] Within a year the events of World War II became the subject of a series of documentaries including actual newsreel footage from battles and daily life at the front.[8] Not until 1954, however, did the Austrian production of Helmut Käutner's *The Last Bridge* (*Die letzte Brücke*) initiate a first wave of feature-length films about the war by German directors. The story about a German doctor in Yugoslavia (played by Maria Schell) who, when confronted with atrocities committed by German soldiers, collaborates with the partisans, strikes an uneasy balance between the motif of innocent Germans as victims and the issue of German resistance as betrayal of the fatherland.

That this was an Austrian production—by the same company that would finance Pabst's *The Last Ten Days*—illuminates the cinematic symbiosis between German-speaking countries (including the Swiss-German film industry). Even prior to Austria's annexation to the German Reich in 1938, its film industry depended on the entire German-speaking realm to amortize the costs of its productions.[9] Within months after the annexation the laws of the *Reichsfilmkammer* and the Reich's cinema law (*Lichtspielgesetz*, see chap. 4) were extended to Austria. This introduced the same controls and prohibitions concerning personnel and thematics exercised in Germany; however, Austrian and Viennese cultural autonomy was tolerated as long as it did not contradict National-Socialist principles. The film industry in return gained excellent financing and advantageous distribution possibilities. Like Germany after the war, Austria too was occupied by the Allies and the film industry came under similar jurisdiction. Contrary to Germany, however, there was little understanding for or interest in rubble films on the part of studios or spectators, and the Soviet administration had no designs for establishing a centralized production unit in Vienna specializing in antifascist films, as was the case in the Eastern Sector of Berlin.[10] The postwar industry was dominated almost exclusively by the sentimental Viennese musical and the Alpine Heimat film. The state regarded the cinema as a purely commercial undertaking, controlled by the trade ministry rather than the education ministry, and taxed it heavily to discourage competition with the more traditional arts. In the course of the fifties, then, Austrian film production became increasingly dependent on and oriented to the West German market with similar peaks and valleys.[11]

With few exceptions—among them Pabst's *The Last Ten Days*—German (and Austrian) war films can be divided into two categories: those about resistance to the political manipulation of the Nazis by idealistic officers or exploited soldiers, and those about heroic or sentimental adventures using the war as a pretext or backdrop.[12] Among the early productions the first type dominated. *Daybreak* (*Morgengrauen*, Victor Tourjansky, 1954) and *The Devil's General* (*Des Teufels General*, Helmut Käutner, 1955), for example, share a view of the common soldier as a simple human being with ties to home, to family, and to children. He is the innocent dupe who does his best to keep out of politics and who, if at all, resists the Nazis through carefully contrived acts of sabotage that will not endanger the comrades at the front. Other war films focused on the officers. *Canaris* (Alfred Weidenmann, 1954) and *Germany Betrayed* (*Verrat an Deutschland*, Veit Harlan, 1955) as well as Pabst's own, inept *Jackboot Mutiny* (*Es geschah am 20. Juli*, produced immediately after *The Last Ten Days*), differentiate the bad SS from the (relatively) good *Wehrmacht* with its non-Nazi officers who engaged in "brave" moments of resistance. The most successful of all these was Paul May's *The Revolt of Corporal Asch* (08/15, 1954), the first part of a trilogy based on an equally popular novel by Hans Helmut Kirst in which a few sadistic military men personify the evil of the authoritarian Nazi system that abuses the honest soldiers. Such efforts to rehabilitate the millions of Germans who found themselves accomplices in the national debacle rely on an image of war as a dehumanizing and fateful event. The eagerness to construct this image around the conventionally rigid oppositions of good and bad and to avoid any suggestion that many of these victims in fact identified with the goals of the cinematic bullies confirmed for the spectators an imaginary relation to the past that exonerated feelings of guilt and responsibility.

Although *The Last Ten Days* was only moderately popular both in Austria and in West Germany, critics consider it among the few noteworthy films of 1955 and recognize it as one of the few of Pabst's many postwar productions that even deserves mention.[13] After a spectacular directing career during the Weimar Republic, Pabst emigrated to France in 1933. Having returned to Austria for family reasons in 1939, he was unable to leave when war was declared and the borders were closed. He found himself in the difficult position of being pressured by Goebbels to direct a film. Later he defended his unremarkable productions during the Third Reich as purely historical films but nonetheless he failed to avoid the stigma of collaboration with the Nazis.[14]

Pabst became interested in directing a film about Hitler as early as 1948, when he was approached by Michael Musmanno, an American military judge at the Nuremberg Tribunal, who suggested that the director make a film about Hitler's final days based on the twenty volumes of testimony he had assembled.[15] Only in 1954 did financial backers come forward who were willing to underwrite the risky project. Carl Szokoll, production manager of the small Cosmopol Film company in Vienna, and investor Ludwig Polsterer were interested in repeating the critical and commercial success they had achieved with their production of Helmut Käutner's *The Last Bridge*. The novelist Erich Maria Remarque, who had neither experience nor expertise in drama or cinema, was commissioned—reputedly at an unusually high cost—to write a scenario from Leo Lania's original film treatment using the material collected by Musmanno, which had in the meantime been published in a semidocumentary account in the United States.[16] For the production firm this promised an opening to the all-important American export market and a patina of authenticity that could protect against any potential attacks owing to the film's "sensitive" nature. For Remarque the project was an opportunity to plead the case of "the good German" (*das andere Deutschland*), of those whose innermost core had not been deformed by fascism.[17] For Pabst it represented an attempt to qualify his own compromised past and to express his humanistic vision of the cinema, which serves "understanding and peace among peoples."[18]

"The last act" of the film's German title refers to the Third Reich's grand finale, those eventful days of final defeat during World War II from April 20–30, 1945, culminating in Hitler's suicide and Germany's capitulation. The film's action is restricted almost exclusively to the Reich Chancellery bunker in Berlin, the center from which Hitler witnessed Germany's defeat while trying to hold together his crumbling empire in its last months. The main historical figures around Hitler are introduced, including Goebbels, Goering, Himmler, and Bormann, as well as military generals and family members like Eva Braun and Magda Goebbels with her children. From Musmanno's text Pabst adapted the intrinsically dramatic situation and the most important episodes and encounters while avoiding the author's tiresome metaphors and speculative commentary. The story follows the growing disintegration of the main protagonists: Hitler's physical deterioration and increasingly erratic behavior, the desertion of loyal cohorts like Goering and Himmler, and the general decline that characterizes social interaction in the bunker. On the one hand, Hitler fantasizes military strategies that will never be realized because of nonexistent war matériel; on the other hand, the military advisors are either too circumspect or too obsequious to admit the hopeless situation. The atmosphere of devout respect and willing submission in the bunker suggests a microcosm of the political forces that were able to sustain the fascist tyranny in Germany for twelve years.

Parallel to this main plot are two subplots that were not adapted from Musmanno's historical account but that rather introduce fictional characters. Richard, a young boy mobilized from the Hitler Youth to defend the city of Berlin in its last moments, stands as a metaphor for the confusion and disillusionment of Germany's youth. Even with his home a ruin, his father miss-

Hitler's isolation and physical deterioration is observed by his guards and by Frederick II in the framed portrait on the right (used by permission of Stiftung deutsche Kinemathek, Berlin).

ing in action, his mother, and his battle-maimed, cynical brother squeezed with thousands of other war victims into the subway tunnels under Berlin, Richard still wants to believe that he is defending a noble principle while fighting for the Reich. When he learns that Hitler, in order to delay the progress of the Soviet troops, has given the SS orders to flood the very subway tunnel where his family has found shelter, Richard makes his way to the Führer's bunker where he encounters Captain Wüst. He also comes to the bunker with a personal request for troop reinforcements in the north. Confronted with the staff officers' ineptitude and Hitler's willful isolation from the war's realities, Wüst recognizes why Germany faces imminent military defeat. When Richard appeals to his sense of honor and challenges him to help save his family, Wüst has reached the limit of his patience. At last face to face with Hitler, he speaks with the voice of "the other Germany," pleads with him and even threatens him so that he is shot by the bodyguards. On his deathbed Wüst articulates—for Pabst—the film's "message," explicitly directing it to the young Richard: "If you ever know peace, don't let them take it away. Never let them take it. Don't say 'Jawohl.' Don't ever say 'Jawohl.' The world can get along without 'Jawohl.' Always keep faith."

GEORG WILHELM PABST'S *THE LAST TEN DAYS*   **133**

The power of Pabst's film derives from its visual metaphors of gradual but inexorable collapse and the illusions of survival set against it. The spectator's attention focuses, of course, on Hitler, not only because he is the central subject of the Third Reich but also because the actor Albin Skoda—who does not physically resemble the person so much as he employs a convincing voice and gestures—is able to translate the historical and emotional excess associated with the figure into a visual representation that is neither grandiose nor demonic. The Hitler of *The Last Ten Days* has a puppetlike quality in his extreme moodiness, swinging back and forth from expansive optimism and determined destructiveness to desperate self-doubt and finally cowardly fear of being captured alive. This quality neither minimalizes his aggressiveness nor exaggerates his authority but rather indicates the destabilization of the power under his control. Pabst shows the Third Reich's disintegration to be a retreat from the complexity of the moment. The underground bunker becomes a site of social dispersion, of regression in which war seems like a game as Hitler and his generals study maps and move phantom armies around it. Similarly the soldiers, guards, and staff still in the bunker live the moment for immediate gratification or denial, plundering the storerooms and shooting those who desert, even after it is clear that the war has been lost. Authority has become a paranoid system of sudden reverses, and those who exercise it are at its mercy. As power relations shift, a new narrative trajectory can begin, that of the loner Captain Wüst, the low-ranking officer who tries to break out of the system of authority.

The bunker is an enclosed, self-sufficient space that seems to be at the film's beginning a kind of oasis. The opening shots of Wüst struggling to reach the bunker in a rain of bombs give way to the safety of its cold sterility and paralysis. Carefully reconstructed on a soundstage according to original drawings, the bunker images not only underscore the film's goal of documentary veracity but also link it to underground domains in other Pabst films, for example to the mine shaft in *Kameradschaft* (1931) or to the robber gang's warehouse in *The Threepenny Opera* (1931). Cut off from the rest of the world, these "protected" spaces function as a dramaturgical device for intensifying the relations between characters and concentrating the spectator's attention on them as if they were under a microscope. In this case the bunker's dim lighting and low ceilings, exaggerated by low-angle shots and tight framing, create an oppressive, claustrophobic atmosphere that, together with dancing shadows on the walls, reinforce the impression of impending doom. Seen through rhythmically alternating high and low-angle shots, the narrow staircase leading down to the bunker serves as a convenient transition from the outside world of war, which penetrates this self-enclosed world only through the increasingly frequent sounds of battle and through the smoke wafting in the ventilating system. Accordingly Wüst enters the bunker in the first scene as if it were the mythological Hades. He relinquishes first his identity papers, then his pistol, stripped of his individuality and self-defenses before descending into this hell.

Pabst uses stairs to suggest a descent into a space where everyday logic no longer functions, and as in his Weimar films the space at the bottom of the stairs is characterized by male camaraderie and sexual license. This is particularly evident in the canteen scenes punctuating the narrative at regular intervals. In counterpoint to the austerity of the spaces associated with Hitler and the close-up and medium shots in those scenes, the canteen is usually filled with noisy throngs of drinking, singing, and carousing soldiers and nurses seen in wide-angle long shots. The last scene in the canteen, immediately after Wüst's pathos-laden death, generates a sense of despair and social dissolution in a particularly effective way. The camera cuts from the infirmary to a pan of wildly dancing legs which are revealed as those of a crowd of drunken revelers engaged in a dance of death. It singles out a nurse who, with a cigarette lasciviously dangling between her lips, throws off her white apron, tears open her blouse, and begins to move sensuously to the mournful tone of the accordion. When the music changes to a jazzy melody, she is joined by a wounded soldier with his head swathed in bandages who thrusts forward his broken arm mounted in a cast as if in a mock *Heil* salute. Another soldier throws himself on the woman and all of them continue dancing as if they were automatons, unable to halt their twitching limbs. Slowly the music changes to a crisp march rhythm, and the crippled soldier's dance turns into goose-stepping. The sequence ends with a chorus of drunken soldiers singing "Heute erobern wir Deutschland/ Und morgen die ganze Welt" [Today we conquer Germany and tomorrow the whole world] superimposed on the image of the goose-stepping cripple. The apocalyptic vision, combining images of debauchery and Nazi icons, elaborates for the spectator the film's dominant imaginary relation that represents the trauma of loss in shocking and grotesque images.

The robotic movements of the dancing cripple and the woman in the canteen sequence have an expressionistic quality that also characterizes Wüst's and Hitler's gestures throughout the film. Interestingly Pabst at first intended to have Werner Krauss in the lead role, the unforgettable Dr. Caligari in Robert Wiene's *The Cabinet of Dr. Caligari* (*Das Cabinet des Dr. Caligari*, 1920).[19] The director planned apparently from the outset to exploit these puppetlike movements, which Krauss had introduced so effectively in the early twenties, in order to stress the narrative's theatricality but also to capture the hypnotic dream state that dominates the characters' actions. Contrasted to this kind of expressionistically stylized acting is the verisimilitude in looks and gesture of other major figures, especially Willy Krause's uncanny resemblance to Joseph Goebbels. In both cases Pabst was more interested in developing types rather than characters with psychologically

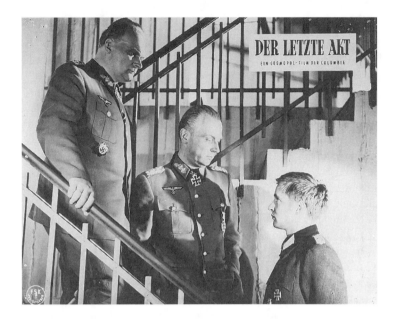

The stairs in the bunker lead down to a space where everyday logic no longer functions (used by permission of Stiftung deutsche Kinemathek, Berlin).

The bunker's canteen is the site of social dissolution and sexual license in the final days of the Third Reich (used by permission of Stiftung deutsche Kinemathek, Berlin).

convincing motivations. Indeed their abstractness reveals Pabst's purpose in employing documentary authenticity as a historical backdrop for an essentially melodramatic narrative. The clearly defined character types and highly coded dramatic situations are discrete elements in the construction of a fantastical atmosphere that plays against the documentary veracity of those last, hectic days of war.

Pabst's care in editing, in finding the significant detail, or in investing an everyday gesture with meaning lends the narrative its visual coherence. Like the stair motif, the telephone switchboard is a charged visual image of contact, transition, and verbal communication. It recurs often in close-up shots situated immediately prior to or after scenes in Hitler's rooms and usually marks the intrusion of some catastrophic news from the outside world. The subway space also takes on connotative force as a repetitive structuring device. In contrast to the bunker, it is portrayed early in the film as a space where the solidarity of the victims and human respect are still asserted. When an SS unit dynamites the subway, it is transformed into a scene of chaos, accompanied by a soundtrack of dramatic orchestral music and muffled screams. Not unlike the rhythm of suspense in a disaster movie, the editing plays on the spectator's desire to watch while hoping the inevitable catastrophe can be avoided. The sequence of quick long shots resembles closely the parallel scene near the end of Staudte's *Rotation,* and both could be considered a homage to Fritz Lang in whose *Metropolis* (1926) a similar catastrophe occurs when water comes rushing into the underground city. Pabst returns again at the end of the film to the subway space in a parallel montage with scenes of Hitler dictating his "political testament" and preparing his suicide. Submerged in water, two victims attempt unsuccessfully to save themselves by grasping a sign that reads "Wir schwören—Treue dem Führer" [We swear loyalty to the Führer], and finally a slow pan of the still water in the now flooded tunnel passes another sign reading *Schweig* [silence (quoting a widespread, antispying poster campaign during the last years of the Third Reich)] as the sound of slowly dripping water emphasizes the silence. The juxtaposition of Hitler's willful murder of women, children, and war invalids in the subway tunnel refuge and his self-inflicted death precisely because the war has already been lost is cruelly underscored by the signs' ironies and represents Pabst's strongest indictment of German guilt for the crimes of National Socialism.

These objects and details—stairs, switchboard wires, the subway space, signs—take on an anthropomorphic life of their own in contrast to the character types who become progressively dehumanized. Yet, like in most serious films of the fifties, the details quickly assume a transparent symbolism in order to stress the moralism of the pointed finger. Thus, at moments of tension or conflict the film narrative appeals to authorities, real or imagined. Behind Hitler, for example, hovers the portrait

The SS floods the Berlin subways, destroying an alternative underground site where solidarity reigned (used by permission of Stiftung deutsche Kinemathek, Berlin).

of Frederick II, the eccentric eighteenth-century Prussian king whom Hitler admired as a great, lonely military and political leader. Several times he is referred to as a historical example of perseverance during periods of political pressure and as an excuse for Hitler's own irrational behavior. On another plane the film itself is framed by a portraitlike image of Captain Wüst shot from above: at the film's beginning surrounded by clouds of smoke as he waits to enter the bunker and again at the end superimposed over the smoke and flames engulfing Hitler's funeral pyre. Wüst's youthful face, framed with curly hair, rises phoenixlike out of these flames while a voice-over intones his earlier words "Always keep faith, never say 'Jawohl,'" and the rich orchestral music subsides first to a dissonant chord and then to a trumpet call and ominous drum roll.

This final image of apotheosis shows how the film narrative seems unable to choose between its tragic framework and the melodramatic structure. Pabst's original film conception projected Hitler as an Elizabethan tragic hero who, replete with stagy monologue, must pay the price for his hubris in the eponymous last act.[20] A usurper of power like Richard III, a murderous Macbeth with no qualms or guilt, this was to be the Hitler whose tragedy brings about the disintegration of the world around him. Later, however, Pabst shifted from the tragic dimension of his material into a melodramatic mode, a reductive form of tragedy.[21] The denouement of the Third Reich, at least in this version, does not occur in the clash of contradictory forces through which guilt and catharsis achieve a delicate balance but rather it unrolls in an enclosed, insulated world where good and evil are binary opposites and vice is duly punished. Typical too for the melodramatic structure is the film's fundamental plot conflict. Pitted against Wüst's obsession with virtue and responsibility for others is Hitler's unabashed egomania. Yet both the sacrificial hero (Wüst) and the villain (Hitler) pursue the same ideological goals: the redemption of Germany and the German people and, in particular, traditional values like family and home.[22] Melodrama, however, can encompass such inconsistencies because rather than their causes it stresses affects like pathos, victimization, and resignation. By implementing the melodramatic structure, then, Pabst is able to transform the historical issues of power and legitimacy, turning them inward as personalized issues of family and the individual.

To make *The Last Ten Days* into a domestic melodrama in which the private conflict conceals a national tragedy shifts the center of attention from Hitler to Richard and Wüst, from Hitler's loss of control and his errors to the victims who are helpless objects of events that destroy their world. Richard's family constellation—displaced mother, war-maimed brother, and unnamed father—diegetically invites surrogates. The absent father, whom one may assume was killed in the war, throws the system (familial and social) into turmoil and allows Hitler to establish as the surrogate Father a domestic economy of a different sort for twelve years. Wüst's past is sketched in during a conversation with Major Venner, the cowardly and opportunistic officer responsible for bunker communications who turns out to be Wüst's half brother by the same mother (the father is never mentioned). The narration positions Wüst as Richard's nominal big brother in a coalition against the Father. He responds to Richard's cry for help to save what is left of the family in its underground refuge but fails to displace the usurper. His brief moment of resistance in the attack on Hitler leads to his death. The fact that Hitler is deposed at the end through a deus ex machina (his suicide) is a familiar narrative reversal that invites a deletion of the past to enable a positive vision of the future, condensed into Wüst's call for resistance and faith.

The deflection of attention from the past parallels the motif of sight and blindness. Hitler refuses to see what the maps show, claiming that his generals pull the wool over his eyes and relying instead on his premonitions (*Vorsehung* or prevision). At one point Goebbels flatters him with an astrologer who can see the future in the planets' configuration, while the

Führer constantly demands blind fanaticism from those around him. Wüst, meanwhile, is furious that Hitler has never gone into the battlefields to see the devastation for himself. Formally, the film's dramaturgy of the look picks up on this truncation of sight. Unlike Pabst's Weimar films, where the omnipresent mirrors, windows, and reflecting surfaces set in motion a complex interplay of the seen and the not-seen, the shown and the not-shown, in order to heighten the indeterminacy and ambiguity of the look, in *The Last Ten Days* there is no splitting of perception in this way. Rather than transferring the look from one actor to another, it is directed offscreen, unreceived by other characters or by the audience: Hitler gazes into an undefined and presumably mythical thousand-year Reich; Frederick II's steely gaze in the portrait focuses on an unknown reference point in his past or future; and Wüst, in his apotheosis, also stares into the space of a better future. This look, not unlike Gloria's in *To New Shores*, is deflected beyond the frame. It confirms the narrative's refusal to engage history, to *see* the forces responsible for fascism and at the same time it foregrounds the verbal text's didactic platitudes and the music track's melodramatic excess. Similarly the film's composition reveals few examples of the fluid editing so characteristic of the early Pabst. The frequent pans and traveling shots and the many unusual camera angles do not compensate for the static, highly posed images and the predictable transitions. For a director who established his reputation with admirably innovative visual editing in the Weimar cinema, such restraint in visual images suggests either a serious compromise in his cinematic values or a distrust of the audience that by the midfifties had grown accustomed to the lowest common denominator of industry standards as represented in a film like *Black Forest Girl*.

The affirmation of knowing nothing about the past describes an imaginary strategy that insists on denial of political responsibility and complicity and distinguishes the film more than anything else as a contribution to the process of social restoration under way in the fifties. Insofar as Pabst uses Wüst and Richard as primary figures of spectator identification—their points of view dominate the camera perspectives—he invites the spectator to share this position of disguising the problematic past in order to seek salvation in an ambiguous future, and this ten years after the end of the war. To achieve this, the director must write off the entire generation of fathers (there is not one adult male in the film who is not maimed, seriously compromised, or otherwise marked as clearly evil except for Wüst, who dies) and portray the youth (Richard) as victimized by the system of political power. True to the melodramatic form—and one might assume that this is the main reason for the director to have employed it—the real site of conflict (complicity in and guilt for the Nazi past) is rendered invisible. While Pabst clearly recognizes the conflict, its terms remain abstract and impersonal, excerpted from the larger context, just as the actors in the drama remain isolated in the bunker. Characteristically the realism of melodrama is one-dimensional, while questions of historical import are complex and demand subtlety. Thus, at the same time the spectator identification with Wüst and Richard allows a recognition of the forces that oppress, the melodramatic conflict of good and evil types robs them of historical specificity. This reproduces the sentimental, moralistic perspective typical for the fifties war film.

Produced in 1955 and scheduled for its premiere on the tenth anniversary of Germany's capitulation, *The Last Ten Days* is situated within the larger problematic concerning the tortured public discourse about the Nazi past that was prevalent in print and visual media of the fifties and which would become a central concern for the younger generation of New German Cinema directors. Hence, it would be too facile to read the film exclusively as Pabst's attempt to atone for what he might have felt to be his personal complicity for remaining in Austria and cooperating with Goebbels's film industry during the Third Reich. Rather, it addresses the historical spectator in the process of constituting an imaginary relation to the experience of capitulation that in the public consciousness had not yet been clearly defined as a defeat or a liberation.

The semidocumentary portrayal of the bunker mentality and of the corruption of all authority as the logical consequences of National Socialism was a departure for the period war film and a powerful means of gaining access to fascism by playing on the visual fascination with its primary representatives. *The Last Ten Days* is unusual in this context because of its claim to authenticity in the address of a historically documented episode and — here Pabst's excellent sense of casting plays a role — because of the actors' ability in recreating the major historical figures. To be sure, it shares with two Soviet features that also treat the last days of the war — Grigori Alexandrov's *Meeting on the Elbe* and Mikhail Chiaureli's *The Fall of Berlin* (both 1949) — an excessively schematic portrayal of the main characters, but in contrast to the Soviet films, it condenses the action in time and place by concentrating on the small details and gestures of the protagonists. Moreover, after Charles Chaplin's very early satire *The Great Dictator* (1940), Pabst's was the first feature film to present the Nazi leadership in a fictional narrative and to do so convincingly at that. Not until over twenty years later did German directors once again turn their attention to this subject matter when Joachim Fest produced *Hitler, A Career* (*Hitler — eine Karriere*, 1977), a tendentious documentary about National Socialism as the mad caper of a small elite that "somehow" gained power over an entire nation, and when Hans-Jürgen Syberberg completed his monumental, seven-hour *Our Hitler* (*Hitler — ein Film aus Deutschland*, 1977), a highly demanding essayistic reflection on the constitution of history and historical consciousness in postwar Germany.

At the time it was released, *The Last Ten Days* prompted quite a bit of interest both nationally and internationally with festival screenings in Locarno and Edinburgh.[23] It met with a very mixed response among the West German and Austrian audiences, for it obviously raised extracinematographic expectations and reflections.[24] First, its documentary quality evoked too realistically memories of the past, and second, it touched a public anathema, the question of collective guilt, without making concessions to the adult generation that was supposed to answer for the guilt.[25] Melodramatic conventions demand a clear polarity between corruption and innocence that here becomes a generational conflict. On the one hand, those who hold power are utterly decadent, if not insane. On the other, Richard, a child despite his uniform, remains the helpless and disillusioned victim who never finds the means to control his destiny. In between is Wüst, a young man who may have provided a vehicle of identification for many in the audience who wanted to think they resisted or who at least wished they had, but his direct confrontation with Hitler must still have been perceived in 1955 as pure fantasy. Furthermore, Pabst's optimism that the youth of Germany would find the power to change a society already well on the way to restoring the structures of authority and legitimacy has an aura of unreality about it. Finally, the film narrative's pathos-laden closure with Wüst's appeal to "Keep faith" raises important questions as to the object or content of that faith, for the hope of resistance to injustice and misuse of power remains undefined. The film does not prevent forgetting the past but rather projects an imaginary resolution that helps avoid an all too precise or obsessive recollection of the past that could undermine the present.

Part 4

The East German Cinema

10

The Authenticity of Autobiography: Konrad Wolf's *I Was Nineteen*

ONRAD WOLF'S AUTOBIOGRAPHICAL feature *I Was Nineteen* (*Ich war neunzehn*, 1968) presents a striking counterpoint both to Staudte's family history in *Rotation* and to Pabst's melodrama in *The Last Ten Days*. All three films focus centrally on questions of guilt and responsibility for World War II and specifically for the crimes perpetrated in the name of National Socialism. Both of the earlier films seek to explain the position of the "common man" who became trapped in the logic of complicity while they construct an imaginary position of resistance for the spectator. For Staudte this imaginary position allows the spectator to condemn unequivocally the Nazi past while shifting attention to a younger generation that will avoid the fathers' failures. For Pabst it provides a psychological motivation for historical amnesia while transferring the entire problem onto the abstract and philosophical level of human redemption. Like Staudte, Wolf belongs to the tradition of antifascist realism that represents the richest contribution made by the East German DEFA studios to the postwar German cinema. Like Pabst, he condenses his narrative into a period of several days at the turning point of the German capitulation in order to use the situation's inherent drama as a backdrop to the process of personal insight and transformation. Yet Wolf's film, produced in 1967 as the DEFA studio's formal contribution to the fiftieth anniversary of the Russian Revolution, not only employs a different approach to spectatorship but also reconfigures the question of responsibility within the broader problematic of German identity. Thus, the film addresses both the generational shift in the cinema audience and the specific cultural practices in the German Democratic Republic (GDR) during the late sixties.

If West Germany's cinema during the fifties was characterized by escapism and sentimentality, then East Germany's is best described as overtly partisan and ideologically functional. After the strong start in the late forties the development of the DEFA studios and of cinema aesthetics during the next twenty years was subordinated—as was the entire cultural sphere—to the political priorities defined by the Socialist Unity Party (SED). The party's cultural program was called Socialist Realism, a combination of explicitly articulated philosophical assumptions about the didactic nature of art and a set of normative guidelines for judging the quality of specific works in fulfilling the didactic project.[1] To understand the power of official cultural policies in the GDR during this time, it is crucial to recognize two things: first, the program was, at least on a rhetorical level, flexible enough to adapt to the changing political conditions both domestically and internationally (e.g., the 1953 uprising in East Berlin, the process of de-Stalinization initiated in 1956, the building of the Berlin Wall in 1961, the challenge of a New Left movement in West Germany in the midsixties, and the onset of détente in the late sixties); and second, the majority of artists who lived and worked in the GDR either supported the precepts of Socialist Realism as a framework for articulating the utopian possibilities of their situation or tolerated them as necessary constraints in the politically charged atmosphere of cold-war Europe.

In the context of the cinema Socialist Realism prescribed clearly enunciated message films that avoided dialectical and historicizing discourses. After the founding of the GDR as a state in 1949 the politburo issued its first major statement concerning film production on July 27, 1952. The official call for the revitalization of the progressive German cinema was followed by a film conference organized in September by the Central Committee. Charging that the DEFA studios were too oriented toward the past, the conference resolution stressed the need for contemporary subjects about the working class in the transformation to socialism.[2] Despite the rhetorical flourish, this position neither picked up where the Weimar experiments in progressive political filmmaking had broken off with Brecht and Dudov nor did it encourage the attempts in early DEFA antifascist films to develop innovative formal techniques. Quite to the contrary, under the conservative influence of Georg Lukács's well articulated views on European realism there was a clear skepticism toward the early Soviet experiments of the twenties and the Brechtian tradition in what was defined as the national heritage of socialist culture.[3] Hence, the imaginary strategies of the majority of fifties productions can be subsumed under the concept of "revolutionary romanticism," positing the specific as the general and defining potential solutions as the existing reality. The resistance to engaging openly the real conflicts and contradictions within GDR society corresponded to the suspicion toward if not outright rejection of formal innovation for representing the increasingly complex reality. Conventional linearity and simple forms of spectatorial identification dominated narrative patterns, so that frequently the films looked like old UFA productions but with a "class conscious" content. In some instances they could hardly be distinguished, at least on an aesthetic level, from the features coming out of West Germany, especially in regards to visual, acting, and musical style.

A few films were able to avoid the characteristic pathos and functionalism, and these were often the best and most popular DEFA productions: antifascist features like Slatan Dudov's *Stronger Than the Night* (*Stärker als die Nacht*, 1954), Heiner Carow's *They Called Him Amigo* (*Sie nannten ihn Amigo*, 1958), and Konrad Wolf's *Stars* (*Sterne*, 1959); literary adaptations like Wolfgang Staudte's *The Subject* (*Der Untertan*, 1952) and Konrad Wolf's *Lissy* (1957); and Gerhard Klein's topical Berlin films *Alarm in the Circus* (*Alarm im Zirkus*, 1954), *A Berlin Romance* (*Eine Berliner Romanze*, 1956), and *Berlin — Schönhauser Corner* (*Berlin — Ecke Schönhauser*, 1957).[4] Typical for these films was their insistence on psychologically and individually motivated characters. Dramaturgical decisions were made in the film text itself through mise-en-scène or editing so that little was left to the spectator's imagination. Realistic settings and technical sophistication created an uninterrupted and emotionally moving dramatic action, while particularly in historical narratives problems were resolved from a clear ideological perspective.

One of the major problems confronting the East German film industry was the open border to West Germany and the competition it implied (at least in the border regions and in Berlin). Surprising as it may seem, among the DEFA productions in the fifties were also musical comedies, adventures, and detective stories aimed at inducing the audience to stay at home. The impact of de-Stalinization after 1956 with its implications for more critical approaches in the cultural sphere was short-lived. At the party's cultural conference in 1957 and again at the Second Feature Film Conference in July 1958, high-level functionaries criticized the alleged middlebrow taste of many DEFA productions and their lack of convincing heroes with whom spectators could identify.[5] While this assessment opened the door for discussions about the nature of Socialist Realism in the cinema, in fact they quickly bogged down in unproductive arguments such as how many weaknesses a protagonist might possess and still be considered a positive hero. More important were the moves undertaken to decentralize the administrative control of feature film productions, resulting in the sixties in relatively autonomous, self-managed production groups within the DEFA studios.[6]

Not until after the Berlin Wall was erected in 1961 did GDR functionaries consider the situation stable enough internally to tolerate the kind of experimentation that New Wave Polish cinema or Soviet directors had implemented successfully after 1956. Younger directors in the GDR began to respond to the increasingly sophisticated demands of the film audience with more conflicted narratives and visually complicated compositional strategies. Frank Beyer's working-class comedy *Carbide and Sorrel* (*Karbid und Sauerampfer*, 1964); Wolf's adaptation of Christa Wolf's controversial novel about a young woman's suicide attempt, *Divided Heaven* (*Der geteilte Himmel*, 1964); and Günther Rücker's nostalgic portrait of a young schoolteacher returning after the war, *The Best Years* (*Die besten Jahre*, 1965) are only some of the productions that introduced a modernized film language to articulate the interpersonal conflicts typical of the differentiated reality in the GDR. This concession to a more critical function for the cinema, however, proved to be a brief interlude when serious economic disjunctures led to a crackdown in the cultural sphere. In December 1965 the party clamped down on the creative energies that had emerged during the first half of the decade in a carefully orchestrated plenary session. Couched in the familiar jargon of cultural functionaries, the critique was a defensive ideological assault aimed at "skepticism," the "superficial reflection" of reality, and the "unconvincing resolution" of contradictions in literature, the theater, and especially the cinema.[7] A number of completed films were never distributed, others were interrupted midway in production, and the popular cinema magazine *Film und Fernsehen* came under attack for its broad coverage of Western cinema.[8] As a result of the attack filmmakers retreated to less controversial subjects: historical topics and children's stories.[9]

This is where Konrad Wolf's narrative about the last days of the war fits in. He had quickly advanced as one of the major figures among the first generation of young GDR filmmakers who began their careers in the mid-fifties. Son of the writer Friedrich Wolf, who as a Jewish Communist fled to Moscow in 1933, and trained at the Moscow Film Academy, he had an impeccable record for a stellar career in the young socialist republic. Wolf also had talent and a commitment to film art. He established his reputation at DEFA through a series of prizewinning films concerning the historical decision for or against fascism.[10] From this strong position he was able to champion cinematic innovations introduced by such Soviet directors as Mikhail Romm and Andrei Tarkovsky within an otherwise very conservative studio situation.[11] *I Was Nineteen* was Wolf's tenth feature, his most personal film, and also, as became obvious during the seventies, a pivotal work in his development as a film artist. An antifascist narrative, it reflects not only his own proclivity to engage a dialogue with German history but also the ongoing strength of such historical topics in the GDR cinema. This is demonstrated by the continuity in the production of films like Gerhard Klein's *The Gleiwitz Case* (*Der Fall Gleiwitz*, 1961) about an SS conspiracy against a Polish radio station, which provided Hitler with the excuse he sought to begin the war; Wolf's own adaptation of his father's drama about anti-Semitism in the Weimar Republic *Professor Mamlock* (1961);

Frank Beyer's adaptation of Bruno Apitz's concentration camp novel *Naked among the Wolves* (*Nackt unter Wölfen*, 1963); and Joachim Kunert's adaptation of Dieter Noll's war novel *The Adventures of Werner Holt* (*Die Abenteuer des Werner Holt*, 1964). Unlike these historical films about the Nazi past, however, *I Was Nineteen* eschews dramatic conflicts and the narrative structure of a didactic parable in order to introduce a more problematic relation between the hero, his point of view, and the spectator.

Despite the filmmaker's protestations to the contrary, *I Was Nineteen* suggests in its thematic and formal markings an autobiographical narrative.[12] Like Wolf, the nineteen-year-old protagonist, Gregor Hecker, comes to a defeated Germany as an officer in the propaganda corps of the triumphant Red Army in April 1945. Having grown up in Moscow, where his German parents resettled eleven years earlier, he returns now a stranger to his "home" and at home in another country. In a series of seven loosely connected segments covering the dramatic days immediately preceding the German capitulation he encounters a variety of Germans who make him aware of his ambiguous feelings toward them and toward Germany. A process of self-discovery and self-questioning begins: what does "home" mean in this unknown, native country? In short, the narrative plays on the autobiographical project of constituting the self as an imaginary Other through the process of representing private experience.[13] Formally the film announces its status as a personal, retrospective narrative already in the title. The self-reflexive pronoun "I" and the preterit "was" emphasize the double inscription of subjectivity as an old and a new ego. The intermittent voice-over as well, speaking in the past and addressing the spectator in the present, sustains the oscillation between memory and presence. Finally, the intertitles introducing each episode (e.g., April 16, 1945) not only signify the events as authentic but also suggest a personal, diary-like style for the narrative. In fact, Wolf's wartime diary did provide the point of departure for the film idea, although, as he emphasized repeatedly, it also drew on the experiences of others.[14] More importantly, the director's aim was to filter the recollection of past events through a present-tense narrator in order to objectify the subjectivity of personalized memory. Thus, he utilizes the sense of the here-and-now inherent in the diary form but combines it with the distance of an autobiographical narration that assumes the separation of a more mature self reflecting on its past relation to reality. This notion of meaning production in the context of cinematic autobiography and spectator positioning is one of the film's central issues.

The first segment, dated April 16, 1945, consists of three "events" interrupted by archival footage of a nighttime battle that serve both as exposition of characters and situation and as a structural introduction to the film's formal narrative strategies. Gregor Hecker is a Soviet intelligence officer who, as a native speaker of German, has the task of addressing the

The film's protagonist, a Soviet officer and a German-Jewish exile, encounters his first German outside Berlin, a young girl who wants to commit suicide after Germany's defeat (used by permission of the Bundesarchiv-Filmarchiv Berlin, from the former Staatliches Filmarchiv der DDR).

Gregor encounters another kind of German, the mayor and his wife who have just removed the swastika from their red flag to greet the Red Army properly (used by permission of Stiftung deutsche Kinemathek, Berlin).

enemy troops over a mobile loudspeaker, imploring them to surrender their weapons and to end the already lost war. The first segment is accompanied on the soundtrack by Gregor's electronically amplified voice, appealing—as a fellow German ("I am a German")—to his enemies' sense of trust.[15] This amplified, diegetical voice gives way, however, to a quiet voice-over in which Gregor introduces himself as described above. The disjuncture between his two voices, between the emphatic public pronouncement of his German identity and the intimate biographical confession that he grew up in Moscow, establishes aurally the dilemma the protagonist will have to resolve in the course of the narrative.

The images meanwhile generalize the nature of his struggle toward self-identity as social process with political ramifications. The first scene includes, for example, a long take of a peaceful river landscape. An unrecognizable dark point in the background of the long shot comes closer and closer, revealing a raft floating on the river with a hanged German soldier dangling from a makeshift gallows. The close-up of a sign around his neck announces: "Deserter. I am a Russian slave." The collision between Gregor's appeal to surrender and the visual confirmation of the potential consequences for those who respond to his appeal demonstrates the limits of his undertaking but also names at the very outset one way he will be perceived by the Germans he encounters: as a deserter who betrayed the fatherland. The third scene underscores the vulnerability of this position. A German soldier—in the script described as resembling Gregor closely—assaults the protagonist, who is saved in the nick of time when his comrade and fellow officer Sasha shoots the attacker. The internal struggle Gregor faces in defining the self parallels the life-and-death struggle into which he is drawn with this young German. The point of departure in this process of relating the self to the Other is posed and reposed in the first segment as a parable about an outsider returning home. The displaced German in a Soviet uniform is saved at this point from his German attacker only by the intervention of his Soviet comrade, suggesting in a historiographical subtext the official GDR explanation of its own genesis after the end of the war.

The introductory image of a river landscape is apt for an autobiographical narrative. The metaphor of the flowing river expresses that unity of origin and destiny that traditionally motivates the search for self based on a reading of past experience. The narrative's laconic structure, the lack of an obvious narrative will formulating the causality of events, heightens the sense of sincerity behind the search and counteracts the pull toward synthesis and totality inherent in autobiography. Similar to, but more central for the narration than the river metaphor are the frequent images of roads or traveling shots along roads that punctuate the episodes. *I Was Nineteen* is a film about a journey during which the protagonist is confronted by "typical" Germans. In his encounters Gregor is less a participant than a witness and in this respect provides an obvious point of access for the spectator.

The slow, deliberate pan of the room where an old woman committed suicide out of fear (segment 2), for example, mirrors Gregor's perspective: the observer searching for details. Besides being passive, the protagonist is naive. He cannot comprehend why someone would choose death just as Germany is being liberated by the Soviet Army and he can only stammer a few optimistic generalities when the young refugee who discovered the suicide asks him what will become of her after the war ends. His lack of voice beyond the distorted sound of the microphone and the intimate voice-over registers the perplexity and helplessness of the young, inexperienced outsider who has not yet found his way.

If the hero represents the voyeur, the outsider looking in, as a model of specular cognition, his naiveté establishes the authority of the first-person report because his helplessness seems authentic. This is not official history but personal experience. An epistemological stance that purports to tell the truth or intends to have the spectator believe that it is the truth informs the whole undertaking. It becomes the measure of the reality represented in the film, for authenticity creates an atmosphere of immediacy and also of the historical verity of a situation.[16] In this connection the documentary footage takes on a specific function as an alternative to and yet a confirmation of the protagonist's personalized narrative. The third segment, one of the most striking and also most challenging in the film, illustrates the point. Dated April 24, 1945, it consists of four independent episodes connected only loosely by the location: the Sachsenhausen concentration camp near Oranienburg. The first episode shows a small group of Soviet infantry about to execute a German soldier whom they suspect is a guard at the camp. Gregor's friend and fellow officer, Vadim (a Jewish teacher of German from Kiev), intervenes, but they impatiently push him away and shoot the soldier. Gregor, whose face appears only once in a close-up at the end of the scene, remains an impassive bystander, beyond the visual field of the execution. The sequence ends with the loud gun shot and an abrupt cut to a long take of an extreme low, wide-angle perspective of the Sachsenhausen camp gate. Gregor's voice-over explains that they arrived too late, after all the prisoners had been evacuated by the SS: "But we will get the guilty ones. What will they say?"

Gregor's question introduces footage from the documentary film *Death Camp Sachsenhausen* (*Todeslager Sachsenhausen*, Richard Brandt, 1946). A camp executioner responds to questions posed by a commission of Soviet officers, explaining impassionately and in excruciating detail exactly how prisoners were gassed at the camp. There is no commentary on this interrogation, but the footage is interrupted twice by close-up images of Gregor, first standing under a shower with his eyes closed and later slowly wiping his wet face with a towel. The stark contrast invites associations on the part of the spectator: Gregor's washing away of the camp commander's words and images, the impossibility of innocently showering after the descriptions of showers spewing poisonous gas in the camp's execution rooms, a flood of tears in view of the enormity of the crime described by this subaltern. The mixture of memory and documentary complicates the autobiographical genre, introducing an additional "witness" besides the protagonist and beyond his immediate experience.[17] The obvious framing of the footage as documentary—indicated by a printed title, the eerie background music (composed by Boris Blacher for the original documentary film), and the distinctly different quality of the camera work—establishes an authority of the document that surpasses the subjectivity of personal recollection. At the same time, however, by integrating this document without commentary into the protagonist's process of recollection, his memory strives for a more authentic quality through its juxtaposition to "objective truth."

The third episode in this segment returns to Gregor's voyeuristic experience, confronting him with another view of the German responsibility for crimes against humanity. Here Vadim "interrogates" a landscape architect who lived near Sachsenhausen during the Third Reich. His defense of defeatism, couched in the abstract vocabulary of philosophical pessimism, represents within the narrative the position of the isolated intellectual who capitulates to an ill-concealed conformity in the face of social injustice. Once again, Gregor remains aloof, venturing a response only after Vadim draws attention to his father who had emigrated from Germany: "There are people who will change the situation," Gregor interjects, followed by a Russian curse directed at the architect. In addition, the camera undercuts the architect's lofty and sophisticated speech, focusing in close-ups on his carefully groomed profile, on his delicately manicured hands, on Gregor paging through a book of caricatures, and on Sasha who has fallen asleep in a chair while the folk song he put on the record player, "Ännchen von Tharau," accompanies the architect's self-justificatory monologue. The fourth and shortest episode shows, finally, a strong reaction on Gregor's part, certainly motivated by the architect's valorization of helplessness. Vadim begins to recite Heinrich Heine's famous poem "Ich hatte einst ein schönes Vaterland" [I once had a beautiful fatherland] to Gregor, who angrily finishes the last verses: "Es war ein Traum" [it was a dream]. Vadim's Heine citation expresses his love of German culture, but for Gregor it is mere sentimentality, the dream that Heine—who one hundred years earlier was also an exile—regarded Germany to be. Gregor's aggressive response to Vadim's reminder that this is his home—including the concentration camps and the intellectuals like the architect, but also Heine and familiar folk songs—indicates the ambiguity of his search for self-identity and the difficulty he confronts in reconciling Germany as imaginary and as reality.

Autobiography implies the question "where do I belong" as much as "who am I?" In this case the protagonist's search for identity becomes the process of identifying with the home from which he is estranged, that is, of determining what *Vaterland* means. Diametrically opposed to the generic characteristics of the Heimat film elucidated in chapter 8, the film's working title was nonetheless "Heimkehr 45" (Homecoming 45). For Wolf, however, home has less to do with geography than with politics and ideology. Gregor's experience of otherness, his sense of distrust and shame in the initial encounters described above, gradually give way to feelings of empathy and solidarity. The fifth segment, the celebration of the traditional May 1 Labor Day but also of the imminent military victory, offers a good example of the parameters within which this hesitant discovery of the self through the Other takes place. The festive occasion is an opportunity for the Soviet officers and soldiers to relax together while preparing a huge feast. The images stress the strong sense of community as they all share in preparing dumplings, singing choruses, and drinking toasts. During the feast a Soviet general enters, followed by five German political prisoners from a nearby concentration camp, emaciated and unsure of themselves in these surroundings. Later he introduces Gregor as a German comrade, and it turns out that one of the prisoners indeed knew his father before 1933. Gregor is embarrassed and can barely respond to the older man's astonished questions; and when the general proposes that he make a toast, Gregor can come up with nothing better than an awkward "To my mother!" Heimat, of course, is that lost place of childhood, family, and identity, which Gregor here asserts unconsciously in the association of this unknown figure from his father's past with a common political commitment and his mother. The association takes on an even more emphatic symbolic quality in the next sequence.

A tipsy Gregor leaves the party and playfully walks along the terrace balustrade, balancing uncertainly until he falls to the ground. As the camera focuses on his face, his mother chastises him for his carelessness. The mother's voice, detached from the narrative events, registers a movement to a prior moment in the protagonist's life. Unlike Gregor's embodied voice-over, this disembodied voice speaks from a position of superiority and inaccessibility, but also one that is associated with his voicelessness. Diegetically the "vision" of the mother results from his fall, but psychologically the momentary regression positions Gregor to redefine himself as German. The mother's voice, which reminds him that he was precocious—smoking and drinking alcohol at an early age—evokes his earlier immaturity. Surrounded by darkness, temporally immobilized by the impact of the fall, Gregor is thrown back into the vulnerable position of the child, the position from which he first learned to distinguish the self from the Other, the subject from the object. That fall from plenitude, from the unquestioned certainty of self in the mother-child bond, parallels Gregor's need to learn how to integrate the contradictory feelings he has toward Germany and to find a positive way to accept himself as German. This narrationally unusual sequence is situated between two crucial memories for Gregor: after he is reminded of his father

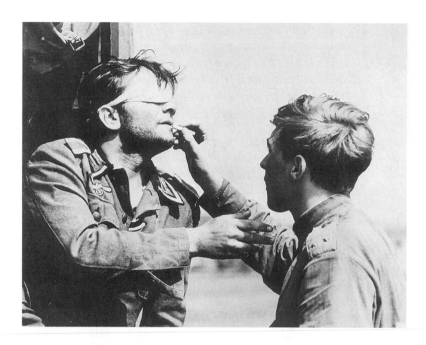

Gregor offers a blinded German soldier a cigarette in a gesture of reconciliation (used by permission of Stiftung deutsche Kinemathek, Berlin).

by one of the Germans who was imprisoned for his leftist political convictions and before he overhears Vadim discussing with another prisoner his concern about how to teach school children about "Goethe and Auschwitz. Two German names, two names in one language." Gregor's search for the self becomes a process of re-cognizing that difference.

For Wolf difference is a political category, and the film's last two segments designate in unambiguous terms exactly where he draws the political boundaries. The sixth segment contrasts two political traditions in Germany, that of the "progressive" and "reactionary" German. Two of the prisoners represent the positive tradition. The first is an older man, a German partisan from the Spanish Civil War who has been appointed mayor by the Soviet Administration in a small village outside Berlin. When Gregor's unit drops him off there, he requests that they play from the truck's loudspeaker a recording of the Rio Jarama song:

> And later and always and everywhere
> That workers are sitting together

The Battle of Jarama song will sound,
Will inflame all hearts for the struggle.
And sometime then, when the hour has come,
When we have chased all the ghosts away,
The whole world will become the Jarama Front,
Just like in those days of February.[18]

The solidarity song, memorializing those who sacrificed their lives in the unsuccessful war against Franco, is also a call to vindicate their unjust deaths, and as such the parallel to the antifascist struggle against Hitler is explicit. The old man, left behind and clearly facing an inimical environment, represents the repetition of defeat but also the continuity of struggle for a working-class victory. Moreover, the slow crescendo of the marching music coupled with the very slow pull-back dolly of the camera in the truck, focusing on the partisan who becomes smaller and smaller as the vehicle drives off, creates a high level of pathos for this struggle. The other, younger prisoner represents a counterpart to the older man. In a short sequence he asks Gregor what he plans to do after the war. When Gregor does not respond, he states his conviction that the schools are the most important challenge. In other words, he points to the continuity of the political struggle into the future through the education of the young.

Counterposed to these progressive Germans who sustain the memory and hope of class solidarity are the reactionary ones who continue the war even after it has been lost. In the last episode of this segment Gregor's group encounters a Soviet guard unit waiting to be relieved of duty now that the major battles have ended. They become the surprised victims of a last, desperate ambush by German soldiers trying to escape from Berlin. Once again the camera underscores the drama with a low-angle freeze shot of a Soviet officer hit by the enemy's bullets. The battle sounds go silent, and the freeze frame dissolves into a slow motion shot of the dead officer's fall, a beautiful dancelike movement that resorts to pathos in order to memorialize the death of a comrade. The ongoing struggle against fascism will not end with the official capitulation.

The final segment maintains this distinction between the progressive and reactionary German but qualifies it in a significant way. Gregor's intelligence unit takes up its position at a farm on a hill outside Berlin, and he begins to address the soldiers fleeing along the road down below, calling on them to surrender.[19] Compared to the similar appeal in the opening sequence, his voice now sounds less editorial and more personal. Gregor's contribution to the struggle for Germany has taken on a new dimension through his exposure to a variety of situations in his putative home. He is also more successful now, for deserting soldiers stream to the farm and abandon their weapons. Once again two of the prisoners take on symbolic roles to illustrate typical attitudes. An older officer surrenders by ritually handing over his dagger, stressing in an almost comical manner a formal relationship based solely on protocol between the Germans and the Soviets. Another soldier, however, addresses Gregor as *Landsmann* (fellow countryman) when he arrives, establishing a link of national identity between the two soldiers of opposing armies. The sole German in the film to be identified by name (Willi Sommer, a very commonplace name) as well as by a distinct Berlin working-class speech pattern, he represents the proletarian Everyman. Deceived by the Nazis, associated with the guilt of having supported the war effort, Willi faces his punishment as a prisoner of war with resignation but also with a fortitude drawn from the example of Gregor:

WILLI:	To Russia, huh?
GREGOR:	Yes.
WILLI:	It'll last a couple years, huh?
GREGOR:	It won't be easy.
WILLI:	Oh well, you were already there.[20]

This is the same soldier who responds to Gregor's inquiry about why he had not given up earlier by saying "People learn slowly." Then he demonstrates that (some) Germans can learn, even if it is a tardy lesson. When an errant SS group attacks from the road, Willi grabs an automatic weapon and, to Gregor's surprise, helps him return the SS's fire. Afterward the correct German officer remarks "Germans shooting at Germans, you should be ashamed," to which Willi replies: "You can lick my German ass!"

The understated class distinction, barely alluded to here, is generalized in the closing sequence once again as the opposition of the progressive and reactionary German. Following the SS attack, Gregor discovers that Sasha has been killed by a stray bullet. Angry and stricken with grief at the death of his comrade, he grabs the microphone and in his longest speech of the entire film gives vent to his hate toward those who cannot learn: "Why can't you stop; we'll get you; we'll find you; we'll search you out; I won't forget you; I'll be right behind you." The emotional outbreak summarizes the dichotomous we/you split of the antifascist who sees the ongoing struggle even after the enemy has been defeated on the battlefield. But the shift in pronouns from "we" to "I" also marks Gregor's new-found understanding that his struggle will be in Germany together with German antifascists. Consequently, when Willi asks him to drop off a letter for him at home (*zu Hause*) in Berlin, Gregor's response confirms his acceptance of this home as well: "I will find it. For sure." Gregor's "we" is not only that of the victorious Red Army but also that of solidarity with the Germans who have learned a lesson from the experience of war. The film's last image shows the long line of prisoners marching off into the horizon. The camera travels back and up to an extreme long and high shot while Gregor's voice-over, like a parenthesis, splits off from the diegesis and shifts to the discursive level. His search is over and a new beginning is indicated: "I am a German. I was nineteen." The last shot visually reinforces the journey context, directing the spectator's attention beyond the film to the long road on which Gregor's truck bumps along slowly.

Antifascism enjoyed a high status in the East German cultural consciousness, especially among intellectuals. It was a historical discourse that focused on the class character of fascism while identifying the liberation from it almost exclusively with the Communist resistance.[21] Early antifascist films like Staudte's *Rotation* described those who were on the "wrong" side of the struggle but underwent a process of change. After realizing the innate barbarism of fascism, the hero ultimately makes the choice for peace and a new social order. Others, like Kurt Maetzig's two-part biographical film *Ernst Thälmann* (1954–55) about the leader of the German Communist Party murdered by the Nazis, filled in a gap in popular historical knowledge for the mass of Germans who knew little about the "invisible" side of the Third Reich, the organized resistance. There is no doubt that this antifascist commitment played a significant role in the reeducation and definition of a new identity undertaken in the first decade of the GDR. By 1961, when the Berlin Wall was built and the GDR borders were closed to protect its economic and political sovereignty, this model of antifascist narrative was no longer convincing for a society claiming to be socialist. For one thing, the majority of adult Germans had endured the Third Reich as a matter of survival, its capitulation as a national defeat, and the ensuing years as a continuing struggle to survive. Few film narratives addressed this side of the GDR reality, at least not until later in the eighties.[22] Furthermore, the division of Germany along geopolitical lines in the context of the cold war called for a new patriotism and a different view toward pacifism. The old models based on identificatory conversion stories or documentary evidence had exhausted their usefulness. Finally, by the mid-sixties a new generation born after 1945 and raised in the GDR no longer accepted the conventionalized heroism of the antifascist canon, which must have seemed at best self-righteous and at worst self-deceptive to them in a society increasingly defined by paranoid power politics.

Wolf was aware of these deficits; in fact, his concern was precisely to find a spectator position for the younger generation by selecting and organizing his material on the antifascist struggle from a contemporary perspective. Hence, the manner in which he establishes audience identification is crucial for the film's impact. There are several strategies he implements to solicit the spectator's activity in producing the film's meaning. First, Wolf avoids the clichés of the combat film by not emphasizing the dramatic action on the battlefield, common to the West German war film, and by not celebrating larger-than-life figures, widespread in the DEFA antifascist tradition. Wolf's characters move on the periphery of the war, and his protagonist's passivity is anything but heroic. The actor Jaecki Schwarz, who plays Gregor Hecker with great restraint, projects the kind of unsure, searching figure with whom a young audience could identify. So too the director is less interested in the facts of the war than the protagonist's subjective responses, including confusion, bewilderment, and strong emotions like hate and contempt. The autobiographical framework assumes a perceiving subject, not an active subject, and the conventions of autobiographical remembering lead the spectator to a position that parallels the filmmaker Wolf as the paradigmatic spectator of his own past and to a model for interpretative activity. Similarly, the film's documentary quality, with its "you are there" effect and black-and-white photography, reinforces the narrative's truth value by making the spectator a witness to the events. Finally, Wolf introduces young people as victims of the war who suffer the perversions of fascism.

Germany's future is the children, traumatized by the final skirmishes between the Red Army and the SS units (used by permission of Stiftung deutsche Kinemathek, Berlin).

Wolf's project was aimed at explaining to a younger generation why the historical struggle against fascism waged by his generation still implicated them. The autobiographical structure allowed him to formulate an individual's personal search for home, for Germany, into a general issue of national identity. For Wolf this was no longer the issue of the Nazis versus the Soviet liberators but rather of East versus West Germany. Gregor develops an affirmative attitude toward Germany by recognizing the historical split between an ideologically progressive and reactionary tradition. For East German ideology the national question posed a similar dilemma. While during the fifties the official party program assumed that the two German states would inevitably be reunited, after the Berlin Wall was built, this position became increasingly difficult to maintain.[23] The shared language, history, culture, and family ties between the two German states, however, at the same time provided the basis for a constant source of comparison of the two economic and political systems. Wolf's film presents a moral argument couched in politically utopian terms for distinguishing between friends and enemies based on the ideological solidarity against imperialism, represented implicitly by the West German state. Wolf establishes a specular structure that assumes a parallel between the young spectator of 1968 and his autobiographical persona. Gregor has already made a political choice for socialism and now he learns to decide who his *Landsleute* or fellow citizens are. Like Gregor, the GDR spectator is positioned to regard the personal question "who am I?" as the political question "where do I belong?"

I Was Nineteen was one of DEFA's most popular releases, especially in that period of restrictive cultural policies after 1965 when very few controversial or challenging films were released. Within eight months after its premiere (February 1968) over 2.5 million spectators saw the feature in 15,141 screenings, and Wolf, together with scenarist Wolfgang Kohlhaase and cameraman Werner Bergmann, received the GDR's National Prize (First Class) for their contribution.[24] Interestingly the public reception as much as the film itself seems in retrospect to have signaled important changes in cinema entertainment that would lead to the revitalization of film art in the GDR during the seventies (see chap. 11). Even before the film was released, concerns were voiced that the war genre had already played itself out and that this feature would therefore not reach its intended public.[25] Partially to counteract that concern but also because the filmmaker identified with this project so personally, Wolf and his team launched a major campaign to gain public attention for the film with essays, interviews, and a press kit.[26] After its release there were the predictable objections that the protagonist's passivity did not offer a strong enough appeal for identification, that the film's political message was not explicit enough, and that the German soldiers were portrayed in too sympathetic a

THE AUTHENTICITY OF AUTOBIOGRAPHY

manner. More common, however, were the many discussions generated after screenings or the letters published in newspapers that seemed to confirm Wolf's conviction that innovative narrative structures would be able to elicit the interest of the younger audience.[27] The imaginary space created by the awkward, autobiographical protagonist allows for the political as personal, affirming the subjectivity of personal experience as a utopian value. Within the cultural discourse of the GDR that tended to subordinate the individual to the general, this valorization of the private and intimate was in itself a political innovation that the cinema public appreciated.

11

Discipline and Gender:
Hermann Zschoche's *On Probation*

WOLF'S AUTOBIOGRAPHICAL FEATURE *I Was Nineteen* is symptomatic for the GDR cinema of the late sixties in the way it displaces the central conflict into a historical plot. Not until the
change of regime in the early seventies did the context for cultural activities once again provide a space for critical, topical films. Restric-
tion and censure gave way to efforts at modernization in the German Democratic Republic that acknowledged conflict potential within the society.
A willingness to accept détente with the West and economic reform was
soon coupled with assurances to intellectuals and artists that the party leadership recognized their relative autonomy both in the choice of subject matter and in formal questions.[1] Already by the end of the sixties the constraints
of the didactic model of Socialist Realism had become apparent. Films by a
young generation of filmmakers anticipated such shifts in a turn to the
everyday concerns of everyday people. The young construction worker in
Rainer Simon's *Normal People* (*Gewöhnliche Leute*, 1969), the novice resi-
dent doctor in Lothar Warneke's *Dr. med. Sommer II* (1969), or the ambulance driver in Roland Gräf's *My Dear Robinson* (*Mein lieber Robinson*,
1970), for example, are individuals who confront their (socialist) environment in a way that began to expose its limitations as a set of historically conditioned pressures. This interest in a new kind of cinematic realism was reflected in the slight upturn in audience attendance at the end of the sixties,
the first increase to be measured in years for DEFA productions.[2]

After the harsh chastisement in 1965–66, the DEFA studios were
cautious in responding to changes in cultural policy.[3] Nonetheless in the
early seventies interesting productions were released with innovative visual
effects and controversial subject matter that attracted new spectators and
raised audience expectations. *The Third* (*Der Dritte*, Egon Günther, 1972),

The Keys (*Die Schlüssel*, Egon Günther, 1973), *The Legend of Paul and Paula* (*Die Legende von Paul und Paula*, Heiner Carow, 1973), and *Life with Uwe* (*Leben mit Uwe*, Lothar Warneke, 1974), for example, addressed topical issues and moments of crisis in their protagonists' daily lives. That all of these box office successes dealt with partner relations points to the growing interest among the cinema audience in films reflecting personal conflicts rather than historical struggles. The inclusion of dream sequences and even surrealistically inspired scenes—suggesting a mix of Claude Lelouche and Ingmar Bergman as the major foreign influences rather than New German Cinema directors from the West—introduced a new dimension of visual playfulness into the GDR cinema. Moreover, the emphatic focus on an individual's self-assertion against social norms and assumptions paralleled a kind of documentary realism in establishing social context through details and gestures.

This combination of playfulness and serious questioning about the limits to self-realization in the GDR dominated artistic production in the seventies. In the cinema it brought forth a series of important "small" films, idiosyncratic contributions without strong narrative lines or traditional structure in the manner of the early French *nouvelle vague*. The reception was enthusiastic. Although cinema attendance was by the midseventies down two-thirds compared with 1950 and thus had followed the general trend in Europe, the steady decrease tapered off, and despite the competition from television programming the audience erosion during the eighties was under control.[4] Indeed, Kurt Maetzig, one of the older generation of East German filmmakers and an important functionary in the DEFA studios, could justifiably claim in 1980 that the GDR film was no longer the Cinderella of the Eastern European cinema.[5] The quality and impact of DEFA films produced in the late seventies reflected a deepening awareness of modern forms of alienation that had developed within a socialist or post-capitalist society, for example, *Sabine Wulff* (Erwin Stranka, 1978), *Seven Summer Freckles* (*Sieben Sommersprossen*, Hermann Zschoche, 1978), *All My Girls* (*Alle meine Mädchen*, Iris Gusner, 1979), *Til Death Do Us Part* (*Bis dass der Tod uns scheidet*, Heiner Carow, 1979), and *Our Short Life* (*Unser kurzes Leben*, Lothar Warneke, 1980).[6] The fact that the protagonists in all these films were strong women bears witness to a critical sensibility for the complex relation between women and society as a paradigm for representing more generally the yearning for difference and otherness in a closed society like East Germany where monotony and habit dominated the everyday.

Hermann Zschoche's 1981 film *On Probation* (*Bürgschaft für ein Jahr*) shows how the demands of a nonconforming woman disrupt social expectations. Extending a popular topos that literary and cinematic narratives had already firmly established, it opens up questions about the continuity of historically derived gender distinctions in a socialist society.[7] The first GDR "woman's film" was Egon Günther's *Lot's Woman* (*Lots Weib*, 1965) in which a young woman demands a divorce from her husband when she realizes that their loveless relationship is demeaning for them both. Many of the most successful DEFA films of the seventies went on to deal with a working and/or married woman whose experience of some kind of private crisis leads to a confrontation with authorities or with self-appointed guardians of propriety. Learning to articulate their own wishes and desires in the face of resistance from all sides, no matter how inadequate the attempt, elicits from these "heroines" doubts and inhibitions, and through visual and narrative strategies of identification the spectator is invited to accompany the protagonists in this learning process. Konrad Wolf's 1979 *Solo Sunny* was among the most influential of these films, the story of a young woman who pursues her dream of becoming a rock singer despite the professional and personal defeats she encounters. The film's combination of excellent acting, good music, and contemporary issues with a blunt insistence on the right to demand that society must also acknowledge an individual's self-interest seemed to signal in the late seventies an important ideological shift in popular entertainment films.

The focus on women who constantly experience their own vulnerability, who isolate themselves from others rather than trying to change them or themselves, is a radical reversal of the traditional positive hero in DEFA films. It also indicates an implicit revision of the orthodox Marxist view on the primacy of class oppression as the trigger of social transformations. In the most popular GDR films of the seventies the many provocative women figures are concerned not with class issues but with the fundamental experience of sexual discrimination and gender conflict in their private lives, and this experience is portrayed as normal rather than extraordinary. Moreover, by calling attention to private problems in the realm of interpersonal relationships, it became possible for filmmakers to account for negativity and failure, aspects of the "human condition" the revolutionary romanticism of Socialist Realism tended to exclude in its stress on the political struggles and triumphs in constructing the "New Man." As a result, an ideological and aesthetic space opened up for raising questions about society's responsibility toward the individual in contrast to the conventional position of seeking meaningful resolutions to narrative conflicts in the individual's integration into a harmonious utopia.

Zschoche belongs to the second generation of directors who debuted in the sixties. Typical for a DEFA career, he first completed several prizewinning children's films and then gathered together a team with whom he continued to work regularly, including cameraman Günter Jaeuthe and composer Günther Fischer. With a sharp sense for the irony of everyday banalities in the GDR, many of his feature films address problems of young people.[8] *On Probation*, however, is aimed at a more mature audience and a critique of their middlebrow values and compromises.

The protagonist, Nina Kern, is an extreme example of the kind of dramatic figure who challenges the comfortable conventions and presuppositions about human needs with which institutions rationalize their interventions in the name of social stability. A twenty-seven-year old woman, divorced from an abusive, alcoholic husband and socializing with a group of young dropouts, she has lost custody of her three young children after many warnings from child welfare agencies. At a hearing called to finalize the children's institutionalization in state-run homes, Nina argues for a last chance to prove that she can become a responsible mother. One of the lay jurors assigned to the juvenile commission is impressed by what appears to be Nina's honest remorse. She convinces her reluctant fellow juror to join her in taking on the personal responsibility of helping Nina put her life in order so that she can "prove" herself and regain custody of the children.[9] Nina's adjustment to the demands of a working mother is not without friction. During the day she is preoccupied by a menial but strenuous job. At her daughter's nursery she encounters the (female) director's disinterest and arrogance toward her daughter's special needs. The husband of a friend in her apartment building tries blackmail to solicit sexual favors. Moreover, Nina herself is not the easiest or most grateful person to help. During a wild party she forgets her daughter, who runs away, and she betrays her reliable but boring lover for a passionate but short fling with another man. Finally, there are setbacks in Nina's efforts to learn housekeeping and budgetary restraint under the tutelage of her guarantors, moments that try their patience and throw the goal of their efforts into question. The film narrative ends on a sober and ambiguous note, neither celebrating the protagonist's small victories nor minimizing the personal price she pays in the process.

The first scene sets a number of crucial formal and contextual parameters for what is to come. In a languid, almost continuous take lasting several minutes the camera pans and tracks around the anonymous room in which Nina's case is being discussed, pausing to examine the different participants as they speak or react. The slow but rhythmical alternation between the camera's movement and its static watchfulness establishes a distant, observant relation between the spectator and what is seen. In effect, this relation places the spectator in the position shared by the various commissioners, consultants, and juvenile authorities grouped around the table to deliberate the custody issue. The sequence begins in medias res as the chair of the juvenile commission calls the meeting to order with a tired voice: "Let's get started again. . . . The Kern case, pretty hopeless. . . . Loss of custody, etc., etc." The setting, the camera work, and the direct sound suggest the tradition of the reportage film, drawing on its appeal to documentary

Nina is a single mother with a menial but strenuous job washing subway cars (used by permission of Stiftung deutsche Kinemathek, Berlin).

authenticity in order to present "the Kern case" as just another of the daily proceedings, to be dealt with as quickly and as effortlessly as possible.[10]

Equally foregrounded in this narrative discourse of authenticity is Nina Kern's presence as a dramatic character who will organize the imaginary strategies for the spectator. She enters the room, clearly upset and intimidated by the situation, seats herself at the table, and listens while an off-voice reads a biographical report sketching in (for the commission and the spectator) the past history of her childhood, marriage, and later asocial behavior. The camera remains fixed on Nina, pinning her down as it slowly zooms in closer and closer on the face whose features change as she remembers the events with shame, humiliation, or anger. Nina is mute. She swallows several times in embarrassed silence and once even starts to interrupt before catching herself and slumping back in her seat. The authority's voice meanwhile is both the point of discursive origin, relating Nina's history for her, and inaccessible, spoken from a vantage point that is invisible and apparently omniscient. The disjuncture between the off-voice, invested with the authority to summarize this woman's life as an inadequate mother, and the image of the woman forced to listen to this voice, situates the narrative problematic from the outset within the context of female voicelessness in the regime of power relations and maternity.

When the (male) chair does allow Nina Kern to speak after her case has been summarized, she is inarticulate. Her (spoken) language is repetitious; her sentences are short; she hesitates frequently and can do little more than assert that she wants her children back. The chair interrupts and asks her symptomatically to speak a bit louder. Nina lacks a voice in a society that identifies speech with paternalistic authority and mastery. In a later scene this point is made explicit when Nina half jokingly asks her live-in lover Werner about an ambiguous grammatical construction. He responds by asking her what she wants to say, that is, what she *means*, and Nina answers: "That I don't feel well." Her discomfort *in* language is one consequence of her rejection of the conventional female roles of wife, parent, and (monogamous) sexual partner. Nina experiences another consequence as well: the institutional diligence in containing and managing her resistance against the coercion imposed by such a language. Nina does not articulate meaning in this language and she is therefore excluded from the symbolic power and privilege associated with speech. Yet, as the narration will elaborate, her resistance and disruptions are potentially more valuable for negotiating the everyday than the stable order of power represented by those who control language in this opening sequence.

The second scene reiterates the split between a disembodied (male) voice-off and Nina's image. Low pans and crane shots of Nina descending the staircase in the administrative building, flanked by Werner and her neighbor and family friend Mrs. Braun, are coupled on the sound track with the chair's voice-over reading the commission's final report that recommends further study of the case. The intrusion of this administrative voice on Nina's image (the sympathetic victim) animates the process of spectatorial identification that characterizes the rest of the narration. The spectator's imaginary activity becomes aligned with Nina's resistance to institutional interventions and against the disciplinary organization of everyday life in the name of normalcy and propriety. The series of loosely connected episodes that comprise the main part of the narrative present the everyday life of this working mother struggling to rehabilitate herself to the juvenile agency's satisfaction. Like Konrad Wolf, Zschoche is a careful observer with a keen eye for details rather than for heroic or dramatic conflicts. He fashions out of this laconic formal principle a space where ambiguity and ambivalence can elicit a skeptical attitude on the spectator's part.

The narrative amplifies the structural oppositions established in the introductory sequences in order to undermine an indulgent legitimation of social authority, even in the sensitive area of child neglect. Although the film does not dwell on the past history of Nina's child abuse, it in no way excuses it. Besides the details in the opening report, only one other scene refers to it, a dream montage triggered by Nina's guilt about this past.[11] Moreover, the report as well as Mrs. Braun's comments in a later scene suggest that Nina is acting out the trauma of inadequate mothering from her own childhood. The narrative, however, stresses the protagonist's will to revise the past. Like the empathetic juror Irmgard Behrendt, the spectator is positioned in the opening sequences to identify with the protagonist's decision to regain her children because she has truly understood the importance of this family bond. That from the outset her children want to return home emphasizes the conflict between social control and the private sphere. Nina's relationship to the youngest child, Mireille, is open and trusting. Her son René has a mature, protective attitude toward his mother despite the accusation of negligent parenting and, although Jacqueline has serious adjustment problems, she too yearns to rejoin her mother. The children whom the state is protecting, then, reinforce the impression that their mother has something much more valuable to offer them than the security and orderliness provided in juvenile institutions. The dilemma posed by the ambiguous ending asks to what extent individuals in this kind of society can assert their will against the power of established social agencies and historically entrenched gender prejudices.

Within the dichotomy of male speech and female voicelessness there is a whole series of behavioral characteristics associated with lack of control and subjectivity developed around Nina's character. She frequently acts impulsively, for example. After the hearing she learns that the two jurors will be "visiting" her apartment with a juvenile agency official, so she grabs a brush to paint the children's toy shelf. In her eagerness, however, she replaces the dolls and stuffed animals before the paint is dry. Similarly, she finds all sorts of hackneyed tricks to freshen up the living room so that she can impress the "guests", for example, tacking curtains with taped up hems to the sides of windows and smearing pieces of wood with black shoe polish so that they look like the coal briquets she forgot to buy for the heater. This kind of hectic behavior—conveyed with humor through quick cutting and the stark strumming of a string bass—points to an appealing personality with a touch of naiveté and a lot of warmth. Later, when Nina is reunited with Mireille, her excitable character gains a further dimension of emotional spontaneity. She weeps on embracing her daughter; she acquiesces when Mireille insists on having sandwiches for lunch, in opposition to the nursery's rule; and she plays with Mireille on her roller skates although the passers-by in the street look askance.

Nina's lack of voice, in other words, is recuperated through the portrayal of internal vitality and dynamism. Although the actress Katrin Sass does not embody the typical alluring female in her dumpy and slightly dated clothes, the positive attributes of impulsiveness and spontaneity reflect conventional gender prejudices that value women for their strong inner emotions. Nina protests the injustice to which her children are subject. She is angry when a female colleague feels she must have an abortion after her lover turns out to have deceived her about being married. She is insulted when Irmgard proposes that she give up a child for adoption. The narrative produces its momentum by positioning the spectator, on the one hand, to identify with these "human" responses as opposed to bureaucratic inflexibility and male egotism and, on the other, to anticipate her bonding within the family as a successful, nurturing mother that presupposes her ability to control such responses. This ambivalence toward the power of female emotions as a source of destabilization but also as the guardian of human passions characterizes a fundamental contradiction in the constitution of the film's imaginary relations.

Nina's emotional strength is clearly linked with qualities of interiority. Her femininity derives from a subjective plenitude or wholeness related to her maternal role, but one that she must demonstrate to the authorities. This interiority makes her dependent on and sets her off against male characters like Werner and Peter who regulate and control the bounds of the acceptable. The lovers' diametrically opposed values are exposed when Nina wants to celebrate the news that Mireille will return home for Christmas by stopping in at a bar for a drink and a snack. Werner, forever the careful and responsible partner, argues that it is wasteful to buy restaurant food when they have something at home to eat.

NINA: Do you really want to ruin my whole evening because of one mark?

WERNER: I find it irrational . . .

NINA: I want a hamburger, now. And if you keep talking like that, I'm going to chuck the whole place. On such a day!

The simplistic equation of desire with the irrational grounds Werner's conformity, as indicated in an event that takes place parallel to this exchange. Two men seated at the same table impertinently grab Nina's hamburger without a word while she is talking with Werner. Not he but the outraged Nina resists by having the waitress kick them out. Werner's inability to respond to emotions also influences his interaction with Mireille. The child's boredom with a jigsaw puzzle elicits from him, for example, the pithy moralism that "what you start, you must carry through to the end."

Lack of imagination and reliance on ritualistic responses characterize the lay juror Peter Müller as well. A family man with housebound wife and young daughter, he is appalled and upset to discover how the juvenile agency with which he is cooperating intrudes on Nina's privacy. Yet, he approaches life's more difficult challenges with the same attitude he does his professional responsibilities as a construction engineer. Problems are tasks to be mastered efficiently with principles, and he has no patience when Nina resists or fails to conform to his expectations of proper behavior. Thus, like the juvenile authorities, he applies what are no more than arbitrary rules meant to sustain socially constructed norms at the expense of individual difference. Zschoche clearly shows the limitations of such middlebrow attitudes in a scene that pits the strength of Nina's intuition against Peter's rigidity. Excited by the prospect that the two older children will be visiting, she suddenly decides to rearrange all the furniture with Peter's help. Against his advice she insists that they move the clothes cupboard to a small niche, where it ends up fitting with just a bit of leeway (*Spielraum* or, literally, space to play). Then Peter decides the bed should be moved to the corner. Nina estimates immediately that it is too large for the space, while he hops about with a tape measure, and after much commotion she is indeed right: "You forgot the leeway, didn't you?" Peter's inability to accord that space for flexibility is a fundamental flaw in his principle of efficiency and ultimately it leads him to abandon Nina mercilessly when, in a time of confusion and hurt, she gets drunk and insults him.

If the protagonist's childlike spontaneity places her in a much more favorable light than do the paternalistic stability and discipline of Werner and Peter, it is also the very source of the vulnerability that creates the obstacles to her reintegration. She is helpless, for example, when confronted by the authority of an institutional system. Irmgard has to argue for her against the arrogant director of the nursery to readmit Mireille for day care so that she can continue working. Later Nina herself confronts the director because Mireille complains, only to discover that the school's compulsive orderliness allows no room for what she considers as her child's rightful sense of privacy (the children are expected to use the toilets only at appointed times and in front of the other children). Faced with the intractability of this authority and the very real threat of losing the child care, she retreats and even excuses herself, a hard-learned lesson in the strategies of self-denial necessary for living within the arbitrary rules of power. Nina also cannot plan. She has never learned to budget money and is threatened with having her television repossessed because of missed payments, so Irmgard instructs her in a simple system of accounting for each month's expenses. Yet when Mireille fights with Peter's daughter over a doll carriage, Nina abandons the system and purchases the same expensive toy for her own child. Similarly, it is Irmgard who confronts Nina's former husband and threatens him with police reprisals if he does not pay his child support. Nina, quite to the contrary, made a practice of subsidizing her husband's drinking even after their divorce. In each case, Nina, who is intimidated by authority and overwhelmed by feelings of sympathy, has neither the emotional fortitude nor the verbal skills to defend herself.

The goal of "probation," then, is to domesticate the protagonist and to discipline her in the conventional gender role of the mother with all its attributes of dependency and self-denial.[12] The first sequence after the introduction symbolically sets this agenda. Nina unlocks her front door, enters the apartment, locks the door, goes directly to the window, and lowers the key on a string to Mrs. Braun, who lives below and will unlock her door

Nina is caught between the institutional regimentation of the day-care director and the disciplinary empathy of the court's representative (used by permission Deutsches Institut für Filmkunde, Frankfurt).

from outside the next morning. This routine, repeated two more times in the narrative, is a form of voluntary entrapment, here implicitly an acquiescence to self-confinement in the home in the name of reestablishing the maternal function. To regain that status, Nina must learn to recognize boundaries. In fact, throughout the film she is constantly reminded about the limits of acceptable behavior. The voice-off in the opening sequence already defined her earlier lifestyle as asocial, that is, beyond the norm: alcohol, promiscuity, child neglect, disorderly home. Because she revolted against domestic drudgery and asserted control over her sexuality, the juvenile authorities removed her children and placed them in state homes.

Nina conforms. She finds a job whose monotony is underscored by the way Zschoche returns briefly but repeatedly to images of her washing subway cars with the same tired gestures. She celebrates the Christmas holidays with a tree, puts her apartment in order, makes her purchases on a budget, avoids her former group of friends, and stops drinking. Despite her efforts, she suffers the disapproving looks and remarks of those around her. The visit by the social worker who must determine whether her home is in order before Mireille can return is, for example, a humiliating experience both for Nina and for the two jurors who watch as the social worker goes through the cupboards, counts the bedsheets, and examines the corners for dust. When Nina plays with Mireille, either the neighbors complain about the noise or strangers on the street make critical remarks about her "unseemly conduct." On an unannounced visit to the Müllers's apartment to seek help from Peter in resisting the sexual advances of Mrs. Braun's husband, she perceives how out of place she is in these surroundings. Peter's wife has nothing to say to her, and Nina realizes how remote her problems are from this island of familial repose when Mrs. Müller discretely removes the "good" ashtray from the coffee table so Nina does not soil it with the cigarette she is nervously smoking.

Two separate episodes underscore the obstacles to Nina's resolve to conform. Although she avoids the clique of dropouts with whom she previously identified, they literally break in upon her one evening to dance and drink. Her protests quickly subside, and she joins them. One of the young men with whom she flirted at the party returns, and she quickly falls in love with him. Heiner, unlike Werner, is able to communicate well with the children and he shares Nina's desire for adventures. Unfortunately Zschoche casts Nina in the most conventional role of the female lover who completely loses self-control to her passion. In a truly silly scene she falls on her knees after a long kiss and begs Heiner to help her because she loves him so much. The situation once again reveals how this film constructs femininity as the interiority that promises emotional intensity and plenitude (to men). At the same time, however, this interiority is premised on dependency and loss of self, the foundation for the very power relations that contain the interiority in the name of stability and the maternal function. The consequences of the fundamental ambiguity of this femininity quickly come to haunt Nina. After leaving Mireille alone to go dancing with Heiner, all of her efforts to conform come undone. Mireille awakens and, frightened at being alone, is perched to jump out the window. Werner discovers Mireille, waits for Nina to return, and then realizes that he has been betrayed. The dramatic catastrophe is complete when Irmgard and Peter arrive the next morning at Mrs. Braun's bidding and discover a dishevelled, beer-drinking Nina who can only express her contempt for everything they represent: "You were just waiting for this. So I'm drinking. I went dancing for two hours. Every night two beers in front of the TV. You can shove it! . . . I'm not drunk. I hate myself. Sometimes I admire you. Always so regular and on time. And sometimes you make me puke."

Although *On Probation* presents itself as a documentary case study, its emplotment follows more closely that of a classical drama with exposition (the introduction), complication (Mireille at home), crisis (the affair with Heiner), reversal (abandoned by Heiner), and resolution (Nina's renunciation). Because Zschoche deemphasizes the drama's continuity with his abrupt cutting and attention to small details, dramaturgical contrasts among characters rather than situations dominate the conflict. From this perspective Nina confronts a series of characters who in various degrees are determined to change her. For all of the male characters Nina represents a force that must be regulated in one way or another. The commissioner has the legal authority to judge and to discipline Nina in her role as mother. Peter Müller treats her as a "case," a systemic failure that can be rectified and function smoothly. The various men involved with Nina exploit her for their own ends: the former husband needs her money; the first lover Werner seeks the stability of a nuclear family through her; the second lover Heiner derives his sense of worth from her attention; the neighbor Mr. Braun preys on her for sex. Among the female characters the social worker and the day-care director, like the other agents of institutional power, are contemptuous and condescending toward Nina. Mrs. Braun and Mrs. Müller provide contrastive roles as resigned wife and mother, the former compromised by a pandering husband and the latter at the service of her husband.

The sole mediating figure in this constellation is Irmgard Behrendt, a middle-aged, single woman and music teacher who neither judges nor uses Nina but rather takes an interest in her as an individual. She recognizes

Nina is also caught between her divorced husband's alcoholic dependency and her lover's sexual possessiveness (used by permission of Stiftung deutsche Kinemathek, Berlin).

from the very first encounter something creative and valuable in this person. Furthermore, she initiates the idea of probation and carries through the responsibility that will permit Nina to regain custody of her children. On the one hand, there is a clear suggestion that loneliness motivates Irmgard's activities, that she sublimates an emptiness in her own life by assuming the personal responsibility for Nina. On the other, several details point specifically to Irmgard as a practicing Christian with a commitment to social values, a fact that would not have gone unnoticed by the GDR audience. When she mentions "God" in an early dialogue with Peter, for instance, he immediately asks her if she belongs to a church, and a later sequence introduces her accompanying a pastor who sings a hymn at a seniors' home.[13]

Irmgard is the only character who empathizes with Nina and even admires her, providing the main vehicle for critical audience identification with the protagonist. In one episode she agrees to baby-sit Mireille for an afternoon and must confront the harsh reality of child care firsthand: the disinterest on the part of adults toward the child in a crowded public bus, the tiresome games the child plays to get what she wants, the energy necessary to supervise and occupy the child constantly. Irmgard realizes by observing Nina that her will power and vitality are admirable qualities to be nourished. Thus, it is no accident that, following Nina's outburst, the camera cuts to a scene in which a talented music pupil tells the disappointed Irmgard that on his father's advice he has decided to pursue soccer rather than to become a concert pianist because it promises easier success. And slightly later Irmgard watches the way Nina coaxes the tired Mireille to walk home by pretending they are jumping over their shadows. In a brief moment of abandon Irmgard too tries "jumping over her shadow," but quickly catches herself, looks around to see if anyone was watching, and continues on her way after straightening her hair.

The understated visual metaphor restates concisely the issue at stake in Zschoche's film: the need for society to learn to tolerate the emancipatory power of desire, even when it undermines society's rules. Nina's voicelessness, her feminine interiority is the counterpart to her ability to transgress boundaries. As she herself warns Irmgard in another context, this is a quality she shares with children: they too know no boundaries! In a sense, then, Nina's socialization as a mother recapitulates the process of growing up: learning to respect limits, to accept responsibility, and to deny the self. The problem for Nina as well as for the textually inscribed spectator is to channel the imaginary power of transgression into a tolerable mode of existence, one that allows for or even sustains the contradiction between an individual's sensitivities and a society's tendency to preserve the system. By the end of the narrative, however, Nina has failed. Contrary to many of the seventies films featuring strong female protagonists, Zschoche's heroine surrenders, abandoning the dream of a family and resigning herself to isolation. When she and her children encounter Irmgard several months later in the penultimate sequence, Nina jokes to her that they are a "real family, only without a man." The import of defeat admits a serious betrayal, for she confides to Irmgard that she will keep only two of the children, giving up Jacqueline for adoption. Yet, when Jacqueline asks her mother in the brief last sequence whether she will be fetching them home soon, Nina assents with a slight nod, and the image freezes on a close-up of her sad, lifeless face. The narrative closure of the freeze frame confirms the irreducible disparity between desire and reality on Nina's part, while its suggestion of provisionality returns the spectator to the documentary fiction of the case study that continues beyond the moment frozen in time.

At the end of the film Nina has lost the self-assurance that her claims to desire and independence are legitimate. Zschoche, however, constructs the narration in such a way that the spectator perceives this defeat and her betrayal of Jacqueline as a challenge aimed against a system of coherence that denies individual self-realization. The series of contrasts between the protagonist and her opposites substantiates the gulf separating the state's or society's investment in its power and the spectator's identification with the protagonist's vitality. By formulating the manifestations of this

The final image is a freeze frame of the troubled Jacqueline, whom Nina has decided to give up for adoption (used by permission of Stiftung deutsche Kinemathek, Berlin).

power as constructions, as arbitrary and reversible, Zschoche invites the spectator to imagine other possibilities beyond the provisional freeze frame. The state's paternalistic sovereignty, the hierarchy of public and private concerns, and issues of socialization within the GDR become the object and the problem of the film's imaginary operation. More specifically, the film locates the problem in the way social structures were being lived on a daily basis in the GDR. The early integration of women into the labor force as well as extensive legal protection of women's equality exacerbated contradictions between the rhetoric of the (nuclear) family and protectionist social policies for children.[14]

Although On Probation is not strikingly sophisticated in its technical craft, it does expose the complexity of these contradictions by thematizing female excess in a positive way and ironically playing on familiar images or situations in the GDR everyday. This may account for some professional critics' unenthusiastic response to the film who cited the reductionism and caricature used for characterizing many of the secondary figures. Just as frequent was the concern with the valorization of a social outsider through the figure of Nina with her absolutist demands.[15] Such criticism reflects a position with a longstanding tradition in Socialist Realism that directly relates a hero's positive traits to the moral impact on the spectator rather than focusing on the imaginary activity textually inscribed in a film. Beyond that, however, it is possible to trace in films produced by DEFA around this time a growing interest in socially marginal characters. Young dropouts or rock singers move in the small pockets of subcultural life; they live in run-down apartments and frequent the bar scene; their nonconformist demands on the system are presented as understandable and valid. This paradigm change in Marxist aesthetics shifts the notion of typicality from a perspective at the center to one at the margin of society. No longer derived from a model of social harmony that restricts otherness to political or class identification, it becomes instead a category that stresses the otherness of gender, age, profession, and lived experience in order to test the boundaries of the imaginary within an increasingly stagnant, oppressive society. On Probation contributed to the process of negotiating this change from an affirmative aesthetics of the acceptable to representations of difference by positing the present as the negative pole in a historical evolution aimed at the not-yet-achieved.

An additional aspect of marginality, and one that throws a somewhat different light on its value in enunciating an imaginary position for the spectator, inflects the gender relations upon which this marginality builds. Nina is marginal not only because of her prior asocial behavior toward the children but also and primarily because she is a woman. Zschoche, like his other male colleagues at DEFA responsible for the remarkable series of "women's films," instrumentalizes the female protagonist as the site of discursive representation. He constructs a rigid binary opposition along the terms of silence and voice, interiority and exteriority, emotional excess and denial, indulgence and entrapment, spontaneity and stability, private and public, in which the female figure is identified with the first field. This offers the opportunity for presenting and analyzing contradiction, but it also erases the potentially more interesting, hypothetical area between the opposing terms. Hence, the director does not fall into the practice of transforming his protagonist into an object of desire and visual pleasure in order to arrest her in a passive role, as was the case in *To New Shores* and *Black Forest Girl.* Instead he thematizes the arbitrary, constructed nature of external authority as opposed to a more valuable psychic reality anchored within femininity. Yet, Zschoche is still bound to an essentialist tradition of gender representation that posits the feminine beyond the realm of historically constructed and situated fictions.

Undoubtedly this can be related to the lack of an alternative cinema and of strong women directors in the GDR. As in other socialist countries, film production was exclusively a state-controlled enterprise until 1990, and there existed no facilities for producing or exhibiting independent film projects. Substantial but almost invisible involvement by women in the film industry was to be found among scriptwriters, many of whom gained entry through prior literary activity. Although the Babelsberg film academy enrolled almost equal numbers of male and female students in the eighties, many of the women found employment in traditional female occupations (editing, design, etc.). Those women who completed their studies in the field of feature film directing usually were channeled into television or children's film production.[16] The few exceptions—documentarists Gitta Nickel and Helke Misselwitz and directors Iris Gusner and Evelyn Schmidt— did not address questions concerning gender images, the gaze, and the hierarchy of vision that have dominated the feminist and women's films in the West. Rather they remained within a more traditional framework of issues like (single) motherhood and (failed) marriages. Even until the collapse of the GDR they shared with male colleagues like Zschoche an interest in formulating imaginary positions so that spectators register perturbations or spaces of resistance in the dominant order. Within this framework a protagonist like Nina Kern, even if burdened by traditional gender attributes, offers a position of female agency and perspectival knowledge that qualify manifestations of institutionalized power.

Part 5

The New German Cinema

12

Beyond Spectacle: Alexander Kluge's
Artists under the Big Top: Perplexed

HE FIFTIES IN West Germany began in 1948 with the Currency Reform and ended in 1962 with the first crisis. When high government
officials were found personally responsible for unconstitutional
searches in the offices of the country's leading news magazine *Der
Spiegel*, it shook confidence in the Federal Republic's democratic structures and led during the sixties to a fundamental political realignment in
the governing institutions.[1] The postwar period of restoration with its combination of political conservatism, economic vitality, and blind forgetting
of the past was over. The year 1962 also marked a watershed in West German cinema culture. That year a group of frustrated young cinephiles and
filmmakers presented at the Oberhausen Film Festival a manifesto articulating their desire and commitment to liberate the West German film from
the industry's conventions and commercialism. The coincidence of these
two events is not as arbitrary as it might seem. The political culture of the
fifties gave rise to state-supported film policies such as subsidies and prizes
in order to ensure that false traditions continued and that new beginnings
were discredited (see chap. 9, n. 4). The fact that no new wave cinema or
group of young filmmakers had been able to assert itself in postwar West
Germany, as was the case in Italy, France, England, Poland, Czechoslovakia, and even to some extent in East Germany's DEFA studios, was only the
most visible effect of these policies. Beyond this the film industry itself was
facing a serious crisis by the early sixties. Having reached prewar production levels already by 1953, production peaked in 1958 with 115 features,
even though the smaller, postwar market was estimated to absorb no more
than 80–90 films a year. Two years later the number of tickets sold was on
the decline, and fiscal year 1961 showed a dramatic decrease in both productions and earnings.[2]

The film industry's response was to continue on the path of least resistance, pursuing a policy of compromise in the interest of light entertainment, while government agencies advocated their conception of film as a mass medium subject to social taboos and restrictions. As a result the extension of UFA and Hollywood styles into the fifties gave way in the sixties to the widespread copying of foreign genres which were increasingly competing with German fare: the Edgar Wallace series of detective films, the German westerns based on novels by Karl May, family entertainment featuring popular stars (e.g., Heintje or Freddy), and later in the sixties soft pornography.[3] Rigorous escapism and infantilism were the common denominator, a trend that could hardly turn around the deteriorating financial situation of commercial producers or attract young filmmakers with alternative visions.

The economic indicators were providing signals of an impending disaster. The West German cinema, which had evolved as a distributor dominated industry during the fifties, experienced in 1961 the collapse of five major domestic distributors, leaving only three others—one fused with an American company—to divide up the market. Not surprisingly, foreign produced features filled the screens, especially American movies. Concurrently cinemas were closing at an alarming rate, their numbers dropping from 7,085 in 1959 to less than half that in 1971 (3,314), and those remaining were concentrated in the larger urban centers. Finally, ticket sales slipped from a peak of 817.5 million in 1956 to 161.4 million in 1971, and as a result the number of movies seen per person each year dropped from a high of 15.6 in 1956 to 2.6 in 1971.[4] Of course, this tendency was apparent in all European common market countries. The expansion of television programming in the course of the sixties coupled with changing consumer patterns (travel, car ownership, improved housing) led to more differentiated use of leisure time. Not only were movies no longer the favored form of entertainment, but the group most regularly frequenting them was shifting from the middle-aged to the younger, so that the cinema was quickly becoming a mainstay of youth culture.[5] Unlike other European countries, however, West Germany had no serious cinema culture to counteract the pull of the commercial media and their homogenization. The indigenous art film tradition had been interrupted by the war, and the most rudimentary institutional facilities—a film academy for training young professionals, a cinematheque, archives, and a serious film journal—were nonexistent.

The Oberhausen Manifesto of 1962 was an optimistic document with its conviction that a "new film" would be created.[6] Claiming that "Papas Kino ist tot!" [Daddy's cinema is dead], the twenty-six signatories described less a coherent group with a program than a generational cleavage in which a young guard was demanding access to the means of production. The sentimental image of a family struggle in which the sons usurp the fathers resonates with tensions of the postwar German family, but the patricidal gesture also indicates how naive the signatories were about the relation between the film industry's structures and their demands for renewal. The total absence of any professional or union organizations as well as of a marketing strategy for an alternative film culture would seem virtually to have condemned the Oberhausen protesters to failure.

Their stagy performance nonetheless hit a nerve. In the first half of the sixties a cultural ferment was beginning that touched not only the cinema but also the established theater (documentary drama), literary discussions (political writing), and the universities (Critical Theory). After the abstinence of the fifties the amnesia about the Holocaust showed signs of subsiding, if for no other reason than the first large-scale court trials of concentration camp commanders from Auschwitz and Maidanek commenced (1963–65). A gap opened between the younger generation's demand for answers and the older generation's need for stability, and it widened with the radicalization of young people through the Vietnam War protests later in the sixties. At the same time the onset of the Grand Coalition—an alliance between West Germany's two major center and left-of-center parties that dominated parliamentary politics from 1966 to 1969—shifted the opposition to the margins, beyond the traditional political and cultural institutions.[7]

In this context the Oberhausen Manifesto found a sympathetic audience. With skillful lobbying in government agencies, much of it under the guidance of Alexander Kluge, the ministry of the interior announced the formation of the "Kuratorium junger deutscher Film" on February 1, 1965, a commission composed of government functionaries, church representatives, and film critics that would distribute production subsidies in the form of loans to young directors with artistic ambitions. In addition, state funding was provided for two film academies in Berlin and Munich and for an archive in Berlin (Stiftung Deutsche Kinemathek). Meanwhile, other nongovernmental initiatives were meeting with success. The journal *Filmkritik*, founded in 1960 as a German counterpart to the Parisian *Cahiers du cinéma* and one of the rallying points for the Oberhausen Manifesto supporters, was making progress not only in fostering a group of critical film journalists but also in generating a broader interest in art and new wave cinema. In 1963 the Arsenal Kino opened in Berlin and slightly later the Kino im Stadtmuseum in Munich, two program cinemas modeled on the Paris Cinémathèque. During the next ten years many municipalities began to support Kommunale Kinos or cinemas under community patronage that sponsored screenings of noncommercial films and specifically of young German directors. In 1966, forty-two production firms of young directors formed a collective (Arbeitsgemeinschaft neuer deutscher Spielfilmproduzenten) to gain more influence in bargaining for their interests. This was followed in 1970 by the Syndikat der Filmemacher, representing some

300 television and film directors, and the Filmverlag der Autoren, a collectively owned distributor for films by young directors. Thus, by the end of the decade it was possible to speak of a new wave German cinema, the Young German Film, with funding sources, its own organizations, and a skeletal network for distribution and exhibition.

Despite the real struggles and obstacles faced by an alternative film culture in West Germany, the unspoken strategy of establishing a decentralized, subversive, and oppositional cinema remained intact. Yet when the first new wave feature-length films finally began to appear in 1966, it became clear that this was not a collective undertaking. What the Young German Filmmakers shared was less a subject, style, or even tone than the impoverished conditions of production and a common rejection of the routine and conformity endemic to the film industry. Small budgets, on location filming, direct sound, and nonprofessional actors were not symptoms of a systematic attack on the commercial cinema but rather the compromises of underfunding. More than anything, however, the Young German Filmmakers were committed to the *Autorenfilm* or *auteur* cinema, that is, to a notion derived from literature that emphasizes the individual filmmaker's freedom and responsibility for all aspects of production.[8] Beyond that there were few domestic models to whom they could look for guidance. The "problem" films by Georg Tressler (*The Hooligans* [*Die Halbstarken*], 1956) and Ottmar Domnick (*Jonas*, 1957), which critically addressed the repressive atmosphere of the fifties; Bernhard Wicki's antiwar film *The Bridge* (*Die Brücke*, 1959); and Will Tremper's political thriller *Escape to Berlin* (*Flucht nach Berlin*, 1961) reflected neither the rigor nor the formal originality the young filmmakers found so inspiring in the French *nouvelle vague*, the Brazilian *Cinema Nôvo*, or the British Free Cinema.

The Oberhausen Manifesto had accomplished to a large extent what it set out to do. Young German directors began to win prizes at international film festivals in Cannes and Venice in 1966; in 1967 a new debut film a month was being released in Germany, Paris cinephiles were taking note, and the Mannheim Film Festival showcased the Young German Film; *Der Spiegel* featured a cover story on the Young German Film in its last issue of 1967, and the autonomous but state-funded Goethe Institute began circulating a package of fifteen feature films by young directors that traveled successfully to London, Prague, Rome, and Paris. By this point the German cinema had seen more directorial debuts than during all the previous postwar years, and as many as 50 percent of West Germany's films were being produced outside the commercial industry.[9] Although the film industry continued to turn out its own brand of entertainment, effectively excluding art films from commercial distribution in West German cinemas, and although the Oberhausen model underwent numerous setbacks and changes owing to industry competition and government meddling, what matured into the internationally celebrated New German Cinema of the seventies traces its origins to that first awkward conviction in the possibility of creating a new film.

Alexander Kluge was one of the prime movers in organizing alternative conditions of production and reception for the West German cinema. Having studied history and music and completed a doctorate in law in 1956, he gained his first studio experience as an apprentice to Fritz Lang, who had returned to Berlin to film his two-part Indian epic in the late fifties. Kluge began making experimental short films in the early sixties, a form he has consistently cultivated, but he launched his public career first as a prizewinning author of documentary fiction.[10] Together with Edgar Reitz and Detten Schleiermacher (also Oberhausen signatories) he established and directed the film department at the Hochschule für Gestaltung in Ulm, a short-lived heir to the Bauhaus school of the twenties.[11] When in 1966 Kluge's first feature-length film, *Yesterday Girl* (*Abschied von gestern*), was released, it was considered the first important Young German Film. Like Jean-Marie Straub's *Not Reconciled* (*Nicht versöhnt*, 1965) and Hans-Jürgen Pohland's *Cat and Mouse* (*Katz und Maus*, 1967), it addresses the legacy of the fascist past in the present. The title (literally, farewell to yesterday) is typical for Kluge's irony in a film that observes how the indelible traces of "yesterday" pursue a young woman who resists but ultimately resigns to the social strictures of West German society. Moreover, the film's intertextual montage—a mixture of documentary sequences, improvisations, interviews, historical references, and fictional scenes accompanied by written titles, voice-over commentaries, and musical quotes—would become his signature style in an oeuvre that stands out for its idiosyncrasy and commitment to freeing the cinema from conventional modes of film expression.[12]

Kluge's second film, *Artists under the Big Top: Perplexed* (*Die Artisten in der Zirkuskuppel: ratlos*, 1968) was even less coherent than his previous feature and hence more controversial because of the international acclaim it received.[13] A parable about the artist's struggle to combine theory and practice, to protect the work of the imagination against economic exigency, it is at one and the same time the story of an unsuccessful circus entrepreneur and an allegory of Kluge's trajectory from the art of the written word to that of the image. Frustrated by the political and aesthetic dogmatism of the emerging student Left, with his film essay he was attempting to defend the social function of (cinema) art as utopian design against the impasse of traditional cultural forms in post-Holocaust society. The episodic story concerns Leni Peickert, a young circus artist who plans a "reform circus" as a monument to her father who died while performing on the high trapeze. Three times she sets out to accomplish her goal and each time she learns a new lesson about the vicissitudes of art in a media-dominated, capitalist society. She finally abandons her project of reforming the circus in order to protect her utopian dream and takes a job at a public television studio as an interim solution while awaiting the changes she envisions.

This rather simplistic, even fairy-tale-like plot with its didactic presentation of the protagonist's struggle belies the textual heterogeneity and structural fragmentation that characterize its form. Causality and the relation of the parts to the whole no longer depend on mimetic representation but rather on a highly developed sense of playful contrast and association. Neither is the eccentric protagonist a strong presence or vehicle of spectator identification but rather a means of connecting disparate parts. The film breaks with formulas of illusionistic narrative and melodramatic subject positioning that dominated the German cinema since the Weimar period. In fact, it is no accident that the look and texture of Kluge's film bear resemblance to the 1932 *Kuhle Wampe* film by Dudov and Brecht, that collective project whose dialectic of political form and social content was a radical revision of representational realism under the pressure of new forms for the reproduction of reality (see chap. 3). Not only does Kluge consciously look back to the silent cinema as an alternative to bourgeois forms of high culture (very early he claimed to make silent films with sound!) but he could be characterized as the most consistent heir in Germany to Brecht's reflections on film aesthetics and the commodification of art in capitalism.[14] Both are concerned with subverting the status of the image as an autonomous, consumable reflection of reality in order to reanimate the relation between production and reception as an active, cognitive process in the spectator's imagination.

The most striking quality of *Artists under the Big Top: Perplexed* is its dispersed, discontinuous editing. The use of all available cinematic means—image, dialogue, voice-over, music, noise, silence, printed titles, portrait photos, trick shots—suggests a relativity of word and image: both are necessary for the narrative rationale but they are not redundant. Kluge's laconic logic undermines the illusionism of the commercial cinema but reveals in turn a strong sensuousness. Often motivated by intensely emotional music, the linking of associations creates a web of memory meant to provoke the spectator into a more active participation in constructing the film. Corresponding to this emphasis on the imaginary work of the spectator, and this is a second striking quality of the film, is its reinscription of visual pleasure. Although thematizing exhibitionism and visibility through the focus on the circus, Kluge undermines the visual opulence characteristic of the commercial cinema with a restrained camera, ascetic images, intentionally mismatched shots, or disjuncture of image and sound. The narrational fragmentation also interrupts the traditional specular unity of the viewer. The female protagonist, as in many Kluge films, provokes disruption because she refuses to discredit any experience. This wise "fool's" innocence promotes identification only insofar as her desire to learn is a position of strength offered to the spectator as a behavioral model. Kluge's belief that aesthetic perfection and synthetic totality exclude the role of the spectator motivates his practice of filmmaking as much as it does Leni Peickert's efforts to reform the circus.[15] The domestication of human fantasy through narrative illusion and consumerist attitudes operates in both through mechanisms of fascination. The allegorical circus as well as the film itself demonstrate how the leap into imaginary space might break down the conventions of spectator absorption that such mechanisms motivate. Thus, *Artists* intentionally resists both Hollywood allure and televisual directness, describing instead the imaginary, utopian space yet to be occupied by the spectator.

Despite the film's opaque coding it is possible to outline a schematic formal structure. The protagonist's professional concerns and her reflections on the possibility of their success can be clustered into four groups (sequences 6–12, 16–29, 36–46, 56–63) set off by interludes or connecting links (sequences 13–15, 30–35, 47–55) and framed by a prologue and an epilogue (sequences 0–5, 64–67).[16] The prologue provides a para-

The circus motif thematizes exhibitionism and visibility, but the restrained camera and ascetic images undermine visual opulence (used by permission of Stiftung deutsche Kinemathek, Berlin).

Leni Peickert dreams of a "reform circus" that escapes the commodification of art in a media-oriented, consumer society (used by permission of Stiftung deutsche Kinemathek, Berlin).

digmatic example of how Kluge organizes his dramaturgy according to a disorienting puzzle method and at the same time it introduces the various meaning fields that will resurface throughout the film.

The first sequence (0) consists of four elements: the introduction of the film's protagonist by means of a frontal portrait shot of actress Hannelore Hoger, a musical motif from Verdi's opera about betrayed love, *Il Trovatore*, played on a harmonium, Hoger's voice-over reading a text, and the film credits followed by two printed texts, the last being the film title itself. The "perplexed" of this title might well describe the spectator's attitude after the short introduction in which none of the elements "fit" together. Yet spectatorial curiosity, conditioned by conventions of narrative cinema, will immediately begin to seek connections between that which is seen, heard, and read. The recited text, contrasted with the image of the actress, describes a male look: "I saw in her eyes a tenderness that I recognized immediately as love. So I held her body tight in my arms and kissed her genitals like in earlier times." The camera then cuts to a printed text ("They worked their way up to here. Now they don't know what to do. Simply exerting oneself is useless.") and then to the film title. The helplessness expressed in the first printed text points in two directions, toward the (male) desire described by the (female) voice-over and toward the film title's circus artists under the big top. Both are confronted with a blockage: the actress trapped in the sexual economy of the patriarchal gaze and the artist constrained by tradition. Yet, just like the interrogative attitude of the spectator that constantly produces and tests possible meanings, the cinema machine continues to yield a string of sounds and images. In other words, the fundamental principle of construction is here inscribed in the spectator positioning: the combination of image, voice, music, and text does not produce fixed meaning but questions about meaning, stressing textual enunciation and discursive activity on the spectator's part.

The following three sequences in the prologue take up other blockages and provide them a name as the dominant meaning field: the work of mourning or *Trauerarbeit*. The "inability to mourn" is a concept introduced in the midsixties specifically in the context of the apparent blockage on the part of Germans to face the issue of complicity in crimes against humanity perpetrated in their name during the Third Reich.[17] Derived from psychoanalysis but shifted onto the plane of collective sociopsychology, it refers to the painful emotional process of working through loss owing to separation, a process not so much of forgetting the lost object as recombining memories of it in the present. The film's first example of *Trauerarbeit* refers to this historical dimension of loss (sequence 1). Documentary footage of "The Day of German Art" (unidentified for the spectator), a gala parade in 1939 celebrating fascist art, shows Hitler and his entourage reviewing troops and watching a procession of historically costumed figures and larger than life monumental statues. The background music, consisting of an especially maudlin rendition of the Beatles song "Yesterday," which cuts to the rich tonality of a duet from *Il Trovatore*, "derealizes" the pomp of the documentary sequence and the cultural revolution for which it stands. The camera cuts abruptly to a fast motion traveling shot of a snow-covered plain (Battle of Stalingrad) while a female voice-over comments: "He [Hitler] was such fun, for the big and for the small. Millions laughed at him. Who will weep for him now?" Here the pain associated with memory, in particular with that of the Third Reich, issues from a catastrophe and a rupture that has not been worked through. The combination of iconic Nazi images, of the vacant and "chilly" landscape of German defeat, of sentimentalized popular music, and the tragic vengeance quoted by the opera suggests a relation through the associations that refer to this past.

The second example of *Trauerarbeit* in sequence 2 concerns Manfred Peickert, who will only later be identified as the protagonist's father. A trapeze artist, he pursues restless dreams of something completely new and different in the circus, for example, raising elephants with a balloon to the top of the tent where they can dance. The following series of circus act shots are accompanied variously by off-voices explaining how famous circus artists were killed while performing their acts: victims of art who will be mourned. The camera then returns to Manfred and to his trapeze act as an off-voice tells how, one day seized by melancholy, he too falls to his death. The film stock switches to black and white (up to this point the second sequence describing Manfred's utopian circus was in color), and a hand-held camera tilts down in the jerky motion of a fall until there is an abrupt cut to a bird's-eye shot of what gradually can be made out as a coffin in state. Printed titles (citations from Schiller, Hegel, Nietzsche), music (a Schumann piano excerpt, a tango, and a circus overture), and old prints sustain the multivocality that characterized the first sequence. Manfred's artistry, like that of the other circus acts shown, is committed to innovation and perfection, to an Enlightenment heritage related to the goals of the French Revolution that idealized man's domination over nature.[18] The valorization of performance becomes a pure abstraction in his dream of "something entirely new" that can elicit "a new feeling," and its logical consequence is potential self-destruction since success is measured by the audience's heightened expectation of risks and accidents. Manfred's melancholy, the cause of his death, results from the awareness of this unresolvable tension. The rupture of the father/daughter relation through his death motivates the work of mourning which Leni's "reform circus" represents.

The final example of *Trauerarbeit* points directly to Manfred's aesthetic idealism. In the briefest of the first sequences (sequence 3) a series of historical illustrations—their very materiality connoting pastness and loss—shows, among other things, old circuses, a hot air balloon, and a crashed airplane. The montage is framed by two fast motion shots of circus tents being dismantled at night and horses being loaded in trucks while the male off-voice repeats the printed text of sequence 0, now with a slight shift in tense: "They had worked their way up to here. Now they didn't know what to do. Simply exerting oneself is useless." Anticipating Leni Peickert's attempts to renew the circus, the sequence draws the consequences from the ambivalence attributed to the circus's history (as well as that of German idealism) but also suggests in the slightly altered repetition the possibility of removing the blockage. The circus's consistent reversal of all natural characteristics in the animal kingdom as a proof of human omnipotence with its ancillary pathos of freedom is doomed to failure. Leni Peickert, the artist Kluge's alter ego, is introduced immediately in the next sequence as Manfred Peickert's heir, and she will mourn her father by trying to reformulate his utopia of a new and better circus.

Unlike the postwar Germans who repress the past and unlike Manfred Peickert who idealized the past, Leni will not ignore its perversions and their relevance for the present in her *Trauerarbeit*. Her efforts, however, will come up against historically conditioned limitations. Thus, se-

Portrait images of Napoleon belong to the "meaning field" related to the Enlightenment, the French Revolution, and the notion of dominating nature (used by permission of Stiftung deutsche Kinemathek, Berlin).

quence 4 begins, typically, with a blockage to her forward movement: her car has broken down, and she is awkwardly trying to change a tire. A frontal shot of Leni with a supplicating look in her eyes gives way to a reverse shot and a fast, 180° pan of the passive onlookers watching her but offering no help. These are the skeptical spectators waiting for something to happen, those who in an extended sense will define the limits of her activity as a circus entrepreneur and no less Kluge's textually inscribed spectators. They embody the specular relations of voyeurism with which any performance art, including the cinema, must reckon.

Sequence 5, the prologue's last and the film's most complicated, disorienting sequence, addresses the problematic relation of memory and loss through the trope of elephantine memory. Once again images not rationalized by narrative linearity are interwoven and repeated in a seductive textual rhythm: four excerpts from Sergei Eisenstein's silent film *October* about the Russian Revolution, close-up shots of elephants, shots of elephant acts, and a pan around circus tents and clouds, a night scene, a picture of Napoleon. The soundtrack too continues to mingle voice-over commentary, silence, and familiar music quotes in no obvious synchrony with these images. The modulation between a dramatic story about a circus fire, a passage from Hegel's *Phenomenology of the Mind* concerning human freedom, and the refrainlike repetitions of the phrases "we must not forget" and "sink into the sea" are linked to the already established meaning fields of the catastrophic fascist past, the perversion of German idealism in Nazi culture, and the work of memory. Meanwhile the sensory overload reproduces that perplexity apostrophized in the title while figuring it as a problem of remembering. Even an attentive spectator can no longer comprehend the individual details in the soundtrack's simultaneous layering, for example, of a tango, the spoken description of the circus fire described from the perspective of the elephants, and the altered text of a traditional Christmas carol. Having scrambled many of the cinematic codes of representation, Kluge can at this point begin to reconstruct a story that no longer seeks its unity in plot, character, and motivation but in the production of experience by the spectator who is willing to engage the film's structural challenge and sensuous associations. Seeking correspondences in its improvisations is the imaginary activity that the film insists can be learned.

The film's apparent inaccessibility and the lack of certainty or determinations is a crucial factor in Kluge's aesthetics because in his view the *process* of perception drives understanding and communication. The spectator who perceives correspondences, visual associations, links between sensuous stimuli, also perceives the constructedness of reality and the possibility to modify it. This effort to upset conventional patterns of specular activity in order to redefine the spectator's imaginary relation to the real constitutes both the structure and theme of *Artists under the Big Top: Perplexed*. Animal domestication—a repeated motif in Kluge's films—is the filmmaker's allegorical representation of the spectator's willingness to be guided by habits of seeing. Hence, the film's fragmented form intends not to sow confusion but to undo those habits. For Kluge the ideal spectator watches carefully and seeks a pragmatic position for putting together the pieces. The regular use of the voice-over is a case in point. Three different speakers, male and female, pronounce the texts at random, unidentified with any particular point of view. Sometimes the voice-off explains an image or provides a transition, more frequently it develops its own train of thought in contrast to the image.

The introduction of Manfred Peickert in sequence 2 exemplifies the disjuncture of voice and image. A disembodied male voice explains: "Manfred Peickert is an artist. He has plans." Then a different voice, that of the Peickert actor (Siegfried Graue), relates a dialogue between him and his circus director as the frozen, frontal portrait shot of Peickert begins to move. In a later shot Graue's voice is not synchronized with his lip move-ments until midway into the monologue. This voice-over no longer draws on the documentary principle of the authoritative off-voice invested with knowledge about reality. There is no unity between voice and meaning or voice and character that can disclose a position for the spectator from which to "master" the real and identify with the situation. The "aural" point of view asserts its independence as a position outside the story, sub-verting the redundant bond between eye and ear exploited by the com-mercial cinema and cultivating both the spectator and the protagonist as careful listeners.[19] Moreover, this disembodied authorial narrator never tells a story but rather quotes the gesture of storytelling. The voices' soft tim-bre and cautious intonations emphasize in their very naiveté the awareness that simple storytelling simplifies reality. Finally, the long takes of frontal portrait shots with an actor staring at the spectator set the voice against the power of the frontal look to make the spectator self-conscious as the person being addressed.

Music functions in a related way as a means of disrupting the uni-fied discourse of conventional narrative cinema.[20] Kluge uses exclusively nonfilmic music in the form of quotations in order to comment on the im-ages: circus music, a tango, a hit song, a Christmas song, the International, a Strauss waltz, classical music by Chopin, Mozart, Mendelssohn, and ex-cerpts from a Verdi opera. Musically poetic sounds may contrast with doc-umentary images, creating a dialogue, as in sequence 1 where the newsreel footage from the Third Reich forms a counterpoint to the Beatles' senti-mental song about memory, "Yesterday." That it is sung in Spanish only un-derscores the effort to quote the past while drawing attention to the strate-gies used to forget it. In sequence 23 the music provides an ironic commentary and an anticipatory warning. A pianist sings from act 1, scene 1 of *Il Trovatore* the aria "Be careful!" just when Leni is beginning to build her circus enterprise. As with all quotes in the film—images, texts, or sounds—they are catalysts for associations that are to be produced by the spectator. The film text's incompleteness is the foundation for Kluge's genre of the film essay as construction site.[21] It invites the spectator to initi-ate a dialogue by constructing a point of view from the parts offered, or more precisely, by filling in the spaces or gaps between the parts. Unlike *Kuhle Wampe*, the aim here is neither to persuade nor to convince but rather to begin a process of imagining that cannot yet be represented. As the failure of the reform circus demonstrates, before new forms of artistic production (including the *Autorenfilm*) can develop, the spectator must be willing to engage the medium's discourse and its imaginary operations.

If Leni Peickert's effort to create a reform circus is an allegory for Kluge's struggle to make films, its implications go beyond the dilemma of the Young German Film in 1968. Indeed, Leni's efforts and failures can be read as Kluge's general critique of the historical possibilities for the artist in an industrialized, consumer-oriented society. Leni begins by adopting her father's model. Out of love for "his" circus she trains as a trapeze artist, only to realize that the circus must be more than a mere museum or monument to past achievements. She becomes a circus entrepreneur committed to "realism" rather than sensational spectacle, despite the skepticism she encounters on the part of traditionalists ("Circus animals are only authentic in the jungle," sequence 9). Faced with the constraints of the capitalist market, Leni approaches a Soviet manager for help, but the "socialist" circus cannot afford material solidarity and is organized in any case on formal principles similar to the circus in capitalism. To earn money she signs a contract with a television circus, only to discover that illusion is more important than art in the most advanced electronic media. Similarly, her audition for an overseas troop show (a Hollywood quote) reveals how entertainment is business for profit. Unwilling to abandon her project, Leni changes her strategy, embraces the idea that circus art too is a commodity (rather than a matter of love), and obtains bank loans to finance the undertaking. When her creditors repossess the circus animals to cover unpaid bills, she declares bankruptcy. Leni has to admit that her love for the circus and her commitment to changing its voyeuristic sensationalism and illusionism is not worth the price of its spontaneity and relevance to everyday life. In an allusion to his intellectual debt to Frankfurt School philosophy, Kluge has Leni inherit a large sum of money from a scholarly institute in Frankfurt, allowing her the financial security to build a circus without compromising her aesthetics.[22] The series of acts she develops (sequence 46) include playful, abstract, and sensuous ones, a combination of art as well as subversive politics. Leni must soon acknowledge, however, that the reform circus she envisions is a utopia for which no audience yet exists. She liquidates her holdings and decides that it is more important to struggle against the real obstacles in life than to pursue a dream in the abstract: "Utopia becomes better and better while we wait for it" (sequence 52).

The Greek etymology of the word "utopia" means no place (*ou* + *topos*). Leni's decision to abandon the circus project and seek employment at a television studio is for Kluge not a defeat but the consequence of her insight into the dialectic of utopia. Her choice for "the long march through the institutions" (sequence 66, a reference to one strategy devised by leftist radicals when their hopes for social change did not materialize in the sixties) is a practical compromise intended to avoid an abstract and inflexible opposition between ideological cooptation and aesthetic isolation. In sequence 53 Leni guides her circus elephants across the frontier, but border guards apprehend her, and a tax evasion investigation begins. Her attempt to smuggle the elephants, traditionally identified with long memory, over

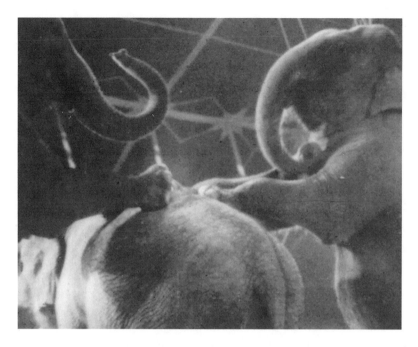

Elephants assume allegorical significance as the repository of memory, pointing to the unfulfilled "work of mourning" (frame enlargement by Kristin Thompson, Madison).

the border (perhaps that of the imagination), is impractical and comes up against the limits set by the authorities.

For Kluge the work of the imagination (art) is to create a place where the unseen (utopia) holds the promise that there can be something other than the unsatisfactory present. For the same reason utopia is always too early, aiming for self-realization but by definition never able to achieve it. Moreover, every utopia is historically conditioned, taking shape as an imaginary space mediated by the corrosion and compromise of experience. The *Trauerarbeit* of the prologue refers to ruptures and losses experienced in the past which qualify this imaginary space. As long as Leni remains in her circus tent, she will not relate to the reality of the past in the present.[23] This dialectical understanding permeates the narrative and visual structure of *Artists under the Big Top: Perplexed*. It also describes Kluge's personal program as a Young German Filmmaker with access to state funding but still without a cinematic public that was willing to move with him beyond the conventions of entertainment and illusionism. Finally, it summarizes his response to the early phase of the sixties student movement. In contrast to the polemical stance demanding the radical politicization of art, Kluge suggests in his film that art should not be confused with politics. When it abandons the utopian project, it loses its very social function as art, as the sphere that articulates (the as yet) nonexisting reality through counterimages and fiction.

The reform circus does not exist but happens. It is event rather than product. Kluge's entire literary and cinematic oeuvre is in this sense his reform circus, promoting the creation of a public sphere or space where experience is organized collectively. In other words, as filmmaker he is more concerned with challenging the structures of spectatorship and reception than with the status of his films as commodities or art. Central to this consideration is Walter Benjamin's and Siegfried Kracauer's concept of distraction as a collective process of reception in the cinema, which they both observed in Weimar Germany. In contrast to the interiority that characterized the privatized relation between the bourgeois subject and the work of art, the distraction of the cinema spectator suggested a historically new mode of perception that superseded the auratic nature of art reception in the nineteenth century.[24] By the fifties this relation too was in a process of metamorphosis. The ruptures and contradictions producing the distracted reception among Weimar's urbanized spectators now structure the very perception of the culture industry's products, substituting for the perceiving subject the economy or exchange of specular images. Thus, reality itself has become abstract and unfathomable as spectacle. Yet, if experience "produces" perception, then according to Kluge it is historical and can be changed by reforming the means of production. The problem, in other words, is not reality but the blockages and insensitivity produced by a particular, historically situated society.

The utopian aspect of his undertaking does not escape Kluge himself. He is aware of the limitations and compromises dictated by a televisual culture where the cinema has become a tertiary discourse that no longer fulfills the function of mediating between high and low culture.[25] The danger of the filmmaker talking to himself about concerns that only interest other intellectuals is ever present. Yet, what seems like a joke in the open ending of *Artists under the Big Top: Perplexed* has become over two decades later a veritable prophecy fulfilled. Leni Peickert together with other members of her circus team work during the day at a television studio, and at night they write serial novels for her newly established business enterprise. Her goal: "Sometime this will all come together: love for a thing, the novels, and television technology" (sequence 63). Leni loses her independence by joining the television studio—the epilogue (sequences 64–67) makes clear that with her ideas she will inevitably confront the bounds of state supervision and public education—but continues to act in a collective with the hope of public resonance. In 1985 Alexander Kluge himself started to produce TV features for one of the newly chartered commercial television networks in West Germany.[26] The circus has moved but the utopia still lives, despite and through the struggle with the dominant means of image production.

13

The Subject of Identity: Margarethe von Trotta's *Marianne and Juliane*

ITH NEITHER AN established art cinema public nor a stable infrastructure for exhibiting their films, the Oberhausen directors of the sixties approached what they perceived as the indifferent cinema public either with a hostile or ingratiating attitude. During the seventies a younger generation of directors was responsible for the unprecedented international regard enjoyed by the New German Cinema. Contrary to Kluge's characteristic collage technique which steered a narrow path between didacticism and avant-garde aesthetics, the next generation pursued other cinematic strategies. Directors like Rainer Werner Fassbinder, Werner Herzog, Volker Schlöndorff, Hans-Jürgen Syberberg, Margarethe von Trotta, and Wim Wenders, to name only the best known, combined the claims to artistic integrity and control inherent in the notion of the *Autorenfilm* with more traditional audience demands for specularity and narrative coherence. Hence, by the early eighties the New German Cinema achieved what had eluded the Young German Filmmakers. It constructed for itself an audience, a social space, a coherent body of themes and distinct formal means of representation. Given the opportunity to make films through state subsidies, the second generation of young directors sought and found ways to address its audience that could confound the experience of isolation and defeat articulated by Kluge in the allegory of *Artists under the Big Top: Perplexed*.

The single most important factor in the flourishing West German cinema of the seventies was the cooperation between independent filmmakers and public television networks. The *Kuratorium* system, introduced in 1965 and revised in 1968, had failed to integrate minimum standards of quality as part of its subsidy system. As a result, the government found itself funding among other things soft pornography and action films because their producers could demonstrate a record of box office success. Modifications of the film subsidy law (*Filmförderungsgesetz*) in 1971 established guidelines for applying quality standards, and the 1974 and 1979 revisions (in conjunction with the *Film/Fernsehabkommen* or film and television agreement) allocated specific amounts of money to the public television networks for coproducing feature films.[1]

This policy confirmed the status of the art cinema as a cultural asset beyond pure entertainment. If the state did not subsidize it as generously as opera houses, theaters, and museums, then at least it recognized art cinema as a potential prestige object for purposes of representation, especially on an international level.[2] At the same time television coproduction protected filmmakers both from direct governmental control and from dependency on the commercial exigencies of the distribution and exhibition chains. The two major West German television networks and the eight regional stations assumed a mediating role, acting as producer or distributor of feature films that would otherwise never have found a public. As government-funded but autonomous utilities with a commitment to public service, they furnished a forum in which filmmakers could engage contemporary social issues, explore historical events, and/or experiment with innovative aesthetic forms. Moreover, the diversity of the television audience as well as the networks' own demands for varied and balanced programming opened up new possibilities for groups that otherwise rarely found public funding, let alone a broad-based audience. This was one of the factors that led to the strong presence of women like Margarethe von Trotta within the New German Cinema but also of gay, documentary, and avant-garde directors.[3] The unique situation of television funding in West Germany contributed to what became arguably the most exciting and original national cinema of the seventies; it also accounts for the strangely hybrid nature of a state-sponsored cinema without commercial constraints.[4] Despite the production boom of high quality films during the early seventies, the New German Cinema was never a commercially viable industry. It accounted for as much as 80 percent of the country's annual production but drew only 4–10 percent of the cinema receipts in the Federal Republic.[5] After ten years of relative stability the situation once again began to deteriorate after the peak year of 1976 with a shift to shoe-box cinemas in the few larger urban centers screening mainly American imports and with a gradual drift among the most successful New German directors to international coproductions supported by foreign (i.e., American) distributors.

In this respect the New German Cinema suggests historical parallels to earlier developments in the German film industry. Like the Weimar cinema, for example, it contributed to redefining the relation between the cultural establishment and popular media. Similar to the expressionist avant-garde, the directors were protected from the full pressure of the market but not entirely independent either in social or economic terms. Under these circumstances both found a space to explore new strategies for narrative film while also examining the social and/or political ramifications of being marginalized. In the seventies this took form through the redis-covery of fascism as the most powerful memory of recent history combined with strong narratives about exemplary heroes who rebel against authority. The quest for self-identity wrought a complex layering of national, familial, and personal trajectories that helped to define a specifically German sub-ject, something the Young German Film in the sixties had never achieved.

There are parallels too between the film industry in the Third Reich and the development in the seventies, despite major differences in the studio system and ideological orientation. The commercial film indus-try's concentration in a monopoly organization, which for the Nazis was a matter of political control of the public sphere, reemerged in the seventies as a matter of market economics and international commerce. Govern-ment intervention, although benign in its form of direct subsidies, prizes, and indirect financing through public television, moved the noncommer-cial cinema dangerously close to an arm of the state. And just as the Holly-wood "dream factory" was the primary competitive influence in the thir-ties, so in the seventies did the New German filmmakers have to confront the American cinema as the dominant source of moving images. Perhaps this explains why the suspicion on the part of young directors toward opu-lent imagery—identified as much with UFA's illusionism in the Third Reich as with Hollywood—gradually dwindled. The typical ascetic "look" and the verbal discourse found in films by Jean-Marie Straub and Danièle Huillet, Harun Farocki, Helke Sander, or even Kluge gave way to more sensuous, specular films. Volker Schlöndorff's *The Tin Drum* (*Die Blechtrommel,* 1979), Helma Sanders-Brahm's *Germany, Pale Mother* (*Deutschland, bleiche Mutter,* 1979), and Fassbinder's *Lili Marleen* (1980), for example, critically refigure seductive images and sounds from Ger-many's fascist past in order to challenge the heritage of the Nazi cinema, and for the first time since the international successes of the early Weimar cinema, German films enjoyed once again critical acclaim beyond their domestic audience.

Margarethe von Trotta's 1981 *Marianne and Juliane* (*Die bleierne Zeit*) typifies the New German Cinema's dilation of personal and national history in the quest for a postwar identity. The story interrogates how the pre-sent is mortgaged to the past in a retrospective narrative about the conflic-tual relationship between two sisters growing up in postwar Germany: one a political terrorist and the other a feminist journalist. Von Trotta shares with other New German directors a political commitment to contemporary so-cial issues as well as a dominant mood of melancholy and loss. The idealism and solidarity of the student movement, which had constituted the immediate context for the Young German Film in the sixties, were dissolving, and their demise seemed to pose stark alternatives that cancelled each other: anger or anxiety, impatience or interiority, extremism or victimization. The rise of urban terrorism and the imposition of government restrictions on civil liberties to control it were developments in the public sphere to which intellectuals and artists were particularly sensitive. Their sense of political exhaustion was accompanied by disillusionment and the general abandonment of utopian energies. In response the vacuum was filled by the idea of repossessing the past, and the New German Cinema became one of the main sites in which this often nostalgic yearning for a lost history was worked through both with seriousness and pathos.[6] Von Trotta's film accommodates this pattern, raising the question whether the repressed past (fascism) or contemporary repression (terrorism) drives German society. Contrary to some other directors, she does not rely on exhibitionism and audience provocation, preferring instead a more traditional psychological and visual realism that tends to strike some critics as artless and modest. Like many women directors in Germany, she is explicitly interested in portraying the private as political, relating the affectivity of historical trauma to the way the subject is formed; yet unlike, say, Jutta Brückner in *Hunger Years* (*Hungerjahre*, 1979) or Jeannine Meerapfel in *Malou* (1981), she does not formulate problems autobiographically but rather as an exploration of the more general dynamics of female socialization.

In contrast to many of the younger feminist directors in West Germany who emerged from the newly established film academies of the sixties, von Trotta followed the more typical career pattern of women in the film industry. She advanced from a stage and film-acting career to coscripting and then codirecting with her husband Volker Schlöndorff (*The Lost Honor of Katharina Blum* [*Die verlorene Ehre der Katharina Blum*, 1975]). She finally assumed full responsibility as director in her highly regarded feature *The Second Awakening of Christa Klages* (*Das zweite Erwachen der Christa Klages*, 1977), a film about a woman who commits a bank robbery to finance a child care center.[7] The network of doublings, parallels, and mirrorings among the women characters became a dominant structural pattern in von Trotta's subsequent films. In *Sisters or The Balance of Happiness* (*Schwestern oder Die Balance des Glücks*, 1979), for example, she adapts it to a family constellation of two sisters with their female bonding and mutual dependencies. In her first features she established a reputation for realistic narratives based on topical, even sensationalistic events such as urban violence, government censorship, and suicide. She unabashedly drew on the archetypal and atavistic symbolism of the family melodrama as well as the investigative plot of the thriller, both of which pit good against evil in a highly emotional conflict. Yet, like Lubitsch in *Passion* or Zschoche in *On Probation*, von Trotta's choice to focus on strong female characters within a psychological drama produces a series of textual configurations that upset both traditional and essentialist images of women.

In *Marianne and Juliane* von Trotta combines conventional melodramatic coding with radical political issues, translating ideological dilemmas into private predicaments. The plot closely follows the political biography of Gudrun Ensslin, a member of the Red Army Faction terrorist group that was responsible for the most spectacular bombings, abductions, and hijackings in West Germany during the seventies. Three of the group's leaders, including Ensslin, were apprehended and incarcerated in one of the world's highest security prisons at the time (Stammheim). Thus, their apparent triple suicide in the fall of 1977 while in solitary confinement was all the more suspect as some kind of government provocation, especially to an educated public that found itself constantly under attack by the conservative German press and by government witch hunts.[8] Filmed only three years after the crisis, much of the West German audience considered von Trotta's film a (largely inadequate) documentary about terrorist politics. More than a decade later the fictionalized story of a terrorist seen through the eyes of her sister seems more than ever to belong to the genre of the quest narrative so popular in the New German Cinema.

The narrative consists of a series of loosely connected flashbacks covering the postwar period from 1945 to 1980 and introduced by a framing device: Juliane Klein stands at the window of her study brooding about her sister Marianne. The memories can be divided into two groups. The first comprises the more or less linear sequence of events during the seventies surrounding Marianne's political radicalization, imprisonment, and death, including Juliane's obsessive search for clues to disprove the suicide claim; the second and much less linear group interrupts this continuity and includes seven sets of sequences from the years 1945, 1947, 1955, and 1968.[9] The flashbacks are not coded with transitions to smooth over the gaps and jumps in temporal logic. Quite to the contrary, the editing is abrupt, with dramatic cuts, elliptical abbreviations, and condensed exposition that qualify the film's realism. In other words the narrative logic is highly subjective in its search for explanations, and von Trotta's realism is closer to the mimesis of the psyche than to a model of verisimilitude. The flashback structure stresses the dislocations of Juliane's memory so that ultimately her reconstruction of the other, of Marianne's past, becomes no less than the process of negotiating the self. The intense relationship of dominance and submission that von Trotta describes reveals a split personality struggling for wholeness. Hence, the complicated polar system of exchanges, reversals, and mutual denial between the sisters is a form of role-playing that leads to the recognition of the self in the Other. In this case the Other is a family member as well as a politically defined enemy, and the erasure of difference proposed by the narrative creates an imaginary unity with implications for a postwar national identity as well.

The flashbacks to the sisters' youth, all triggered in Juliane's mind by encounters with the imprisoned Marianne, suggest a strong sibling rivalry but also an equally strong identification between the two sisters as victims. The fifth flashback, temporally the earliest "memory"—of the mother protecting them in an air-raid shelter during an aerial bombing at the end of the war—shows two vulnerable children at the mercy of a threat unknown to them. Already the first flashback portrays the young girls in 1947 as cohorts, sharing through surreptitious glances to each other an unspoken affinity while their father drones on in an evening prayer. The third flashback, again to 1947, introduces the first hint of competitiveness between the sisters, albeit playful, that will dominate their further relationship. Standing on their heads, their backs to the wall, neither wants to be the first to stand upright; and later they race home to see who will be first. As teenagers their differences are more divisive. Juliane is assertive and independent, defying her father by wearing jeans to school instead of a dress and mockingly cynical about her sister's naive idealism. Marianne is obedient to the authority of her father and the school.

This rivalry will become the strongest characteristic in their adult relationship and for Juliane it marks her sister as the extreme Other. Marianne marries Werner, has a child, and spends her time as a housewife, while Juliane has a live-in friend, Wolfgang, and becomes involved in feminist reform projects. The neat dichotomy between the rebellious and abiding sisters begins to dissolve, however, when Marianne joins a terrorist group, abandoning her husband and child. In a sense she appropriates the role of the tough, defiant daughter, while Juliane in the meantime has adopted, as she says, an "almost bourgeois lifestyle." The irony of this reversal is nowhere more acute than in the scene when Marianne invades Juliane's and Wolfgang's apartment in the middle of the night with two terrorist companions. The impatient ringing of the doorbell, the accusatory silences and abrupt gestures, the harsh voices and grating noise exaggerated by the soundtrack set off Marianne's radical bravado from Juliane's comfortable, orderly existence. When the intruders leave just as quickly as they appeared, Marianne's farewell—"sleep on"—comments not only on the nighttime interruption but also on her understanding of Juliane's feminist politics.

The narrative suggests that for both sisters the identity as rebellious outsider derives from their tormented family dynamics. Marianne and Juliane grow up in a classically patriarchal family environment where the father exercises authority with a heavy hand while the repressed mother helplessly looks on. This personalization of political commitment as the result of rebellion against a domineering father runs the risk of reducing ideological conviction to individual psychology. Von Trotta, however, presents a more complicated intersection of personal and social categories, painting in broad strokes the "leaden" atmosphere of the fifties referred to in the film's German title.[10] For example, the authority vested in the father is explicitly connected to the rigor of Protestant ethics. On the one hand, he is a church minister whom the adult Juliane associates in a dream with the fear of a vengeful God. Furthermore, through the flashbacks this God is related in Juliane's memory to anxious feelings elicited by the suffering depicted in a particularly gruesome Grünewald painting of the Crucifixion hanging in the childhood home. On the other hand, the father is the only person whose conscience does not deny the German guilt for the Third Reich. In a prayer he thanks God for releasing them from their self-imposed slavery (National Socialism), and he later screens a film in a school class about the German concentration camps. Finally, it is the father who first articulates doubt about the official explanation of Marianne's suicide in prison. In other words, the paternalistic image of the postwar family condensed into the father figure resonates with the strong tradition of German Protestantism. It defines not only the framework of moral severity and self-loathing in which von Trotta places Marianne's political terrorism but also the willingness to suffer and sacrifice, which motivates Juliane's search for truth.[11]

Von Trotta includes visual and narrative references to other institutional discourses beyond the nuclear family and the Protestant Church in constructing an image of the "leaden" time of the fifties. The flashback to the screening of Alain Resnais's 1955 documentary *Night and Fog* for the young students contrasts with a parallel scene at school in the same flashback. An insolent Juliane, who challenges the teacher by asking why they spend their time reading a melancholy, metaphysical poem about rootlessness rather than a poem that directly addresses the most recent German past, is asked to leave the classroom.[12] Contrary to the father's Protestant insistence on "confessing" the ugliness of the past to "expatiate" its guilt (even if only indirectly through the documentary film's voice-over soundtrack), the school is shown to comply with the historical amnesia encouraged more generally in a society committed to forgetting the past. In another flashback Juliane is reading Jean-Paul Sartre's play *Les Jeux sont faits* (*The Chips Are Down*), a reference to existential philosophy, which was the major signifier in the fifties for intellectual nonconformity. Finally, in what must be visually the most pointed demonstration of Juliane's rebellious otherness, she accepts a whispered wager from Marianne at the school's final ball and takes to the dance floor without a partner, diffidently waltzing around the ballroom alone to the surprise and disapproval of the other guests.

In *Marianne and Juliane* von Trotta is concerned with contextualizing a past in order to bring into play its absence in the political discourse of the present. Her referent is the fifties but the drama that sustains the film's plot emerges in the context of the sisters' role reversal and its gradual resolution in the seventies. Here too the filmmaker uses carefully placed and familiar references to establish the social discourses within which she situates the personal confrontation. A few brief sequences sketch in the siblings' different trajectories. A flashback to 1968 (the seventh and last of the "memories" noted as such in the scenario) once again shows the two sisters watching a film, this time consisting of excerpts from a documentary about the victims of American napalm bombings in North Vietnam—in particular children. The allusion, of course, is to the German student movement in the late sixties, which derived much of its early energy from protests against American imperialism in the Vietnam War. On a deeper level, though, the documentary film echoes the sisters' own experience of vulnerability and victimization as "innocent" victims in the earlier 1945 flashback. The diegetic parallel to the previous film screening about the victims in German concentration camps interweaves these memories with a similar moral reprehensibility and aligns the spectator's position with the sisters' response of shocked disgust. At this point, however, the sisters' paths separate and the possibilities for spectatorial identification become complicated. Although the link is never specified, here apparently is the beginning of Marianne's politicization, which leads to guerilla training in Beirut and her return to Germany as a member of an underground terrorist group.[13] Two other sequences show Juliane who meanwhile has become involved in a women's collective editing a feminist journal and an activist in abortion issues.[14] She too has joined an oppositional movement that emerged from the student Left, but rather than taking up arms, Juliane has taken up the pen in the pursuit of reasoned enlightenment. The subsequent encounters between the two adult women reveal their politically antithetical views but also their psychological similarity.

Von Trotta's film elucidates neither the political terrain of terrorist activities nor the ideological convictions that drove them. Indeed, the allusions to Marianne's terrorism remain unusually vague, in the vein of having thrown bombs. She appears only three times as a "terrorist," and in each case von Trotta employs standard coding for clothing, gesture, and movement familiar from television newscasts to represent the abstract idea of terrorism. Otherwise the adult Marianne only appears in jail in the role of a political prisoner rather than as an agent of violent extremism. The exchanges with Juliane all make reference to the issue of terrorism, but they are short, angry, and intermittent. While both are committed to social change, the sisters hurl accusations at one another that oppose the one's revolutionary urgency to the other's reformist patience. The narrative, however, avoids any further direct argument with the political legitimation of terrorism in order to focus more generally on the past sources for the subjective reactions to injustice and victimization.

Marianne, a terrorist whose political convictions and motivations remain vague, is portrayed as a victim of state authority who is melodramatically held in solitary confinement (used by permission of Stiftung deutsche Kinemathek, Berlin).

In the case of National Socialism von Trotta has Juliane draw fairly explicit comparisons between contemporary terrorist practices and historical state terrorism. Early in the narration Juliane dictates into a microphone her notes for an article on the complicity of mothers with Nazi goals while the camera pans over various photographs from the Third Reich of Hitler and children, mothers and children, and fleeing and dead children. Reproduction, as she quotes Hitler, is the women's battle for the endurance of the race. The example of one way women have contributed to their own oppression by serving the wrong political cause suggests early in the narrative a differentiated perspective on how victims are historically engendered. In a later prison visit Juliane angrily denounces Marianne's blind idealism by claiming that she could just as likely have been a member of the Nazi girls' organization (Bund Deutscher Mädchen [BDM]), had she been born only one generation earlier. This charge arises from Juliane's attempt to write an article about her sister, which the latter rejects as just another piece of bourgeois commercialism because it insists on personal history as an explanation for political commitment:

THE SUBJECT OF IDENTITY

MARIANNE: You can't describe me from the perspective of our personal history. My history only begins with the others [Marianne's companions]. . . . The most important thing is reality, don't you understand, not words.

JULIANE: As if our childhood were not a reality. Anyway, I don't believe we can free ourselves from our personal history.

(sequence 70)

This dialogue is interesting for two reasons. First, it opposes in blunt terms two incompatible views of history: the one would willfully construct history out of an imaginary reality and the other would fatalistically imagine the past to give shape to reality. In both cases, reality emerges as a highly arbitrary narrative, which describes in part the controversial nature of the subject von Trotta addresses in her film *Marianne and Juliane*—the personal history of a fictional terrorist. Second, Juliane's written account of her sister, a project which despite encouragement from her editorial colleagues she resisted for a long time, is only the initial rendering of Marianne's story. As spectators we learn nothing more of this account than what is quoted above, but its inadequacy—*because* it is a portrayal only of the Other—is confirmed by the very narration we are watching. This is the second reconstruction of the past, the search for self-identity introduced in the opening frame story. That second story does not only tell the sisters' common history but also Juliane's gradual psychological bonding with Marianne, with the extreme otherness she represents. Moreover, when that frame closes at the narrative's end, the closure itself will become the beginning of a third story, for then Juliane promises Marianne's son to tell him about her, in other words, to try once again, in a different way, to reconstruct her story for the next generation. Here the shift begins from competitiveness to oneness, from difference to sameness. And from this tentative closure von Trotta projects a utopian space for the spectator where the constitution of self-identity becomes part of the process of remembering a national past beyond the polarization figured in the two sisters.

Juliane visits her sister seven times in prison, a sequence of tense meetings, which for the spectator reveals the functioning of an almost magnetic relationship between them. The context of incarceration already suggests the melodrama of victimization, and especially Juliane's first entrance into the prison stresses the way the state uses its authority to impose isolation on those it confines. A stern, matronly guard submits her to a complete body search, guides her down empty halls echoing their footsteps, opens and closes locked gates and doors with a huge chain of clanking keys. The cold lighting and the almost irritating noise level create an oppressive atmosphere that in later prison scenes will be reinforced by the ubiquitous

The sisters' meetings in the prison are tense, emotional encounters opposing Marianne's revolutionary urgency to Juliane's reformist patience (used by permission of Stiftung deutsche Kinemathek, Berlin).

presence of guards watching and taking notes when the two sisters meet. Marianne's refusal to see Juliane this first time marks the low point in their relationship, the outright rejection of any common interest. Yet the similar way the state treats both the prisoner and the visitor as objects of suspicion will become an increasingly powerful source of identity between the two as trapped victims. The subsequent encounters, although not free of recriminations and even physical attack, detail subtle gestures and exchanges that underline the sisters' common bonds.

The final visit finds the sisters facing each other through a pane of glass and barely communicating by means of an electronic intercom. These barriers prevent the physical touching and emotional directness that was possible in the earlier prison encounters. Yet, the spectator sees something else. While Juliane complains to the guard that she can hardly recognize her sister through the glare on the glass, the camera briefly shows in close-up the reflection of Juliane's face superimposed on Marianne's.[15] The fusion of their images contradicts Juliane's statement, but only for the film spectator who is positioned to see the merging rather than the dissolving (*verschwimmen*) that Juliane anxiously perceives. The visual bonding sug-

The sisters' separation is exaggerated visually by physical barriers and tightly framed compositions, while psychologically Juliane identifies more and more strongly with her sister's victimization (used by permission of Stiftung deutsche Kinemathek, Berlin).

gested by this image functions metaphorically in pointing to the psychological bonding that Juliane will experience in the rest of the film. In fact, this is the last time she sees her sister alive, for Marianne is found hanged while Juliane and Wolfgang are on vacation in Sicily.[16] The sisters' last encounter, the film's dramatic high point, takes place in the cemetery chapel where Marianne's body lies in state, still now attended by four armed guards with police dogs. Irresistibly drawn to the coffin, Juliane is riveted by this face while her mother recites a desperate prayer and her father and Wolfgang look on. An abrupt cut to Juliane sobbing uncontrollably in an ambulance introduces her physical and mental collapse, the symmetrical reaction corresponding to her sister's death. Drugged with a sedative, she falls into a dream: the two of them as small children button each others' undershirts while listening to the terrifying sermon of their father. The spectacular music accompanying the climax underscores the passion of the scene as well as the subtext of revenge.[17]

Identity through imitation implies a psychotic dimension of appropriating the Other. Both Wolfgang and Juliane see Marianne's intrusions and later her demands from the prison as an attempt to possess Juliane.

Juliane's final encounter with her (dead) sister in a cemetery chapel still takes place under the watchful eyes of state authority (used by permission of Stiftung deutsche Kinemathek, Berlin).

Gradually, however, it becomes clear that the narration is constructing a double (or doppelgänger) motif with its reversals, symmetries, and mirroring effects. Marianne is a double, both psychologically and politically, a hidden part of the self which Juliane has repressed and which now requires attention on its own terms. Her need to experience sympathetically the pain to which Marianne is subjected on her hunger strike in protest of the solitary confinement, for example, leads her to push a plastic tube down her own throat. Later she will test nooses and tie one around her neck to recreate her sister's hanging. After Marianne's death she studies medical textbooks, collects her belongings from the prison cell, sorting through them meticulously for any clues about the alleged suicide, and conducts hanging experiments with ropes and weights. She even sacrifices her ten-year relationship with Wolfgang when he can no longer tolerate this obsessive behavior that leaves no room for another person. Consistent with the elaborate textual fabric of flashbacks and allusions, von Trotta balances the psychopathology of repressed guilt as it expresses itself in Juliane's extreme introversion with the repression of history on a more general, social plane. After years of research devoted to her sister's death, she finally has what she believes to be sufficient evidence to prove that it was not a suicide. The response of a newspaper editor whom she contacts with the story highlights the public resistance to historical memory but also implicitly throws into question Juliane's single-minded pursuit of the truth: "Topicality means the right story at the right time. Everything else belongs on the dung heap of history . . . or in the history books, for all I care." The political rigor of the one sister leads to incarceration; the moral rigor of the other's search ends in isolation.

Beyond the obvious allusions to solitary confinement in prison and psychological estrangement, the film's thematization of visibility underscore the centrality of isolation and separation. The repeated motif of looking through windows stresses an insider/outsider dichotomy. The opening image, for example, which at first appears to be a blank screen with a vertical line dividing it as a background for the printed credits, is revealed to be a large window with a vertical divider when the camera slowly pulls back into Juliane's study. Outside this window is a façade with many other regularly spaced, empty windows. The prison sequences also stress windows as a frame for looking but not necessarily for seeing: they suggest anonymity on the face of a large building or a barrier by virtue of opaque glass or the glare of light. Similarly, when the sisters watch films or are watched by the prison guards, von Trotta self-consciously formulates the ambiguity of spectatorship as a problem: the power of identification and of control.[18]

The catalyst that draws Juliane out of her isolation and propels the melodramatic narrative toward its tentative closure is Jan, Marianne's orphaned child and a memorial to the consequences of his mother's radical politics. The mutilated or abandoned child is a popular topos in the New German Cinema and is easy to recognize as a metaphor for postwar Germany.[19] Jan hates his mother because he becomes the victim of her violence. After Marianne's husband commits suicide, Juliane places Jan in a foster home and severs all ties to him. Six years later he is intentionally set afire in a vicious attack motivated by political vengeance toward his dead mother. The officially provoked and sanctioned hysteria toward terrorism in West Germany, a publicly camouflaged trauma in the guise of the return of the repressed, is visited upon the innocent, victimized child. After her own quest for the self through the Other has ended, Juliane is now prepared to accept Jan, a sign of the healed disruption between the sisters and an acknowledgement of her responsibility for historical continuity. Haunted by the nightmare of his burning, the defensive, almost mute child in the last sequence tears up a photo of Marianne and aggressively demands from Juliane to know everything about his mother, thus converging the retrospective narration with the temporal frame of the opening sequence.

Jan is the vehicle of utopian energy and implicitly the catalyst that shifts visual memory (the destroyed photo) to discursive practice (knowledge). His conscious decision to ask questions, his desire to know everything, even more than Juliane knows, is a challenge pointing beyond the narrative's fragile resolution. If the melodramatic structure with its many flashbacks focuses on the personal, traumatic consequences of social contradictions—victimization, entrapment, vengeance, sacrifice—it also elides their inconsistencies. Juliane contains the radically Other in order to reconstitute the self but pays the price in total isolation. At the end of the film she has no friends, no collective, no work, and apparently no family. Yet the last scene offers an alternative to Juliane's contemplative solitude in the first scene. Jan, her sister's child, is for Juliane the living memory that she must accept the Other (as opponent, as enemy, as double) and the possibility of contradiction in order to escape the solipsism of identity as sameness. The nature of this closure, and this is the enduring strength of melodrama, can accommodate both the identity through victimization and resistance to victimization.

When it was released in fall 1981, *Marianne and Juliane* was celebrated on the festival circuit as a major German triumph and launched Margarethe von Trotta's international reputation.[20] The popular reception in West Germany, however, was much more restrained. There was little room for the middle ground of enlightened and reasoned discourse on the subject of terrorist violence proposed by von Trotta's film in a public sphere reduced by hysterical official reactions and press self-censorship. While von Trotta never presents Marianne the terrorist as an admirable figure, the narrative does take her seriously. Consequently, opinions split between those who accused von Trotta of sympathy with terrorists and those who perceived the personalization of political issues as a substitution of the personal for the political. Moreover, the resistance or inability to read the text as fiction rather than as documentary—perhaps an understandable lapse in the early eighties when these issues were still perceived in West Germany as relatively contemporaneous—often led to a rejection of the film because of its putative distortion of reality.[21] The film continued to create difficulties both for leftist and feminist critics who were stymied by what they perceived to be the narrative's ambiguity or paradoxes. Those concerned with defining the ideological status of the film as progressive or reactionary foreclosed prematurely the critical and textual negotiations of the text. Furthermore, they failed to account for the fact that von Trotta is less interested in programmatic answers than in charting a space to ask uncomfortable questions at a time in West Germany when marginalizing any critical political activity was on the agenda. Consequently, what sometimes has been perceived as confusion on the filmmaker's part can be described more accurately as her commitment to leaving questions open, to accepting the complexity of holding two opposing views at the same time. Von Trotta defends in the name of compassion or identification with victims of political oppression an ideal of sane, critical inquiry against a vengeful society. That utopia is an imaginary order which arises, however, from the distorted and contradictory values of the material society it presumes to displace.

Other critics, especially Anglo-American ones who are removed from and therefore less apt to be cognizant of the quotidian politics in West Germany, were more concerned with von Trotta's realism. The conventional formal strategies of suspense and spectator identification have been seen as sustaining a stable subject position for articulating reality and therefore as complicit in the dominant ideological mystifications of that reality.[22] This implies epistemological considerations as well as gender issues. Von Trotta chose mainstream forms of specular identification in order to reach a broader public than the more intellectual avant-garde cinema does. In this respect she learned a lesson from the politicized filmmaking of the seventies, which could rely on a relatively coherent and ideologically sympathetic audience. When the youth movement and alternative scene began to disperse, bringing with it not only political fragmentation but also a new discourse of interiority and subjectivity, the polemical edge of oppositional and antiestablishment filmmaking took on a new quality. Feminist directors in particular experimented with various strategies to undermine female representation and gender identity. Von Trotta's work aims not at the deconstruction of "woman" as patriarchal sign but rather at the discourse of female subjectivity where women are active, gendered characters.[23] Her parable of stifled subjectivity throws the self as stable identity into question but does not reject the notion of subject. Von Trotta's quest narrative, figured through the two sisters and coupled with the constitution of identity through history, needs by definition a stable self-image. To reduce that representation of identity itself to an ideology fails to consider that it also points to signs of struggle, to the process of contesting the space of imaginary practices. In this wider sense *Marianne and Juliane* marks a culmination point in the effort to construct the audience for the project of *Trauerarbeit* that Alexander Kluge had envisioned for the cinema in 1968 with his *Artists* film and that the New German Cinema of the seventies consistently sought in the relation between German history, images of history, and German identity.

14

The Archaeology of the Present: Wim Wenders's *Paris, Texas*

WIM WENDERS APPROACHES filmmaking phenomenologically as the art of seeing, subordinating everything—editing, music, narrative, character—to the camera. This cinema of observation, with its sensuality and pathos of the image, refuses psychology, awakens emotions rather than analyzing them, avoids explicit links in order to generate spectator activity. He shares with other New German Cinema directors like Fassbinder and Syberberg an acute awareness of Germany's problematic history vis-à-vis images. The opulent dramaturgy of the fascist cinema dedicated to escapism as well as the hegemony of foreign (i.e., American) images in the consciousness of postwar Germans motivate a desire to examine the way reality and the self are constructed through seeing. In the road movie *Paris, Texas* (1984) Wenders explores, like Margarethe von Trotta, the vicissitudes of identity formation from a specific postwar German perspective. Rather than her psychological realism, however, he has more in common with the chronicle format of Konrad Wolf's quest narrative and with Alexander Kluge's wariness toward visibility and specularity. Wenders's films draw on banal plot structures or rely on the strength of familiar genres like the road movie, the family melodrama, or the Western for their coherence. That Wenders responds to quintessential Hollywood genres is a direct effect of the rupture in German cinematic tradition marked by the Third Reich. The trauma of loss that permeates all his films is related similarly to a sense of stalemate in German history, a generational attitude that in this case accounts for his deemphasis on telling stories and uncertainty about representing the past. This too partially explains the director's cinephilia, his ironic quoting of cinema myths and traditions as signals that bridge the ellipses in his plots.[1]

Wenders's highly charged visual imagination is evident in *Paris, Texas* with its hyperrealistic photography. The exceptional quality of the images produces the aura of psychic landscapes through color and intensity, through the depth of focus that directs the eye, through weightiness and stability even in the many slow traveling shots. As in his films prior to this, the pronounced male psychic landscape is determined by Oedipal displacement.[2] Consumed by guilt and unable to communicate emotionally with another person, the protagonist's displacement begins in Wenders's films with the anxiety toward a woman. The wish for separation, exclusion, and negation engendered by this anxiety characterizes the narcissism or self-centeredness of these heroes and launches them on journeys triggered by the desire to escape emotional bonds to others. In the process they confront a childhood in one form or another of which they are victims. This deflection imposes itself on the narrative and determines the subjective confrontation between a lost family and the consciousness of trying to retrieve it. *Paris, Texas* adapts this basic pattern but departs from it in crucial ways, marking a turning point in Wenders's development as a filmmaker and storyteller. First, there is a definite shift to a stronger, less self-conscious narrative, perhaps influenced by the experience of working on the American production *Hammett* (1982) and certainly positioned at the opposite extreme of *The State of Things* (*Der Stand der Dinge*, also 1982), which literally exorcised narrative logic. As a result, *Paris, Texas* advances toward a synthesis of Wenders's documentary approach to representation and the pull of a fictional story with a beginning and an end. Second, the protagonist begins to externalize his feelings of love and with that surrenders the aggressive defense against the family and filial love. For the first time Wenders attempts to portray the intimacy between a man and a woman, a topic he would pursue further in later films like *Wings of Desire* (*Himmel über Berlin*, 1987) and *Until the End of the World* (*Bis ans Ende der Welt*, 1991). Finally, the film avoids the dense fabric of cinematic quotes that threatened to suffocate *Lightening over Water* (*Nick's Film*, 1980) and his two 1982 features mentioned above. Wenders abandons this ironic tool of distancing in order to celebrate here the high emotionality of myth, a myth which despite the title has more to do with the archaeology of an imaginary Germany than with the American dream.[3]

The first sequences contain some of the film's most striking and dreamlike images. First the spectator sees in an extreme long, high shot a man walking in a sun-drenched desert, straight toward the horizon as if into an infinite nothingness. The camera moves in on his scrubby, unkempt clothes and his unshaven face to capture the air of mad desperation in his figure. A shot/reverse shot to a close-up of a perched hawk transects his sight line with that of the preying bird and is followed by him discarding an emptied water bottle. The initial shots introduce the desert as a metaphor for silence and emptiness, a place of total immobility, except for this man. The meaning-laden images of the hunter and the hunted announce the strong yearning of this loner to continue his journey. The protagonist Travis is a traveler and in the course of the narrative the desire that drives him out of the desert will be revealed.

Wenders's desert is a symbolically endowed visual space, a physical landscape that dwarfs the individual with its magnitude and austere beauty. Travis's rugged appearance conforms to the space: he belongs here. The desert is also an imaginary space, "a deep vast country," Travis will call it later, a faraway place he could at one time only dream of, a place where no one knows him, "somewhere without language or streets."[4] The film's opening images, accompanied by Ry Cooder's mournful guitar, evoke this abstract desert of the mind, this protected space without communication and without connections. The rest of the narrative will follow Travis's painful retreat as he undertakes a journey of "return to the living." A diegetical rupture signals his exit from the desert and reentry into life: Travis faints and after a fade out awakens in a primitive clinic. The doctor hovering over him asks if he knows which side of the border he is on and demands that the patient tell him his name. The doctor's articulation of these fundamental identity issues plunges the spectator into the narration and defines the trajectory of ensuing events and encounters. For Travis, how-

Travis, the rugged loner on a journey, emerges from the depth of his symbolic desert to reenter life (used by permission of Stiftung deutsche Kinemathek, Berlin).

ever, crossing the geographical border (between Mexico and Texas) and the imaginary border (between nonidentity and life) is his symbolic reentry into history. The fact that the clinic is located at Terlingua (or terra lingua, land of language) suggests that he will leave behind the space that denies time, identity, and language. Indeed Travis is a mute, and his disavowal of language is the lived experience of a loss of self and "his story."

Wenders structures the reentry into history via Travis's encounter with his family and his passage back into language. His brother Walt, contacted by telephone from the border clinic, arrives from Los Angeles to pick him up, but their meeting is postponed because Travis has already disappeared from the clinic to continue his journey. The doctor warns Walt—and the spectator—that Travis's exit from "down here," from the real and imaginary desert, will exact a price. Walt finally crosses Travis's path, on both figurative and literal levels, in a visual image when the road he takes and Travis's obsessive beeline intersect. Thus, Walt obstructs the man's journey, erasing his absence and pulling him from nonexistence into existence. Travis's uncomprehending reaction when Walt calls his name and names himself and his relationship as brother delineates not only the as yet undefined identity of Wenders's protagonist but also the childlike quality of

Travis's brother Walt intercepts his trajectory visually and literally (used by permission of Stiftung deutsche Kinemathek, Berlin).

someone who lacks a past. The physical presence of every image, underscored by the slow, languorous camera and saturated colors, corresponds to Travis's reentry into the world of signs; he sees everything anew.

The next sequences follow Walt and Travis as they make their way from the Texas border to Los Angeles, from the desert to the city streets, from a no-man's-land to a metropolis. On the way Travis is transformed into a socialized man: clean-shaven, outfitted with new clothes, and provided with memories by Walt. The process does not advance without resistance. Travis shows no response, for example, to Walt's gentle care or to his meek attempts at intimacy. He takes the first opportunity to sneak away when it presents itself, and Walt finds him once again walking into the distant horizon. Travis refuses to fly with Walt from Texas to Los Angeles, not comprehending the need to "save" time because he has a different sense of temporality. Then he insists they can only continue their trip in precisely the same rental car they had been using earlier, a child's illogic matched only by the equally illogical and bureaucratic rental agent's refusal to give them the same car. Finally, Travis diverts the car from the highway while Walt is sleeping. As if still under the force of an intense longing, he exits into the desert, to a car dump in the Mojave Desert, at an exit that "didn't have a name."

In the meantime Travis is propelled into language by his very proximity to Walt. Finally reacting to his brother's threat to match his silence, he utters his first word: "Paris." This initial verbal utterance is composed of a single word devoid of syntax, without an explicit speaking subject and without a verb. If to speak is to appropriate language, then Travis's first act of appropriation is inaugurated by a proper noun, that is, with a name that exists to designate essence or substance. A proper name, of course, designates a unique thing in its singularity, being *proper* to that thing and denoting *property* and *propriety*. In this case, however, the word Paris is marked by duplicity, for Walt understands Paris to be the capital of France, while for Travis Paris is a place on the map of Texas, the eponymous "Paris, Texas." The name "Paris" is thus both double and duplicitous.

Paris is also the place named on the much-fingered photograph Travis carries with him, an image of a barren piece of land with a for-sale sign, land that Travis had bought years ago by mail. Only later during their trip does Travis recall why he bought the land there: Paris is where his parents first made love, the place where Travis believes he was conceived: "I started out there." But even more than that, Paris represents a linguistic duplicity introduced by his father. Travis relates "Daddy's joke" to his brother: he always told people he had met his wife in Paris, then after a long pause, when everyone was conjuring up images of France, he added Texas and laughed uproariously because of the confusion evoked by the duplication of the proper noun tied to two referents. Travis will later repeat his father's story to his son in a crucial dialogue when he describes his mother, the plain, shy woman who lived out the father's linguistic duplicity as a "fancy woman" from Paris. At that point, however, Travis calls his father's joke by another name, a "sickness" in which he saw his wife as someone other than she was: "he had this idea about her . . . He looked at her, but . . . he didn't see her. He saw this idea." The joke resides in the comma after the proper noun "Paris," the border between dream and reality, between the necessity of knowing one's origins in order to know one's identity and the contingency of all other knowledge. In this sense Travis's desire, his own sickness, and his quest are all contained in these two words "Paris, Texas."

The same duplicity or doubling effect distinguishes Travis's first word in his appropriation of language, for he too smiles to himself when Walt equates Paris with France. Paris *is* a geographical place located on the road map he holds in his hands, it *is* a place anchored in reality, at least nominally for Travis, by the picture showing the vacant property he owns; but at the same time it is also a space just as unconnected to reality as that desert into which he disappeared four years earlier. It is Travis's destination, the object of his desire, and the reason that brings him out of the desert and across the border. In this context Paris is nowhere and anywhere, a space in his mind, the zero point of his life, and the imaginary source of his personal history. Paris is the home Travis seeks to return to, the unruptured past he yearns for, the origin that promises him an identity. Travis, however, has been intercepted by language because his desire to return full circle to his imaginary origin is, of course, impossible. Instead his journey leads him into history, into a narrative that is marked at the beginning by solitude (hawk) and desiccation (empty water bottle). And when he realizes the impossibility of this desire after finding his wife Jane, he discards the image of the vacant piece of land and with it the dream of reuniting his family, those three people connected only by his "idea" of them.

Duplication is the fundamental structuring device of Wenders's entire narrative. The second part of the film, situated in Los Angeles, brings Travis into his past, but he finds a real past rather than the imaginary home he yearns for. He enters into a constellation of characters connected once again through a figure of doubling, through the son Hunter who has two fathers, two sets of parents, for it is Walt and his wife Anne who have raised Hunter as their own child since Travis disappeared four years earlier. Hunter is not active at this point in the film; initially he even resists Walt's and Anne's pressure to interact with Travis. Although the son is unwilling to recognize him as his father, he is the only person in the film who will find an emotional link to him, helping him to discover who he is, that is, to appropriate his identity and his past as a proper father. When Walt wants to screen a super-8 home movie to help Travis remember, Hunter is uninterested: "I've already seen it." Yet during the movie—with its images of Jane as well as the two sets of Hunter's "parents" it is an evocation of the happy past Wenders achieves without using a flashback—he and Travis exchange looks. The intimacy captured on the home movie as their shared memory leads to mutual visual recognition and awakens in Hunter a desire to find his mother.

A new trajectory in the film narrative begins that relates Hunter to Travis, son to father, by their shared object of desire and launches them on a new journey. In order to begin the search for his mother, Hunter positions Travis as father, psychologically, linguistically, and narrationally. It is Hunter who moves toward Travis after the home movie and initiates the first physical contact; it is Hunter who acknowledges linguistically his double paternity by saying "good night Daddy" to both Walt and Travis when he goes to his bedroom; and it is Hunter who tells Anne, while she puts him to bed, that he perceives Travis's love for Jane by the way he looked at her image during the home movie. Most importantly it is Hunter who appropriates George Lucas's *Star Wars* trilogy as a paradigmatic quest narrative for his own situation when he refers to the home-movie image of his mother: "That's only her in the movie . . . a long time ago 'in a galaxy far away.'" The Star Wars theme designates Hunter's role by establishing a framework—based on a popular mythology particularly accessible to children—in which the son, Luke Skywalker, engages in numerous adventures and battles until he discovers his real father in Darth Vader. Hence, the frequent visual quotes of Star Wars icons such as the Star Wars bed sheets, the Jedi pillowcase, and the toy figures with which Hunter acts out battles, represent not just playful nods by a foreign director to the hegemony of Hollywood movie culture but are signifiers strategically introduced when Hunter—here his antonomastic, "speaking" name becomes obvious, like the traveller's name Travis—takes on an active role in the film narrative.

Hunter functions as mentor in defining the nature of the quest and in guiding Travis through it. Travis's own attempts to approach Hunter are clumsy and reap rejection because he is unable to distinguish between the truth and falsity of images. He wants his son to recognize in him the imaginary Father, so he tries to fit the role formally and formulaically, seeking in magazine ads an image he might imitate. These pop culture images, however, the most manipulated form of masculine social identity, do not reveal the proper traits of paternity that he needs. Next he seeks advice from the domestic, a Chicana situated by her work in a rigid hierarchical relationship and by her culture in a consciousness of strong patriarchy. She tells Travis precisely and without hesitation what to wear, how to comport himself, what image to convey in order to be a father. Hunter responds to the masquerade, walking home from school with Travis and imitating his gait, while the camera's lateral panning shots register their distance and proximity. Then the father and son look through an old photo album, an opportunity for Travis to "reconstruct" the family's continuity through images of his own father (also named Travis) and for Hunter to define the difference between death (of the grandfather) and absence (of the mother). This in turn triggers Hunter's desire to find his absent mother and introduces a new narrative trajectory.

The quest to find the mother in Houston not only provides the framework in which father and son will discover each other, but it also offers an alternative goal to Travis's desert, to his imaginary space outside of time and without connections. On their drive to Houston Hunter tells two stories. First he proposes in a gesture of substitution for the father an explanation of the genesis of the cosmos. Contrary to Travis, whose desire was directed toward a return to an originary home in order to undo the rupture in his past, Hunter situates human life within a macrohistorical narrative characterized by change and continuity (the big bang theory of creation). Second, he tells a riddle about the speed of light. If a man were to travel in space at the speed of light for an hour, he would return to earth being only one hour old, whereas a baby who remained on earth would have become an old man. This relativity of time suggests exactly the disparity that casts Hunter the son in the role of mentor for his father and it represents a spatiotemporal flexibility in the search for identity that counters Travis's desert experience outside of time. Later in the film Travis will tell Hunter: "I was hoping to show you that I was your father. You showed me I was." As such, it is only consistent that Hunter recognizes Jane at the bank in Houston where they wait for her, and Hunter guides Travis as they follow her car through the labyrinth of Houston's freeways, echoing the subtext of Homer's *Odyssey*.[5]

For Travis (the son) this journey is an Oedipal search for his father: he reinserts himself into the world in the image of the Father. It is also the search for his son. Meanwhile for Hunter the complicity of his recognition of Travis as father allows for his own, reciprocal constitution as son, for during this journey Hunter also learns to be the son of this father. Two sequences at its outset link Travis's behavior with the resolution of the family drama. Having set out for Houston, Travis insists that Hunter, not he, call Anne and Walt. Anne, realizing instantly that they are losing "their" child, wants to speak with Travis, but he motions to Hunter simply to hang up, to break the connection. The father's practiced gesture of cutting off communication, of retreating from language, is a legacy quickly appropriated by his son. At some level Hunter too seems to perceive that he is what holds Anne and Walt together as a family, and he is willing to sacrifice that "suffocating" security for the adventure of reconstituting the lost family.[6] Later in a motel room Travis gives him a black-and-white Photomat strip print which shows three stereotypical images of the intact family: Travis, Jane, and Hunter. He bequeaths to Hunter a memory frozen in time; the father hands on to the son the representation of the family past. This and the photo of an empty piece of land are among the few possessions he carried with him out of the desert, delineating the points between which Travis wanders. Moreover, like all the other photographic images in this film—Walt's billboards, the super-8 movie, the starkly framed mirror reflections—they serve as an index of subjectivity and incomplete identity.

Before Hunter and Travis begin their journey, the narration provides a number of diegetical and visual clues to what follows. Anne's information, for example, about Jane's practice of sending money from a Houston bank for Hunter on the fifth of each month supplies Travis with the important detail he needs to locate her. From Anne Travis also learns that the day's date is November 1; the evening of All Souls' Day, the day of remembering the dead, is a portentous beginning for the journey into the past. On the way to Walt, from whom he receives money and credit cards for his trip, Travis encounters another man caught in the wilderness of an imaginary space who sums up visually and verbally Travis's dilemma. On a bridge high above a Los Angeles freeway, framed/trapped behind the bars of the bridge railing, this man screams his words at the cars passing below to warn of the "land of no return" awaiting us all. Travis, who has just been forced out of his mutism and into language, pats the logomaniac on the back with empathy but also passes him by. He has already left his desert behind. Finally, after Travis has fetched Hunter from school in his newly acquired used car, the two are conspicuously framed in a medium two-shot against a maze of multilayered freeway overpasses. Visually the deep focus beckons them into the distance, a shot similar to the long perspectives of the Texas desert in the first part of the film. The perpendicular placement of the vehicle in the center foreground of the frame, however, suggests a blockage or barrier at the outset of the journey. Their dialogue, consisting of remarkably short question-answer exchanges and sequences of shot/reverse shots, sums up Travis's desert experience and his desire to locate Jane as well as Hunter's insistence on accompanying him. With that the blockage is cleared, the journey to Houston commences, and the third part of the film begins in which Travis, with Hunter's help, will find Jane in a peep show, return the son to his mother, and then leave.

Wenders unobtrusively develops a series of visual motifs that echo each other throughout the film. One cluster of images indicates connection and movement: the frequent trains that cross Travis's path, the train tracks he walks along, the airplanes he refuses to fly in but which he observes with fascination through binoculars, the bridges and freeways along which he travels, the kinetic neon legs of galloping horses on a motel sign, and of course the vehicles in which he rides. Another cluster of images indicates connection and communication: the electrical wires guiding Travis's path into the horizon, the ubiquitous telephones, and finally the tape recorder by which Travis addresses his final message to Hunter. On the one hand, these images signal a social world characterized by human interaction, relation, and attachment, the very opposite of Travis's desert "without language or streets." On the other hand, Travis cannot participate in the connections signified by such images. His mutism and desire to disappear at the beginning of the film represent the extreme of separation that remains despite the availability of the means to communicate. Travis learns to speak, but he never enters into real dialogue.

If the first two parts of the film are informed by Travis's reluctant entry into language and history, then the last part presents the protagonist in language and with memory. Typically, however, Travis's discourse is monological, and his memory is conventional and topological. Travis discovers Jane in an elaborate peep show, an economy of voyeurism (called the Keyhole Club in the screenplay) in which the male visitor can choose a setting (e.g., hotel pool, diner, kitchen) and type of woman (e.g., nurse, waitress, wife) to indulge his sexual fantasies. The interaction between the visitor and the fantasy object is nonphysical, separated by a one-way mirror and connected only by a telephone receiver. On one level, the peep show serves as a metaphor for the representation of the female which puts the

The carefully framed two-shot suggests a blockage or barrier between father and son that must be removed before the journey can continue (used by permission of Stiftung deutsche Kinemathek, Berlin).

WIM WENDERS'S *PARIS, TEXAS*

male in control of the woman's image. It is the ultimate closed space for narcissistic possession of the Other. The stagelike artifice of the setting and the rigid, photographic-like framing of the woman in the one-way mirror emphasizes the relentless gaze of the camera. Even more it underscores the subject/object dichotomy in Travis's relationship to Jane. On another level, the peep show facilitates Travis's encounter with Jane precisely by separating seeing (through the glass whose opaque surface can be either window or mirror) and speaking (through the telephone). It provides a complexly mediated metaphor for a confessional in which rage and hurt can be articulated because of the distancing device for expressing them.[7] Only in this peep show can their discourse become truth, can communication be established between the estranged partners, because neither one is able to look at and to speak with the other at the same time.

In the first of two visits to the peep show, Travis remains anonymous and barely speaks to Jane: "I don't want anything . . . I want to talk with you," he says, and stares through the one-way mirror. Jane, paid to listen but not to see, assures her client that he can say anything he wants to her. Looking at Jane entrapped by his look, by the framing of the glass, he is moved to tears by her sight, but he also realizes that he cannot look at Jane without feeling jealous, accusing her of prostitution. Travis finally places the telephone receiver on the counter and leaves his peep show booth without a word, reiterating the established pattern of broken connections but also aware that his jealousy is no different than his father's sickness: he looks at Jane but does not see her. Travis's two visits to the peep show are punctuated by "confessions" to his son. In the first he lies drunk on a Laundromat couch while his son sits in the position of psychoanalyst, listening in an armchair. He tells Hunter about his father's Paris joke, about the sickness that was an inability to see his wife and to speak the truth about her. Having lost awareness of the duplicity in his joke, he believed the conjunction between the sign and the thing. For Travis's father Paris, Texas, became Paris, France. In the second confession, this time spoken not to Hunter directly but into a tape recorder because he fears he will not find the right words in Hunter's presence, Travis explains to him that his fear—the fear of his own jealousy—prevents him from joining Jane and Hunter, from reconstructing the family as it was in the home movie and the photographic image.

Travis's journey is also a psychoanalytical itinerary whose stations are amnesia, the gradual accession to language, the establishment of family ties, and exorcism of his fetishes. Reliving the past family trauma helps him regain his memory and with it recover his present identity, but also the guilt and responsibility that replaces his desire. The second visit to the peep show, in which the exposition supplied by the characters' monologues becomes a process of self-exposure, finally provides an explanation for the family's collapse. Travis now speaks into the telephone telling a story, their

THE ARCHAEOLOGY OF THE PRESENT

The end of Travis's journey also reveals the economy of his desire: he finds Jane at the Keyhole Club, an elaborate peep show in which the male visitor can talk with a woman while watching her through a one-way mirror (used by permission of Stiftung deutsche Kinemathek, Berlin).

story, distanced grammatically by the use of the third person pronoun "he." Moreover, during the entire narrative, distinguished on the verbal level by its very conventionality, he turns his chair around so that he does not see Jane. Travis renounces the possibility of narcissistic possession in this theatrical setting because he can only communicate with Jane if he does not look at her body. The restrained editing, consisting of a very few reverse shots blocked by the one-way mirror, visually confirms the disparity between seeing and speaking and reproduces visually the subject/object dichotomy in Travis's monologic discourse. Then Jane, having recognized Travis, tells the story of what happened after he abandoned her and Hunter. She too turns away from his image—now visible through the mirrored glass on her side after they rearrange the lights—while telling an equally banal story. Here in the peep show booth Jane and Travis can finally meet and exchange words full of desire because its artifice guarantees that bodies do not touch and looks do not intersect. Only for a moment between these two stories do their images and looks meet in silence: shot from behind Travis, who looks at the window, his face is superimposed on Jane's as she presses against the mirror surface on the other side, trying to see Travis. The eerie merging of their two faces in the center of the frame—not unlike the fusion of the two sisters' images in the prison in von Trotta's *Marianne and Juliane*—is a symbolic moment of visual communication never achieved on the verbal level. It is also a moment that only the spectator, positioned as a third party outside the frame, can appreciate.

At this point it becomes clear that on a metafilmic level a reversal has taken place. Whereas the first part of *Paris, Texas* is filled with gorgeous but almost silent landscape images characterized by deep focus or lateral movement, these last sequences overflow with Travis's words while the visual track features tight framing, foreshortened perspectives, and cramped spaces. Diegetically this reversal manifests itself in Travis's use of language in his effort to recover the past. Travis tells Hunter in his taped message: "I can't even hardly remember what happened. It's like a gap." And similarly in his dime-novel narration of desire and jealousy in front of Jane he does not explain *why* he ran away, only that "for the first time he wished he were far away. Lost in a deep vast country where nobody knew him. Somewhere without language or streets." The silence without knowledge at the beginning becomes words without desire at the end.

While the initial appropriation of language in the word "Paris" was marked by a doubling of reality and imagination, it has become in the final segment of the film the lived disparity between language and image, the impossibility of bringing together speaking and seeing, word and image, memory and emotion. Here the scopic and metaphysical drive that drew Travis out of that "deep vast country" allows him to look at the unseeable. It creates the context in which Travis sees himself mirrored in Jane, in which he finds himself in order to see the Other: "Travis is sitting in front of a screen, and she's on the screen, or behind it, and is really the object of his imagination."[8] As in all of Wenders's films, woman is the ultimate resistance, an enigma who challenges and destabilizes male identity. Travis cannot see Jane as a mother, yet he knows now through his son Hunter that he is his father and Jane is his mother. Hence, he displaces himself to make room for that maternal love, renouncing his own "image" because it is bound to an absolute, impossible, and destructive longing.

Travis's journey to and with his son has brought him to the point where his act of love is the renunciation of love itself. Having found Jane and reunited mother and son, he has also found the self; however, it is based on separation. Travis watches from a distance—the outsider, the observer—as Jane comes to Hunter, and in the last image he drives off alone into the sunset. Wenders's intentionally heavy-handed quote of all those John Ford Westerns, including Travis's smile, ironically countermands the film's narrative closure. To be sure, there is a utopian quality when Hunter's quest comes to an end in the visual figure of mother and son embracing in a spin, but the circularity of the closure, with Travis abandoning his family once again to return to his solitude, cannot be read realistically.[9] This sentimental family utopia, here privileging the mother-child relationship, suggests a dream logic in which the self has been absented. Bringing the family together is not sufficient; the illusion of plenitude simply offers the possibility of not defining oneself through negation. By creating the image of the father for Hunter, Travis simulates a role for himself. In other words, the family serves as a projection screen that supplies an imaginary position for the self. Travis, like the spectator, watches his life become fiction in the narrative closure, but it is a fiction with unsettling effects, frustrating the formal expectations associated with the genre conditions of the domestic melodrama and the road movie.

Like Wenders's earlier quest films *Alice in the Cities* (*Alice in den Städten*, 1974), *Wrong Movement* (*Falsche Bewegung*, 1975), and *Kings of the Road* (*Im Laufe der Zeit*, 1976), *Paris, Texas* addresses the problematic constitution of male subjectivity in the context of a search for the family bonds of home. Those family bonds are experienced as an Oedipal trauma, and "home" resembles an intrusion of the past in the present. In the case of *Paris, Texas* Wenders has displaced that search for a home to America, but home is in this instance less a geographical place than an imaginary space. As one critic rightly claims, "German history is present, even where it does not appear as such."[10] Germany's historical traumas constantly reappear in the New German Cinema in figures of border crossings, exile, and journey. In this regard the film partakes of the larger postwar discourse on *Vergangenheitsbewältigung* or mastering the past that already preoccupied West German filmmakers like Pabst, Kluge, and von Trotta. More specifically, and this distinguishes *Paris, Texas* from these earlier films as well as from the GDR's antifascist films, it is an attempt to problematize the very language—linguistic and visual—that constructs the imaginary relations for telling the story of the postwar generation in Germany.[11]

It would be too simple to view Wenders's narrative as a chronicle of the postwar generation's unresolved Oedipal complex in Germany but at the same time it does offer insights into the psychopathology of the postwar German family and the psychological deficits and injuries manifested by an entire generation.[12] Most parents of this generation lived the historical experience of the Third Reich through an unusually strong emotional investment of personal and national identity associated with individual self-sacrifice and group destiny. The 1945 defeat and final capitulation represented for many an officially avowed break with the fascist system of sociopolitical domination, but they could not convert so quickly the emotional energy and its attendant psychological desire without paying a price. The ready-made framework of reconstruction introduced by the Occupying Powers sanctioned a convenient and at least partially successful form of sublimation for the guilt, but the parents' repression, silence, and forgetting was visited on the children. The family became the primary stage on which the parents' bewilderment about their role in a past universally condemned by the world was acted out. It provided, on the one hand, a refuge with an outward form of continuity and a surrogate identity projected in the children. On the other hand, the family structure alone could not conceal the parents' frugality of emotions and lack of tenderness resulting from historically invested guilt. The children, in turn, experienced family life and their parents in particular as protectors of authority and empty forms. Moreover, the space of childhood from which the start in life proceeds—at least in the sense of cultural continuity—did not exist for postwar German children.[13] This is the tortured search for *Heimat* already anticipated by the fifties Heimat film configured in *Black Forest Girl* and reconfigured in the eighties by Wenders as a mythic quest.

Paris, Texas was Wenders's most popular and commercially most successful film up to that point.[14] Yet the international success of this multinational feature—German director, American scriptwriter, American, German, and French actors and technical team—confirmed not only an unparalleled sophistication in the production and marketing of the New German Cinema but also a trend that many understood to signal the doom of this new wave cinema in its cultural particularity. The disrupted father-son relationship that Wenders sets in Texas speaks not only to a German phenomenon but also more generally to the dilemma of the modern, ravaged family as a site for the production and reproduction of emotions. Nonetheless, the specific experience of a clear historical rupture in Germany, marked by the absence—literal or figurative—of a generation of fathers, places their children at the cutting edge of the problematic. This factor may even explain why New German Cinema directors, the generation of filmmakers that came of age after 1960, were frequently considered pariahs in their own country while celebrated abroad, for they showed a consistent interest in the crisis of identity and legitimation, both hallmarks of the generational conflict at stake here.[15]

It is surely no accident that the first major success of the West German New Wave was Volker Schlöndorff's *The Young Törless* (*Der junge Törless*, 1966). An adolescent boy, turned over by his father to a surrogate parental authority represented by a boarding school and the older classmates, learns to channel his hypersensitivity into contempt for those around him while escaping into the world of imagination. In *The Tin Drum* (*Die Blechtrommel*, 1979) Schlöndorff projects another disturbed father-son relationship. Not only does Oscar refuse to grow older and to grow up but he also cannot decide who his real father is. This posture of reproach describes as well Werner Herzog's parable of the wild child Kaspar Hauser in *Every Man for Himself or God against All* (*Jeder für sich und Gott gegen alle*, 1974). Thrown into the world without paternity, the victim of the absent father yearns for that original state of undifferentiated preconsciousness that Herzog identifies with nature, a state before the fall into history, and patriarchal law. Hark Bohm's films about adolescents, especially *The North Sea Is Murderous* (*Nordsee ist Mordsee*, 1975), and Wolfgang Petersen's *The Neverending Story* (*Die unendliche Geschichte*, 1984) treat the absent fathers literally—they are invisible—and the genre pattern of adolescent initiation adopted by these films takes on a typically somber, melancholy air. Rainer Werner Fassbinder's entire oeuvre discloses from this perspective an obsessive curiosity about family constellations and the affective politics of subordination and power. Most striking in the context of the father-son dynamic is *I Only Want You to Love Me* (*Ich will doch nur, dass ihr mich liebt*, 1976) based on the sociological case study of a patricide motivated by anger toward an unloving father. Finally, Hans-Jürgen Syberberg's *Our Hitler* (*Hitler, ein Film aus Deutschland*, 1977) constructs Hitler as the collective father figure in a mythic German consciousness. The film's idiosyncratic aesthetic form positions the spectators both as jury and accused in a monumental trial aimed at confronting the postwar denial of this "father."

In *Paris, Texas* Wenders signals a new approach to the problematic father-son constellation beyond the responses of refusal and accusation typified by these earlier films. No longer is it a matter of the fathers' absence or unarticulated negation; it is an attempt to rescue the idealism of *not* forgetting, of turning to one's own beginnings in order to erase false images. From this point of view it is less a film about Travis's existential desire to become a father or Hunter's quest for his mother than a cinematic demonstration of the struggle between the power of images to deny reality and the need for narrative to produce new images. The struggle was anticipated linguistically in Travis's appropriation of a language that has lost authenticity and it was conveyed visually by the disjunction of seeing and speaking in the peep show encounter. Wenders offers no apologies or excuses for his protagonist's faulty memory, he merely substantiates the continued presence of a rupture and its power to affect any relation to reality that is constituted by means of images. The endless, perhaps even hopeless, attempt to erase or to repress the buried past and its images becomes, in turn, the constitutive factor for self-identity as the telling of one's story in the present.

Conclusion

The screening of Wenders's *Paris, Texas* in Germany was delayed over six months until January 1985 by a complicated legal battle between the filmmaker and his West German distributor. Filmverlag der Autoren, the cooperative distribution company established to promote New German Cinema films and to which ironically Wenders belonged as an original stockholder, refused to launch the feature as a major production in first-run cinemas despite its international acclaim. The controversy was symptomatic of the crucial weakness of the hybrid, alternative film culture in West Germany: it was never able to develop a distribution network that could compete with the American multinationals in delivering its productions to the domestic German market. In 1984 the signs of a second postwar crisis in the West German film industry were obvious after the first sharp downturn of the sixties. The cinema's competitiveness was being further exacerbated by the introduction of new electronic media—video, commercial and cable television, satellite reception, interactive computer games. Meanwhile the funding clinch with public television and state subsidies and prizes was drawing the New German Cinema ever closer to a kind of state-sponsored stagnation.

Of course, to speak of the West German film industry in the eighties is deceptive. Production remained (and today still remains) concentrated in craftslike minienterprises without access to new technologies of animation, trick photography, digital imaging, and computer applications. In many cases only about 10 percent of the production costs were covered by ticket sales, whereas the rest drew on various direct and indirect subsidies.[1] Continuing the slippage since the midseventies, the share of domestic features in the West German exhibition market was during the eighties only 10 percent of the total, compared to 40–50 percent for domestic productions in countries like Italy and France. One strategy to compensate for this imbalance was to increase the export attractiveness of West German features. In fact, by the early eighties New German Cinema films were earning about three times as much in export revenues than they were from the domestic market.[2] This not only confirmed the general public's suspicion that the New German Cinema was at worst a creation of foreign cinephiles or at best a phenomenon of purely artistic interest but it also affected the look of the films themselves. Wim Wenders, especially after the critical and international success of *Wings of Desire* (*Der Himmel über Berlin*, 1987), was perhaps the most visible among the New German directors who were adapting Hollywood production values to gain access to international markets and audiences. Other established directors followed suit. Volker Schlöndorff (*Death of a Salesman*, 1985; *A Gathering of Old Men*, 1987; *The Handmaid's Tale*, 1989) and Percy Adlon (*Baghdad Cafe* [*Out of Rosenheim*], 1987; *Salmonberries*, 1991) began producing features with English-language screenplays for English-speaking audiences. Margarethe von Trotta in effect emigrated to Italy where she directs European coproductions (*Paura e amore*, 1988; *L'Africana*, 1990; *Il lungo silenzio*, 1993). Wolfgang Petersen's *The Boat* (*Das Boot*, 1981) and Doris Dörrie's *Men* (*Männer*, 1985) recycled genre clichés of the war film and the comedy of errors that gained them access to the American commercial market. The "old" New German Cinema was no longer oppositional or innovative; indeed it seemed to have lost all connection to German genres, themes, and traditions.

By the end of the decade the political changes in Germany were reconfiguring the terrain for cinema culture. Unification suddenly introduced new competitors (the large pool of talented filmmakers from East Germany seeking state and television funding), an expanded television broadcasting system (new stations in the East), and a different public sphere. At the same time the nineties' political agenda for European integration suggests that traditional national cinemas may be a thing of the past. The DEFA studios were bought out by a French multinational with the intent of producing European film and television programming, while the ongoing negotiations on international free trade relations (GATT) pit the American information and entertainment industries against a persistent but splintered European notion of cultural autonomy.

Germany continues to produce between fifty and seventy feature-length films each year (about the same number as during the fifties), but only about 20 percent actually are distributed in cinemas.[3] Television and video marketing are becoming more and more important as delivery systems for German feature films, and not surprisingly many films look just like television entertainment. The major German-produced box office successes in the nineties feature Germany's best-known television comedians,

CONCLUSION

Otto Walke, Loriot, Helge Schneider, and Hape Kerkeling, and humor is one of the most difficult commodities to export, especially German humor. Younger filmmakers have followed suit, producing comedies and satires with moderate success: Peter Timm's spoof about the East German automobile *Go, Trabi, Go* (1991; part 2, 1992); Detlev Buck's comedy about a provincial policeman *Little Rabbits* (*Karniggel*, 1991); Sönke Wartmann's debut film about a macho who becomes the housekeeper in a women's commune *Alone among Women* (*Allein unter Frauen*, 1991); and Helmut Dietl's parody about the forged Hitler diaries *Schtonk* (1992). In fact the number of cinemagoers is rising. In 1991 more tickets were sold in the united Germany than in the traditionally cinephile France, but the explanation leads back to the dominance of American productions: Germany is the second largest export market for American box office hits after Japan. Thus, although the traditional cinema venues appear to be active, their fare is becoming an increasingly international commodity defined by American production values and professionalism and marketed with American distribution strategies.

Skeptics regard these developments as a sellout of the New German Cinema's critical and aesthetic ideals to commercial interests, while pragmatists see internationalization—which is at best only a partial description of the actual situation—as an adequate or necessary response to the ongoing crisis in the traditional media and to the political and economic shifts of the nineties. From the longer view of historically constituted and changing imaginary relations this is a new turn in the conditions for representation and spectatorship. No longer does the ability to tell a good story well in moving images suffice for the production of a successful film in Germany. When television broadcasts as many as 15,000 films a year in Germany, the cinemas must offer something special, be it the American megahits or the small, thoughtful films European directors have excelled in producing.

The year 1989 emerged as another one of those radical ruptures in German continuity, identity, and memory, and there is good reason to assume Germans will persist in exploring their anxieties and hopes with new narratives and resolutions. If the cinema is one way of imagining the contingencies of the present, then its strategies for constructing a way of seeing in the nineties will bear the traces of those events, as long as moving images do not cease. Just as important is the interpretation of these narrative and visual negotiations. I have proposed in the readings collected here that the cinema invokes the past in order to understand the present. Despite a popular tendency to consider the camera a window on reality and the visible as true, cinematic images are no more than views of how we wish to believe the world to be. Our work as interested and critical spectators is to read and reread these visual texts, taking account of the changing contexts under the pressure of time passing.

Appendix: Film Credits

Passion
(Madame Dubarry)

Released	1919
Producer	Carl Moos, Projektions-AG Union, Berlin
Director	Ernst Lubitsch
Screenplay	Fred Orbing (=Norbert Falk), Hanns Kräly
Cinematography	Theodor Sparkuhl
Set decoration	Kurt Richter, Karl Machus
Costumes	Ali Hubert
Music	Alexander Schirmann
Cast	Pola Negri (Jeanne Vaubernier/Madame Dubarry)
	Emil Jannings (King Louis XV)
	Reinhold Schünzel (Choiseul, Finance Minister)
	Harry Liedtke (Armand de Foix)
	Eduard von Winterstein (Count Jean Dubarry)
	Karl Platen (Guillaume Dubarry)
	Paul Biensfeldt (Lebel, King's Chamberlain)
	Magnus Stifter (Don Diego, Spanish Envoy)
	Willy Kaiser-Heyl (Commander of the Guards)
	Elsa Berna (Duchess Gramont)
	Fred Immler (Duke Richelieu)
	Gustav Czimeg (Duke Aiguillon)
	Alexander Ekert (Paillet)
	Marga Köhler (Madame Labille)
	Bernhard Goetzke
	Robert Sortsch-Plá
Length	2280 meters (original censor length)

The Last Laugh
(Der letzte Mann)

Released	1924
Producer	Erich Pommer, Decla-Film der UFA
Director	Friedrich Wilhelm Murnau
Screenplay	Carl Mayer
Cinematography	Karl Freund, Robert Baberske (assistant)
Set decoration	Walter Röhrig, Robert Herlth
Music	Giuseppe Bucce
Cast	Emil Jannings (doorman, then lavatory attendant)
	Maly Delschaft (his daughter)
	Hans Unterkircher (hotel manager)
	Georg John (night watchman)
	Max Hiller (daughter's fiance)
	Emilie Kurtz (his aunt)
	Olaf Sturm/Hermann Valentin (hotel guests)
	Emmy Wyda (thin neighbor)
Length	2315 meters (original censor length)

Kuhle Wampe or Who Owns the World?
(Kuhle Wampe oder Wem gehört die Welt?)

Released	1932
Producer	Georg M. Höllering, Robert Scharfenberg, Prometheus GmbH/Praesens GmbH
Director	Slatan Theodor Dudov
Dir. of dialog	Bertolt Brecht
Screenplay	Bertolt Brecht, Ernst Ottwald
Cinematography	Günther Krampf
Set decoration	Robert Scharfenberg, Carl P. Haacker
Sound	Carl Erich Kroschke, Fritz Michaelis
Sound editing	Peter Meyrowitz
Editing	Slatan Dudov
Music	Hanns Eisler
Music Director	Josef Schmid
Orchestra	Lewis Ruth Band
Cast	Hertha Thiele (Anni Bönike)
	Martha Wolter (Gerda)
	Lilli Schönborn (Mrs. Bönike)
	Ernst Busch (Fritz)
	Adolf Fischer (Kurt)

Max Sablotzki (Mr. Bönike)
Alfred Schäfer (Franz Bönike)
Willi Schur (Otto, guest at engagement party)
Gerhard Bienert (man with a goatee in the subway)
Martha Burchardi
Karl Heinz Carell
Karl Dahmen
Fritz Erpenbeck
Josef Hanoszek
Richard Hilgert
Hermann Krehan
Paul Kretzburg
Anna Müller-Lincke
Rudolf Nehls
Erich Peters
Olly Rummel
Martha Seemann
Hans Stern
Karl Wagner
Hugo Werner-Kahle
"Das rote Sprachrohr" (agitprop theater group)

Ballads   Helene Weigel, Ernst Busch
Length   2070 meters (original censor length)

To New Shores / Life Begins Anew
(Zu neuen Ufern)

Released	1937
Producer	Bruno Duday, UFA
Director	Detlef Sierck
Asst. Director	Fritz Andelfinger
Screenplay	Detlef Sierck, Kurt Heuser (based on a novel by Lovis H. Lorenz)
Cinematography	Franz Weihmayr
Set decoration	Fritz Maurischat
Costumes	Arno Richter
Sound	Carl-Heinz Becker
Editing	Milo Harbich
Music/lyrics	Ralph Benatzky
Music Director	Erich Holder
Cast	Zarah Leander (Gloria Vane)
	Willy Birgel (Sir Albert Finsbury)

Viktor Staal (Henry Hoyer)
Erich Ziegel (his uncle, Dr. Magnus Hoyer)
Hilde von Stolz (his wife Fanny Hoyer)
Edwin Jürgensen (Governor of Sydney)
Carola Höhn (his daughter Mary)
Jakob Tiedtke (Wells senior, cheese merchant)
Robert Dorsay (his son, Bobby "Pudding" Wells)
Iwa Wanja (Violet)
Ernst Legal (Stout, Henry's friend)
Siegfried Schürenberg (Gilbert)
Lina Lossen (Paramatta prison Director)
Lissi Arna (Nelly)
Herbert Hübner ("Casino" Director)
Mady Rahl (singer at "Casino")
Lina Carstens (street singer in London)
Paul Bildt (melodian player)
Horst Teetzmann, Horst Birr, Hans Kettler, Walter
    Schramm-Duncker, Fritz Hoopts, Franz Stein,
    Claus Pohl, Ekkehart Arendt, Hanns-Maria
    Böhmer, Curt Jürgens, Ilse von Colani, Walter
    Werner, Werner Pledath, Karl Hannemann, Hella
    Graf, Karl Auen, Hans Waschatko, Else Boy, Boris
    Alekin, William Huch, Max Wilhelm Hiller,
    Oskar Höcker, Paul Schwed, Hermann Pfeiffer,
    S. O. Schoening, Lilli Schönborn, Ellen Bang,
    Hildegard Friebel, Hanna Mohs, Thea Truelsen,
    Olga Schaub, Hansjoachim Büttner

Length   2879 meters

Request Concert

(Wunschkonzert)

Released   1940
Producer   F. Pfitzner, Cine-Allianz-Tonfilmproduktion GmbH
Director   Eduard von Borsody
Screenplay   Felix Lützkendorf, Eduard von Borsody
Cinematography   Franz Weihmayr, Günther Anders, Carl Drews
Set decoration   Alfred Bütow, Heinrich Beisenherz
Costumes   Gertrud Steckler
Sound   Walter Rühland
Editing   Elisabeth Neumann

Music Werner Bochmann
Cast Ilse Werner (Inge Wagner)
Carl Raddatz (Captain Herbert Koch)
Joachim Brennecke (Lieutenant Helmut Winkler)
Ida Wüst (Mrs. Eichhorn, Inge's aunt)
Hedwig Bleibtreu (Mrs. Wagner, Inge's
  grandmother)
Heinz Goedecke (radio concert moderator)
Malte Jaeger (Peter Friedrich, schoolteacher)
Hans H. Schaufuss (Hammer, baker)
Hans Adalbert Schlettow (Max Kramer, butcher)
Walter Ladengast (Schwarzkopf, music student)
Albert Florath (physician)
Elise Aulinger (Mrs. Schwarzkopf)
Günther Lüders (Zimmermann, airplane mechanic)
Wilhelm Althaus (Captain Freiberg)
Erwin Biegel (Justav, airplane mechanic)
Ellen Hille (Mrs. Kramer)
Walter Bechmann (waiter)
Vera Hartegg (Hanna Friedrich, Peter's wife)
Vera Comlojer (Mrs. Hammer)
Aribert Mog, Rolf Heydel, Wilhelm König, Erich
  Stelmecke, Ewald Wenck, Wolf Dietrich, Werner
  Schott, Fritz Angermann, Max Wilmsen, Hans
  Sternberg, Franz List, Reinhold Bernt, Erik
  Radolf, Rudolf Vones, Fred Goebel
Request Concert Performers: Marika Rökk, Heinz
  Rühmann, Paul Hörbiger, Hans Brausewetter, Josef
  Sieber, Weiss-Ferdl, Wilhelm Strienz, Albert Bräu
Length 2832 meters

Romance in a Minor Key
(Romanze in Moll)

Released 1943
Producer Hermann Grund, Tobis-Filmkunst GmbH
Director Helmut Käutner
Asst. Director Rudolf Jugert, Siegfried Breuer
Screenplay Willy Clever, Helmut Käutner, based on an idea of
  Willy Clever
Cinematography Georg Bruckbauer
Camera Wolfgang Hewecker

Set decoration	Otto Erdmann, Franz F. Fürst
Costumes	Ludwig Hornsteiner
Sound	Hans Grimm
Editing	Anneliese Sponholz
Music	Lothar Brühne, Werner Eisbrenner
Cast	Marianne Hoppe (Madeleine)
	Paul Dahlke (Madeleine's husband)
	Ferdinand Marian (Michael)
	Siegfried Breuer (Victor)
	Eric Helgar (Michael's brother)
	Karl Platen (Michael's servant)
	Anja Elkoff (Tamara, the singer)
	Elisabeth Flickenschildt (concierge at Madeleine's apartment building)
	Walter Lieck (tall man)
	Ernst Legal (deaf man)
	Hans Stiebner (chubby man)
	Karl Günther (jeweler)
	Hugo Flink (bank president)
	Klaus Pohl (pawnbroker)
	Leo Peukert (cafe head waiter)
	Maria Loja (his wife, the cashier)
	Ethel Reschke (streetwalker)
	Karl Etlinger (bank manager)
	Ernst Rotmund (police commissioner)
	Walter Bechmann (restaurant waiter)
	Hans Parge (shoe salesman)
	Hansi Schündler (shoe saleswoman)
	Rudolf Kalvius (physician)
	Herbert Weissbach (orchestra manager)
	Egon Vogel (flower seller)
	Hanns Waschatko (head of the bank's investigatory committee)
	Helmut Käutner (poet)
Length	2728 meters (original censor length)

Rotation

Released	1949
Producer	Collective Herbert Uhlich, DEFA
Director	Wolfgang Staudte

Asst. Director	Hans Heinrich
Screenplay	Wolfgang Staudte, Erwin Klein
Cinematography	Bruno Mondi
Set decoration	Willy Schiller, Willi Eplinius, Artur Schwarz, Franz Fürst
Costumes	G. Schott
Sound	Karl Tramburg
Editing	Lilian Seng
Music	H. W. Wiemann
Cast	Paul Esser (Hans Behnke)
	Irene Korb (Lotte Behnke)
	Karl-Heinz Deikert (their son, Helmuth Behnke)
	Brigitte Krause (his girlfriend Inge)
	Reinhold Bernt (Lotte's brother, Kurt Blank)
	Reinhard Kolldehoff (Rudi Wille, a Nazi)
	Werner Peters (Udo Schulze, Hitler Youth commander)
	Albert Johannes (personnel manager at the newspaper)
	Theodor Vogeler (secret service operative)
	Walter Tarrach (secret service operative)
	Valeska Stock (midwife)
	Ellen Thenn-Weinig (Mrs. Salomon)
	Klemens Herzberg (Mr. Salomon)
	Hans-Erich Korbschmitt (party operative)
	Maria Loja (landlady)
	Wolfgang Kühne (unemployed actor at wedding)
	Alfred Maack (landlord)
	Siegfried Andrich (SS operative)
	Hugo Kalthoff (SS officer)
	Carlo Kluge (orderly)
	Helmut Hain (bomb shelter guard)
	Georg-August Koch (secret service operative)
	Kitty Franke (refugee)
	Herbert Mahlsbender (prison SS guard)
	Gerd Ewert (adjutant)
	Rudi Beil (soldier)
	Albert Venohr, Hans Emons, Helmuth Bautzmann, Walter Diehl (striking workers)
	Eduard Matzig, Peter Marx, Johannes Knittel, Hans Schille, Gerd Robat, Friedrich Teitge (workers at the print shop)
Length	2375 meters (East German version), 2231 (West German version)

Black Forest Girl

(Schwarzwaldmädel)

Released	1950
Producer	Kurt Ulrich, Berolina-Film
Director	Hans Deppe
Asst. Director	Hans Ohrtmann
Screenplay	Bobby E. Lüthge, based on the operetta by August Neidhardt
Cinematography	Kurt Schulz
Camera	Herbert Geier
Set decoration	Gabriel Pellon
Costumes	Walter Kraatz
Sound	Hans Ebel, Hans Löhmer
Editing	Margarete Steinborn
Music	Leon Jessel, adapted by Frank Fox
Choreography	Hanns Gérard
Make-up	Maria Westhoff, Fred Arnold
Color Adviser	Gerhard Huttula
Cast	Paul Hörbiger (Blasius Römer, choir master)
	Trude von Wilke-Rosswog (Traudel Riederle, his housekeeper)
	Sonja Ziemann (Bärbele Riederle, Bussmann's secretary and Traudel's niece)
	Fritz Kampers (Jürgen, innkeeper at the "Blue Ox")
	Lucie Englisch (Lorle, his daughter)
	Kurt Zehe (Gottlieb, worker at the "Blue Ox")
	Rudolf Prack (Hans Hauser, artist)
	Gretl Schörg (Malwine Hainau, stage star)
	Walter Müller (Richard Petersen, her partner)
	Ernst Waldow (Fritz Bussmann, jeweler and owner of Bussmann & Co.)
	Hans Richter (Theo Patzke, Bussmann's employee)
	Kurt Pratsch-Kaufmann (Herr Staubig, Bussmann's accountant)
	Franz Otto Krüger (master of ceremonies)
	Karl Schöpp (church dean)
	Lydia Veicht's Ballet on Ice
Length	2846 meters

The Last Ten Days

(Der letzte Akt)

Released	1955
Producer	Carl Szokoll, Cosmopol-Film (Vienna)
Director	Georg Wilhelm Pabst
Asst. Director	Peter Pabst
Screenplay	Erich Maria Remarque, based on Michael A. Musmanno's book *Ten Days to Die* (dialogue by Fritz Habeck)
Cinematography	Günther Anders
Camera	Hannes Staudinger
Set decoration	Werner Schlichting, Otto Pischinger, Wolf Witzemann
Makeup	Rudolf Ohlschmidt, Leopold Kuhnert
Music	Erwin Halletz
Sound	Otto Untersalmberger
Editing	Herbert Taschner
Cast	Albin Skoda (Adolf Hitler)
	Gerd Zöhling (Richard)
	Oskar Werner (Captain Wüst)
	Lotte Tobisch (Eva Braun)
	Willy Krause (Josef Goebbels)
	Helga Dohrn (Magda Goebbels)
	Hermann Erhardt (Hermann Goering)
	Eric Suckmann (Heinrich Himmler)
	Kurt Eilers (Martin Bormann)
	Julius Jonak (Hermann Fegelein)
	Leopold Hainisch (General Wilhelm Keitel)
	Otto Schmöle (General Jodl)
	Otto Wögerer (General Ritter von Greim)
	Erik Frey (General Burgdorf)
	Herbert Herbe (General Krebs)
	Erland Erlandsen (Albert Speer)
	Hannes Schiel (Günsche, Hitler's adjutant)
	Guido Wieland (Hitler's doctor)
	Walter Regelsberger (Major Venner, Wüst's half brother)
	Michael Janisch (SS officer)
	Raoul Retzer (the bully, SS guard)
	Ernst Waldbrunn (Hitler's astrologer)
	Eduard Köck (Volkssturm officer)

John van Deelen (Brinkmann)
Lilly Stepanek (Mrs. Brinkmann)
Herta Angst (Jutta, their daughter)
Ernst Pröckl (Wagner, justice of the peace)
Helen Arcon (Hanna Reitsch, pilot)
Franz Messner (bartender)
Martha Wallner (Frieda, waitress)
Otto Kerry (military doctor)
Eduard Spiess (a thin man)
Otto Guschy (Franz, Wüst's driver)
Otto Loewe (secretary)
Peter Holzer (Herbert Spalke)
Elisabeth Epp (Richard's mother)
Inge Kurzbauer(secretary)

Length	3200 meters (Austrian version), 3143 meters (West German version)

I Was Nineteen

(Ich war neunzehn)

Released	1968
Producer	Herbert Ehler, DEFA-Studio für Spielfilme, Gruppe Babelsberg 67
Director	Konrad Wolf
Asst. Director	Doris Borkmann, Rainer Simon
Screenplay	Wolfgang Kohlhaase, Konrad Wolf
Cinematography	Werner Bergmann
Editing	Evelyn Carow
Set decoration	Alfred Hirschmeier
Costumes	Werner Bergemann
Sound	Konrad Walle
Dramaturgy	Gerhard Wolf
Cast	Jaecki Schwarz (Gregor Hecker)
	Vassili Livanov (Vadim)
	Alexei Eiboshenko (Sasha)
	Galina Polskich (female Soviet soldier)
	Jenny Gröllmann (young German woman)
	Mikhail Glusski (Soviet General)
	Anatoli Soloviov (Soviet guard)
	Kalmurska Rachmanov (Dsingis, the driver)
	Rolf Hoppe (Major)
	Wolfgang Greese (landscape architect)

Johannes Wieke (Commander, Spandau fortress)
Jürgen Hentsch (Adjutant)
Kurt Böwe (SS Commander)
Klaus Manchen (blind soldier)
Walter Bechstein, Hermann Beyer (concentration
    camp prisoners)
Afanasi Kotshetkov (Soviet Sergeant)
Dieter Mann (non-com officer)

Length   3262 meters

On Probation
(Bürgschaft für ein Jahr)

Released   1981
Producer   Dorothea Hildebrandt, DEFA Studio für Spielfilm,
            Gruppe Berlin
Director   Hermann Zschoche
Asst. Director   Evelyn Opoczynski, Eleonore Dressel
Screenplay   Gabriele Kotte, based on the novel by Tine Schulze-
            Gerlach
Cinematography   Günter Jaeuthe
Camera   Hans-Joachim Knospe
Set decoration   Dieter Adam
Costumes   Anne Hoffmann
Makeup   Kurt Tauchmann, Christa Grewald
Music   Günther Fischer
Sound   Klaus Tolstorf
Editing   Monika Schindler
Cast   Katrin Sass (Nina Kern)
        Monika Lennartz (Irmgard Behrend)
        Jaecki Schwarz (Peter Müller)
        Jan Spitzer (Werner Horn, Nina's first lover)
        Christian Steyer (Heiner Menk, Nina's second lover)
        Heide Kipp (Mrs. Braun)
        Barbara Dittus (Director of nursery)
        Ursula Werner (Mrs. Müller)
        Angelika Mann (Renate)
        Solveig Müller (social worker)
        Gabriele Methner (Fränzi)
        Dieter Montag (Kern, Nina's former husband)
        Heinz Behrens (Mr. Braun)
        Uwe Kockisch (Dieter)
        Werner Tietze (Chair of the Juvenile Commission)

On Probation, (continued)

> Peter Bause (Director of children's home)
> Michaela Hotz (Mireille)
> Cornelia Förder (Jacqueline)
> Enrico Robert (René)
> Sebastian Reuter (music student)
> Length   2545 meters

Artists under the Big Top: Perplexed
(Die Artisten in der Zirkuskuppel: ratlos)

Released	1968
Producer	Kairos-Film, Munich
Director	Alexander Kluge
Screenplay	Alexander Kluge
Cinematography	Günter Hörmann, Thomas Mauch
Camera	Dietrich Lohmann, Frank Brühne
Sound	Bernd Hoeltz
Editing	Beate Mainka-Jellinghaus
Piano	Liviane Gomorrhi, Hellmuth Löffler
Cast	Hannelore Hoger (Leni Peickert, circus artiste and entrepreneur)
	Siegfried Graue (her father Manfred Peickert)
	Alfred Edel (her friend Dr. Busch)
	Bernd Hoeltz (von Lüptow, her business manager)
	Eva Oertel (Gitti Bornemann, a rich heiress)
	Kurt Jürgens (trainer Mackensen)
	Gilbert Houcke (trainer Houcke)
	Wanda Bronska-Pampuch (Mrs. Saizewa)
	Mr. Jobst (impresario)
	Hans-Ludger Schneider (Korti, bureaucrat from censorship commission)
	Klaus Schwarzkopf (Gerloff, professor)
	Nils von der Heyde (Arbogast, press attaché)
	Marie Luise Dutoit (Swiss circus artiste)
	Peter Staimmer (Perry Woodcock)
	Theodor Hoffa (man with a monocle)
	Maximiliane Mainka/Ingeborg Pressler (clowns)
	Wolfgang Mai (Joe Willkins, dramaturge)
	Tilde Trommler (Lotte Losemeyer, accountant)
	Ingo Binder (Fadil Sojkowski, snake trainer)
	Kurt Tharandt (Böhme, creditor)
	Ina Giehrt (journalist)

commentary spoken by: Alexander Kluge, Hannelore Hoger, Mr. Hollenbeck

Length   2829 meters

Marianne and Juliane
(Die bleierne Zeit)

Released   1981
Producer   Eberhard Junkersdorf, Bioskop-Film and Sender Freies Berlin
Director   Margarethe von Trotta
Asst. Director   Helenka Hummel
Screenplay   Margarethe von Trotta
Cinematography   Franz Rath
Editing   Dagmar Hirtz
Set decoration   Georg von Kieseritzky
Costumes   Monika Hasse, Jorge Jara
Make-up   Bernd-Rüdiger Knoll, Jutta Stroppe
Sound   Vladimir Vizner
Music   Nicholas Economou
                  Georg Friedrich Händel (Lucretia)
Cast   Jutta Lampe (Juliane)
                  Barbara Sukowa (Marianne)
                  Rüdiger Vogler (Wolfgang)
                  Doris Schade (Mother)
                  Verenice Rudolph (Sabine)
                  Luc Bondy (Werner)
                  Franz Rudnick (Father)
                  Julia Biedermann (Marianne at 16)
                  Ina Robinski (Juliane at 17)
                  Patrick Estrada-Pox (Jan at 10)
                  Samir Jawad (Jan at 4)
                  Barbara Paepcke (Juliane at 6)
                  Rebecca Paepcke (Marianne at 5)
                  Margit Czenki, Carola Hembus, Anna Steinmann, Wulfhild Sydow, Ingeborg Weber (magazine co-editors)
                  Satan Deutscher (Karl)
                  Karin Bremer (prison guard)
                  Rolf Schult (newspaper editor)
                  Anton Rattinger (pastor)
                  Lydia Billiet (nurse)
                  Hannelore Minkus (teacher)
Length   2909 meters

Paris, Texas

Released	1984 (in West Germany, 1985)
Producer	Chris Sievernich, Road Movies (Berlin) and Argos Film (Paris) in cooperation with Westdeutscher Rundfunk (Cologne), Channel 4 (London) and Pro-jekt Filmproduktion (Filmverlag der Autoren, Munich)
Director	Wim Wenders
Asst. Director	Claire Denis
Screenplay	Sam Shepard, adapted by L. M. Kit Carson
Cinematography	Robby Müller
Camera Assts.	Agnès Godard, Pim Tjujerman, Martin Schär
Editing	Peter Przygodda
Editing Asst.	Anne Schnee
Set decoration	Kate Altman
Costumes	Birgitta Bjerke
Make-up	Charles Balasz
Sound	Jean Paul Mugel
Sound Asst.	Douglas Axtell
Sound Editor	Dominique Auvray
Music	Ry Cooder
Cast	Harry Dean Stanton (Travis)
	Nastassja Kinksi (Jane)
	Dean Stockwell (Walt)
	Aurore Clément (Anne)
	Hunter Carson (Hunter)
	Justin Hogg (Hunter at age 3)
	Bernhard Wicki (Dr. Ulmer)
	Socorro Valdez (Carmelita)
	Tom Farrell (screaming man)
	Sally Norvell ("Nurse Bibs")
	Sam Berry (gas station attendant)
	Claresie Mobley (car rental clerk)
	Edward Fayton (Hunter's friend)
	John Lurie (bouncer at the bar)
	Sharon Menzel (comedian)
	The Mydolls (rehearsing band)
Length	3964 meters

Notes

Names preceded by asterisks (*) indicate an entry in the chapter bibliographies following the Notes.

Introduction

1. For introductions to the reasons for such a shift in writing history and in historiography, see Certeau, Lloyd. For its impact in the field of film history, see Sorlin, Heath, Mellenkamp and Rosen, Allen and Gomery, and Fero.

2. For a comprehensive introduction to issues of cinematic narration, see Bordwell.

3. For an excellent introduction to the history and issues of cinematic spectatorship, see Mayne; for a comprehensive bibliography, see Bergstrom and Doane.

4. The notion of imaginary activity derives from Jacques Lacan's concept of the imaginary as the virtuality or image of the real that can be known or expressed only through the symbolic registers of language and representation. For a brief but clear explanation of Lacan's imaginary, see Silverman, *Subject of Semiotics*, 157–62.

Chapter 1

1. On the founding of the UFA corporation as a vertical monopoly, see Spiker, 22–27; for an English language summary, see Petley, 29–33. Kreimeier summarizes additional archive material in his history of the UFA corporation; see *Die UFA-Story*, 39–47.

2. Germany lagged behind the United States and other continental countries in attracting the bourgeois audience into the cinemas because of idiosyncrasies in the film industry's economic structure (dominated by foreign production companies) and in the cultural context (resistance by cultural traditionalists). One sign of the postwar expansionism, for example, can be seen in the extraordinary growth in cinemas after 1918. On the economic situation, see Saunders, 20–24; for the cultural resistance, see Heller's and Diederichs's studies on the intellectual response to the cinema during the silent era. Schlüpmann's investigation of the prewar German cinema, *Unheimlichkeit des Blicks*, also discusses (in the

second part) the role of intellectuals in this cultural struggle but from the perspective of aesthetics rather than ideology. For an English-language study on the cultural struggle around the cinema, see Hake, chaps. 2 and 4.

3. On luxury cinemas in the postwar period, see Baacke, 32–37, and the accompanying photographs on 81–104.

4. Characteristic for the obstacles faced by German film exports after the war was the odyssey of *Madame Dubarry*'s distribution: bought for U.S. exhibition by First National Pictures a year after its premiere in Berlin, it was part of a package deal of three Lubitsch films acquired for the then very low price of $40,000. First National tried to camouflage the film's German origin, first as an Italian costume film and then as a "European production" or "continental film"; *Variety* even reported the director's name with the more Polish sounding "Emil Subitch." For a bibliography of the contemporary reception in New York, see *Carringer and Sabath, 56; for sample reviews, see Pratt, 308–10. On the European continent and especially in France the film's reception among critics revolved around the "pernicious distortion" of the French Revolution. For bibliographical sources, see Oms, 19–24. On German hopes about penetrating the American exhibition market, see Saunders, 63–64.

5. Kracauer, *From Caligari to Hitler*, especially the introduction, 3–11. For a critical appraisal of Kracauer's writing on the Weimar cinema, see Hake, chap. 11.

6. Two articles by Thomas Elsaesser are fundamental for this reassessment: "Film History and Visual Pleasure" raises a number of general questions about modifying approaches to Weimar Cinema and "Lulu and the Meter Man" offers a demonstration using Pabst's 1929 film to examine the implications of such questions. More recently, Petro has complicated traditional periodization of the Weimar cinema by focusing on the melodrama and its address to the female audience.

7. Kracauer, *From Caligari to Hitler*, 48–56.

8. See *Paul for some general comments on Lubitsch's narrative structures (but without an explicit theoretical grounding) as well as his bibliography. For a more theoretical discussion that does not focus on Lubitsch specifically, see Nichols, especially chap. 3; and Bordwell, especially chap. 9, an analysis of Lubitsch's 1925 feature *Lady Windermere's Fan*.

9. Theater directors like Max Reinhardt and Leopold Jessner became well-known proponents of modernized and politicized versions of historical and classical plays on Berlin stages after the war. For a discussion of Prussian history in the German cinema, see Marquardt and Rathsack. For a discussion specifically of film treatments of the French Revolution in the Weimar period, see Silberman, "Imagining History."

10. Toeplitz, vol. 1, 63–64.

11. *Hake comes to similar conclusions as mine in an analysis that focuses on *Passion*'s set design, costume, and mass choreography, and she presents compelling historical and structural arguments for the emergence of the period film as a German genre in the Weimar Republic.

12. On Lubitsch's involvement with Reinhardt's theater, see *Prinzler and Patalas, 12–14.

13. Lubitsch, the son of a Berlin textile merchant, had discovered the clothes store as a model for relations of exchange in his early slapstick comedies (for example, *Shoe Emporium Pinkus* [*Schuhhaus Pinkus*], 1916) and continued to invoke it well into the forties (*The Shop Around the Corner*, 1940).

14 The look has been one of the central concepts in psychoanalytical film theories, relating the subject to the spectacle through the spectator's identification with the camera/gaze. Silverman's *Male Subjectivity* is a challenging introduction to these discussions, and in a subsequent article, "What is a Camera?" she insists further on the need to specify historically and culturally the representational logic of the camera and the eye.

15. The fact that this servant/slave, who is presented to Jeanne as a wedding gift by one of the king's lackeys, is black, dressed and played as a Moor with fairy-tale overtones, suggests a further subtext of imperialism and racism within the film, but the role is unique and hardly worked out within the narrative. That the Moor betrays Jeanne, however, seems to indicate less the emancipatory promise of the revolution for oppressed and colonized races than the more general placement of an Other between various agents of power (Jeanne, the nobility, the Republicans). This may have biographical implications for Lubitsch as a Jew in Germany who experienced exclusion.

16. Some versions of the film include a last scene where the executioner (in an ironic flaunting of the protagonist's penchant for display) shows Jeanne's severed head to the crowd and then throws it to them like a football. See, for example, the summary by Helma Sanders-Brahms in *Prinzler and Patalas, 132–36.

17. Lubitsch employs a number of techniques to exploit the voyeurism of this theatricality: the parting of the drapes behind Jeanne to reveal the lavish dinner table when she arrives at Don Diego's palace, the irises (especially to introduce characters, e.g., Choiseul, Gramont, and the king), wipes (double wipes like curtains opening, vertical wipes like a curtain rising—at the opera ball—or dropping—after the wedding ceremony), and the mise-en-scène's formality and symmetry for the procession at Jeanne's introduction to the court.

18. Kracauer, *Die Angestellten*. Irmalotte Guttmann's 1927 empirical study of cinemas in Cologne and Danzig (*Über die Nachfrage auf dem Filmmarkt in Deutschland*, 1928) distinguished a clearly stratified audience of educated, middle-class, and working-class cinemagoers attracted to various genres and theater houses; see Saunders, 157–58.

19. See Elsaesser, "Film History and Visual Pleasure," 68–69, and Heller, 15.

20. See Altenloh. Hansen was among the first to problematize the class and gender make-up of the early silent cinema audience in a way that would sustain this conclusion in "Early Silent Cinema," especially part 2. Using Altenloh's data, Petro, 18–25, similarly suggests an alternative reading of the gendered historical spectator in relation to Kracauer's analysis of the destabilization of male identity in the Weimar cinema. Although her study focuses on the prewar German cinema, Schlüpmann's analysis would apply as well to the transitional phase in the postwar period. Against prevailing views of the primitive cinema's audience as largely working class she proposes rather that it can be defined across class lines by its exclusion from the dominant (bourgeois) forms of cultural activity, and this also implies exclusion based on gender; see Schlüpmann, *Unheimlichkeit des Blicks*, 204.

21. Quoted in *Ernst Lubitsch*, 107.

Chapter 2

1. Anton Kaes makes a persuasive case for at least acknowledging this mass entertainment cinema that traditional Weimar film histories ignore in favor of the distinctive tradition of Weimar art cinema in the introduction to his overview article, "Weimarer Republik," 39–40.

2. For an introduction to expressionism in the arts, see Willett, *Expressionism*, especially chap. 4, and Dube; for an overview of scholarly issues concerning expressionism, see Vietta and Kemper; for an up-to-date bibliography, see *Bibliography of German Expressionism*. Budd's discussion (especially 12–18) of the *Cabinet of Dr. Caligari* as an expressionist and modernist film outlines the major terms of cinematic expressionism.

3. On the distinction between modernism and modernity, particularly as it has emerged in the postmodernism debate, see Schulte-Sasse, especially 5–14. For the specific context in German expressionism, see Bronner and Kellner, 3–39.

4. Historical examples include the already mentioned study by Eisner as well as Kurtz; for a stylistic analysis of the expressionist cinema that counterposes it to the expressionist stage, see Kasten.

5. Besides Kracauer's pathbreaking study *From Caligari to Hitler*, see Monaco, Tudor. On the contradictory and problematic status of the concept "expressionist cinema," see Kaes, "Expressionist Vision."

6. Eisner provides numerous details on personal, professional, and formal interactions between Reinhardt's theater and the expressionist cinema, as the subtitle of her study "The Haunted Screen" indicates.

7. One of the most important sociological effects one could attribute to expressionist films is the fact that they finally drew the middle-class strata committed to traditional culture forms (*Bildungsbürgertum*) into the cinema by legitimating it as an art form in its own right. A number of scholars have collected documents and commented on the unique and tortured relationship between literary intellectuals, the middle-class defenders of culture, and the cinema in Germany: Greve, et al.; Kaes, "Debate about Cinema" (this is a slightly revised translation of the introduction to Kaes, *Kino-Debatte,*); Güttinger; and Heller.

8. Burch and Dana enumerate in brief form the subversive narrative and visual strategies at work in the film; see as well Silberman, "Industry, Text, Ideology," for the broader context of early cinematic expressionism. Recent research into the early German or Wilhelmine cinema indicates that some characteristics associated with innovations in expressionist films had already been introduced and tested as early as 1911. Thompson, for example, presents compelling evidence for the static, painterly approach of the expressionist image as early as 1913, and Elsaesser, "National Subjects," delineates some important lines of continuity. Although he misleadingly insists on the *Caligari* film as an innovative prototype for the horror film genre, Prawer's detailed, structural analysis is a starting point for a consideration of its expressionist elements (especially chap. 6 on the film's iconography). See Budd for a bibliography on literature concerning the *Caligari* film.

9. Following Kracauer, who divides the Weimar cinema into the postwar period (1918–24), the stabilized period (1924–29), and the pre-Hitler period (1929–33),

most commentators agree that 1924 was a pivotal year, although the evidence and reasons vary according to the ideological thrust or evidence of the respective critic. See Kracauer, *From Caligari to Hitler*, 131–37; Spiker, 36–43; Heller 201–5; and Kreimeier, *Die Ufa-Story*, 115–32, for representative details.

10. Kreimeier, *Die Ufa-Story*, calls this tendency "the grand liberal experiment and the grand democratic illusion of the Weimar period" (109). On the notion of cinematic distraction as it relates to this socialization of the audience in the writings of Kracauer and Walter Benjamin, see "Cinema Theory in the Twenties," the special issue of *New German Critique*, especially the articles by Elsaesser, Schlüpmann, Petro, and Hake.

11. The German title, literally "the last man," is poorly rendered by the English distribution title *The Last Laugh*, missing the double ironies implied in the various possibilities of "last." The epilogue is introduced by an intertitle quoting a newspaper obituary in which the will of a millionaire requires that his fortune go to the last man he encounters.

12. For more information on Mayer, see *Hempel, 107–8; and *Spiess. In 1967 a conference on German film expressionism was held at the Mostra di Venezia with many contributions on Mayer; see the proceedings *"Atti del Convegno," with articles by Spiess, Pandolfi, Eisner, Luft, and Rotha, among others.

13. The first two *Kammerspiel* features were directed by Lupu Pick: *Shattered* (*Scherben*, 1921), and *New Year's Eve* (*Sylvester*, 1923).

14. Besides the one formal intertitle introducing the epilogue, there are only three other uses of written words: the decoration on the wedding cake (*den Hochzeitsgästen* or for the wedding guests), the hotel manager's letter explaining to the porter his demotion to lavatory attendant, and the newspaper article announcing the surprising bequest by the American millionaire. The film script is not extant, but three sequences preserved from various sources are reprinted in *Hempel, 119–26. Even in these excerpts it is obvious that Mayer was one of the first German scriptwriters to take seriously the literary nature of screenplays. For the film critics' reception of *The Last Laugh* in Germany, see *Kreimeier, 58.

15. Freund, quoted in *Hempel, 149.

16. Rohmer's detailed analysis of light and composition in Murnau's *Faust* film is a model for the kind of work that could be undertaken for other Murnau films.

17. Some versions of the film do not include the oval mask during the sequence when the porter reads his letter of demotion. The text of the letter (framed by the camera) also reads slightly differently: "Owing to your long years of service the management has decided to give you another post [vacated by our oldest employee who is being transferred to an old people's home]." The center of the text blurs and an oval mask opens showing the "oldest employee" handing in his white smock. The mask disappears and the letter's text reappears in its entirety. See the segmentation (shots 81–84, in French) in *Borde, et al., 37, based on the version available at the Swiss Cinémathèque; the reconstructed version in the Munich Filmmuseum also includes the oval cash.

18. *Bergstrom, 191, discusses Murnau's use of ellipses as part of a highly conventionalized and historically specific system in the Weimar cinema.

19. Kreimeier, *Die Ufa-Story*, 173–75, summarizes the various speculations about who inspired the parodic conclusion.

20. The fact that the American millionaire is called A. G. Monney points to a more explicit level of political allegory in the narrative. AG (*Aktiengesellschaft*) is the German abbreviation for "stock corporation," and corporate money was exactly the remedy offered Germany by the American Dawes Plan to save its collapsing economy in 1924. Widely shared anxieties on the part of intellectuals about the Americanization of German culture resonate in this fictional trope; for the implications in the cinema, see Saunders, chap. 4.

Chapter 3

1. In 1955 *Kuhle Wampe* was rereleased in the German Democratic Republic within a broader discussion about traditions of proletarian culture in the Weimar Republic; see *Herlinghaus. Only ten years later, in the midsixties, did the film become an object of interest in the Federal Republic and, at least initially, it was situated almost exclusively within the scholarly reception of Brecht's artistic endeavors; see *Witte.

2. See Bächlin, 45–54; Spiker, 43–46; and for a description in English, *Murray, chap. 5.

3. Part 3, "The Stabilized Period (1924–1929)" in Kracauer's *From Caligari to Hitler* gives an accurate account of this interaction between new capitalization and changes in the "look" of film productions. For background details on structural changes, see Kreimeier, *Die Ufa-Story*, 190–205.

4. For details about the shortcomings of working-class cultural programs on the part of left-wing parties in the years following World War I, see *Murray, chaps. 3 and 4.

5. For a useful collection of documents on the Social Democratic Party's involvement with film politics during the Weimar Republic, see *Kühn, Tümmler, and Wimmer, vol. 2, 430–69.

6. Heller, 145–56.

7. Münzenberg's polemical pamphlet *Erobert den Film! Winke aus der Praxis für die Praxis proletarischer Filmpropaganda* (Conquer the Film! Practical Hints for the Practice of Proletarian Film Propaganda, 1925) addressed the failure of the working class to enter into a creative relationship with the cinema. The germane documents for the Communist Party positions are collected in vol. 1 of *Kühn, Tümmler, and Wimmer. For an overview, see also *Stoos; for a discussion in English, see *Murray, chap. 6.

8. For a novelist like Alfred Döblin or for the stage director Erwin Piscator the rhetorical innovations in the Soviet film of the twenties inspired and confirmed their efforts at reorganizing perceptual possibilities in other media. For documents on the reception of new Soviet films, see *Kühn, Tümmler, and Wimmer, vol. 1, 277–423; in English, see Willett's discussion of revolutionary Russian influence in the arts in *Art and Politics*.

9. For positive approaches to Jutzi's film, see *Leonard; *Michaelis; and for a highly critical approach, see *Pettifer, "Limits of Naturalism."

10. Another organization, The People's Film Association (Volks-Film-Verband), was established in 1928 with the participation of Left intellectuals to coordinate working-class film activities. Its ambitious program foresaw an independent chain of cinemas, its own film productions, and an audience organization, but after only one year it had to scale down its goals. For documents on the Volks-Film-Verband and its short-lived journal *Film und Volk*, see *Kühn, Tümmler, and Wimmer, vol. 2, 238–300.

11. See producer *Hoellering's explanations about the background to the film's production.

12. The original treatment is printed in *Brecht, *Kuhle Wampe*, 83–88.

13. Because of the financial constraints, shooting lasted almost three quarters of a year with long interruptions (from August 1931 until February 1932), and the technical team and cast worked without pay in order to contain production costs at about one-half the cost of a normal feature film; see *Herlinghaus, 15.

14. Recognizing Dudov's talent, Brecht integrated him into his "work team," as was his habit with talented persons. Dudov staged with Brecht the didactic play *The Measures Taken* (*Die Massnahme*, 1930), worked on the 1931 version of the play *A Man's a Man* (*Mann ist Mann*), contributed to Brecht's film treatment of the *The Threepenny Opera* ("Die Beule"), and participated in discussions about the play *The Mother* (*Die Mutter*, 1932). For details, see *Gersch, 104; *Herlinghaus, 10–11. (Note: in German, the Bulgarian v sound is transcribed with the letter w.)

15. In his book-length essay *The Threepenny Trial*, Brecht presents his most extended and coherent analysis of the film medium's impact on the way art represents reality and the way the reader or spectator sees. The trial, and Brecht's presentation of it, was a brilliant example of applied dialectics that counterposed two ideological institutions, the state justice system with its norms of contract law and copyright protection against the film industry's media practice with its economic exigencies and cultural legitimations. The dispute forced the establishment to face its own contradictions: on the one hand, the artist's individual right to protect the ideal integrity of the creative work of art (the scenario for the film version of *The Threepenny Opera*) and, on the other, the film producer's financial interest in protecting his investment (Pabst's completed film). By admitting the film's commodity character, the court recognized that art in the industrial age was socialized in a new way, and Brecht considered this insight objectively progressive. See *Brecht, *Der Dreigroschenprozess*. By adopting the role of the naive artist for the purposes of the trial, Brecht showed that new technologies and capitalist market mechanisms had removed the means of production from the hands of the artist and in the process destroyed the idealistic and metaphysical ideology of cultural production. The modern artist, like the laborer in industrial society, had no choice but to organize collectively, a commitment he tried to put into practice in his work on *Kuhle Wampe*.

16. See *Adank.

17. Brecht himself emphasized the collective nature of the *Kuhle Wampe* project as part of its political commitment to an alternative to the capitalist mode of production. See *Brecht, *Kuhle Wampe*, 89. The film credits as well as the original poster list Dudov as director, Brecht and Ottwald as scriptwriters, and

Eisler as music composer. The censorship card, however, lists Brecht as director, assisted by Dudov. The film often runs under both Dudov's and Brecht's names, and especially in its postsixties reception it is frequently attributed to Brecht alone.

18. For a taxonomy of rhetorical figures in the Soviet cinema of the twenties, see Bordwell, chap. 11.

19. Brecht proposed that the technological advance of capitalism inserted more and more machines or mechanical processes between the real and human perception of the real. Neither progressive nor regressive in itself, this technology enabled a communicative activity in a social and institutional framework. Although the medium's technology contained the potential of a democratic public organ, capitalist society was using the mass medium to isolate and pacify the listener. See *Brecht, *Der Dreigroschenprozess*, vol. 1, 171–77. For an elaboration of Brecht's reflections on the cinema within a broader theoretical context, see *Silberman; *Groth and Voigts.

20. On the concept of social *gestus* and its differentiation in the Epic Theater and cinema, see *Mueller, chap. 4.

21. Originally the film addressed the abortion issue more directly, but the titles and dialogue concerning the State's laws controlling the woman's body and the relationship between money and access to abortion were censored. This might account for the apparently anomalous status of this associative sequence. For a list of the film's censored material, see Klaus, vol. 3, 127.

22. *Kuhle Wampe* was finally released for distribution on April 25, 1932, after several cuts were made in the original version. It premiered in Berlin on May 30, and enjoyed a very successful run throughout Germany. Ten months later, in March 1933, it became one of the first films to be forbidden by the National-Socialist Reich ministry for propaganda. For documents on the censorship controversy, including examples of press responses, see the following collections: *"Dokumente zum Zensurgang"; *Brecht, *Kuhle Wampe*, 103–67; and *Kühn, Tümmler and Wimmer, vol. 2, 130–85. Kracauer's critical evaluation published contemporaneously in the *Frankfurter Zeitung* (April 4, 1932) can be found in the German edition of Kracauer's *Von Caligari zu Hitler*, ed. Karsten Witte (Frankfurt: Suhrkamp, 1979), 536–41. Brecht travelled to Moscow to attend the film's world premiere there on May 14, 1932, but it was not received very positively; see two Soviet reviews in *Wyss, 157–59.

23. Some of the first films produced in the Third Reich even echo situations, techniques, and the *gestus* from *Kuhle Wampe*, for example, Hans Steinhoff's *Hitler Youth Quex (Hitlerjunge Quex)*, Franz Seitz's *SA-Mann Brand*, and Franz Wenzler's *Hans Westmar* (all 1933).

24. Precisely the images of a mass sports rally led some critics to compare this film with Nazi images of sports events, for example in Leni Riefenstahl's documentary of the 1936 Berlin Olympic Games (*Olympia*, 1938). See Kracauer, *From Caligari to Hitler*, 246–47; Eisner, 335; and *Pettifer, "Against the Stream," 62. In my view such a comparison disregards the film structure as analyzed in the text and ignores the fact that images are perceived in a context.

25. Brecht's influence on the cinema can be traced back to the post-1968 politicization of the public sphere. In West Germany directors like Alexander Kluge,

Jean-Marie Straub/Danièle Huillet, Rainer Werner Fassbinder, Harun Farocki, and Helke Sander owe much to the Brechtian model. The most radical and consistent student of Brecht's aesthetics, however, was Jean-Luc Godard, and through his films, especially *Tout va bien* (1972), he mediated much of the theoretical tradition for which Brecht stands in the French, the Anglo-American, and the Latin American cinemas. In the midseventies Brecht and *Kuhle Wampe* played an important role as an example for possibilities and limitations of political filmmaking among English and French film scholars, see for example, the special issue of *Screen* on *"Brecht and a Revolutionary Cinema," as well as *Walsh. For a retrospective overview, see *Mueller, 103–25.

Chapter 4

1. Sirk left Germany in 1938 and began producing films in Hollywood in 1942. His American domestic melodramas, all produced during the fifties, include *All I Desire* (1953), *Magnificent Obsession* (1953), *All That Heaven Allows* (1955), *Written on the Wind* (1956), *The Tarnished Angels* (1957), and *Imitation of Life* (1958). During the late sixties a growing interest in the Hollywood melodrama initiated the critical rediscovery of Sirk as auteur. A first hiatus was marked by the special "Douglas Sirk" issue of *Screen* 12, no. 2 (Summer 1971), including articles pertinent to the German years by *Halliday, "Notes on Sirk's German Films," and *Elsaesser, "Postscript" (on Sirk's earlier career in the German theater). In 1972 a major retrospective of Sirk's films took place at the Edinburgh Film Festival, accompanied by the publication of a collection of essays by *Mulvey and Halliday.

2. The central sources for administrative and economic history of the film industry in the Third Reich are Becker; Spiker (especially part B, 80–239); and to a lesser degree, Courtade and Cadars, 7–37; and Drewniak. Important collections of documents include Wulf (part 2); Albrecht, *Der Film im Dritten Reich*. English treatments can be found in M. S. Phillips; Petley, chap. 3; and Welch, part 1.

3. Wetzel and Hagemann, 44 n.4, estimate that between eighty to one hundred films from the Weimar period were censored within the first year of the Third Reich.

4. On the continuity between censorship in the Weimar Republic and the Third Reich, see Barbian; on film censorship laws, see Albrecht, *Nationalsozialistische Filmpolitik*, 510–22; and for a detailed comparison of the Weimar and Nazi laws, see Maiwald.

5. The postproduction system of predication or evaluation (*Prädikatisierung*) was a particularly important aspect for encouraging high quality production through tax incentives and at the same time influencing public reception processes. See Courtade and Cadars, 17–18; Becker, 96–97.

6. Rentschler, "Eigengewächs à la Hollywood," especially 209–15, provides background for the challenge American films presented throughout the Third Reich in his discussion of Paul Martin's *Glückskinder* (*Children of Fortune*, 1936, a remake of *It Happened One Night*). For further examples of the competitive American influence, see Witte, "Film im Nationalsozialismus."

7. Courtade and Cadars, 31.

8. Although their number decreased steadily after 1936, films continued to be imported from the United States until 1939, so that both film professionals and the cinema audience were familiar with American comedies, musicals, and other genres. Goebbels cut off American film imports definitively in 1939 after Anatole Litvak's *Confessions of a Nazi Spy* was released in Europe.

9. For Sierck's own explanation of his move into the cinema, see *Halliday's series of interviews (a kind of autobiography in interview form) collected in *Sirk on Sirk*, especially 46–49.

10. Sources with material on Sierck's German years include *Stern; *Masson; *Pithon in a special focus issue on Sirk; *Bourget's biocritical survey; and *Läufer, the first German-language monograph with material based on interviews with Sirk and his wife. Interviews with Sirk that deal also with the German years include: *Sirk, "Entretien," by Daney and Noames; *Sirk, "Interview"; *Sirk, "Entretien," by Biette and Rabourdin; and *Sirk, "Entretien," by Decaux and Villien. *Koch has critically addressed the aporias and outright mistakes in the reception of Sierck's work in the German theater and cinema among both Anglo-American and West German film scholars.

11. Important articles on Sirk and melodrama include *Elsaesser, "Sound and Fury"; *Willemen; *Mulvey, "Notes"; and *Brandlmeier. Referring to "the Sirk factor," *Gledhill, especially 7–13, has examined the various stages and critical positions in this intersection of melodrama theory and Sirk's films.

12. Many of Sierck's German films show a predilection for New World mythology: besides the quotations from the Western genre in *To New Shores*, *Final Accord* begins in New York and *La Habanera* is set in Puerto Rico. *Bourget, 11, suggested that these may have been subtle signals on Sierck's part to Hollywood, and indeed it was Warner Brothers who invited him to do a remake of *To New Shores* in 1939, a project, however, that never materialized. It ought to be remarked that indigenous people are invisible in Sierck's colonial Australia. Even in *La Habanera* there is at least a token, albeit romanticized role for the Spanish-speaking peasants who work in the fields (in the background) and sing the title song (in German!).

13. The German text of the quoted passages:

> Man fürchtet, ich könnt' die behüteten Neffen
> im Himmelbett oder im Spielsalon treffen,
> ich könnt' sie verführen mit tausend Listen,
> zu etwas, das sie vielleicht doch noch nicht wüßten.
> . . .
> So bin ich am ganzen Leibe ich,
> So bin ich und so bleibe ich, yes, Sir!
> So wie ich hier stehe, so bin ich eben, yes, Sir!
> Die Schönheit ist mir nicht umsonst gegeben, no, Sir!

14. Modlewski discusses the relationship of silence and hysteria in the general context of films with female protagonists.

15. The German text:

> Immer warten nur die Menschen, die wirklich lieben!
> Kommst du noch nicht?

Wie die fallenden Tropfen am Ärmel zerstieben!
Ich stehe im Regen und warte auf dich, auf dich!
Auf allen Wegen erwart' ich nur dich, immer nur dich!

16. *Mulvey, "Notes," 54.

17. Frequently critics classify *To New Shores* together with other Nazi films addressing the decadence of English society. Typical for such an approach is the chapter "Das perfide Albion" in Courtade and Cadars, 172.

18. On images of women in the cinema of the Third Reich, see Hollstein, 196–98; Stöckl; Romani, 28–36; and Friedman, "Männlicher Blick," especially 55–59.

19. Hull, 124, suggested the influence of Josef von Sternberg in the "look" of Sierk's German films, especially in the use of light; *Koch, 121, however, criticizes this comparison between Sierck and Sternberg and she identifies the former's lighting qualities with an "authoritarian dramaturgy of the look."

20. For details on the crisis year 1936–37, see Spiker, 147; Becker, 128–30; Kreimeier, *Die Ufa-Story*, 300–306; and Petley, 61.

21. On Zarah Leander's star personality, see *Rhode; *Sanders-Brahms; Romani, 85–86; and Beyer, 151–95. Leander became the highest paid UFA star with the unusual privilege of receiving part of her salary in hard currency paid directly to her Swedish bank. When Goebbels pressured her to relinquish this privilege and to become a German citizen in 1942, she left Germany for Sweden, where she remained for the rest of the war.

22. In her memoirs Leander relates some of the specifics about how UFA constructed her public image as a star in preparation for the film's premiere. See *Leander, *So bin ich*, 56–58; as well as *Leander, *Es war so wunderbar*, 150–51. Economically *To New Shores* was both a domestic and export success, and it won the first prize at the Venice Film Festival in 1937.

23. In November 1936, Goebbels officially forbade all culture criticism (reviews of books, theatrical productions, films, etc.) in favor of what he called "chronicles," a step that only confirmed a practice that had began already in 1933. What went under the name of film criticism rarely rose above plot summary and the organized celebration of specific films for publicity purposes. As a result, there are virtually no records or sociological data to draw on for evaluating actual audience response to a specific film except box office receipts.

Chapter 5

1. On the economic history of the film industry in the Third Reich, see chap. 4, n. 2; on Winkler's role specifically, see Spiker, 162–68; and for an English summary, Petley, 75–81.

2. On the economic role of German film exports, see Drewniak, 691–95; and on the film politics pursued in the occupied areas, see Kreimeier, *Die Ufa-Story*, chap. 28. On the quality and importance of German newsreel production during World War II, see Barkhausen, chap. 18.

3. The most comprehensive categorization was undertaken by Albrecht, *Nationalsozialistische Filmpolitik*.

4. *Request Concert* was one of the films banned by the Allies from public distribution in Germany after 1945 because of its propaganda content. It was shown on public television for the first time in 1974 (Norddeutscher Rundfunk) and is now commercially available on videotape as well.

5. Goebbels, "Der Film als Erzieher," speech of October 12, 1941, in Albrecht, *Nationalsozialistische Filmpolitik*, 480 (my translation).

6. See *Hippler, *Betrachtungen zum Filmschaffen*, 34. Hippler reports in his memoirs that Goebbels even contributed to the scenario and dialogues; see *Hippler, *Die Verstrickung*. The cast included competent and well-known actors, among them Ilse Werner in the lead role who gained a reputation as the simple and loyal German "girl-next-door." For information on Werner, see Beyer, 242–82. The technical team also included old hands, although cameraman Franz Weihmayr reveals none of the finesse he used in *To New Shores* and other Sierck films.

7. E.g., Toeplitz, vol. 3, 280; and Witte, "Gehemmte Schaulust," 10–13.

8. For biographical background, see Hull, 146.

9. See Courtade and Cadars, 259.

10. Leiser, 62.

11. Polan, 91, discusses typologies for the American war film of the forties, including the war romance. Many of his conclusions could be considered in light of the Third Reich cinema as well. My emphasis on the fascist narrative, however, distinguishes between the two contexts (one could also compare Soviet productions from the same period). This does not exclude areas of overlap but it does account for fundamental differences in the cinema apparatus and conditions of film reception.

12. For general references to images of women in the Third Reich cinema, see chap. 4, n. 18.

13. Polan, 68–69.

14. For a discussion of the Other in constructing National-Socialist identity in the cinema, see Friedman, *L'Image*, especially 177–79.

15. Prox, 81.

16. For essays on the German revue film and its musical dimension, see Belach.

17. The lead actress in *Request Concert* describes the popular radio program in her autobiography; see *Werner, 106–7.

18. The third and last radio program, the longest in the film, illustrates the way music is employed as a unifying force through an ideal of easy comprehension and with the help of familiar concert and film stars. The program consists of short excerpts from the following selections:

1. after the initial trumpet fanfare opening the program Marika Rökk sings a suggestive love song, "Eine Nacht im Mai," from her successful prewar musical film of the same title;

2. the popular film trio Heinz Rühmann, Hans Brausewetter, and Josef Sieber sing their well-known song "Das kann doch einen Seemann nicht erschüttern";

3. Eugen Jochum directs the Berlin Philharmonic Orchestra in the Overture to *The Marriage of Figaro* (intercut with the crucial scene at Helmut's hospital bedside when Inge finally figures out the misunderstanding that led her to believe Koch had forgotten her, thus establishing a parallel between the comic opera's happy ending and the resolution soon to be achieved in the film narrative);

4. the Munich cabarettist Weiss-Ferdl (Ferdinand Weisheitinger) offers his spoof "Ich bin so froh, ich bin kein Intellektueller" which ends with the refrain "a little bit of stupidity is worthwhile;"

5. a clarinetist plays a comic musical solo which sounds like laughter;

6. film star Paul Hörbiger sings the hit "Apollonerl" while accompanying himself on the accordion;

7. after the concert moderator (played by the real "Wunschkonzert" moderator Heinz Goedeke) announces the new births for the week, the film cuts to a children's chorus dressed in traditional folk costumes who sings the lullaby "Schlafe, mein Prinzchen, schlaf ein," intercut once again with kitsch images representing a cross section of the listening public: a grandmother reading to two children, an old woman with an Iron Cross hanging around her neck who sits at her window crocheting, Friedrich's platoon in a bunker, and Hanna Friedrich sitting in a chair and nursing her newborn infant;

8. following a further commemoration by the moderator for all the mothers of fallen sons, Wilhelm Strienz, one of the most popular stage voices at the time, sings "Gute Nacht, Mutter" (by Werner Bochmann);

9. finally, the concert concludes with the entire studio audience singing and swaying as one body with Norbert Schultze to the anti-British march "Wir fahren gegen Engelland," while the film blends into the final images—a familiar apotheosis from the documentary genre in which a series of fades of boats, planes, trains, ships, and flags suggest imminent military victory.

19. See *Regel, 12.

20. *Wunschkonzert* grossed the enormous sum of over 7.2 million Reichsmarks during its first year of distribution; see tables in Albrecht, *Nationalsozialistische Filmpolitik*, especially 410. A book publication based on the film, *Wir beginnen das Wunschkonzert für die Wehrmacht*, also sold over 200,000 copies.

21. Although it was not unusual for propaganda films to receive multiple distinctions, four of them for a single film was not the rule by any means. They served not only to draw public attention to a particular film but also meant valuable tax rebates for the production company. Documents from the files of the secret police indicate that they carefully monitored public reaction to *Request Concert*; see the document on the favorable response recorded in February 1941, reproduced in English in Leiser, 158–59. Another document from the propaganda ministry included the following recommendation: "*Request Concert* should be carefully dealt with and presented as one of the most important films of recent times. It is no mere feature film, as it pursues the fate of many people from the Olympics to the war," quoted in Welch, 120.

Chapter 6

1. Research on the Nazi propaganda film has been more successful in relating aesthetic principles to problems of representation and reception in the cinema. See the early study by Isaksson and Furhammer; Neale's critical response; and essays in Konlechner and Kubelka. Lowry presents one of the first theoretically informed investigations into the Nazi entertainment film; Witte's overview "Film im Nationalsozialismus" stresses the multiplicity of discourses in the cinema of the Third Reich.

2. Others include Harald Braun, Erich Engel, Rolf Hansen, Werner Hochbaum, Herbert Selpin, and Wolfgang Staudte. Käutner's reputation as a premier film *artist* has been argued by Leiser, 20; the East German critics *Freund and Rohrmoser; and *Harmssen (a discussion on the occasion of a West German television retrospective of Käutner's films in 1975).

3. On Käutner's aestheticism, see two crucial articles by *Witte, "Die Filmkomödie" and "Ästhetische Opposition." *Witte makes a similar argument in his more sustained overview of Käutner's entire film production in "Im Prinzip Hoffnung."

4. For details on Käutner's biography, see *Cornelsen; *Völker; a brief English summary is provided by *Gillett. A complete filmography was prepared by *Koschnitzki.

5. Film historians who have celebrated Käutner's achievement in the Third Reich include Courtade and Cadars, 232; Hull, 233–44; Gregor and Patalas, 280; and Toeplitz, vol. 4, 237–38. French critics have been especially lavish in their praise: an early article by *Marcorelles compares him with Jean Cocteau and Nicholas Ray; Mitry, vol. 5, 327–29, considered *Romance in a Minor Key* one of the few successful Maupassant adaptations of world cinema; and Sadoul, vol. 6, 31, called it the best film to come out of the Third Reich.

6. *Maupassant, "Les Bijoux" (first published in 1883). Maupassant was not one of the foreign writers "recognized" in the Third Reich. Only two other films produced during that period were based on his stories, Wolfgang Liebeneiner's *Yvette* (1938) and Willi Forst's *Bel Ami* (1939).

7. Besides the obvious literary antecedents of this provincial domestic tragedy in Gustave Flaubert's *Madame Bovary* and Theodor Fontane's *Effi Briest*, two earlier German films—both directed by Paul Czinner with Elizabeth Bergner in the lead role—also treat a woman who, caught between a boring husband and an acclaimed musician, is driven to suicide: *Nju* (1924) and the 1932 remake *The Dreaming Mouth* (*Der träumende Mund*). The allusion to the dreamy smile in the latter film's title refers to the same mysterious power that attracts Michael to Madeleine, tracing a direct lineage to the Käutner film.

8. On point of view in the classical narrative cinema, see Heath, 92–98; and Silverman, *Subject of Semiotics*, 201–15.

9. On the authoritarian personality in the context of (German) fascism, see Reich; Adorno.

10. The editing in this sequence reinforces the gesture of looking with shot/reverse shots in close-up of their faces. The emphasis on sight and vision is underscored in many of the film's close-up shots by masked lighting that frames the eyes in a strip of light while the rest of the face recedes in shadow.

11. In the original script, Madeleine addresses the poet in this scene as Maupassant, a detail that would have created a dizzying *mise-en-abîme* effect in the narration. Presumably it was not included in the final version because the French author was considered degenerate (*entartet*) by the censors. (Note: the original script is available at the Stiftung deutsche Kinemathek, Berlin.)

12. The original German text was written by Käutner with music by Lothar Brühne (originally published by Edition Filmton in Baden-Baden) and apparently was performed in concert and on radio; now it is distributed by Wiener Bohème Verlag, a subsidiary of UFA-Musikverlage (Munich). The German text:

> Eine Stunde zwischen Tag und Träumen
> soll sich meine Seele zu Dir wenden,
> will mein Herz ich auf die Reise senden,
> hin zu Dir.
> Diese Stunde will ich nie versäumen,
> schon am Morgen will ich an sie denken,
> laß mich täglich sie aufs neue schenken
> Dir und mir . . .
> All mein Sehnen soll den Weg umsäumen,
> seiner weiten Reise Kraft zu spenden.
> Bitte schick es nicht mit leeren Händen
> heim zu mir.

13. On the structural components of the classical narrative, see Bordwell, "Classical Hollywood Style," in Bordwell, Staiger, and Thompson, 1–84.

14. The original screenplay includes a final sequence in which Michael visits Madeleine at the hospital where she lies unconscious and in a voice-over asks her to marry him. Moreover, in an elaborate press booklet distributed for publicity purposes prior to the film's release there are similar indications that Madeleine will recover to learn that Michael wants to marry her, and they will live "happily ever after." See *Helmut Käutner. The press material is available in the Archive of the Deutsches Institut für Filmkunde, Frankfurt.

15. Goebbels reportedly considered the film both defeatist because of the suicide attempt and demoralizing for soldiers who were stationed away from their families because of the portrayal of a wife's infidelities. *Harmssen quotes Käutner directly on Goebbels's antipathy toward him and the difficulties in getting the film released.

16. See *"Starke Auslandserfolge." Käutner's film placed before the other favorite, Julien Duvivier's *Manhattan*, in the final balloting.

17. See Drewniak, 35–38.

18. Käutner himself claims this escapism for his work as a veritable program. *Harmssen quotes him at length about the filming of *Under the Bridges* in the suburbs of Berlin during the last weeks of the war: "*Unter den Brücken* is actually my favorite film. Anyone who sees it today would not be able to understand that at the time, when there was no future any more and Germany's final collapse was a question of days, it was possible to film such a simple, almost idyllic story. . . . When I really think about it, what we did arose from the film makers' stubbornness to allow any of the horror which surrounded us to seep into our work."

Chapter 7

1. For historical background on the Allied occupation policies, see Laqueur; Grosser; and Engelmann.

2. For details on the orders concerning the cinema issued by the Allied Control Commission, see Pleyer, 19–23; and the excellent selection of documents in Hauser.

3. On the early years of DEFA, see Baumert and Herlinghaus, 9–22; Wolf, 247–51; and Mückenberger, "Zeit der Hoffnungen." For a brief account in English based on Kersten, *Das Filmwesen*, see Liehm and Liehm, 76–83.

4. On the hardnose policies of the American film industry concerning distribution of its films for profit in postwar Germany, see Guback, 128–31.

5. The UFI film conglomerate was scheduled to produce forty-six films in 1945, and despite film stock shortages, damaged studio parks, and diminished film personnel, shooting was under way, films were awaiting release, and new projects were being planned up to the very end in April 1945. For lists of rereleases and new releases in the various occupation zones, see Pleyer, 427–60; and Kersten, *Das Filmwesen*, 375.

6. For details, see *Auf neuen Wegen*; Wilkening.

7. An isolated example is Gustav von Wangenheim's feature *Fighters* (*Kämpfer*, produced in the Soviet Union in 1936 and released under the Russian title *Borzy* in 1938), filmed in Soviet exile with German actors and technicians. The difficulties facing political film people in Hollywood, including German emigres, have been amply documented; see for example the two volumes by Horak.

8. There has been ample documentation on the continuity of personnel from UFA to both the East and West German postwar film industry. See Mückenberger, *Zur Geschichte*, 20–31; Schnurre; and Knochenrath. On the hopes for the new German film, see the discussions at the first conference of German scriptwriters held in 1947, *Der deutsche Film*; and for a critical treatment of the ideological and aesthetic constraints that determined these discussions, see Brandlmeier, "Und wieder Caligari."

9. Gersch, 93.

10. For further details on Staudte's film activities during the Third Reich (as well as an up-to-date filmography and bibliography), see *Netenjakob, 15–22.

11. Staudte adapted visual effects associated with German cinematic expressionism like acute camera angles and stark shadows. One critic stressed the background of Staudte's films as the heritage from his acting career under Max Reinhardt and Erwin Piscator during the twenties. See *Witte.

12. Financial and technical questions took priority over possible ideological suspicions in the commercial exploitation of "nonpolitical," wartime UFA material after 1945. Sovexport-Film continued the highly profitable practice of distributing older German productions until DEFA was turned over completely to German hands in 1952. In the Western zones this practice was even more widespread, and by the late seventies UFA films produced during the Third Reich had become a major staple of television programming in West Germany.

Although DEFA's reputation rests on its early antifascist films, it also produced UFA-type comedies. Films like *The Girl Christine* (*Das Mädchen Christine*, Arthur Maria Rabenalt, 1949); *Don't Dream, Annette* (*Träum nicht, Annette*, Eberhard Klagemann, 1949, also an UFA remake using footage shot before the collapse); and *A Quartet of Five* (*Quartett zu fünft*, Gerhard Lamprecht, 1949) were meant to compete with the light entertainment features that dominated Western production by this time. For an early East German assessment of such film fare, see "In jeder Filmproduktion," in Maetzig, 212–14.

13. *Staudte, [on *Rotation*]. Although he worked in East Berlin for DEFA, Staudte continued to live in West Berlin as did many of his DEFA colleagues.

14. *"Wolfgang Staudte," 44.

15. For background to Brecht's return to East Berlin, see Mittenzwei, *Leben des Bertolt Brecht*, vol. 2, 279–98.

16. The scene alludes to Polly's betrothal to the robber baron Macheath in a dock warehouse in the *Threepenny Opera*. It begins with a guest transforming a window curtain into a makeshift wedding veil for Lotte as he sings several verses from the *Threepenny Opera* wedding duet; after a political speech about the injustice of unemployment, it closes with another song ("Denn wovon lebt der Mensch," from the "Threepenny Finale") about the inhumanity of capitalist exploitation. The shooting script includes a shot preceding the wedding party which shows a poster with the title "300 Performances of 'The Threepennny Opera'" and introductory music from the musical. This script is available at the Stiftung deutsche Kinemathek in Berlin and differs substantially from the printed script (*Staudte, "Rotation"). The latter also deviates significantly from the finished film.

17. Besides the five newspaper headlines that punctuate the narrative chronology, Staudte employs other kinds of printed matter, including the already mentioned graffiti, two posters in a subway, the placards at the demonstration, a list of fallen soldiers and battle dates, and Kurt's death warrant. The radio announcement of the Battle of Berlin and the Nuremberg Party Congress also belong to this kind of narrational information. The exclusive use of diegetic music and song and the dramatic effectiveness of noise and silence reinforce the authentic quality that these editing practices lend the film. Jens Thiele suggests that the scriptural images might be considered a film within the film documenting public events as a commentary on the protagonist's private biography; see *Thiele, 131.

18. Some critics have read the last shot, where Helmut and Inge walk down the same path as Hans and Lotte twenty years earlier but turn to the left fork rather than the right one, as Staudte's coded signal for his hope for a socialist Germany; see Witte, 149. Staudte himself denied this partisan reading and suggested instead he only wanted to indicate that the younger generation was taking a different path from that of the parents, see *"Wolfgang Staudte," 42.

19. Other early DEFA films that project onto young people the ability to resolve problems or begin again after the destruction of the war include Gerhard Lamprecht's *Somewhere in Berlin* (*Irgendwo in Berlin*, 1946); Hans Müller's *1–2–3 Corona* (1948); and Hans Deppe's *Die Kuckucks* (1949).

20. These include Staudte's first postwar film, *The Murderers Are among Us*; Kurt Maetzig's *Doomed Marriage* (*Ehe im Schatten*, 1947, the most popular accord-

ing to audience figures and foreign distribution statistics; Erich Engel's *Blum Affair (Affaire Blum,* 1948); and Maetzig's *Life in the Ticking (Die Buntkarierten,* 1949). See Hochschule für Film und Fernsehen, 90; and table 1 in Kersten, *Das Filmwesen,* 346–47.

21. Two scenes were cut from the film under Soviet pressure. Staudte included a short dialogue among Hans and his coworkers about the Berlin Olympics in 1936 followed by excerpts from Leni Riefenstahl's *Olympia* documentary film showing the entrance march of the nations into the stadium (footage similar to that used in *Request Concert!*). His point was to motivate Hans's membership in the Nazi Party not only as a private decision but also as a consequence of the regime's international recognition. The Soviet censors were concerned that such a scene could be understood as an apology for National Socialism because of tacit international approval. The second cut concerned a sequence in the penultimate scene when Hans gives Helmut a suit of clothes. Staudte had included a shot of the father burning the son's uniform as he says: "That is your last uniform." The Soviet censors objected here to the pacifist message, especially at a time when Soviets were establishing an East German police force. See *"Wolfgang Staudte," 40–41.

22. For contemporary East German reviews, see Mückenberger, *Zur Geschichte,* 274–93. For West German reviews, see *Orbanz, *Wolfgang Staudte,* 111–16.

23. See the exchange of letters in *Fernseh-Film* 17 (June 5, 1958).

24. On June 20, 1948, a currency reform was introduced into the three Western zones and the Western sectors of Berlin without prior warning. Four days later the Soviet Military Administration blocked all land access to Berlin in protest against the breach of the Allied Control Commission's authority in the city. The Berlin Blockade and Airlift, thus, became the most visible signs of cold-war tensions. On May 12, 1949, the Soviets ended the blockade, but in the meantime decisive steps had been undertaken in the West to establish a separate West German state. On May 23 the *Grundgesetz* (constitution or Basic Law) was instituted and on September 7, the parliament of the Federal Republic of Germany was seated. In response to that an East German constitution and the parliament of the German Democratic Republic were established on October 7, 1949.

25. Not only the dialogues but also the camera work in the last two scenes are especially unimaginative. Like all the scenes in which political positions are articulated, including Kurt's "speeches," the camera remains static and the editing relies almost exclusively on shot/reverse shots or over-the-shoulder shots. Staudte was most successful in the realm of representing the everyday and telling stories, not of grand politics. Where the politics become subordinated to an idea, the link to the visual narration weakens. After years of ideological encoding during the Third Reich, many directors sacrificed subtlety in favor of expressing or showing directly their ideals.

Chapter 8

1. Helmut Käutner's *In Those Days (In jenen Tagen,* 1947), Peter Pewas's *Street Encounters (Strassenbekanntschaften,* 1948), and R. A. Stemmle's *Berlin Ballad (Berliner Ballade,* 1949) are the classic examples of rubble films produced

with licenses in the Western zones. For further details on the these and other *Trümmerfilme*, see Pleyer as well as Brandlmeier, "Von Hitler zu Adenauer."

2. Historians tend to identify either 1945 (the collapse of the Third Reich) or 1949 (the establishment of the two German states) as the crucial starting point for the postwar development in Germany, but there is good reason to consider the currency reform in 1948 as the crucial rupture in popular German consciousness. This position has been argued most forcefully by social historians, e.g., Broszat, Henkel, and Woller.

3. Strictly speaking there were no UFA productions between 1945 and 1954 because of Allied insistence on the decartelization and reprivatization of the state-owned film conglomerate. In 1953 what was left of the 138 UFI-controlled companies was auctioned off at cut-rate prices, and a much scaled-down UFA production and exhibition company once again emerged. By 1962 it was bankrupt and bought by the Bertelsmann publishing cartel, which proceeded to liquidate the assets of the production unit while retaining the profitable UFA cinema chain. For details on the UFI decartelization process, see Kreimeier, *Kino und Filmindustrie*, 178–85; and his revised account in *Die Ufa-Story*, 445–54; as well as Hauser. The latest chapter in UFA's postwar history saw Bertelsmann announce in December 1992 the formation of a new production company called "Ufa Babelsberg GmbH." See H.-J. Rother, 87.

4. Not only did the number of foreign films screened in Germany after the currency reform supersede rereleases and new releases of German films, but also the number of exhibition days for foreign films accounted in 1949, for example, for 90 percent of the total. See Pleyer, 85–86.

5. Höfig, 94, reckons that of the 1206 German-language films produced in West Germany, Austria, and Switzerland between 1947 and 1960 as many as one quarter were Heimat films. For an excellent taxonomy of the Heimat film genre, see *Seesslen.

6. On the origin of the word "Heimat" and the literary antecedents of the Heimat film, see Höfig, 3–28; Rossbacher.

7. On the role of nature in the mountain film, see Rentschler, "Hochgebirge und Moderne."

8. On Hans Deppe's biography, see *Kurowski; Höfig, 168. For a complete listing of Deppe's films, see the entry in Bock, *Cinegraph*.

9. The film industry organ *Film-Echo* named *Black Forest Girl* the most successful picture of the year 1950 (Nr. 47–48, 1950: 1139) and reported 14 million tickets sold by August 1952 (Nr. 31, 1952: 692), compared to an average of 3–4 million tickets per film. This made it the most popular German production since 1945. Deppe's *Green Is the Heather* (*Grün ist die Heide*) did even better in the following years. For an insightful reading of the latter Heimat film, see *Bliersbach, 33–46.

10. Höfig, 167, table 11.

11. The original 1917 operetta was by August Neidhardt with music by Leon Jessel. The 1933 film was directed by Georg Zoch based on a screenplay by Franz Rauch. Buschmann, 129, mentions an even earlier, silent version from 1920.

12. Most of the exterior shooting was done in the Black Forest village of St. Peter near Freiburg, while the interiors were completed in Berlin studios. Interestingly many of the Heimat film production companies were situated in West Berlin, Germany's largest metropolis and, considering the postwar geopolitics of the divided and enclosed city, the one with the least access to "nature." This might be a gauge of the extent to which Heimat films were aimed at the nostalgia of urban cinemagoers. Perhaps only coincidentally St. Christopher, the namesake of the village, is the patron saint for protection against sudden death as well as for achieving prosperity.

13. The fact that orchards blossom in spring while the St. Cecilia festival would have to be celebrated in November according to the church calendar and that Bärbele's "fresh" apples at the spring costume ball were a fall harvest are only some of the many inconsistencies in the plot. Obviously the narrative takes place outside of time. Scenarist Bobby E. Lüthge, credited with the script to *Black Forest Girl*, wrote over 200 screenplays from the twenties to the fifties in almost every genre. It is unclear whether the above inconsistencies are in the script or the result of sloppy editing.

14. Gottlieb is played by Kurt Zehe, a wrestler reputedly over seven feet tall and weighing 375 pounds. In the course of the fifties he became a fixture in comic Heimat films, playing the caricatural village idiot.

15. Höfig, 74, quotes a 1952 dissertation by Wirth which reports that a survey showed *Black Forest Girl* was the most popular film of 1951 in all regions of West Germany *except* the Black Forest. Apparently the proximity to the real geographical space diminished the audience's appreciation for the film's idealizations.

16. The use of dialect coloring to suggest regionalism is particularly nonsensical in this Black Forest film, since it uses Berlin, Viennese, Munich, and Swabian accents.

17. Schmieding, 27, uses this apt phrase to characterize the political abstinence of the fifties cinema, adapting it from the historian Hermann Heimpel. For a useful documentation of the West German cinema in the fifties as experienced in a microcosm in the city of Bochum, see Bessen.

18. The credits list a special color consultant for the film, and indeed the color photography in general and in the ice revue sequence and landscapes in particular is excellent. *Barthel, 90, claims that the film stock was smuggled in from East Germany, presumably because the black market price was much cheaper than the commercially available domestic stock.

19. Rudolf Prack, of Viennese background, made his film debut in Austria in 1937 and was a recognized star by 1950, having received his first Bambi prize in 1949. Sonja Ziemann (alias Alice Toni Selma) was groomed as a child star, making her debut in the early forties in song and dance roles. With *Black Forest Girl* she too was heaved into stardom. In 1950 he was forty-eight years old, whereas she was only twenty-five. Nonetheless, Ziemann-Prack became the incarnation of the sweet and dashing "German couple" in the early fifties, to the point where fanzines referred to them as "Zieprack." Prack's elegant manners and romantic flair seemed to represent an ideal of male attractiveness at the time, and the fact that he was considerably older than his female opposite sug-

gested stability and responsibility, conveying the impression that he had learned something from past experience.

20. Besides Höfig's structural profile of the Heimat film and *Bliersbach's sociopsychological analysis, scholarly studies on the fifties German cinema include Osterland; Meyer; Wiest-Welk; and Westermann.

21. Höfig, 117. On the competition between the new television medium and the established cinema in Germany, see Hickethier, "Vom Ende des Kinos."

22. On the critical Heimat film in the New German Cinema, see Rentschler, *West German Film*, 103–28; and on the immensely popular television series *Heimat* (1984) by Edgar Reitz, see Kaes, *Deutschlandbilder*, 171–204. Achternbusch's films, mostly set in rural Bavaria and including the whole spectrum of peasant caricatures, are more directly descended from the thin slapstick tradition in the German cinema and theater (i.e., Karl Valentin). Bockmeyer's *Vulture Wally* (*Geierwally*, 1987) is a remake and the ultimate parody of this popular Heimat film subject.

Chapter 9

1. Pre-Nazi films about World War I include Luis Trenker's *Mountains in Flames* (*Berge in Flammen*, 1931); Gustav Ucicky's *Dawn* (*Morgenrot*, 1933); and Pabst's own pacifistic *Westfront 1918*. During the Third Reich war films were a staple item, especially right before and after hostilities began in 1939. Regel has discussed a number of patterns in war films produced during the Third Reich; for a more general introduction to the history of German war films, see Silberman, "Shooting Wars."

2. The few remigrés were less inhibited about producing hardhitting films on the Nazi past. Peter Lorre, Robert Siodmak, and Frank Wisbar returned to West Germany from the United States to make films that dealt with guilt and responsibility for the war, and the Swiss Bernhard Wicki produced the most important fifties antiwar film in West Germany (*The Bridge* [*Die Brücke*], 1959). On remigrés, see Göttler, 182–84.

3. See Kreimeier, *Kino und Filmindustrie*, 108–29; and Bredow, "Filmpropaganda."

4. The state financial guarantees were a governmental attempt to support the chronically undercapitalized production sector in the film industry. The plan failed because it covered the costs of high-risk projects rather than encouraging quality. The program invited irresponsibly high costs by guaranteeing a minimum 7.5 percent profit margin for the producer based on production outlays, no matter what a film earned in distribution. For a presentation of the *Bürgschaft* subsidy system, see Herringer; for critiques, see Dost, Hopf, and Kluge, 103–5; Berger, "Bürgen heisst zahlen."

5. One of the first such films was Zoltan Korda's 1939 British war film *Four Feathers*, which played in Germany for the first time in 1950. American features followed quickly, including such popular ones as *The Halls of Montezuma* (Lewis Milestone, 1951, under the German title *Okinawa*); *From Here to Eternity* (Fred Zinnemann, 1953, under the German title *Verdammt in alle Ewigkeit*); and *The Caine Mutiny* (Edward Dmytryk, 1954, under the German title *Die*

Caine war ihr Schicksal). On the role of American war films distributed in West Germany during the early fifties, see Schmieding, 35–54; Barthel, 204–6.

6. Schmieding, 36.

7. They include Geza von Bolvary's *Fritz und Friederike* (1952); Johannes Alexander Hübler-Kahle's *Mike Joins up* (*Mikosch rückt ein*, 1952); and Georg Jacoby's later *Three Days Confinement* [*Drei Tage Mittelarrest*] (1955).

8. These documentary compilation films include *Both Sides of the Runway* (*Beiderseits der Rollbahn*, Jonas and Stegemann, 1952); *Our Rommel* (*Das war unser Rommel*, Wiganko, 1953); *Til Five After Twelve* (*Bis fünf Minuten nach zwölf*, Gerhard Grindel, 1953); and *The German G.I.* (*So war der deutsche Landser*, Albert Baumeister, 1955).

9. One film historian estimates that the domestic, Austrian market covered only 10–15 percent of the production costs before 1938, see Drewniak, 21.

10. There were three rubble films (*Trümmerfilme*) produced in Austria, *The Trial* (*Der Prozess*) about historical anti-Semitism (G. W. Pabst, 1947); *The Widow Farmer of Sonnhof* (*Die Sonnhofbäuerin*) about returning refugees (Wilfried Frass, 1948); and *Duel with Death* (*Duell mit dem Tod*) about the resistance (Paul May, 1949).

11. Like West Germany, Austria faced the market pressures of foreign imports and releases or rereleases of earlier features as well as competition from the West German industry itself. During the consolidation phase in the early fifties a Film Agreement with the Federal Republic regulated the number of films exported by each side, about fifteen a year in each direction. After the Austrian State Contract was signed with the Allied Powers in 1955, ending the occupation and establishing the country's sovereignty, the industry peaked in 1956 with thirty-seven feature-length films, including the highly successful *Sissi* series starring Romy Schneider. Parallel to the development in West Germany, the introduction of publicly financed television broadcasting in 1955 marked the beginning of the industry's decline, although with a lag of two to three years. Film critics and historians often do not distinguish between the Austrian and the German cinema, neglecting important details of the symbiotic relationship between the two. On the history of the Austrian cinema and its film industry, see the two historical presentations by Fritz as well as Steiner.

12. Thiel presents in brief format a more complex typology in "Acht Typen."

13. For general, retrospective treatments of Pabst's works that concur on the singular success of *The Last Ten Days* among his late productions, see *Agel, 140; *Amengual, 59–62; *Atwell, 138–42; *Aubry and Pétat, 359–60; *Buache, 93; *Cozarinsky, vol. 2, 760–61; and *Groppoli, 101–4.

14. Pabst was involved with three productions in the Third Reich: *Komödianten* (1941), *Paracelsus* (1943), and *The Molander Affair* (*Der Fall Molander*, 1944, the uncut footage was destroyed in the chaos of the war's end). On Pabst's biography and for discussions of his most important films, see *Rentschler.

15. See *"Hitler war kein Kasperle." Leo Lania mentions the year 1948 at which time the question arose about filming Musmanno's book in *Bachmann, 75.

16. *Musmanno. On Remarque's role in writing the scenario, see *Owen, 269; on the controversy about the quality of Remarque's (unpublished) screenplay and

the revisions that were undertaken but never acknowledged, see *"Hitler. Story von Remarque."

17. See *Owen, 266; and *Remarque's own comments about his concern at the time to foster the image of "the good German" as a basis for preventing a recurrence of fascism.

18. Pabst in *Cinema*, n.s. 28 (Milan, December 15, 1949), quoted in *Amengual, 101.

19. See the notes to *"Filmographie," 21.

20. *"Hitler war kein Kasperle," 37.

21. On the literary and dramatic sources of melodrama, see Rahill; Brooks; for an introduction to the terms of cinematic melodrama, especially with reference to the family structures that play a role in Pabst's film, see "Dossier on Melodrama"; and the sources mentioned in chap. 4, n. 11.

22. There is an unsettling resemblance between Wüst's heroics in this film and Pabst's portrayal of the historical Caroline Neuber in *Komödianten* (1941) who devotes her life to the cause of developing a national German theater in the late eighteenth century. See *Gleber's discussion of this film.

23. At the 1956 Edinburgh Film Festival, *The Last Ten Days* (British distribution title: *Ten Days to Die*) won a Gold Medal as one of the best non-American feature films, and Albin Skoda won a Golden Laurel as best actor of the year for his portrayal of Hitler.

24. Even before production began, the film project was the object of not a little publicity. Conservative critics were apprehensive that it would be an anti-German film making Hitler's death into a source for box office profits, while liberal critics were concerned that Hitler on the screen would provoke Nazi nostalgia. For details, see *"Hitler. Story von Remarque."

25. Most of the journalistic discussion after the film's premiere ignored the film and addressed the political issue of Germany's recent past. All critics seemed to agree that *The Last Ten Days* had major artistic flaws, but such judgments quickly shifted into moralistic arguments, ranging from total rejection of the film's "falsifications" to its embrace as reminder and warning. Spectator reactions registered at the premiere screening were reported generally as negative: the events seemed fantastical and very far away, as if from another planet! A special, closed showing in Munich was reported to have elicited strong criticism from Hitler's personal chauffeur (Erich Kempa) about the film's lack of documentary authenticity: there was no large canteen in the bunker, the nurses never had time to dance with soldiers or SS members, the subway tunnel in Berlin was blasted three days *after* Hitler's death, etc. See *"Unfug der 'Dokumentarfilme.'" A collection of written responses by eleven spectators (mostly educated professionals) was published under the title *"Der letzte Akt."

Chapter 10

1. For a theoretical and historical introduction to Socialist Realism from an East German perspective, see Pracht; and for a brief summary of the historical shifts, see Tate.

2. Party concern for the development of the GDR cinema was motivated largely by the campaign against "formalism" in the arts, which had begun in 1950 and was aimed against the threat of ideological seepage from the West. Its effect in the short run was to stifle almost any creative efforts. DEFA productions distributed in the GDR fell from ten in 1950 to eight in 1951 and to six in 1952. After the 1952 conference, however, the ideological situation began to ease and DEFA production figures rose consistently thereafter to peak in 1959 at twenty-six feature films. Also, by the end of the fifties DEFA was becoming involved in television films and international coproductions. See Baumert and Herlinghaus, 23–39. For a more recent overview, see Schenk, "Mitten im kalten Krieg."

3. For background on what was referred to in the East German context as the "realism debate," see Mittenzwei, *Der Realismus-Streit*. For a summary in English of the pertinent positions, see Livingstone.

4. For background on the conditions of production for these films, see Lohmann, "Neue Haltungen."

5. See Baumert and Herlinghaus, 41–53. The critique was directed at the hard-hitting, critical Berlin films mentioned above and the danger perceived by the party of Western decadence in such youth-oriented, rebellious features.

6. Kersten, "Entwicklungslinien," 39.

7. On the impact of the Eleventh Plenary from the contemporaneous East German perspective, see Baumert and Herlinghaus, 55–62; a somewhat later assessment is provided by Lohmann, "Die DEFA-Spielfilme." After 1989 the Eleventh Plenary became a major focus of critical examination among intellectuals and artists because it seemed to bear the seeds of collapse; see Agde's collection of essays and documents, in particular Wolf's 1966 letter to the Party Committee in the DEFA studios, 374–81, and Renk's essay, 201–12.

8. Eight of the twelve censored films were reconstructed and showcased at the 1990 Berlinale International Film Festival. In 1987 Heiner Carow's feature *The Russians Are Coming* (*Die Russen kommen*) was released in the GDR after its distribution was blocked in 1968. The Soviet intervention in Prague in August of that year, supported by the GDR government, led to this measure, although the film has much in common with Wolf's feature. With a very subjective use of camera and sound Carow contrasts the anxiety of a young German boy toward Soviet soldiers with their generosity toward him in the last days of the war.

9. DEFA developed a strong reputation for high quality, feature-length films for children and young adults, including Western genre films in which the Indians always were the "good guys" such as Josef Mach's 1965 *The Sons of the Great She-Bear* (*Die Söhne der grossen Bärin*) and Richard Groschopp's 1967 *Chingachgook—The Great Snake* (*Chingachgook — Die grosse Schlange*). On the development of the children's film studio at DEFA, see Jungnickel.

10. For an overview of Wolf's career and a discussion of his entire oeuvre in English, see *Silberman; for a West German introduction, see *Gregor; for an East German discussion of the early films, see *Tok; and for the late films, see *Richter.

11. Wolf referred frequently to Romm's *Nine Days of One Year* (1961) as an important inspiration for his 1964 film *Divided Heaven* (*Der geteilte Himmel*),

and Tarkovsky's biographical film *Ivan's Childhood* (1962) could well have exemplified for him the power of historical biography. Additionally, Wolf had been interested in Italian neorealism since his earliest films. In the case of *I Was Nineteen*, Roberto Rossellini's *Paisà* (1946) seems to have exerted some influence in the episodic structuring, the image of the hanged deserter, and the documentary style.

12. In a prerelease interview Wolf insisted that the film was not autobiographical, see *Wolfe and Kohlhaase, 959. For biographical material related to this film, see *Köppe and Renk, especially the introductory essay by Klaus Wischnewski and the photographs and documents on the film *I Was Nineteen* (136–47).

13. The status of autobiographical narration in the cinema is not settled. Using a traditional definition of classical autobiography, Bruss proceeds to show how film autobiography is a form of historical biography because it lacks the essential self-referentiality inherent in language. Although this argument foregrounds some crucial distinctions, there are two reasons to consider this film autobiographical. First, Wolf employs the immediacy of the image to radicalize the very role-playing Bruss finds essential in the written autobiography; Wolf must confront the remembered self as Other, as stranger, if in no other way than in the actor who plays his persona. Second, rather than considering autobiography a genre (either in its normative or descriptive sense), one can consider it a mode of understanding or a specular structure in which the author (or filmmaker in this case) becomes the subject of his own understanding.

14. Wolf's wartime diaries, written in Russian, cover the period from February 1943 to April 18, 1945. The relevant portions for *I Was Nineteen* were first published as background material to the film in an internal publication of the East German Academy of Arts. See Wolf, "Tagebuchnotizen," in *Ruschin, 5–25.

15. The shooting script for *I Was Nineteen* was published as part of the discussion material for the Academy of Arts: see Kohlhaase and Wolf, "Ich war neunzehn," in *Ruschin, 29–64.

16. *G. Wolf, responsible for the film's dramaturgy, stressed the formative role of authenticity both as a stylistic principle and a moral claim in his production notes. Wuss (especially 294–332) discusses what he calls the "authenticity effect" (*Authentie-Effekt*) as the general trend toward a documentary style in films from socialist countries during the sixties. Although none of his examples come from the GDR, *I Was Nineteen* shares many of the characteristics he elaborates.

17. This is also an issue of consistency in narrative perspective. A different kind of break in point of view occurs in the fourth segment, the long episode in the Spandau fortress. While Gregor and Vadim are negotiating with the German military officers in one part of the fortress, the camera follows one of the adjutants when he leaves in order to inform the SS commander about what is happening. The two following scenes allow Wolf to show the SS's desperate situation, which logically could not have been witnessed by Gregor.

18. *Ruschin, 55 (my translation). The song is sung by the well-known actor/singer Ernst Busch, whose voice was also heard in the 1932 *Kuhle Wampe*.

Aber später und immer und überall,
wo Arbeiter sitzen beisammen,

wird erklingen das Lied der Jaramaschlacht,
wird zum Kampfe die Herzen entflammen.
Und einmal dann, wenn die Stunde kommt,
wo wir alle Gespenster verjagen,
wird die ganze Welt zur Jarama-Front,
wie in den Februartagen.

19. See *Wulff, 139–43, for an informal close reading of the final sequence and its spatial relations.

20. Wolf fails to mention these prisoners are marching off to forced labor or death in Stalin's gulags; this might seem surprising in a 1967 film, eleven years after the revelations of Stalin's crimes. Official disclaimers notwithstanding, the Stalinist past in the Soviet Union remained a fundamental taboo in the GDR, thus, it was a blind spot in the historical consciousness of filmmaker Konrad Wolf, who identified emotionally and ideologically with the Soviet Union.

21. For a discussion of the cultural status of antifascism in the literary sphere and its repressed relationship to Stalinism, which has many parallels in the cinema, see Silberman, "Writing What."

22. Ulrich Weiss's *Your Unknown Brother* (*Dein unbekannter Bruder*, 1981), Frank Beyer's adaptation of the Hermann Kant novel *Held for Questioning* (*Der Aufenthalt*, 1983), Michael Kann's *Stielke, Heinz, 15* (1987), and Siegfried Kühn's *The Actress* (*Die Schauspielerin*, 1988) are examples of films that try to address in the eighties the psychosocial dimension of complicity or resistance, neither demonizing nor heroizing those who were involved on either side of the war.

23. For a brief history of the changing attitudes toward the national question in the GDR, see Hacker.

24. The average audience figures for a successful DEFA film in the sixties was 1 million spectators. See *Wolf and Kohlhasse. The film's international release was crucially undermined by the events in Prague in August 1968, when Soviet troops quelled the Prague reformist efforts. There was little sympathy for a positive portrayal of the Soviet military for years to come.

25. The concern about reaching young spectators was not just theoretical; in the late sixties about 75–80 percent of the cinema spectators were under twenty-one. See *Bisky and Netzeband.

26. See Geisler's critical commentary on the press campaign in *Ruschin, 93–96.

27. For a selection of such responses, see *Ruschin, 78–87. Wolf's film was the object of one of the first broad-based empirical surveys of audience reactions by a sociologist. See Netzeband, "Einstellungen Jugendlicher," in *Ruschin, 87–93.

Chapter 11

1. For details on the political change of regime, see Staritz, 198–203. The new head of state, Erich Honecker, made a crucial statement in December 1971 at a congress of cultural functionaries that there are "no taboos in the realm of art and literature," marking the first time in the history of GDR cultural policies that the party relinquished its position as arbiter in ideological questions.

2. Wätzold, 182–83.

3. On the changes ushered in at 1972 Film and Television Congress and its impact on film production, see Lohmann and Weiss.

4. A sociological study noted that the cinema was at this time twice as popular in East Germany as in West Germany with about the same number of cinemas per person, see Deja-Löhhöffel, 70. The attendance figures are also attributable to the more liberal import policy of Western European and American feature films in the eighties. DEFA itself produced between 50–60 films/year, of which approximately 15–18 were cinema features (including 3–4 children's features), and the remaining two thirds were commissioned for television. GDR cinemas screened about 140–50 releases each year, so that DEFA productions made up only 10–15 percent of the total while films from other socialist countries accounted for another 60 percent. See Kersten, "Entwicklungslinien," 54; and Bisky, 37. Because of its geopolitical situation the East German public enjoyed wide access to films via television. Most of the country received not only two East German channels (with about 800 films a year) but three West German channels as well. As in the rest of Europe, television had become in the GDR by the late seventies the dominant leisure-time medium so that cinemas had to devise new means of attracting a public that was increasingly younger. This included film clubs, luxurious showcase cinemas in larger urban centers, and film festivals. More importantly, film was no longer understood to be primarily a vehicle for information, agitation, and propaganda, functions television had taken over. This was most visible in the shift of historical and biographical themes from the cinema to television programming.

5. Maetzig, 389.

6. This trend was not unrelated to the crisis in the cultural sphere precipitated by the expatriation of dissident poet Wolf Biermann in 1976. The resulting rupture and polarization between intellectuals and the political power holders had a lasting effect throughout the eighties. See Naumann and Trumpler. For an overview of the seventies cinema, see Wischnewski; and for a focus on the ups and downs of cultural policy in the DEFA studios, see Bretschneider.

7. On the literary antecedents for female protagonists, see Herminghouse. For a brief summary of "woman's films" see Kersten, "Role of Women"; more critical overviews are presented by Leonhard, 60–71; and Schieber, 267–74.

8. For an insightful discussion of Zschoche's films prior to *On Probation*, see *Prochnow; additional biographical and filmographical information can be found in the Zschoche article in Bock.

9. Civil courts in the GDR included citizen representatives (*Schöffen*) who were elected as lay judges or jurors to participate in the proceedings. Under certain circumstances they could suggest a form of probation for the defendant in which they or peers from the defendant's workplace would guarantee (*bürgen*) the individual's improvement with conditions and responsibilities clearly spelled out. The "Bürgschaft" in the film's title refers to this type of guarantee and not to the kind of probation familiar in the American court system. On the GDR legal system, see the entries "Strafensystem" and "Rechtswesen" (part C) in Zimmermann as well as Brunner.

10. The scenario is based on *Schulze-Gerlach's 1978 novel of the same title, drawn from a real case study; however, the novel's protagonist and narrative authority is not Nina Kern but the lay juror Irmgard Behrend.

11. The dream sequence reveals one way in which Nina's voicelessness is displaced, here into the role of the listener. One of the jurors asks Nina why the older daughter refuses to eat chocolate. Obviously embarrassed, she avoids an answer, but shortly thereafter a sound montage reveals the source of her discomfort. Threatening chords of rock music and the cacophony of adult voices are interspersed with a child's cries of "Mama, Mama." It is a flashback—consisting of dark, distorted images—to one of Nina's parties where, to silence the child, a man pushes chocolate into her mouth while Nina weakly protests. The only retrospective scene showing the protagonist's earlier negligence toward her children (albeit filtered through a dream), it places her in a helpless position of listening. Related to the role of Nina as a listener rather than a speaker is also the film's careful dramaturgy of noise. Often the sound track is full of miscellaneous street or radio noise. The separation of sound from visible sources stresses Nina's lack of control, her exclusion from discursive authority posited in language. For an insightful and detailed discussion of gender-specific issues of voice, sound, and noise in the cinema, see Silverman, *Acoustic Mirror*.

12. Reviews of the film tend to distort this process by describing it as a positive experience toward social integration. The scriptwriter, Gabriele Kotte, however, confirmed this disciplinary aspect: "Our interest was how a young woman became involved in a situation, in part through her own fault but in part unknowingly, from which she truly wants to escape. For her this means renouncing almost everything that defines her personality, in other words, living from hand to mouth and the drive to live each day fully." Other comments from this discussion after a public showing of the film corroborate that at least some spectators also understood the film to be about institutional discipline in everyday life. See the comments from a discussion at Kino International in Berlin, GDR, *"Leben nach Regeln." For a complete list of GDR reviews of *On Probation*, see *Filmografischer Jahresbericht 1981*, 287–88.

13. Such scenes were relatively rare in topical DEFA films, where religion and religious persons rarely if ever played a positive role. Not until 1988 did DEFA release a major feature film that thematized the church (Lothar Warneke, *Bear Ye One Another's Burdens* [*Einer trage des anderen Last* . . .]). Relations between the GDR government and the Protestant and Catholic Churches were strained until 1978, when the state officially accepted the churches' right to contribute to the "humanistic aims" of the socialist society. The year Zschoche's film was released, 1981, witnessed the beginning of the Protestant Church's involvement in a controversial, non-state-sanctioned peace movement that increasingly attracted participation from citizens who did not or would not identify with the officially organized antiwar program. Ultimately this led to the broad protest movement resulting in the collapse of the Berlin Wall and German unification. For background information on GDR church politics, see Henkys; Nitsche.

14. On the history and status of women in the GDR, see Kuhrig and Speigner; Helwig.

15. E.g., *Gehler; *Mihan's collective review of films with strong women figures outside the mainstream; and *Blazejewski. Zschoche's film went on to win

prestigious prizes at several festivals in 1982: the Second GDR National Spielfilmfestival (best director, screenplay, sets, and costumes), the GDR Critics' Prize as the best contemporary DEFA film, and two prizes at the (West) Berlinale International Film Festival (the Silver Bear for Katrin Sass and the Catholic Film Bureau's Interfilm Prize).

16. The first woman to direct a DEFA film was Bärbel Bergmann with her children's feature *The Agate* (*Die Achatmurmel*, 1959). Ingrid Reschke was the first female student enrolled in the directing program at the Babelsberg film academy. Her first production was the children's film *David and the World Champion* (*David und der Weltmeister*, 1962); she was killed in an automobile collision in 1971 after having completed three further features.

Chapter 12

1. For background and documents on the impact of the *Spiegel* controversy, see Seifert; for an English-language discussion, see Schoenbaum.

2. For statistics on the development of the West German film industry during the fifties, see Höfig, 92, 448 (table 4), and 451 (table 9); as well as Herringer, 15. On the signs of crisis in the early sixties, see Dost et al., 111–15; and Koch, 32–37.

3. On commercial films of the sixties, see Bredow, "Zwischen Kitsch und Krise." On detective films, see Grob.

4. In 1963, 70 percent of the films screened in West Germany were foreign produced (Herringer, 17); other figures are from the *Filmstatistisches Jahrbuch.

5. For demographic statistics on the sixties audience according to its age, education, and employment background, see Kroner, 146–47; and Prokop, 169–79.

6. For details of the Oberhausen Manifesto, see Koch, 63–67; it is discussed in English by Dawson, and by Rentschler, "Critical Junctures." For the English translation of the Manifesto, see Rentschler, *West German Filmmakers*, 2.

7. For background on the role of the German student movement and the formation of a political and cultural opposition, see McCormick, 30–42.

8. Hansen, "Cooperative Auteur Cinema," 37 n. 4, distinguishes the usages of the *auteur* notion in French and Anglo-American contexts in contrast to the West German usage of *Autor*. For an extended discussion of the *Autorenfilm*, see Brauerhoch.

9. On the early successes of the Young German Film, see Courtade; and Elsaesser, *New German Cinema*, 20–27 (also 95–98 on Kluge). The ten-page cover story in the December 25, 1967 issue of Germany's most important news magazine *Der Spiegel* represented a crucial contribution for publicizing and legitimating the German new wave cinema; see the English translation "Young German Film."

10. On Kluge's biography, see *Lewandowski, *Alexander Kluge*, 7–14; and in English *Fiedler. For bibliographic information, see *Böhm-Christel, 325–60, including a list of the pertinent reviews of *Artists under the Big Top: Perplexed* (346–48); and Arnold, ed., "Alexander Kluge," 145–63. In English two focus issues of journals have presented writings by and about Kluge's diverse literary,

theoretical, and cinematic projects as well as comprehensive filmographies and bibliographies: *Liebmann, "Alexander Kluge"; and *Hansen, "Special Issue."

11. The Institut für Filmgestaltung in Ulm was supposed to have been developed under Fritz Lang's direction, but he abandoned the project when it became clear that the school was not interested in narrative film form. The Institute formally opened in October 1962. It ceased functioning along with the rest of the university in 1969 because of financial and political pressure. For information on the Institute, see *Koetzle; on Kluge's concept of the curriculum, see *Kluge, "Die Utopie Film." For a short description in English of the Institute's beginnings, see *Kluge, "Early Days."

12. For overviews of Kluge's films, see the article on Kluge in Bock; *Lewandowski, *Die Filme*; *Hummel (a special Kluge issue of *Kinemathek*); and *Richter and Wysseier. For a discussion of *Yesterday Girl*, see *Hansen, "Space of History."

13. The film received in 1968 the Golden Lion at the Venice Film Festival (the first German film to receive this honor after Leni Riefenstahl's *Triumph of the Will* in 1936!) and in 1969 the German government prize, *Filmband in Gold*. The journalistic response to the film made a real effort to account for the dispersed dramaturgy and associational montage techniques but generally complained about its elitist, intellectual approach. Excerpts from four important newspaper reviews are included in *Hummel, 17–21. See also *Handke's scathing critique.

14. On the silent film, see *Hummel, 7. *Hansen, "Reinventing the Nickelodeon," 193, regards this film as Kluge's most "comprehensive homage" to the pre–World War I "cinema of attractions." Kluge refers frequently to Brecht and to the Brechtian tradition; for details on this relationship in the context of the later film *The Female Patriot* (*Die Patriotin*, 1979), see *Stollmann, 245–64. He also pointed out very early his affinity with another filmmaker in the Brechtian tradition, Jean-Luc Godard; see "Wort und Film," in *Kluge and Eder, 9–27, (1965) (in English, "Word and Film," *October* 46: 83–95). Both Godard and Kluge have adapted Brecht's epic techniques but the relationship is more that of a parallel evolution of cinematic language than of imitation. Kluge's thematic reservoir has little in common with Godard's, and the latter's fascination with American film history finds no echo in Kluge's work.

15. *Schlüpmann, 145, examines in her extended discussion of gender issues in *Artists* the string of scenes that critically reflect on the role of the actress in show business.

16. The sequence numbering refers to the "Dialogue List" in *Kluge, *Die Artisten*, 11–53.

17. Mitscherlich and Mitscherlich.

18. Associations with flight—the trapeze act, a stranded hot air balloon in this and the next sequences, and airplanes in later sequences (e.g., 3, 14, 18, 19)—belong to the image cluster or meaning field related to the Enlightenment notion of dominated nature. The cluster also includes the many shots of animals performing contrary to their "nature," for example, an elephant standing on its head or walking on two legs like a human being, and the images of Napoleon

with the associations of the Imperator as omnipotent (sequence 5 and 54). Kluge discusses the historical roots of the circus in the French Revolution in *Lewandowski, *Die Filme*, 46; and in *Negt and Kluge, 456; see also the off-screen commentary in sequence 27 of the film.

19. *Hansen's discussion—in "Space of History"—of the voice-over commentaries and the "aural" point of view in *Yesterday Girl* also applies to *Artists*.

20. For general comments on Kluge's use of music as well as a description of the parenthetical music structure in sequence 2, see *Hohlweg, 55–56; and Norbert Schneider, 201–4.

21. On Kluge's theory of the spectator composing the film, see *Liebman, "Why Kluge?" 14. Contrary to the self-consciousness this process of construction elicits in the spectator's imaginary activity, Kluge resists problematizing or foregrounding his own privileged, controlling position as the one who creates the texture of gaps that the spectator/listener must reassemble to produce meaning.

22. *Liebman, "Why Kluge?" 17, characterizes *Artists under the Big Top: Perplexed* as the filmmaker's manifesto for his convictions about the cinema as art. He goes on to discuss briefly the grounding of Kluge's views in cultural theories of Theodor W. Adorno and the Frankfurt School's Critical Theory. On Kluge and the Frankfurt School, see also *Hansen, "Alexander Kluge: Crossings."

23. In sequence 49 Leni and her business manager evaluate the speeches presented at a circus congress. The documentary shots of the congress, however, show the last regular meeting of the literary "Gruppe 47" in 1967, an ironic allusion for insiders but also an indication that the issues addressed in the film go beyond the narrow confines of the circus. The repetition of the phrase in the speeches "I would like to meet the person who can prevent us from saying something after Auschwitz" refers to Adorno's controversial rhetorical question about the nature of poetry after Auschwitz. For Kluge's most sustained examination of the relationship of the Germans to their history, see *Kluge and Negt, 361–769.

24. See Benjamin, 217–51. For a discussion of distraction, see Schlüpmann, "Phenomenology of Film," 102–3. Kluge develops his theory of the public sphere most consistently in *Negt and Kluge. For an introduction in English to this concept in the context of the cooperative film project *Deutschland im Herbst* (1978), organized by Kluge, see Hansen, "Alexander Kluge, Cinema"; as well as English excerpts from the later Kluge film *The Female Patriot* (*Die Patriotin*, 1979), in *Kluge, "On Film."

25. *Negt and Kluge, 187–91.

26. The program was called "Hour of the Filmmakers: Film History—Film Stories" and was broadcast on the cable station SAT 1. In 1988 Kluge developed a series of 20–25 minute segments for his own program called "Ten to Eleven" on the commercial RTL network. Kluge comments on this irony in a 1987 interview in *Richter and Wysseier, 5. For background in English on Kluge's television work, see *Morse. For a general discussion of the relationship between cinema and television broadcasting, see Hickethier, "Die Zugewinngemeinschaft."

Chapter 13

1. Between 1974 and 1979 46 million Marks were invested by the television networks in seventy-four coproductions. Besides coproductions networks purchase completed features and subcontract work for series. Especially during the seventies this put some television administrators into the position of executive producers for the cinema; Peter Märthesheimer, Joachim von Mengershausen, Günter Rohrbach, Eckhardt Stein, and Gunther Witte, for example, were some of the most important administrators who supported risky or challenging projects by young directors. See Pflaum.

2. It has frequently been noted that the New German Cinema was a creation of foreign cinephiles, in particular of Anglo-American critics, festival directors, and universities. The Goethe Institute and Inter Nationes, two government-funded but autonomous institutions responsible for representing the culture of the Federal Republic of Germany abroad, were instrumental in providing access to New German Cinema films and directors by sponsoring film packages and arranging tours of directors to foreign countries. For an early appraisal, see Rentschler, "American Friends"; for a more recent note, see Elsaesser, *New German Cinema*, 290–92.

3. For background on the emergence of a women's cinema and explicitly feminist films in the context of the New German Cinema, see Knight.

4. There is quite a body of material in English on the formation and impact of the New German Cinema. Early overviews include Rentschler, *West German Film*; Sandford; Franklin; Corrigan; and Phillips. Elsaesser's *New German Cinema* (1989) is the most comprehensive investigation to date and includes an extensive bibliography.

5. Elsaesser, *New German Cinema*, 36. Annual statistics are published in the *Filmstatistisches Taschenbuch*.

6. There have been several excellent studies on Holocaust and historical discourses in the New German cinema including Kaes, *Deutschlandbilder*; Santner; Coates, 108–55; McCormick; and Frieden et al., vol. 2, part 2, 163–289.

7. For biographical background on Margarethe von Trotta, see the early introduction and interview by *Möhrmann, 195–202; and *Donner's biographical essay. Other overviews of von Trotta's work include *Schiavo; *Moeller; *Gehler; and *Quart.

8. For background on West German terrorism as a revolutionary project, see Fetscher and Rohrmosser; and on the Red Army Faction specifically, see Aust. For journalistic and research sources on West German terrorism, see Backes and Jesse, vol. 1, part 5. Von Trotta met Christiane Ensslin, Gudrun's sister, while filming footage of the burial of the suicides with Volker Schlöndorff for his contribution to the omnibus project *Germany in Autumn* (*Deutschland im Herbst*, 1978). Although Christiane Ensslin is not mentioned in the credits, she apparently advised von Trotta on the scenario, even visiting the set during filming, as mentioned in an interview with actress Jutta Lampe. See *Weber and Weber, 95–96.

9. See the scenario, included in *Weber and Weber, 11–76. Each of these scenes is listed and numbered in the scenario as a memory (*Erinnerung*). In addition

there is Juliane's dream after her collapse (also set about 1947), and Jan's nightmare about being set afire.

10. The German title, *Die bleierne Zeit* (The Leaden Time) quotes a phrase from the elegy "Der Gang aufs Land" by the Romantic poet Friedrich Hölderlin, which draws a parallel between the "leaden" time in an unnamed past and the troubled present. Von Trotta's title implies a similar double-edged reference to the inhibitions of the fifties restoration in postwar Germany and the public reaction to terrorism in the seventies. The phrase has come to characterize the seventies in general.

11. In *Godard von Trotta remarked that "Protestant education teaches a strict morality, the strict search for truth"; in a later interview she reiterated the Protestant aspect that characterizes the sense of entrapment and prejudice in many of her films; see *von Trotta, "Ich wollte," 170. Elsaesser, *New German Cinema*, 232–37, discusses briefly the Protestant element in von Trotta's films.

12. The poetic references are to Rainer Maria Rilke's "melancholy" poem "Herbsttag" (1902), recited in front of the class by Marianne); Bertolt Brecht's "Ballade von der 'Judenhure' Marie Sanders" (1935); and Paul Celan's "Todesfuge" (1952). The imprisoned Marianne mentions this last poem once again—she has forgotten some lines—as a reminder to Juliane of their shared childhood but also of their shared sense of responsibility for the victims of the Holocaust. Besides the film title and the Resnais documentary, there are additional literary and historical references in the narrative: the teenager Juliane reads Sartre; the adult Juliane has a portrait of Rosa Luxemburg hanging above her desk, which points to an alternate kind of revolutionary activism in the seventies (von Trotta would make a biographical film about Luxemburg in 1986); and the published scenario begins with an epigram by Ingeborg Bachmann. This fabric of citations with strong resonances for an educated public of von Trotta's generation in postwar West Germany counteracts what could be understood as an overdetermined causal link between family psychology and political biography.

13. The guerilla training sequence—the narrative's weakest—consists of a pan of the Beirut skyline, shots of Marianne and Karl driving a jeep through a desert, and a shot of Marianne emerging from a store and pursued by Arab children who want to touch her golden hair. Meanwhile Marianne's voice-over reads a letter to Juliane expressing her admiration for the Al-Fatah and their revolutionary solidarity. The images suggest a poor caricature of the political issues behind terrorism, using media clichés popularized by the press and the television evening news. They seem strangely out of place in a film that otherwise avoids engaging the politics of terrorism.

14. These scenes have been criticized as especially weak in portraying feminist politics. Von Trotta explained, apparently as an excuse, that she asked a woman from the West German Communist Party (DKP) to write them for her; see *von Tratta, "Das bisschen Leben," 18.

15. Coates, 206–13 and 222–28, reads von Trotta's film through its images of horror, death, and the uncanny; he considers it a homage and implicit critique of Ingmar Bergman's *Persona*, especially in this superimposition of the two women's faces, which quotes Bergman and his theme of self-loss and reconstitution of the self.

16. The brief images of the couple on the Mount Etna volcano amid the smoke and wind might be intended as a metaphor for imminent danger, ready to "explode," or as another literary reference to Hölderlin, this time to the central motif in his "Empedokles" fragment. In either case, the allusion would be unusually obscure. Images in this sequence of the Sicilian restaurant and fishing village, however, are notable for their crowded spaces with many people, unlike any of the images of Germany, which tend to be enclosed and relatively empty (prisons, rooms, courtyards, etc.). The contrast between the "leaden" atmosphere of the North and the light, noisy, busy atmosphere in the South is subtle but effective.

17. The text, sung in Italian, is a soprano solo excerpt from Handel's oratorio *Lucretia*: "Already in my breast this dagger begins to do its cruel duty; and yet I feel my heart shuddering more with grief at my unavenged defeat than with horror at the approach of death. But if it be not granted me in this world to punish the tyrant, to crush the impious one, then from hell with more hideous example will I hurl darts whose fatal wounds will fell him dead. Raging and merciless from hell I will wreak my revenge." In fact, the film narrative echoes more precisely the Antigone-Ismene conflict with its overtones of individual resistance to state authority than that of Lucretia, but the sense of the recitative points to the emotions that will carry the rest of the film. Von Trotta assisted Volker Schlöndorff with his contribution to the film *Germany in Autumn* (1978), a satiric episode about anxious functionaries censoring a television production of Sophocles' *Antigone* because of its criticism of state violence.

18. *Linville discusses some of these motifs and their relation to the (gendered) spectator in the film.

19. Werner Herzog's Kaspar Hauser is the most salient example of the orphaned and maltreated child, but there are many others including the young girl in Wenders's *Alice in the Cities* (*Alice in den Städten*, 1973); the autobiographical child in Sanders-Brahms's *Germany Pale Mother*; and Schlöndorff's Oskar in *The Tin Drum*.

20. The film premiered at the Biennale in Venice and won the Golden Lion as well as the director's, FIPRESCI, and OCIC prizes. Von Trotta was only the second German woman to receive the Golden Lion after Leni Riefenstahl's *Triumph des Willen* (1936). Jutta Lampe and Barbara Sukowa also were accorded the Golden Phoenix for their superb acting. In the meantime it has won perhaps more prizes than any other film to emerge from Germany during this period.

21. Although von Trotta argued that the film was not authentic in a documentary sense, she insisted that she did want to show the increasingly inhuman treatment of terrorists in West German prisons; see *von Trotta, "Rebellinnen," 32. For the most blatant example of how a critic both misread *Marianne and Juliane* as documentary and overlooked the sympathetic treatment of terrorist motivations, see *Delorme. *Schultz-Gerstein and *Buchka offer representative West German reviews from the time the film was released.

22. Although some of the discussions of von Trotta's film in English (the British distribution title is *The German Sisters*) draw incorrect conclusions based on a faulty understanding of the German situation, they do present some challenging arguments. Besides those already mentioned, see *Harris and Sklar; *DiCaprio; *Seiter; and *Kaplan.

23. Von Trotta has resisted attempts to label her work as feminist or as part of a "women's cinema" because she perceives this as a way of ghettoizing films by women. Moreover, she has consistently rejected the notion of "woman's film" (*Frauenfilm*) except as an economic descriptor for the discrimination that is typical of the low budgets women filmmakers receive for their projects (see *von Trotta, "Das bisschen Leben," 17). In a short diary entry from May 1982, von Trotta defined her concept of a female aesthetic in the following tentative terms: "If there is anything at all like a female aesthetic form as far as films are concerned, then for me it lies in the choice of themes, also in the attention, the respect, the sensitivity, the care with which we approach the people whom we show, also the kind of actors we choose. . . . The essential point is, however: we do not separate between reason and emotion, large and small events, we have retained something of the antihierarchical conception of the matriarchy" (my translation). See *Weber, 103–4.

Chapter 14

1. There is an abundant literature on Wenders's cinematic career; for presentations with material on *Paris, Texas*, see *Devillers; *Petit, Dubois, and Delvaux; *Künzel; *Buchka; *Geist; *Rauh; and *Grob. For biographical information, international bibliography, and filmography, see *Jansen and Schütte, 315–67.

2. *Corrigan sketches out a psychoanalytic model based on Wenders's *Lightening over Water* (in German, *Nick's Film*, 1980) for analyzing the Oedipal aggression in his films. In an essay on America as the Other, *Elsaesser comments on the narcissistic strategies in the three Wenders films *Alice in the Cities* (*Alice in den Städten*), *The American Friend* (*Der amerikanische Freund*), and *Paris, Texas*.

3. *Grob, 246, characterizes the film as a "German-Romantic story" that on the visual level translates the visible into the poetic. Wenders claims that this preference for mythic over cinematic quotation was an intentional decision on his part while writing the script with Sam Shepard and while working with cinematographer Robby Müller; see *Wenders, "Wenders à la recherche," 14. Nonetheless, there are fairly clear references to Nicholas Ray's *Johnny Guitar* in the peep show sequence, to John Ford's *The Searchers*, to the plot in Michelangelo Antonioni's early features *Il Guido* and *L'Avventura*, and to the atmosphere in Edward Hopper's paintings.

4. All references to dialogues can be found in *Sievernich.

5. The parallel character constellation of Odysseus, Telemachus, and Penelope is not entirely accidental. Wenders mentioned that he was reading the *Odyssey* in winter 1982, while writing the first thirty-page treatment for what would become the screenplay of *Paris, Texas*; see *Wenders, "Entretiens," 10; and *Wenders, "Abschied," 59, 66.

6. The normalcy of Walt and Anne's household suggests the home as a familial cocoon. Yet the house sits poised on the edge of a mountain, and Travis spends his time there looking through binoculars into the abyss below or at the airplanes taking off nearby! Originally the film narrative focused on the relationship between the brothers Travis and Walt and their gradual role reversal after Walt

abandons Anne to pursue Hunter and Travis; see *Wenders, "Wenders à la recherche," 14–15, for Wenders's description of this earlier version. Remnants of that original idea seem to survive in the final cut, for example, Travis dresses as a father in Walt's suit and uses his credit cards, while Walt's wife Anne is French (reproducing in reality the father's "idea" of his wife from Paris). Also, Walt is a professional billboard advertising contractor. His enormous images stimulate desire where it does not (yet) exist through representation, whereas Travis's existing desire is an imaginary that cannot be shown. Among the billboards the spectator can see at Walt's business is a huge portrait of Barbra Streisand in her role as Yentl (another story about searching for identity).

7. The peep show is an example of the collaboration between scriptwriter Sam Shepard and Wenders, melding the former's poetry of feelings with the latter's ironic stance. The Keyhole Club is an imaginary combination of the peep show format familiar in European cities, telephone sex services in the United States, and photo sex shops around Houston. On the attribution of credit for the screenplay and on the fantasy of the peep show, see Wenders's explanations in *Wenders, "Wenders à la recherche," 11–12; and *Wenders, "Wim Wenders." Parts of the script were being written during the filming itself, a not unusual practice for Wenders; on the process of adapting these parts of Shepard's script, see *Carson. *Geist, 111–25, analyzes the collaborative effort on the *Paris, Texas* script.

8. Wenders, quoted in *Wenders, "Wim Wenders," 5.

9. Some critics actually condemned the film for suggesting that children belong to their biological parents. They claim that there is no logic to support Travis taking Hunter away from loving parents (Walt and Anne) so that he can rejoin a single working mother, Jane, who had explicitly abandoned him because she felt she could not mother him adequately. From this perspective Jane is pressed into maternal responsibility by a jealous husband, a position argued most forcefully by *Wellershoff. Seen as a mythic narrative, however, logic requires Jane to relinquish the child after her break with Travis in order to motivate his return to heal their rupture. Travis, in turn, recognizes his responsibility to create the conditions under which the mother and child can be together. The utopian quality of their embrace in the last sequence is qualified not only by the exclusion of the father but also by the emphatic shift in colors from the dominant reds prior to this scene to blacks and a foggy background. The purple sunset of the last image corresponds to Travis's final, ironic smile and does not undermine this somber note.

10. Elsaesser, *New German Cinema*, 216. Chapter 7, "The New German Cinema's Germany," is pertinent in this context and includes brief comments on Wenders's films as well (228–32). *Wenders, "Der amerikanische Traum" (an essay he wrote at the same time he was preparing *Paris, Texas*), reflects on the utopian image of America as an imaginary vision.

11. That Wenders filmed this narrative in the United States based on a text by the celebrated American writer Sam Shepard does not undermine this view of the film's German specificity. Beyond the personal and commercial ties Wenders had developed in the States after having lived there for seven years, the "ideological subtext" already hinted at in his earlier *Kings of the Road* is pertinent. There the two protagonists recall that the Americans colonized the German unconscious in their postwar occupation of the country. Written large, the Oedipal relationship between West Germany and the United States, between

the New German Cinema and Hollywood, resonates throughout *Paris, Texas*. Shepard's input was crucial for addressing the father-son rivalry, a theme he had touched on in several plays—most prominently in *True West* and *Buried Child*—and also later in his screenplay for the Robert Altman film *Fool for Love* (1985); and the language and diction of *Paris, Texas* is quintessential Shepard. Nonetheless, the specific form of the family constellation and the calculated disruptions of spectator positioning are signals of German particularity in the cinematic text of *Paris, Texas*. On Shepard, see *Watt.

12. Michael Schneider has investigated the ramifications of this generational malaise; and Santner, chap. 2, has extended the discussion of generational markings in Germany's political unconscious.

13. The German psychoanalyst Alexander Mitscherlich has called this social formation "the fatherless society." Using David Riesman's analysis of alienation and the individual in mass society as a point of departure, he traced in advanced industrial societies a general tendency for the father to disappear while other institutions assume his authority functions. The consequence is a pattern of infantile regression in which the child's ego development is weakened so that critical and self-critical faculties remain underdeveloped while narcissistic desire dominates. See Mitscherlich, *Auf dem Weg*, chap. 7.

14. Wenders's was the first German film in the thirty-seven-year history of the Cannes Film Festival to be chosen the sole winner of the Golden Palm, and internationally the distribution rights were bought up with unusually high bids. Other important prizes at Cannes included the FIPRESCI, the International Ecumenical Jury, and Prix Léon Moussinac; in Germany Robby Müller received the German Camera Prize, the film received the Deutscher Filmpreis (Silver) and the Gildepreis; and in England Wenders received the British Academy Award for best director of a foreign film.

15. The critical reception of *Paris, Texas* was not uniform. Professional French critics celebrated the film as an event of unparalleled magnitude. The major cinema journals outdid themselves in presenting dossiers, interviews, background articles, and reviews (*Cahiers du cinéma* 360/361, Summer 1984; *Positif* 283, September 1984; *La Revue du cinéma* 397, September 1984; *Films*—Cinécritique 29, September/October 1984). The American reception among film critics was restrained, concentrating on Wenders's appropriation of a programmatically American myth while failing to recognize that "America" can represent different imaginary constructs on either side of the Atlantic; see *Canby's two typical reviews. In Germany, on the other hand, *Paris, Texas* was perceived as Wenders's most German film since *Kings of the Road*. West German critics were unified in their admiration of the film's aesthetic appeal. Otherwise, they split between those who saw it as a successfully modernized but too long version of Snow White (see *Baumgart) and those who rejected its alleged patriarchal ideology (see n. 9).

Conclusion

1. In the late seventies regional governments began to introduce their own subsidy systems as an economic incentive to stimulate the local film industry: e.g., Berlin in 1977, Bavaria and Hamburg in 1979, North Rhein-Westfalia in 1980. For details on the West German subsidy system in the late seventies and early eighties, see Hundertmark and Saul, 9–20, esp. 18. For statistical information

through 1989, see Neckermann. Since 1990 all five new federal states in the East have developed local film centers and subsidy systems modelled after the old federal states; see the articles in the special section "Filmkultur" of *Film und Fernsehen* 4 (1993): 4–19.

2. For details on the export competition, see Orf.

3. For additional statistical information, see Neumann, 250–51.

Chapter Bibliographies

Chapter 1: Ernst Lubitsch

Carringer, Robert, and Barry Sabath. *Ernst Lubitsch: A Guide to References and Resources.* Boston: G. K. Hall, 1978.

Eisenschitz, Bernard. *Lubitsch.* Paris: L'Avant-Scène du cinéma, 1967.

Ernst Lubitsch. Paris: Cahiers du Cinéma/Cinémathèque française, 1985.

Fink, Guido. *Ernst Lubitsch.* Florence: La Nuova Italia, 1977.

Hake, Sabine. *Passions and Deceptions: The Early Films of Ernst Lubitsch.* Princeton: Princeton University Press, 1992.

Madame Dubarry. Magazin 1 of *Die Ufa 1917–1945,* ed. R. Rother. Berlin: Deutsches Historisches Museum, 1992.

Nacache, Jacqueline. *Ernst Lubitsch.* Paris: Edilig, 1987.

Negri, Pola. *Memoirs of a Star.* Garden City: Doubleday, 1970.

Paul, William. *Ernst Lubitsch's American Comedy.* New York: Columbia University Press, 1983.

Prinzler, Hans Helmut, and Enno Patalas, eds. *Lubitsch.* Munich: Bucher, 1984.

Simsolo, Noël. "Ernst Lubitsch—Période allemande." *Revue de cinéma* 405 (May 1985): 75–82.

Steiner, Hanns. *Madame Dubarry: Eine Erzählung.* Berlin: Buch-Film Verlag, n.d. [1920?].

Verdone, Mario. *Ernst Lubitsch.* Translated from the Italian by Fabienne Chabartier, Pierre A. Marchal, and Barthélémy Amengual. Paris: Serdoc, 1964.

Weinberg, Herman G. *The Lubitsch Touch.* New York: Dulton, 1968. Reprint, New York: Dover, 1977.

Chapter 2: Friedrich Wilhelm Murnau

"Atti del Convegno di Studi su Carl Mayer." *Bianco e nero* 29 (1968), Part 1 = Nr. 7–8: 1–90, Part 2 = 9–10: 177–240, Part 3 = 11–12: 177–259.

Bergstrom, Janet. "Sexuality at a Loss: The Films of F. W. Murnau." *Poetics Today* 6, no. 1–2 (1985): 185–203.

Borde, Raymond et al. *Le cinéma réaliste allemand.* Lyon: Serdoc, 1965.

Buffa, Michelangelo. "Analisi fondata sulla successiva divisione in sintagmi." *Filmcritica* (Rome) 25, no. 246 (July 1974): 233–41.

Courtade, Francis. *Cinéma Expressioniste.* Paris: Henri Veyrier, 1984.

Domarchi, Jean. *Murnau.* Anthologie du Cinéma 1. Paris: L'Avant-Scène du cinéma, 1966.

Eisner, Lotte H. *Murnau.* London: Seeker and Warburg, 1973. Revised and enlarged translation of the 1964 French version.

Fieschi, Jean André. "Murnau." In *Cinema: A Critical Dictionary*, ed. Richard Roud, vol. 2, 704–20. New York: Viking, 1980.

Güttinger, Fritz. "Mayers Missverständnis." In *Der Stummfilm im Zitat der Zeit*, 193–204. Frankfurt: Deutsches Filmmuseum, 1984.

Hempel, Rolf. *Ein Autor schreibt mit der Kamera* [Carl Mayer]. Berlin, GDR: Henschelverlag, 1968.

Jameux, Charles. *Murnau.* Paris: Editions Universitaires, 1965.

Kreimeier, Klaus, ed. *Friedrich Wilhelm Murnau: 1888–1988.* Exhibition catalog. Bielefeld: Bielefelder Verlagsanstalt, 1988.

Spiess, Eberhard. "Carl Mayer: Ein Filmautor zwischen Expressionismus und Idylle." *Filmblätter* 11 (1979): 3–38.

Tone, Pier Giorgio. *Friedrich-Wilhelm Murnau.* Florence: La Nuova Italia, 1976.

Chapter 3: Slatan Dudov and Bertolt Brecht

Adank, Thomas. "Hanns Eisler und die Musik in Kuhle Wampe." In *Erobert den Film!*, ed. Neue Gesellschaft für bildende Kunst, 65–67. Berlin: NGBK, 1977.

Brecht, Bertolt. *Der Dreigroschenprozess: Ein soziologisches Experiment. Schriften* 1. Vol. 21, Grosse kommentierte Berliner und Frankfurter Ausgabe. Frankfurt: Suhrkamp and Berlin: Aufbau, 1992.

——. *Kuhle Wampe: Protokoll des Films und Materialien.* Ed. Wolfgang Gersch and Werner Hecht. Frankfurt: Suhrkamp, 1969.

"Brecht and a Revolutionary Cinema." Special issue of *Screen* 15, no. 2 (summer 1974).

"Dokumente zum Zensurgang *Kuhle Wampe* vom 17. März bis 21. April 1932." *Filmwissenschaftliche Mitteilungen* 4 (1962): 771–820.

Eisenschitz, Bernard. "A qui appartient le monde?" *L'Arc* 55 (1973): 24–31. Trans. Kari Hanet under the title "Who Does the World Belong to? The Place of a Film," *Screen* 15, no. 2 (summer 1974): 65–73.

Gersch, Wolfgang. *Film bei Brecht: Bertolt Brechts praktische und theoretische Auseinandersetzung mit dem Film.* Munich: Hanser, 1975.

Groth, Peter, and Manfred Voigts. "Die Entwicklung der Brechtschen Radiotheorie 1927–1932." In *Brecht-Jahrbuch 1976*, 9–42. Frankfurt: Suhrkamp, 1976.

Happel, Reinhold. "*Kuhle Wampe oder Wem gehört die Welt?* Eine exemplarische Analyse." In *Film und Realität in der Weimarer Republik*, ed. Helmut Korte, 169–212. Munich: Hanser, 1978.

Herlinghaus, Hermann. *Slatan Dudow*. Berlin, GDR: Henschelverlag, 1965.

Hoellering, George. "Making *Kuhle Wampe*. An Interview." By Ben Brewster and Colin MacCabe. *Screen* 15, no. 4 (winter 1974–1975): 71–79.

Knopf, Jan. "Anhang: Film." In *Brecht Handbuch: Lyrik, Prosa, Schriften*, 505–15. Stuttgart: Metzler, 1984.

Kühn, Gertraude, Karl Tümmler, and Walter Wimmer, eds. *Film und revolutionäre Arbeiterbewegung in Deutschland 1918–1932*. Dokumente und Materialien. 2 vols. Berlin, GDR: Henschelverlag, 1978.

Leonard, Yvonne. "Die verdoppelte Illusion. Der proletarische Film zwischen Traumfabrik und Wirklichkeit." In *Erobert den Film!*, ed. Neue Gesellschaft für bildende Kunst, 48–64. Berlin: NGBK, 1977.

Michaelis, Margot. "*Mutter Krausens Fahrt ins Glück*: Eine exemplarische Analyse." In *Film und Realität in der Weimarer Republik*, ed. Helmut Korte, 103–68. Munich: Hanser, 1978.

Mueller, Roswitha. *Bertolt Brecht and the Theory of Media*. Lincoln: University of Nebraska Press, 1989.

Murray, Bruce A. *Film and the German Left in the Weimar Republic: From "Caligari" to "Kuhle Wampe"*. Austin: University of Texas Press, 1990.

Pettifer, James. "Against the Stream—*Kuhle Wampe*." *Screen* 15, no. 2 (summer 1974): 49–64.

———. "The Limits of Naturalism." *Screen* 16, no. 4 (winter 1975–76): 5–11. On *Mutter Krausens Fahrt ins Glück* and *Kuhle Wampe*.

Silberman, Marc. "The Politics of Representation: Brecht and the Media." *Theatre Journal* 39, no. 4 (December 1987): 448–60.

Stoos, Toni. "'Erobert den Film!' oder Prometheus gegen UFA & Co." In *Erobert den Film!*, ed. Neue Gesellschaft für bildende Kunst, 4–47. Berlin: NGBK, 1977.

Walsh, Martin. *The Brechtian Aspect of Radical Cinema*. London: British Film Institute, 1981.

Witte, Karsten. "Brecht und der Film." *Bertolt Brecht I*. Special issue of *Text und Kritik* (1972): 81–99.

Wyss, Monika. *Brecht in der Kritik*. Munich: Kindler, 1977.

Chapter 4: Detlef Sierck

Bourget, Jean-Loup. *Douglas Sirk*. Paris: Edilig, 1984.

Brandlmeier, Thomas. "Das Ufa-Melodram der dreissiger Jahre." In *Die Ufa 1917–1945*, ed. R. Rother. Magazin 14, 2–8. Berlin: Deutsches Historisches Museum, 1992.

Elsaesser, Thomas. "Postscript." *Screen* 12, no. 2 (summer 1971): 20–28.

———. "Tales of Sound and Fury: Observations on the Family Melodrama." *Monogram* 4 (1972): 2–15.

Gledhill, Christine. "The Melodramatic Field: An Investigation." In *Home Is Where the Heart Is: Studies in Melodrama and the Woman's Film*, 5–39. London: British Film Institute, 1987.

Halliday, Jon. "Notes on Sirk's German Films." *Screen* 12, no. 2 (summer 1971): 8–13.

———. *Sirk on Sirk*. New York: Viking, 1972.

Koch, Gertrud. "Von Detlef Sierck zu Douglas Sirk." *Frauen und Film* 44/45 (October 1988): 109–29.

Läufer, Elizabeth. *Skeptiker des Lichts: Douglas Sirk und seine Filme.* Frankfurt: Fischer, 1987.

Leander, Zarah. *Es war so wunderbar: Mein Leben.* Hamburg: Hoffmann and Campe, 1973.

——. *So bin ich und so bleibe ich.* Gütersloh: Bertelsmann, 1958.

Masson, Alain. "Un triste et profond murmur d'applaudissements." *Positif* 259 (September 1982): 12–15.

Mulvey, Laura. "Notes on Sirk and Melodrama." *Movie* 25 (winter 1977–78): 53–56.

Mulvey, Laura, and Jon Halliday, eds. *Douglas Sirk.* Edinburgh: Edinburgh Film Festival, 1972.

Pithon, Remy. "Les constantes d'un style: Sur quelques films allemands de Douglas Sirk." *Cinema* 3 (Zurich 1978): 12–25.

Rhode, Carla. "Die grosse Liebe—Zarah Leander." In *Wir tanzen um die Welt*, ed. Helga Belach, 134–36. Munich: Hanser, 1979.

Sanders-Brahms, Helma. "Zarah." In *Jahrbuch Film 81/82*, ed. Hans-Günther Pflaum, 165–72. Munich: Hanser, 1981.

Sirk, Douglas. "Entretien avec Douglas Sirk." Interview by Serge Daney and Jean-Louis Noames. *Cahiers du cinéma* 189 (April 1967): 19–25 and 67.

——. "Entretien avec Douglas Sirk." Interview by Jean-Claude Biette and Dominique Rabourdin. *Cahiers du cinéma* 293 (October 1978): 13–22.

——. "Entretien avec Douglas Sirk." Interview by Emmanuel Decaux and Bruno Villien. *Cinématographe* 80 (July/August 1982): 24–30.

——. "Interview." By Michael Stern. *Bright Lights* 6 (winter 1977–78): 29–34.

Stern, Michael. *Douglas Sirk.* Boston: Twayne, 1979.

Willemen, Paul. "Towards an Analysis of the Sirkian System." *Screen* 13, no. 4 (winter 1972/73): 128–34.

Chapter 5: Eduard von Borsody

Hippler, Fritz. *Betrachtungen zum Filmschaffen.* Berlin: Max Hesses Verlag, 1942.

——. *Die Verstrickung: Einstellungen und Rückblendungen.* Düsseldorf: Verlag Mehr Wissen, 1981.

Regel, Helmut. "Zur Topographie des NS-Films." *Filmkritik* 10 (1966): 5–19.

Werner, Ilse. *So wird's nie wieder sein: Ein Leben mit Pfiff.* Bayreuth: Hestia, 1982.

Wunschkonzert. Magazin 17 of *Die Ufa 1917–1945*, ed. R. Rother. Berlin: Deutsches Historisches Museum, 1992.

"Zur Aufnahme des Films *Wunschkonzert.*" In *Film im Dritten Reich*, ed. Gerd Albrecht, 192–93. Karlsruhe: Doku-Verlag, 1979.

Chapter 6: Helmut Käutner

Cornelsen, Peter. *Helmut Käutner: Seine Filme, sein Leben.* Munich: Heyne, 1980.

Freund, Rudolf, and Kurt Rohrmoser. "Die Sehnsucht der kleinen Leute. *Unter den Brücken* und Käutner's 'leise Opposition' vor 1945." *Film* 68 (May/June 1968) 13: 36–38.

Friedman, Régine Mihal. "Die Ausnahme ist die Regel. Zu *Romanze in Moll* (1943) von Helmut Käutner." *Frauen und Film* 43 (December 1987): 48–58.
Gillett, John. "Helmut Käutner." *Film Dope* 29 (March 1984): 20–21.
Harmssen, Henning. "Im Slalom durch die Nazizeit. Zu Helmut Käutner und seinen Filmen im Dritten Reich." *Die neue Zürcher Zeitung* (June 20, 1975): 73–74; (June 27, 1975): 73.
Helmut Käutner: Romanze in Moll. Press book. Berlin: Tobis Bild und Text-Information, [1942?].
Jacobsen, Wolfgang, and Hans Helmut Prinzler, eds. *Käutner.* Berlin: Volker Spiess, 1992.
Koschnitzki, Rüdiger. *Filmographie Helmut Käutner.* Wiesbaden: Institut für deutsche Filmkunde, 1978. An updated version appears in *Käutner,* ed. Wolfgang Jacobsen and Hans Helmut Prinzler, 274–311. Berlin: Volker Spiess, 1992.
Marcorelles, Louis. "Kautner [sic] le Dandy." *Cahiers du cinéma* 73 (July 1957): 26–29.
Maupassant, Guy de. "Les Bijoux." In *Contes et Nouvelles,* vol. 1, 764–71. Paris: Gallimard, 1974.
"Starke Auslandserfolge des deutschen Films." *Der Film-Kurier* (July 18, 1944): 1–2.
Völker, Klaus. "'Wir spielen . . .' Helmut Käutners Leben." In *Käutner,* ed. Wolfgang Jacobsen and Hans Helmut Prinzler, 8–33. Berlin: Volker Spiess, 1992.
Wischnewski, Klaus. "Ein Augenblick der Freiheit oder Helmut Käutners *Romanze in Moll.*" In *Mitten ins Herz: 66 Liebesfilme,* ed. Helga Hartmann and Ralf Schenk, 170–73. Berlin: Henschelverlag, 1991.
Witte, Karsten. "Ästhetische Opposition: Käutners Filme im Faschismus." *Sammlung: Jahrbuch für antifaschistische Literatur und Kunst* 2 (1979): 113–23.
———. "Die Filmkomödie im Dritten Reich." In *Die Literatur im Dritten Reich,* ed. Horst Denkler, 347–65. Stuttgart: Reclam, 1976.
———. "Im Prinzip Hoffnung: Helmut Käutners Filme." In *Käutner,* ed. Wolfgang Jacobsen and Hans Helmut Prinzler, 62–109. Berlin: Volker Spiess, 1992. On *Romanze in Moll* see 74–78.

Chapter 7: Wolfgang Staudte

Borde, Raymond, Freddy Buache, and Francis Courtade. *Le cinéma réaliste allemand.* Lyon: Serdoc, 1965.
Buchka, Peter. "Wolfgang Staudte." In *Ansichten des Jahrhunderts: Film und Geschichte in 10 Porträts,* 185–95. Munich: Hanser, 1988.
Knietzsch, Horst. *Wolfgang Staudte.* Berlin, GDR: Henschelverlag, 1966.
Netenjakob, Egon. "Ein Leben gegen die Zeit." In *Staudte,* ed. Eva Orbanz and Hans Helmut Prinzler, 11–129. Berlin: Wissenschaftsverlag Volker Spiess, 1991.
Orbanz, Eva, ed. *Wolfgang Staudte.* Berlin: Volker Spiess, 1977.
Orbanz, Eva, and Hans Helmut Prinzler, eds. *Staudte.* Berlin: Wissenschaftsverlag Volker Spiess, 1991.
Staudte, Wolfgang. [on *Rotation*]. *Deutsche Filmkunst* 2 (1955). Reprint, in *Wolfgang Staudte,* ed. Eva Orbanz, 85–86, Berlin: Volker Spiess, 1977.

———. "Rotation." *Filmstudio* 49 (April 1, 1966): 47–63; 50 (July 1, 1966): 36–64.

———. *Rotation.* In *Vier Filmerzählungen nach bekannten DEFA-Filmen*, ed. Ellen Blauert, 279–80. Berlin, GDR: Henschelverlag, 1969.

———. "Wolfgang Staudte." Interview by Ulrich Gregor and Heinz Ungureit. In *Wie sie filmen: Fünfzehn Gespräche mit Regisseuren der Gegenwart*, ed. Ulrich Gregor, 19–53. Gütersloh: Sigbert Mohn, 1966.

Thiele, Jens. "Die Lehren aus der Vergangenheit: *Rotation* (1949)." In *Auf der Suche nach Werten*, ed. Werner Faulstich and Helmut Korte, 126–47. Frankfurt: Fischer, 1990.

Witte, Karsten. "Ein Traum von Realismus. Wolfgang Staudte wird 75 Jahre." In *Im Off: Texte vom Sehen und Hören*, 146–52. Frankfurt: Fischer, 1985. Originally published in *Die Zeit*, October 9, 1981.

Chapter 8: Hans Deppe

Aktionsgruppe Film am Bildungszentrum Nürnberg and Kino Meisengeige, ed. *Wo ewig der Wildbach rauscht: Der deutsche Heimatfilm und seine Ideologie.* 2d ed. Nürnberg: Bildungszentrum, 1977.

Barthel, Manfred. "Mehr Täler als Höhen. Der deutsche Heimatfilm." In *So war es wirklich*, 89–106. Munich: F. A. Herbig, 1986.

Bliersbach, Gerhard. "Grüne Heide und Silberwald: Wird alles wieder gut?" In *So grün war die Heide*, 33–49. Weinheim: Beltz, 1985.

Kaschuba, Wolfgang, ed. *Der deutsche Heimatfilm: Bildwelten und Weltbilder. Bilder, Texte, Analysen zu 70 Jahren deutscher Filmgeschichte.* Tübingen: Ludwig-Uhland Institut für Empirische Kulturwissenschaft, 1989.

Kurowski, Ulrich. "Nicht nur 'Grün ist die Heide.'" *Filmkorrespondenz* 3 (1977).

Seidl, Claus. "Das Pfeifen im Walde. Das deutsche Genre: der Heimatfilm." In *Der deutsche Film der fünfziger Jahre*, 52–102. Munich: Heyne, 1987.

Seesslen, Georg. "Der Heimatfilm: Zur Mythologie eines Genres." In *Sprung im Spiegel: Filmisches Wahrnehmen zwischen Fiktion und Wirklichkeit*, ed. Christa Blümlinger, 343–62. Vienna: Sonderzahl, 1990.

Strobel, Ricarda. "Heimat, Liebe und Glück: *Schwarzwaldmädel* (1950)." In *Auf der Suche nach Werten*, ed. Werner Faulstich and Helmut Korte, 148–70. Frankfurt: Fischer, 1990.

Chapter 9: Georg Wilhelm Pabst

Agel, Henri. *Les Grands cinéastes.* Paris: Editions Universitaires, 1960.

Amengual, Barthélemy. *Georg Wilhelm Pabst.* Paris: Seghers, 1966.

Atwell, Lee. *G. W. Pabst.* Boston: Twayne, 1977.

Aubry, Yves, and Jacque Pétat. *G. W. Pabst.* Paris: Editions l'Avant-Scène, 1968.

Bachmann, Gideon, ed. "Six Talks on G. W. Pabst." Special issue of *Cinemages* 1, no. 3 (1955).

Buache, Fredy. *G. W. Pabst.* Lyon: Serdoc, 1965.

Cozarinsky, Edgardo. "G. W. Pabst." In *Cinema: A Critical Dictionary*, ed. Richard Roud, vol. 2, 752–61. New York: Viking, 1980.

"Filmographie G. W. Pabst." *Filmkunst* 18 (1955).

Gleber, Anka. "Masochism and Wartime Melodrama: *Komödianten* (1941)." In *The Films of G. W. Pabst*, ed. Eric Rentschler, 175–83. New Brunswick, N.J.: Rutgers University Press, 1990.

Groppoli, Enrico. *Pabst.* Florence: La nuova Italia, 1983.

"Hitler. Story von Remarque." *Der Spiegel* 7 (February 9, 1955): 34–35.

"Hitler war kein Kasperle." *Der Spiegel* 41 (October 6, 1954): 37–39.

"*Der letzte Akt*—noch nicht das letzte Wort." *Das Wochenend,* May 25, 1955.

Musmanno, Michael. *Ten Days to Die.* Garden City, N.Y.: Doubleday, 1950.

Owen, C. R. *Erich Maria Remarque: A Critical Bio-Bibliography.* Amsterdam: Rodopi, 1984.

Remarque, Erich Maria. "Be Vigilant." *Prevent World War III* 48 (summer 1956): 17–18.

Rentschler, Eric, ed. *The Films of G. W. Pabst: An Extraterritorial Cinema.* New Brunswick, N.J.: Rutgers University Press, 1990.

"Unfug der 'Dokumentarfilme.'" *Der Fortschritt* (Düsseldorf), June 16, 1955.

Chapter 10: Konrad Wolf

Bisky, Lothar, and Günter Netzeband. "Helden-Menschen wie wir: Zur Aufnahme des DEFA-Films 'Ich war neunzehn' durch Jugendliche." *Neues Deutschland,* April 24, 1968. A slightly longer version appeared in *Sonntag* 48 (August 4, 1968): 4–5.

Gregor, Ulrich. "Konrad Wolf: Auf der Suche nach der Heimat." In *Film in der DDR,* ed. Peter W. Jansen and Wolfram Schütte, 77–98. Munich: Hanser, 1977.

Hoff, Peter, Friedrich Salow, and Renate Georgi, eds. *Konrad Wolf: Neue Sichten auf seine Filme.* Berlin: Vistas, 1990.

Kasjanowa, Ludmilla, and Anatoli Karawaschkin. "Konrad Wolf." In *Begegnungen mit Regisseuren,* 132–86. Berlin, GDR: Henschelverlag, 1974.

Köppe, Barbara, and Aune Renk, eds. *Konrad Wolf: Selbstzeugnisse, Fotos, Dokumente.* Berlin, GDR: Henschelverlag, 1985.

Micheli, Sergio. *Il Cinema nella Repubblica Democratica Tedesca: Trenta anni di attività della DEFA (1946–1976).* Rome: Bulzani Editore, 1978.

Richter, Rolf. "Konrad Wolf." In *DEFA-Spielfilm-Regisseure und ihre Kritiker,* vol. 2, 250–87. Berlin, GDR: Henschelverlag, 1981–83.

Ruschin, Thomas, ed. *Der Film "Ich war neunzehn": Intention und Wirkung.* Berlin, GDR: Deutsche Akademie der Künste zu Berlin, 1968. Includes: treatment, 5–28; diary excerpts, 5–25; script, 29–64; audience responses and evaluation, 78–93.

Silberman, Marc. "Remembering History: The Filmmaker Konrad Wolf." *New German Critique* 49 (1990): 163–91.

Tok, Hans-Dieter. "Konrad Wolf." In *Regiestühle,* ed. Fred Gehler, 111–28. Berlin, GDR: Henschelverlag, 1972.

Wolf, Gerhard. "Fakten und Überlegungen zur Dramatugie des Films 'Ich war neunzehn.'" In *Der Film "Ich war neunzehn,"* ed. Thomas Ruschin, 64–71. Berlin, GDR: Deutsche Akademie der Künste zu Berlin, 1968.

Wolf, Konrad. "Künstler und Gesellschaft." Interview by György Fenyves. *Beiträge zur Film- und Fernsehwissenschaft* 3 (1985): 179–82. Originally published in Hungarian, *Filmvilág* 24 (1968).

———. *Sag' Dein Wort: Dokumentation—eine Auswahl*. Hermann Herlinghaus, ed. Special issue of *Aus Theorie und Praxis des Films*. Potsdam-Babelsberg: DEFA, 1982.

———. "So sehe ich unseren Film." *Neues Deutschland* January 3, 1968. Reprinted in *Der Film "Ich war neunzehn"*, ed. Thomas Ruschin, 71–74. Berlin, GDR: Deutsche Akademie der Künste zu Berlin, 1968.

Wolf, Konrad, and Wolfgang Kohlhaase. "Gespräch mit Konrad Wolf und Wolfgang Kohlhaase." Interview by Günter Netzeband. *Sinn und Form* 34, no. 5 (September/October 1982): 953–63. The interview was conducted July 1967.

Wulff, Hans J. "Ein Brief zu *Ich war neunzehn*." In *Konrad Wolf: Neue Sichten*, ed. Peter Hoff et al., 133–45. Berlin: Vistas, 1990.

Chapter 11: Hermann Zschoche

Blazejewski, Carmen. "Bürgschaft für ein Jahr." *Podium und Werkstatt* 12 (1982): 105–19.

Filmografischer Jahresbericht 1981. Berlin: Henschelverlag, 1984.

Gehler, Fred. "Bürgschaft für ein Jahr." *Sonntag*, October 11, 1981.

"Leben nach Regeln oder von der Hand in den Mund" [audience reactions to *On Probation*]. *Sonntag*, November 1, 1981.

Mihan, Hans-Rainer. "Sabine, Sunny, Nina und der Zuschauer: Gedanken zum Gegenwartsfilm der DEFA (1)." *Film und Fernsehen* 8 (1982): 9–12.

Prochnow, Christoph. "Hermann Zschoche: Ironie und Sinnlichkeit." In *DEFA-Spielfilm-Regisseure und ihre Kritiker*, ed. Rolf Richter, vol. 1, 224–41. Berlin, GDR: Henschelverlag, 1981–83.

Schulze-Gerlach, Tina. *Bürgschaft für ein Jahr*. Berlin: Union Verlag, 1978.

Spoden, Madina. "Bürgschaft für ein Jahr." *Aus Theorie und Praxis des Films* 5 (1982): 36–44.

Zschoche, Hermann. "Was heisst hier Liebe?" *Junge Welt*, September 30, 1981.

Chapter 12: Alexander Kluge

Böhm-Christel, Thomas, ed. *Alexander Kluge*. Frankfurt: Suhrkamp, 1983.

Fiedler, Theodor. "Alexander Kluge: Mediating History and Consciousness." In *New German Filmmakers*, ed. Klaus Phillips, 195–229. New York: Ungar, 1984.

Filmstatistisches Jahrbuch. Wiesbaden: Spitzenorganisation der Filmwirtschaft, 1972.

Handke, Peter. "Augsburg im August: trostlos." *Film* (Velber) 1 (1969): 31–32.

Hansen, Miriam. "Alexander Kluge: Crossings between Film, Literature, Critical Theory." In *Film und Literatur: Literarische Texte und der neue deutsche Film*, ed. Sigrid Bauschinger, Susan L. Cocalis, and Henry A. Lea, 169–96. Bern: Francke, 1984.

———. "Reinventing the Nickelodeon: Notes on Kluge and Early Cinema." In "Alexander Kluge," ed. Stuart Liebman, 179–98. Special issue of *October* 46 (fall 1988).

———. "Space of History, Language of Time: Kluge's *Yesterday Girl* (1966)." In *German Film and Literature*, ed. Eric Rentschler, 193–216. New York: Methuen, 1986

———, ed. "Special Issue on Alexander Kluge." *New German Critique* 49 (winter 1990).

Hohlweg, Rudolf. "Musik für den Film—Film für Musik: Annäherung an Herzog, Kluge, Straub." In *Herzog/Kluge/Straub*, ed. Peter W. Jansen and Wolfram Schütte, 52–61. Munich: Hanser, 1976.

Hummel, Christoph, ed. "Alexander Kluge." *Kinemathek* 63 (September 1983).

Kluge, Alexander. *Die Artisten in der Zirkuskuppel: ratlos*. Munich: Piper, 1968.

———. "The Early Days of the Ulm Institute for Film Design." In *West German Filmmakers on Film*, ed. Eric Rentschler, 111–12. New York: Holmes and Meyer, 1988.

———. "On Film and the Public Sphere." Trans. Thomas Y. Levin and Miriam Hansen. *New German Critique* 24/25 (fall/winter 1981/82): 206–20.

———. "Die Utopie Film." *Merkur* 201 (1964): 1135–46.

Kluge, Alexander, and Klaus Eder. *Ulmer Dramaturgien: Reibungsverluste*. Munich: Hanser, 1980.

Kluge, Alexander, and Oskar Negt. *Geschichte und Eigensinn*. Frankfurt: Zweitausendeins, 1981.

Koetzle, Michael. "In Gefahr und grösster Not . . . Alexander Kluge und das Ulmer Institut für Filmgestaltung." *Text + Kritik* 85/86 (1985): 111–23.

Lewandowski, Rainer. *Alexander Kluge*. Munich: Beck/text + kritik, 1980.

———. *Die Filme von Alexander Kluge*. Hildesheim: Olms Presse, 1980.

Liebman, Stuart, ed. "Alexander Kluge." Special issue of *October* 46 (fall 1988).

———. "Why Kluge?" In "Alexander Kluge," ed. Stuart Liebman, 5–22. Special issue of *October* 46 (fall 1988).

Morse, Margaret. "Ten to Eleven: Television by Alexander Kluge." In *1989 American Film Institute Video Festival*, 50–53. Los Angeles: The American Film Institute, 1989.

Negt, Oskar, and Alexander Kluge. *Öffentlichkeit und Erfahrung: Zur Organisationsanalyse von bürgerlicher und proletarischer Öffentlichkeit*. Frankfurt: Suhrkamp, 1972.

Richter, Robert, and Hans Wysseier, eds. *Filmwerkschau Alexander Kluge/Cinéaste allemand*. Basel: Cinélibre, 1987.

Schlüpmann, Heide. "'What Is Different Is Good': Women and Femininity in the Films of Alexander Kluge." In "Alexander Kluge," ed. Stuart Liebman, trans. Jamie Owen Daniel, 129–50. Published in German as "'Unterschiedenes ist gut.' Kluge, Autorenfilm und weiblicher Blick," *Frauen und Film* 46 (February 1989): 4–20.

Stollmann, Rainer. "Alexander Kluge als Realist." In *Alexander Kluge*, ed. Thomas Böhm-Christel, 245–78. Frankfurt: Suhrkamp, 1983.

Chapter 13: Margarethe von Trotta

Buchka, Peter. "Ein deutsches Familienalbum." *Die Süddeutsche Zeitung*, October 2, 1981.

Delorme, Charlotte. "Zum Film 'Die bleierne Zeit' von Margarethe von Trotta." *Frauen und Film* 31 (February 1982): 52–55. Trans. Ellen Seiter under the title "On the Film *Marianne and Juliane* by Margarethe von Trotta," *Journal of Film and Video* 37 (spring 1985).

DiCaprio, Lisa. "Baader-Meinhof Fictionalized." *Jump Cut* 29 (February 1984): 56–59.

Donner, Wolf. "Blick für Frauen." *Zeit Magazin* 47 (November 13, 1981): 46–52.

Gehler, Fred. "Margarethe von Trotta." In *Regiestühle international*, 225–58. Berlin, GDR: Henschelverlag, 1987.

Godard, Colette. "En mémoire d'une soeur absente: Les Années de plombe de Margarethe von Trotta." *Le Monde* (March 23, 1982): 17.

Harris, Adrienne, and Robert Sklar. "Marianne and Juliane." *Cinéaste* 12, no. 3 (1983): 41–44.

Kaplan, E. Ann. "Discourses of Terrorism, Feminism, and the Family in von Trotta's *Marianne and Juliane*." In *Women and Film*, ed. Janet Todd, 258–70. New York: Holmes and Meier, 1988.

Linville, Susan E. "Retrieving History: Margarethe von Trotta's *Marianne and Juliane*." *PMLA* 106, no. 3 (May 1991): 446–58.

Möhrmann, Renate. "Margarethe von Trotta." In *Die Frau mit der Kamera: Filmemacherinnen in der Bundesrepublik Deutschland*, 195–202. Munich: Hanser, 1980.

Moeller, Hans-Bernhard. "The Films of Margarethe von Trotta: Domination, Violence, Solidarity, and Social Criticism." In *Women in German Yearbook* 2, 129–49. Lanham, Md.: University Press of America, 1986.

Quart, Barbara Koenig. "The Development of a Major Director: Margarethe von Trotta." In *Women Directors: The Emergence of a New Cinema*, 93–128. New York: Praeger, 1988.

Schiavo, Maria. *Margarethe von Trotta*. Turin: AIACE, 1985.

Schultz-Gerstein, Christian. "Vom Abtanzball zu El-Fatah." *Der Spiegel* 38 (September 14, 1981): 226–29.

Seiter, Ellen. "The Political Is Personal." *Journal of Film and Video* 37 (spring 1985): 41–46. Reprinted in *Films for Women*, ed. Charlotte Brunsdon, 109–16. London: BFI, 1986.

von Trotta, Margarethe. "Das bisschen Leben, das ich brauche." Interview by Alice Schwarzer. *Emma* (January 1982): 10–18.

——. "Ich wollte von Anfang an Filme machen." Interview by Renate Fischetti. In *Das neue Kino—Acht Porträts von deutschen Regisseurinnen*, 160–74. Frankfurt: tende, 1992.

——. "Rebellinnen wider eine bleierne Zeit." Interview by Reiner Frey and Christian Göldenboog. *Filmfaust* 24 (October/November 1981): 29–36.

——. "'Von Zeit zu Zeit muss ich den Baum schütteln, ob noch alle Früchte dran sind.' Gespräch mit Margarethe von Trotta." Interview by Renate Mundzeck. In *Als Frau ist es wohl leichter, Mensch zu werden*, ed. Heike Mundzeck, 52–98. Reinbek: Rowohlt, 1984.

Weber, Hans Jürgen. *Heller Wahn: Ein Film von Margarethe von Trotta*. Frankfurt: Fischer, 1983.

Weber, Hans Jürgen, and Ingeborg Weber, eds. *"Die bleierne Zeit": Ein Film von Margarethe von Trotta*. Frankfurt: Fischer, 1981.

Chapter 14: Wim Wenders

Baumgart, Reinhart. "Der lange Film zum Kürzen." *Die Zeit,* January 11, 1985.

Buchka, Peter. *Augen kann man nicht kaufen: Wim Wenders und seine Filme.* 2d ed. Frankfurt: Fischer, 1985.

Canby, Vincent. "Directors Evoke Many Americas." *New York Times,* November 11, 1984.

———. "*Paris, Texas* from Wim Wenders." *New York Times,* October 14, 1984.

Carson, L. M. Kit. "Paris Texas Diary." *Film Comment* 20, no. 3 (June, 1984): 60–63.

Corrigan, Timothy. "Cinematic Snuff: German Friends and Narrative Murders." *Cinema Journal* 24, no. 2 (winter 1985): 9–18.

Devillers, Jean-Pierre. *Berlin, L.A., Berlin: Wim Wenders.* Paris: Samuel Tastet, 1985.

Elsaesser, Thomas. "American Graffiti und Neuer Deutscher Film—Filmemacher zwischen Avantgarde und Postmoderne." In *Die Postmoderne: Zeichen eines kulturellen Wandels,* ed. Andreas Huyssen and Klaus R. Scherpe, 319–26. Reinbek: Rowohlt, 1986.

Geist, Kathe. *The Cinema of Wim Wenders: From Paris, France to "Paris, Texas".* Ann Arbor, Mich.: UMI Research Press, 1988.

Grob, Norbert. *Wenders.* Berlin: Volker Spiess, 1991.

Jansen, Peter W., and Wolfram Schütte, eds. *Wim Wenders.* Munich: Hanser, 1992.

Künzel, Uwe. *Wim Wenders: Ein Filmbuch.* 2d ed. Freiburg: Dreisam-Verlag, 1985.

Petit, Catherine, Philippe Dubois, and Claudine Delvaux. *Les Voyages de Wim Wenders.* Crisnée, Belgium: Editions Yellow Now, 1985.

Rauh, Reinhold. *Wim Wenders und seine Filme.* Munich: Heyne, 1990.

Sievernich, Chris, ed. *Paris, Texas.* Berlin: Road Movies/Greno, 1984.

Snyder, Stephen. "Wim Wenders: The Hunger Artist in America." *Postscript* 6, no. 2 (winter 1987): 54–62.

Watt, Stephen. "Simulation, Gender, and Postmodernism: Sam Shepard and *Paris, Texas*." *Perspectives in Contemporary Literature* 13 (1987): 73–82.

Wellershoff, Dieter. "Fromme Lügen. Zur Diskussion: Wim Wenders' *Paris, Texas*." *Die Zeit,* February 15, 1985.

Wenders, Wim. "Abschied von der dröhnenden Stimme des alten Kinos. Aus einem Gespräch mit Wolfram Schütte." Interview by Wolfgang Schütte. In *Die Logik der Bilder,* Wim Wenders, 53–67. Frankfurt: Verlag der Autoren, 1988. Originally published in *Frankfurter Rundschau,* November 6, 1982.

———. "Der amerikanische Traum." In *Emotion Pictures: Essays und Filmkritiken,* 141–70. Frankfurt: Verlag der Autoren, 1986.

———. "Entretien avec Wim Wenders." Interview by Michel Ciment and Hubert Niogret. *Positif* 283 (September 1984): 8–15.

———. *Die Logik der Bilder: Essays und Gespräche.* Frankfurt: Verlag der Autoren, 1988.

———. "Wenders à la recherche d'un lieu: Entretien sur *Paris, Texas*." Interview by Alain Bergala, Alain Philippon, and Serge Toubiana. *Cahiers du cinéma* 360/361 (summer 1984): 10–17.

———. "Wim Wenders: An Interview." By Katherine Dieckmann. *Film Quarterly* 38, no. 2 (1984): 2–7.

General Bibliography

Adorno, Theodor W. *The Authoritarian Personality.* New York: Norton, 1969.

Agde, Günter, ed. *Kahlschlag: Das 11. Plenum des ZK der SED 1965.* Berlin: Aufbau Taschenbuch Verlag, 1991.

Albrecht, Gerd, ed. *Der Film im Dritten Reich: Eine Dokumentation.* Karlsruhe: Doku-Verlag, 1979.

——. *Nationalsozialistische Filmpolitik: Eine soziologische Untersuchung über die Spielfilme des Dritten Reiches.* Stuttgart: Ferdinand Enke Verlag, 1969.

Allen, Robert Clyde, and Douglas Gomery. *Film History: Theory and Practice.* New York: Knopf 1985.

Altenloh, Emilie. *Zur Soziologie des Kino: Die Kino-Unternehmen und die sozialen Schichten ihrer Besucher.* Jena: n.p., 1914.

Arnold, Heinz Ludwig, ed. "Alexander Kluge." Special issue of *Text + Kritik* 85/86 (January 1985).

Auf neuen Wegen: 5 Jahre fortschrittlichen deutschen Film. Berlin, GDR: Deutscher Filmverlag, 1951.

Aust, Stefan. *Der Baader Meinhof Komplex.* Hamburg: Hoffmann und Campe, 1986.

Baacke, Rolf-Peter. *Lichtspielhausarchitektur in Deutschland: Von der Schaubude bis zum Kinopalast.* Berlin: Frölich and Kaufmann, 1982.

Bächlin, Peter. *Der Film als Ware.* Basel: Burg-Verlag, 1945.

Backes, Uwe, and Eckhard Jesse. *Politischer Extremismus in der Bundesrepublik Deutschland.* 3 vols. Cologne: Verlag Wissenschaft und Politik, 1989.

Barbian, Jan-Pieter. "Filme mit Lücken: Die Lichtspielzensur in der Weimarer Republik." In *Der deutsche Film,* ed. Uli Jung, 51–78. Trier: Wissenschaftlicher Verlag, 1993.

Barkhausen, Hans. *Filmpropaganda für Deutschland im Ersten und Zweiten Weltkrieg.* Hildesheim: Olms, 1982.

Barthel, Manfred. *So war es wirklich: Der deutsche Nachkriegsfilm.* Munich: F. A. Herbig, 1986.

Baumert, Heinz, and Hermann Herlinghaus, eds. *Zwanzig Jahre DEFA-Spielfilm.* Berlin, GDR: Henschelverlag, 1968.

Becker, Wolfgang. *Film und Herrschaft: Organisationsprinzipien und Organisationsstrukturen der nationalsozialistischen Filmpropaganda.* Berlin: Spiess, 1973.

Belach, Helga, ed. *Wir tanzen um die Welt: Deutsche Revuefilme 1933–1945.* Munich: Hanser, 1979.

Benjamin, Walter. *Illuminations.* Ed. Hannah Arendt. Trans. Harry Zohn. New York: Schocken, 1969.

Berger, Jürgen. "Bürgen heisst zahlen—und manchmal auch zensieren: Die Filmbürgschaften des Bundes 1950–1955." In *Zwischen Gestern und Morgen,* ed. Jürgen Berger et al., 80–97. Frankfurt: Deutsches Filmmuseum, 1989.

Berger, Jürgen, Hans-Peter Reichmann, and Rudolf Worschech, eds. *Zwischen Gestern und Morgen: Westdeutscher Nachkriegsfilm 1946–1962.* Frankfurt: Deutsches Filmmuseum, 1989.

Bergstrom, Janet, and Mary Ann Doane, eds. "Spectatrix." Special issue of *Camera Obscura* 20/21 (May–September 1989).

Bessen, Ursula. *Trümmer und Träume: Nachkriegszeit und fünfziger Jahre auf Zelluloid: Deutsche Spielfilme als Zeugnisse ihrer Zeit.* Bochum: Studienverlag Dr. N. Brockmeyer, 1989.

Beyer, Friedemann. *Die UFA-Stars im Dritten Reich: Frauen für Deutschland.* Munich: Heyne, 1991.

Bibliography of German Expressionism: Catalogue of the Library of the Robert Gore Rifkind Center for German Expressionism at the Los Angeles Country Museum of Art. Boston: G. K. Hall, 1990.

Bisky, Lothar. "Trends of Film Culture in the GDR." In *Studies in GDR Culture and Society* 8, ed. Margy Gerber, 37–45. Lanham: University Press of America, 1988.

Bliersbach, Gerhard. *So grün war die Heide: Der deutsche Nachkriegsfilm in neuer Sicht.* Weinheim: Beltz, 1985.

Bock, Hans-Michael, ed. *Cinegraph: Lexikon zum deutschsprachigen Film.* Munich: text + kritik, 1984ff.

Bordwell, David. *Narration in the Fiction Film.* Madison: University of Wisconsin Press, 1985.

Bordwell, David, Janet Staiger, and Kristin Thompson. *The Classical Hollywood Cinema: Film Style and Mode of Production to 1960.* New York: Columbia University Press, 1985.

Brandlmeier, Thomas. "Und wieder Caligari ... Deutsche Nachkriegsfilme 1946–1951." In *Der deutsche Film,* ed. Uli Jung, 139–66. Trier: Wissenschaftlicher Verlag, 1993.

———. "Von Hitler zu Adenauer: Deutsche Trümmerfilme." In *Zwischen Gestern und Morgen,* ed. Jürgen Berger et al., 32–59. Frankfurt: Deutsches Filmmuseum, 1989.

Brauerhoch, Annette. "Der Autorenfilm: Emanzipatorisches Konzept oder autoritäres Modell?" In *Abschied vom Gestern,* ed. Hans-Peter Reichmann and Rudolf Worschech, 154–67. Frankfurt: Deutsches Filmmuseum, 1991.

Bredow, Wilfried von. "Filmpropaganda für Wehrbereitschaft: Kriegsfilme in der Bundesrepublik." In *Film und Gesellschaft in Deutschland*, ed. Wilfried von Bredow and Rolf Zurek, 316–26. Hamburg: Hoffmann und Campe, 1975.

———. "Zwischen Kitsch und Krise. Vorstudien zum westdeutschen Film der 60er Jahre," *Kürbiskern* 1 (1970): 90–114.

Bredow, Wilfried von, and Rolf Zurek, eds. *Film und Gesellschaft in Deutschland: Dokumente und Materialien*. Hamburg: Hoffmann und Campe, 1975.

Bretschneider, Jürgen. "VEB Kunst—aus der Traum." In *Babelsberg*, ed. Wolfgang Jacobsen, 289–314. Berlin: Argon, 1992.

Bronner, Stephen Eric, and Douglas Kellner, eds. *Passion and Rebellion: The Expressionist Heritage*. South Hadley, Mass.: Bergin, 1983.

Brooks, Peter. *The Melodramatic Imagination*. New Haven: Yale University Press, 1976.

Broszat, Martin, Klaus-Dietmar Henkel, and Hans Woller, eds. *Von Stalingrad zur Währungsreform: Zur Sozialgeschichte des Umbruchs in Deutschland*. Munich: Oldenbourg, 1988.

Brunner, G. *Einführung in das Recht der DDR*. 2d ed. Munich: Beck, 1979.

Bruss, Elizabeth W. "Eye for I: Making and Unmaking Autobiography in Film." In *Autobiography: Essays Theoretical and Critical*, ed. James Olney, 296–320. Princeton, N.J.: Princeton University Press, 1980.

Budd, Mike, ed. *The Cabinet of Dr. Caligari: Texts, Contexts, Histories*. New Brunswick: Rutgers, 1990.

Burch, Noël, and Jorge Dana. "Propositions." *Afterimage* 5 (spring 1974): 43–44.

Buschmann, Christa. *Es leuchten die Sterne: Aus der Glanzzeit des deutschen Films*. Munich: Heyne, 1979.

Certeau, Michel de. *The Writing of History*. Trans. Tom Conley. New York: Columbia University Press, 1988. Originally published as *L'Ecriture de l'histoire* (Paris: Gallimard, 1975).

"Cinema Theory in the Twenties." Special issue of *New German Critique* 40 (winter 1987).

Coates, Paul. *The Gorgon's Gaze: German Cinema, Expressionism, and the Image of Horror*. Cambridge: Cambridge University Press, 1991.

Corrigan, Timothy. *New German Cinema: The Displaced Image*. Austin: University of Texas Press, 1983.

Courtade, Francis. *Jeune cinéma allemand*. Lyon: Serdoc, 1969.

Courtade, Francis, and Pierre Cadars. *Geschichte des Films im Dritten Reich*. Trans. Florian Hopf. Munich: Carl Hanser, 1975. Shortened from *Histoire du Cinéma Nazi* (Paris: Eric Losfeld/Le Terrain Vague, 1972).

Dawson, Jan. "A Labyrinth of Subsidies: The Origins of New German Cinema." *Sight and Sound* 50/51 (winter 1980/81): 14–20.

Deja-Löhhöffel, Brigitte. *Freizeit in der DDR*. Berlin: Holzapfel, 1986.

Der deutsche Film: Fragen, Forderungen, Ansichten: Bericht vom ersten Deutschen Film-Autoren Kongress am 6.–9. Juni 1947. Berlin: Henschelverlag, 1947.

Diederichs, Helmut H. *Anfänge deutscher Filmkritik*. Stuttgart: Verlag Robert Fischer and Uwe Wiedleroither, 1986.

"Dossier on Melodrama." *Screen* 18 (summer 1977).

Dost, Michael, Florian Hopf, and Alexander Kluge. *Filmwirtschaft in der BRD und in Europa: Götterdämmerung in Raten.* Munich: Hanser, 1973.

Drewniak, Boguslav. *Der deutsche Film 1938–1945.* Düsseldorf: Droste, 1987.

Dube, Wolf-Dieter. *Der Expressionismus in Wort und Bild.* Stuttgart: Klett-Cotta, 1983.

Eisner, Lotte H. *The Haunted Screen: Expressionism in the German Cinema and the Influence of Max Reinhardt.* Berkeley: University of California Press, 1969.

Elsaesser, Thomas. "Film History and Visual Pleasure: Weimar Cinema." In *Cinema Histories, Cinema Practices,* ed. Patricia Mellenkamp and Philip Rosen, 47–48. Metuchen, N.J.: University Publications of America, 1984.

———. "Lulu and the Meter Man: Louis Brooks, Pabst and *Pandora's Box.*" *Screen* 24, no. 3–4 (July–October, 1983): 4–36. Reprinted in a shorter version as "Lulu and the Meter Man: Pabst's *Pandora's Box,*" in *German Film and Literature: Adaptations and Transformations,* ed. Eric Rentschler, 40–59 (New York: Methuen, 1986).

———. "National Subjects, International Style: Navigating Early German Cinema." In *Before Caligari,* ed. Paolo Cherchi Usai and Lorenzo Codelli, 338–354. Pordenone: Edizioni Biblioteca dell'Immagine, 1990.

———. *The New German Cinema: A History.* New Brunswick, N.J.: Rutgers University Press, 1989.

Engelmann, Bernt. *Wir hab'n ja den Kopf noch fest auf dem Hals: Die Deutschen zwischen Stunde Null und Wirtschaftswunder.* Cologne: Kiepenheuer and Witsch, 1987.

Faulstich, Werner, and Helmut Korte, eds. *Auf der Suche nach Werten: 1945–1960.* Fischer Filmgeschichte 3. Frankfurt: Fischer, 1990.

Fero, Marc. *Cinema and History.* Berkeley: University of California Press, 1989.

Fetscher, Iring, and Günter Rohrmosser. *Ideologien und Strategien.* Analysen zum Terrorismus 1. Opladen: Westdeutscher Verlag, 1981.

"Filmkultur." *Film und Fernsehen* 4 (1993): 4–19.

Filmstatistisches Taschenbuch. Wiesbaden: Spitzenorganisation der Filmwirtschaft.

Franklin, James. *New German Cinema: From Oberhausen to Hamburg.* Boston: Twayne, 1983.

Frieden, Sandra, et al. *Gender and German Cinema: Feminist Interventions.* 2 vols. London: Berg, 1992.

Friedman, Régine Mihal. *L'Image et son juif: Le Juif dans le cinéma nazi.* Paris: Payot, 1983.

———. "Männlicher Blick und weibliche Reaktion: Veit Harlans *Jud Süss.*" *Frauen und Film* 41 (December 1986): 50–64.

Fritz, Walter. *Geschichte des österreichischen Films.* Vienna: Bergland, 1969.

———. *Kino in Österreich: Film zwischen Kommerz und Avantgarde.* Vienna: Österreichischer Bundesverlag, 1984.

Gerber, Margy, ed. *Studies in GDR Culture and Society* 8. Lanham: University Press of America, 1988.

Gersch, Wolfgang. "Die Anfänge des DEFA-Spielfilms." In *Film- und Fernsehkunst der DDR,* ed. Hochschule für Film und Fernsehen der DDR, 87–111. Berlin, GDR: Henschelverlag, 1979.

Göttler, Fritz. "Westdeutscher Nachkriegsfilm: Land der Väter." In *Geschichte des deutschen Films*, ed. Wolfgang Jacobsen et al., 171–210. Stuttgart: Metzler, 1993.

Gregor, Ulrich, and Enno Patalas. *Geschichte des Films*. Gütersloh: Sigbert Mohn Verlag, 1962.

Greve, Ludwig et al., eds. *Hätte ich das Kino! Die Schriftsteller und der Stummfilm*. Stuttgart: Klett, 1976.

Grob, Norbert. "Das Geheimnis der toten Augen: 13 Aspekte zum deutschen Kriminalfilm der sechziger Jahre." In *Abschied vom Gestern*, ed. Hans-Peter Reichmann and Rudolf Worschech, 72–97. Frankfurt: Deutsches Filmmuseum, 1991.

Grosser, Alfred. *Deutschland Bilanz: Geschichte Deutschlands seit 1945*. 4th ed. Munich: Hanser, 1972.

Guback, Thomas H. *The International Film Industry: Western Europe and America since 1945*. Bloomington: Indiana University Press, 1969.

Güttinger, Fritz. *"Kein Tag ohne Kino": Schriftsteller über den Stummfilm*. Frankfurt: Deutsches Filmmuseum, 1984.

Guttmann, Irmalotte. *Über die Nachfrage auf dem Filmmarkt in Deutschland*. Berlin: Gebrüder Wolfssohn, 1928.

Hacker, Jens. "Die DDR und die nationale Frage." In *Die Last der Geschichte. Kontroversen zur deutschen Identität*, ed. Thomas M. Gauly, 140–66. Cologne: Verlag Wissenschaft und Politik, 1988.

Hake, Sabine. *The Cinema's 3rd Machine: Writing on Film in Germany 1907–1933*. Lincoln: University of Nebraska Press, 1993.

Hansen, Miriam. "Alexander Kluge, Cinema and the Public Sphere: The Construction Site of Counter History." *Discourse* 6 (fall 1983): 53–74.

———. "Cooperative Auteur Cinema and Oppositional Public Sphere: Alexander Kluge's Contribution to *Germany in Autumn*." *New German Critique* 24/25 (fall/winter 1981/82): 36–56.

———. "Early Silent Cinema: Whose Public Sphere?" *New German Critique* 29 (spring/summer 1983): 147–84.

Hauser, Johannes. *Neuaufbau der westdeutschen Filmwirtschaft 1945–1955*. Pfaffenweiler: Centaurus Verlagsgesellschaft, 1989.

Heath, Stephan. *Questions of Cinema*. Bloomington: Indiana University Press, 1981.

Heller, Heinz B. *Literarische Intelligenz und Film: Zu Veränderungen der ästhetischen Theorie und Praxis unter dem Eindruck des Films 1910–1930 in Deutschland*. Tübingen: Max Niemeyer, 1985.

Helwig, Gisela. *Frau und Familie: Bundesrepublik—DDR*. 2d ed. Cologne: Verlag Wissenschaft und Politik, 1987.

Henkys, Reinhard, ed. *Die evangelische Kirche in der DDR: Beiträge zu einer Bestandsaufnahme*. Munich: Christian Kaiser, 1982.

Herminghouse, Patricia. "Wunschbild oder Porträt? Zur Darstellung der Frau im Roman der DDR." In *Literatur und Literaturtheorie in der DDR*, ed. Peter Uwe Hohendahl and Patricia Herminghouse, 281–334. Frankfurt: Suhrkamp, 1976.

Herringer, Hans-Peter. *Die Subventionierung der deutschen Filmwirtschaft*. Köln/Opladen: Westdeutscher Verlag, 1966.

Hickethier, Knut. "Vom Ende des Kinos und vom Anfang des Fernsehens: Das Verhältnis von Film und Fernsehen in den fünfziger Jahren." In *Zwischen Gestern und Morgen*, ed. Jürgen Berger et al., 282–315. Frankfurt: Deutsches Filmmuseum, 1989.

———. "Die Zugewinngemeinschaft: Zum Verhältnis von Film und Fernsehen in den sechziger und siebziger Jahren." In *Abschied vom Gestern*, ed. Hans-Peter Reichmann and Rudolf Worschech, 190–209. Frankfurt: Deutsches Filmmuseum, 1991.

Hochschule für Film und Fernsehen der DDR, ed. *Film- und Fernsehkunst der DDR: Traditionen, Beispiele, Tendenzen*. Berlin, GDR: Henschelverlag, 1979.

Höfig, Willi. *Der deutsche Heimatfilm 1947–1960*. Stuttgart: Ferdinand Enke, 1973.

Hollstein, Dorothea. *"Jud Süss" und die Deutschen: Antisemitische Vorurteile im nationalsozialistischen Spielfilm*. 2d ed. Frankfurt: Ullstein, 1983.

Hopf, Florian. "Medien-Konzerne." In *Bestandsaufnahme: Utopie Film. Zwanzig Jahre neuer deutscher Film / Mitte 1983*, ed. Alexander Kluge, 495–510. Frankfurt: Zweitausendeins, 1983.

Horak, Jan-Christopher. *Anti-Nazi-Filme der deutschsprachigen Emigration von Hollywood 1939–1945*. Münster: MAkS Publikationen, 1984.

———. *Fluchtpunkt Hollywood: Eine Dokumentation zur Filmemigration nach 1933*. Münster: MAkS Publikationen, 1984.

Hull, David Stuart. *Film in the Third Reich: A Study of the German Cinema 1933–1945*. Berkeley: University of California Press, 1969.

Hundertmark, Gisela, and Louis Saul, eds. *Förderung essen Filme auf . . . Positionen—Situationen—Materialien*. Munich: Ölschläger, 1984.

Isaksson, Folke, and Leif Furhammer. *Film and Politics*. New York: Praeger, 1971.

Jacobsen, Wolfgang, ed. *Babelsberg: Ein Filmstudio 1912–1992*. Berlin: Argon, 1992.

Jacobsen, Wolfgang, Anton Kaes, and Hans Helmut Prinzler, eds. *Geschichte des deutschen Films*. Stuttgart: Metzler, 1993.

Jansen, Peter W., and Wolfram Schütte. *Film in der DDR*. Munich: Hanser, 1977.

Jung, Uli, ed. *Der deutsche Film: Aspekte seiner Geschichte von den Anfängen bis zur Gegenwart*. Trier: Wissenschaftlicher Verlag, 1993.

Jung, Uli, and Walter Schatzberg, eds. *Filmkultur zur Zeit der Weimarer Republik*. Munich: Saur, 1992.

Jungnickel, Dirk. "Aspekte des DEFA-Kinderfilmschaffens." In *Filmland DDR: Ein Reader zu Geschichte, Funktion und Wirkung der DEFA*, ed. Harry Blunk and Dirk Jungnickel, 83–93. Cologne: Verlag Wissenschaft und Politik, 1990.

Kaes, Anton. "The Debate about Cinema: Charting a Controversy (1909–1929)." *New German Critique* 40 (winter 1987): 7–33.

———. *Deutschlandbilder: Die Wiederkehr der Geschichte als Film*. Munich: text + kritik, 1987. Published in English as *From Hitler to Heimat: The Return of History as Film* (Cambridge, Mass.: Harvard University Press, 1989).

———. "The Expressionist Vision in Theater and Cinema." In *Expressionism Reconsidered: Affinities and Relationships*, ed. Gertrud Bauer Pickar and Karl Eugen Webb, 89–98. Munich: Fink, 1979.

———. "Film in der Weimarer Republik: Motor der Moderne." In *Geschichte des deutschen Films*, ed. Wolfgang Jacobsen et al., 39–100. Stuttgart: Metzler, 1993.

———. *Kino-Debatte: Texte zum Verhältnis von Literatur und Film 1909–1929.* Tübingen: Max Niemeyer, 1978.

Kasten, Jürgen. *Der expressionistische Film: Abgefilmtes Theater oder avantgardistisches Erzählkino? Eine stil-, produktions- und rezeptionsgeschichtliche Untersuchung.* Münster: MAkS, 1990.

Kersten, Heinz. "Entwicklungslinien." In *Film in der DDR,* ed. Peter W. Jansen and Wolfram Schütte, 7–56. Munich: Hanser, 1977.

———. *Das Filmwesen in der sowjetischen Besatzungszone Deutschlands.* Bonn: Bundesministerium für Gesamtdeutsche Fragen, 1963.

———. "The Role of Women in GDR Films since the Early 1970s." In *Studies in GDR Culture and Society* 8, ed. Margy Gerber, 47–64. Lanham: University Press of America, 1988.

Klaus, Ulrich J. *Deutsche Tonfilme: Filmlexikon der abendfüllenden deutschen und deutschsprachigen Tonfilme nach ihren deutschen Uraufführrungen.* Vol. 3, *Jahrgang 1932.* Berlin: Klaus, 1990.

Knight, Julia. *Women and the New German Cinema.* London: Verso, 1992.

Knochenrath, Hans-Peter. "Kontinuität im deutschen Film." In *Film und Gesellschaft in Deutschland,* ed. Wilfried von Bredow and Rolf Zurek, 286–92. Hamburg: Hoffmann und Campe, 1975.

Koch, Krischan. *Die Bedeutung des "Oberhausener Manifestes" für die Filmentwicklung in der BRD.* Frankfurt: Peter Lang, 1985.

Konlechner, Peter, and Peter Kubelka, eds. *Propaganda und Gegenpropaganda im Film 1933–1945.* Vienna: Österreichisches Filmmuseum, 1972.

Kracauer, Siegfried. *Die Angestellten: Aus dem neuesten Deutschland.* 1930. Reprint, Frankfurt: Suhrkamp, 1974.

———. *From Caligari to Hitler: A Psychological History of the German Film.* Princeton: Princeton University Press, 1947.

Kreimeier, Klaus. *Kino und Filmindustrie in der BRD: Ideologieproduktion und Klassenwirklichkeit nach 1945.* Kronberg: Scriptor, 1973.

———. *Die Ufa-Story: Geschichte eines Filmkonzerns.* Munich: Hanser, 1992.

Kroner, Marion. *Film—Spiegel der Gesellschaft? Inhaltsanalyse des jungen deutschen Films von 1962–1969.* Heidelberg: Quelle and Meyer, 1973.

Kuhrig, Herta, and Wulfram Speigner. *Zur gesellschaftlichen Stellung der Frau in der DDR.* Leipzig: Verlag für die Frau, 1978.

Kurtz, Rudolf. *Expressionismus und Film.* Berlin: Verlag der Lichtbildbühne, 1926. Reprint, Filmwissenschaftliche Studientexte, vol. 1, Zurich: Hans Rohr, 1965.

Laqueur, Walter. *Germany Today: A Personal Report.* Boston: Little, Brown, 1984.

Leiser, Erwin. *"Deutschland erwache!" Propaganda im Film des Dritten Reiches.* 2d ed. Hamburg: Rowohlt, 1978. Trans. Gertrud Mander and David Wilson under the title *Nazi Cinema* (London: Secker and Warburg, 1974).

Leonhard, Sigrun D. "Testing Borders: East German Film between Individualism and Social Commitment." In *Post New Wave Cinema in the Soviet Union and Eastern Europe,* ed. Daniel J. Goulding, 51–101. Bloomington: Indiana University Press, 1989.

Liehm, Mira, and Antonin Liehm. *The Most Important Art: East European Film after 1945.* Berkeley: University of California Press, 1977.

Livingstone, Rodney. "Georg Lukács and Socialist Realism." In *European Socialist Realism*, ed. Michael Scriven and Dennis Tate, 13–30. Oxford: Berg, 1988.

Lloyd, Christopher. *Explanation in Social History*. Oxford: Basil Blackwell, 1986.

Lohmann, Hans. "Neue Haltungen und Ausdrucksformen im Kinospielfilm." In *Film- und Fernsehkunst der DDR*, ed. Hochschule für Film und Fernsehen der DDR, 173–93. Berlin, GDR: Henschelverlag, 1979.

——. "Die DEFA-Spielfilme der sechziger Jahre." In *Film- und Fernsehkunst der DDR*, ed. Hochschule für Film und Fernsehen der DDR, 309–42. Berlin, GDR: Henschelverlag, 1979.

Lohmann, Hans, and Wolfgang Weiss. "Kinospielfilme der siebziger Jahre." In *Film- und Fernsehkunst der DDR*, ed. Hochschule für Film und Fernsehen der DDR, 365–421. Berlin, GDR: Henschelverlag, 1979.

Lowry, Stephen. *Pathos und Politik: Ideologie in Spielfilmen des Nationalsozialismus*. Tübingen: Niemeyer, 1991.

McCormick, Richard W. *Politics of the Self: Feminism and the Postmodern in West German Literature and Film*. Princeton: Princeton University Press, 1991.

Maetzig, Kurt. *Filmarbeit: Gespräche, Reden, Schriften*. Ed. Günter Ägde. Berlin, GDR: Henschelverlag, 1987.

Maiwald, Klaus-Jürgen. *Filmzensur im NS-Staat*. Dortmund: Nowotny, 1983.

Marquardt, Axel, and Heinz Rathsack, eds. *Preussen im Film*. Reinbek: Rowohlt, 1981.

Mayne, Judith. *Cinema and Spectatorship*. London: Routledge, 1993.

Mellenkamp, Patricia, and Philip Rosen, eds. *Cinema History, Cinema Practices*. American Film Institute Monograph 4. Metuchen, N.J.: University Publications of America, 1984.

Meyer, Barbara. "Gesellschaftliche Implikationen bundesdeutscher Nachkriegsfilme." Ph.D. diss., Frankfurt University, 1964.

Mitry, Jean. *Histoire du cinéma*. 5 vols. Paris: Delarge, 1980.

Mitscherlich, Alexander. *Auf dem Weg zur vaterlosen Gesellschaft: Ideen zur Sozialpsychologie*. Munich: Piper, 1963. Trans. Eric Mosbacher under the title *Society Without the Father* (New York: Harcourt World and Brace, 1969).

Mitscherlich, Alexander, and Margarete Mitscherlich. *Die Unfähigkeit zu trauern. Grundlagen kollektiven Verhaltens*. Munich: Piper, 1967. Trans. Beverley R. Placzek under the title *The Inability to Mourn: Principles of Collective Behavior* (New York: Grove, 1975).

Mittenzwei, Werner. *Das Leben des Bertolt Brecht*. 2 vols. Frankfurt: Suhrkamp, 1987.

——. *Der Realismus-Streit um Brecht: Grundriss der Brecht-Rezeption in der DDR 1945–1975*. Berlin: Aufbau Verlag, 1978.

Modlewski, Tania. "Time and Desire in the Woman's Film." *Cinema Journal* 23, no. 3 (spring 1984): 19–30.

Monaco, Paul. *Cinema and Society: Germany and France during the Twenties*. New York: Elsevier, 1976.

Mückenberger, Christiane. "Zeit der Hoffnungen: 1946–1949." In *Das zweite Leben der Filmstadt Babelsberg*, ed. Ralf Schenk, 9–49. Berlin: Henschelverlag, 1994.

———, ed. *Zur Geschichte des DEFA-Spielfilms 1946–1949: Eine Dokumentation.* Potsdam: Hochschule für Film und Fernsehen, 1976.

Naumann, Gerhard, and E. Trumpler, eds. *Biermann und kein Ende: Eine Dokumentation zur DDR Kulturpolitik.* Berlin: Dietz, 1991.

Neale, Stephen. "Propaganda." *Screen* 18, no. 3 (1977): 9–40.

Neckermann, Gerhard. *Filmwirtschaft und Filmförderung: Strukturveränderungen—Daten.* Berlin: Vistas, 1991.

Neue Gesellschaft für bildende Kunst, ed. *Erobert den Film! Proletariat und Film in der Weimarer Republik.* Materialien zur Filmgeschichte 7. Berlin: NGBK, 1977.

Neumann, Hans Joachim. "Ästhetische und organisatorische Erstarrung: Der deutsche Film in den 80er Jahren." In *Der deutsche Film,* ed. Uli Jung, 247–66. Trier: Wissenschaftlicher Verlag, 1993.

Nichols, Bill. *Ideology and the Image: Social Representation in the Cinema and Other Media.* Bloomington: Indiana University Press, 1981.

Nitsche, Hellmuth. *Zwischen Kreuz und Sowjetstern: Zeugnisse des Kirchenkampfes in der DDR (1945–81).* Aschaffenburg: Paul Pattloch, 1983.

Oms, Michel. "Le Cinéma boche." *Les Cahiers de la Cinémathèque* 32 (spring 1981): 19–24.

Orf, Ewald. "Stiefkind Export." In *Förderung essen Filme auf,* ed. Gisela Hundertmark and Louis Saul, 87–94 Munich: Ölschläger, 1984.

Osterland, Martin. *Gesellschaftsbilder in Filmen: Eine soziologische Untersuchung des Filmangebots der Jahre 1949–64.* Stuttgart: Ferdinand Enke, 1970.

Petley, Julian. *Capital and Culture: German Cinema 1933–45.* London: British Film Institute, 1979.

Petro, Patrice. *Joyless Streets: Women and Melodramatic Representation in Weimar Germany.* Princeton: Princeton University Press, 1989.

Pflaum, Hans Günther. "Innenansichten der Filmförderung." In *Abschied vom Gestern,* ed. Hans-Peter Reichmann and Rudolf Worschech, 138–51. Frankfurt: Deutsches Filmmuseum, 1991.

Phillips, Klaus, ed. *New German Filmmakers.* New York: Ungar, 1984.

Phillips, M. S. "The Nazi Control of the German Film Industry." *Journal of European Studies* 1, no. 1 (March 1971): 37–68.

Pleyer, Peter. *Deutscher Nachkriegsfilm 1946–48.* Münster: C. J. Fahle, 1965.

Polan, Dana. *Power and Paranoia: History, Narrative, and the American Cinema, 1940–50.* New York: Columbia University Press, 1986.

Pratt, George C. *Spellbound in Darkness: A History of the Silent Film.* 2d revised ed. Greenwich, Conn.: New York Graphic Society, 1973.

Pracht, Erwin. *Einführung in den sozialistischen Realismus.* Berlin, GDR: Dietz, 1975.

Prawer, Siegbert S. *Caligari's Children: The Film as Tale of Terror.* Oxford: Oxford University Press, 1980.

Prokop, Dieter. *Soziologie des Films.* Neuwied: Luchterhand, 1970.

Prox, Lothar. "Melodien aus deutschem Gemüt und Geblüt." In *Wir tanzen um die Welt,* ed. Helga Belach, 73–86. Munich: Hanser, 1979.

Rahill, Frank. *The World of Melodrama.* University Park: Pennsylvania State University Press, 1967.

Regel, Helmut. "Autoritäre Muster." *Filmkritik* 11 (1966): 650–53.

Reich, Wilhelm. *The Mass Psychology of Fascism*. Trans. Vincent R. Carfagno. New York: Farrar, Straus and Giroux, 1970.

Reichmann, Hans-Peter, and Rudolf Worschech, eds. *Abschied vom Gestern: Bundesdeutscher Film der sechziger und siebziger Jahre*. Frankfurt: Deutsches Filmmuseum, 1991.

Rentschler, Eric. "American Friends and the New German Cinema. A Study in Reception." *New German Critique* 24/25 (fall/winter 1981–82): 7–35.

——. "Critical Junctures Since Oberhausen: West German Film in the Course of Time." *Quarterly Review of Film Studies* 2 (spring 1980): 141–56.

——. "Eigengewächs à la Hollywood." In *Babelsberg*, ed. Wolfgang Jacobsen, 207–22. Berlin: Argon, 1992.

——. "Hochgebirge und Moderne: Eine Standortbestimmung des Bergfilms." In *Filmkultur zur Zeit der Weimarer Republik*, ed. Uli Jung and Walter Schatzberg, 195–214. Munich: Saur, 1992.

——. *West German Film in the Course of Time*. Bedford Hills: Redgrave, 1984.

——, ed. *German Film and Literature: Adaptations and Transformations*. New York: Methuen, 1986.

——, ed. *West German Filmmakers on Film: Visions and Voices*. New York: Holmes and Meyer, 1988.

Richter, Rolf. *DEFA-Spielfilm-Regisseure und ihre Kritiker*. 2 vols. Berlin, GDR: Henschelverlag, 1981–83.

Rohmer, Eric. *L'Organisation de l'espace dans le "Faust" de Murnau*. Paris: Union Générale d'Editions, 1977. Trans. Frieda Grafe and Enno Patalas under the title *Murnaus Faustfilm: Analyse und szenisches Protokoll* (Munich: Hanser, 1980).

Romani, Cinzia. *Die Filmdivas des Dritten Reichs*. Trans. Friederike Blendinger. Munich: Bahia Verlag, 1982. Originally published as *Le Dive del Terzo Reich* (Rome: Gremese Editore, 1981).

Rosen, Philip, ed. *Narrative, Apparatus, Ideology: A Film Theory Reader*. New York: Columbia University Press, 1986.

Rossbacher, Karlheinz. *Heimatkunstbewegung und Heimatroman: Zu einer Literatursoziologie der Jahrhundertwende*. Stuttgart: Klett, 1975.

Rother, Hans-Jörg. "Sehnsucht nach UFA?" *Film und Fernsehen* 2 (1993): 86–87.

Rother, Rainer, ed. *Die Ufa 1917–1945: Das deutsche Bilderimperium*. Berlin: Deutsches Historisches Museum, 1992.

Sadoul, Georges. *Histoire générale du cinéma*. 6 vols. Paris: Denoël, 1946–54.

Sandford, John. *The West German Cinema*. Totowa, N.J.: Barnes and Noble, 1980.

Santner, Eric L. *Stranded Objects: Mourning, Memory, and Film in Postwar Germany*. Ithaca: Cornell University Press, 1990.

Saunders, Thomas J. *Hollywood in Berlin: American Cinema and Weimar Germany*. Berkeley: University of California Press, 1994.

Schenk, Ralf. "Mitten im kalten Krieg: 1950–1960." In *Das zweite Leben der Filmstadt Babelsberg*, ed. Ralf Schenk, 51–157. Berlin: Henschelverlag, 1994.

——. ed. *Das zweite Leben der Filmstadt Babelsberg: DEFA-Spielfilme 1946–1992*. Berlin: Henschelverlag, 1994.

Schieber, Elke. "Anfang vom Ende oder Kontinuität des Argwohns: 1980–1989." In *Das zweite Leben der Filmstadt Babelsberg*, ed. Ralf Schenk, 265–326. Berlin: Henschelverlag, 1994.

Schlüpmann, Heide. "Phenomenology of Film: On Siegfried Kracauer's Writings of the 1920s." *New German Critique* 40 (winter 1987): 97–114.

———. *Unheimlichkeit des Blicks: Das Drama des frühen deutschen Kinos*. Basel: Stroemfeld/Roter Stern, 1990.

Schmieding, Walther. *Kunst oder Kasse: Der Ärger mit dem deutschen Film*. Hamburg: Rütten and Loening, 1961.

Schneider, Michael. "Väter und Söhne, posthum: Das beschädigte Verhältnis zweier Generationen." In *Den Kopf verkehrt aufgesetzt oder Die melancholische Linke*. Darmstadt: Luchterhand, 1981. Trans. Jamie Owen Daniel under the title "Fathers and Sons Retrospectively: The Damaged Relationship between Two Generations," *New German Critique* 31 (winter 1984): 3–51.

Schneider, Norbert Jürgen. *Handbuch Filmmusik: Musikdramaturgie im Neuen Deutschen Film*. Munich: Ölschläger, 1986.

Schnurre, Wolfdietrich. *Rettung des deutschen Films*. Stuttgart: Deutsche Verlags-Anstalt, 1950.

Schoenbaum, David. *The Spiegel Affair*. Garden City, N.Y.: Doubleday, 1968.

Schulte-Sasse, Jochen. "Modernity and Modernism, Postmodernity and Postmodernism: Framing the Issue." *Cultural Critique* 5 (winter 1986–87): 5–22.

Scriven, Michael, and Dennis Tate, eds. *European Socialist Realism*. Oxford: Berg, 1988.

Seifert, Jürgen, ed. *Die Spiegel-Affäre*. 2 vols. Freiburg: Walter, 1966.

Silberman, Marc. "Imagining History: Weimar Images of the French Revolution." In *Framing the Past: The Historiography of German Cinema and Television*, ed. Bruce A. Murray and Christopher J. Wickham, 99–120. Carbondale: Southern Illinois University Press, 1992.

———. "Industry, Text, Ideology in Expressionist Film." In *Passion and Rebellion*, ed. Stephen Eric Bronner and Douglas Kellner, 374–83. South Hadley, Mass.: Bergin, 1983.

———. "Shooting Wars: German Cinema and the Two World Wars." In *1914/1939: German Reflections of the Two World Wars*, ed. Reinhold Grimm and Jost Hermand, 116–36. Madison: University of Wisconsin Press, 1992.

———. "Writing What—For Whom? 'Vergangenheitsbewältigung' in GDR Literature." *German Studies Review* 10, no. 3 (October 1987): 527–39.

Silverman, Kaja. *The Acoustic Mirror: The Female Voice in Psychoanalysis and Cinema*. Bloomington: Indiana University Press, 1988.

———. *Male Subjectivity at the Margins*. New York: Routledge, 1992.

———. *The Subject of Semiotics*. New York: Oxford University Press, 1983.

———. "What is a Camera?, or: History in the Field of Vision." *Discourse* 15, no. 2 (spring 1993): 3–56.

Sorlin, Pierre. *The Film in History*. Oxford: Blackwell, 1980.

Spiker, Jürgen. *Film und Kapital: Der Weg der deutschen Filmwirtschaft zum nationalsozialistischen Einheitskonzern*. Berlin: Volker Spiess, 1975.

Staritz, Dietrich. *Geschichte der DDR 1949–1985*. Frankfurt: Suhrkamp, 1985.

Steiner, Gerhard. *Die Heimat-Macher: Kino in Österreich 1946–1966*. Vienna: Verlag für Gesellschaftskritik, 1987.

Stöckl, Ula. "Appell an Wünsche und Träume." In *Wir tanzen um die Welt*, ed. Helga Belach, 94–118. Munich: Hanser, 1979.

Tate, Dennis. "'Breadth and Diversity': Socialist Realism in the GDR." In *European Socialist Realism*, ed. Michael Scriven and Dennis Tate, 60–78. Oxford: Berg, 1988.

Thiel, Reinhold E. "Acht Typen des Kriegsfilms." *Filmkritik* 11 (1961): 514–19.

———. "Was wurde aus Goebbels' Ufa?" *Film aktuell* 3 (1970).

Thompson, Kristin. "*Im Anfang war* . . . : Some Links between German Fantasy Films of the Teens and the Twenties." In *Before Caligari*, ed. Paolo Cherchi Usai and Lorenzo Codelli, 138–61. Pordenone: Edizioni Biblioteca dell'Immagine, 1990.

Toeplitz, Jerzy. *Geschichte des Films*. 5 vols. Berlin, GDR: Henschelverlag, 1973ff.

Tudor, Andrew. "The Famous Case of German Expressionism." In *Image and Influence: Studies in the Sociology of Film*, 155–79. London: George Allen and Unwin, 1974.

Usai, Paolo Cherchi, and Lorenzo Codelli, eds. *Before Caligari: German Cinema, 1895–1920*. Pordenone: Edizioni Biblioteca dell'Immagine, 1990.

Vietta, Silvio, and Hans-Georg Kemper. *Expressionismus*. 2d ed. Munich: Fink, 1983.

Wätzold, Wolfgang. "Aufgaben des Lichtspielwesens im entwickelten System des Sozialismus." In *Sozialistisches Menschenbild und Filmkunst: Beiträge zu Kino und Fernsehen*, ed. Hartmut Albrecht et al., 182–83. Berlin, GDR: Henschelverlag, 1970.

Welch, David. *Propaganda and the German Cinema 1933–1945*. Oxford: Clarendon, 1983.

Westermann, Bärbel. *Nationale Identität im Spielfilm der fünfziger Jahre*. Frankfurt: Lang, 1990.

Wetzel, Kraft, and Peter Hagemann. *Zensur: Verbotene deutsche Filme 1933–1945*. Berlin: Volker Spiess, 1978.

Wiest-Welk, Georga. "Das Bild der Mutter im westdeutschen Nachkriegsfilm." In *Die Massenmedien und ihre Folgen*, ed. Alphons Silbermann, 33–99. Munich: Ernst Reinhardt, 1970.

Wilkening, Albert. *Geschichte der DEFA von 1945–1950*. [Potsdam]: VEB Defa, 1981.

Willett, John. *Art and Politics in the Weimar Period: The New Sobriety 1917–1933*. New York: Pantheon, 1978.

———. *Expressionism*. London: World University Library, 1970.

Wirth, Eugen. "Stoffprobleme des Films." Ph.D. diss., University of Freiburg, Freiburg, 1952.

Wischnewski, Klaus. "Träumer und gewöhnliche Leute: 1966–1979." In *Das zweite Leben der Filmstadt Babelsberg*, ed. Ralf Schenk, 213–63. Berlin: Henschelverlag, 1994.

Witte, Karsten. "Film im Nationalsozialismus: Blendung und Überblendung." In *Geschichte des deutschen Films*, ed. Wolfgang Jacobsen et al., 119–70. Stuttgart: Metzler, 1993.

———. "Gehemmte Schaulust. Momente des deutschen Revuefilms." In *Wir tanzen um die Welt*, ed. Helga Belach, 7–52. Munich: Hanser, 1979. Trans. J. D. Steakley and Gabriele Hoover under the title "Visual Pleasure Inhibited," *New German Critique* 24–25 (fall/winter 1981–82): 238–63.

Wolf, Dieter. "Gesellschaft mit beschränkter Haftung." In *Babelsberg*, ed. Wolfgang Jacobsen, 247–70. Berlin: Argon, 1992.

Worringer, Wilhelm. *Abstraktion und Einfühlung: Ein Beitrag zur Stilpsychologie.* Munich: Piper, 1908.

Wulf, Joseph. *Theater und Film im Dritten Reich: Eine Dokumention.* Gütersloh: Sigbert Mohn Verlag, 1964. Part 2: Film.

Wuss, Peter. *Die Tiefenstruktur des Filmkunstwerks: Zur Analyse von Spielfilmen mit offener Komposition.* Berlin, GDR: Henschelverlag, 1986.

"Young German Film." Trans. Joachim Neugroschel. *Film Comment* 6, no. 1 (spring 1970): 132–44. Originally published as "Junger deutscher Film," *Der Spiegel* 53 (December 25, 1967).

Zimmermann, Hartmut. *DDR-Handbuch.* 2 vols. 3d ed. Cologne: Verlag Wissenschaft und Politik, 1985.

Index

Kings of the Road (Im Laufe der Zeit) (Wenders), 227, 284n.11, 285n.15
Kirst, Hans Helmut, 131
Klagemann, Eberhard, 265n.12
Klein, Gerhard, 147–48
Kluge, Alexander, xvi, 183, 198, 200, 213, 227, 256n.25; career, 185. *Yesterday Girl*, 185. *See also Artists under the Big Top: Perplexed*
Kohlhaase, Wolfgang, 160
Korda, Zoltan, 269n.5
Kotte, Gabriele, 276n.12
Kracauer, Siegfried, 15, 196; *Die Angestellten*, 16; *From Caligari to Hitler*, 4, 16; on *Passion*, 5–6, 15
Krauss, Werner, 135
Kuhle Wampe or Who Owns the World? (*Kuhle Wampe oder Wem gehört die Welt?*) (Dudov/Brecht), xiii, 52, 62, 104–5, 186, 194; alternative cinema, xvi; montage, 43–45; noncommercial cinema, 35; plot 39; production context, 38–39; reception, 46–48, 254n.1; rhetorical structure and spectatorship, 40–42, 46. *See also* Spectatorship
Kühn, Siegfried, 274n.22
Kunert, Joachim, 149
Kuratorium junger deutscher Film, 183, 198

Lady Windemere's Fan (Lubitsch), 250n.8
Lampe, Jutta, 282n.20
Lamprecht, Gerhard, 35, 265nn.12, 19
Lang, Fritz, 28, 185, 278n.11; *Metropolis*, 23, 33, 38, 137
Lania, Leo, 132, 270n.15
Last Bridge, The (*Die letzte Brücke*) (Käutner), 130
Last Laugh, The (*Der letzte Mann*) (Murnau), xiii, 41, 84; editing, 28; epilogue, 32; lighting, 28; modernist crisis, 25, 30–31, 33; plot, 24; production context, 22–23; script, 25; structural oppositions, 29–30; visual effects, 26–27. *See also* Spectatorship
Last Ten Days, The (*Der letzte Akt*) (Pabst), xv, 145; claustrophic mise-en-scène, 134; documentary quality, 134, 137, 141; editing, 137, 140; family narrative, 139; plot, 132–33;

production context, 131–32; reception, 142. *See also* Excess; Melodrama; Spectatorship
Leander, Zarah, 51, 64
Legend of Paul and Paula, The (*Die Legende von Paul und Paula*) (Carow), 163
Lelouch, Claude, 163
Liebeneiner, Wolfgang, 115, 262n.6
Life with Uwe (*Leben mit Uwe*) (Warneke), 163
Life in the Ticking (*Die Buntkarierten*) (Maetzig), 106, 266n.20
Lightening over Water (*Nick's Film*) (Wenders), 215, 283n.2
Lili Marleen (Fassbinder), 200
Lissy (Wolf), 147
Litvak, Anatole, 258n.8
Little Rabbits (*Karniggel*) (Buck), 233
Loriot, 233
Lorre, Peter, 269n.2
Lost Honor of Katharina Blum, The (*Die verlorene Ehre der Katharina Blum*) (Schlöndorff/Trotta), 201
Lot's Woman (*Lots Weib*) (Günther), 164
Lubitsch, Ernst, xiii, 28, 82–83, 201; and Max Reinhardt, 7; career, 6–7; mass scenes, 14–15. *See also Passion*
Lucas, George, 220
Ludendorff, Erich, 3
Lukács, Georg, 146
Lungo silenzio, Il (Trotta), 232
Lüthge, Bobby E., 268n.13
Lützkendorf, Felix, 69
Luxemburg, Rosa, 281n.12

Mach, Josef, 272n.9
Maetzig, Kurt, 106, 158, 163, 265n.20
Magnificent Obsession (Sirk), 257n.1
Malou (Meerapfel), 201
Man Whose Name Was Stolen, The (*Der Mann, dem man den Namen stahl*) (Staudte), 102
Marian, Ferdinand, 88
Marianne and Juliane (*Die bleierne Zeit*) (Trotta), xvi, 226; doubling and sibling rivalry, 203, 205, 207, 208–10, 212; narrative structure, 202–3, 207, 210–11; partriarchal family, 203–4; plot, 202; reception, 212–13; role reversals, 203, 205; terrorism, 202, 205–6, 211–12; victim motif, 203,

Books in the Contemporary Film and Television Series